Bijan's controls uncertainty by requiring that customers make appointments (see box in Chapter 13). Photo courtesy of Bijan's, New York.

Lee Iacocca of Chrysler Corporation (see box in Chapter 3). Photo courtesy of Chrysler Corp.

Employees making hamburgers at McDonald's (see discussion on standardization and formalization in Chapter 4). Photo courtesy of McDonald's.

ORGANIZATION THEORY
Structure, Design, and Applications

Other Prentice Hall books by the same author:

Organizational Behavior: Concepts, Controversies, and Applications,
4th Edition (1989)
Training in InterPersonal Skills: TIPS for Managing People at Work
(1989)
Management: Concepts and Applications, 2nd Edition (1988)
Personnel/Human Resource Management, 3rd Edition
(with David DeCenzo) (1988)
Essentials of Organizational Behavior, 2nd Edition (1988)
Organization Theory: Readings and Cases (with Penny Wright) (1987)
The Administrative Process, 2nd Edition (1980)
Managing Organizational Conflict: A Nontraditional Approach (1974)

THIRD EDITION

ORGANIZATION THEORY

Structure, Design, and Applications

STEPHEN P. ROBBINS

San Diego State University

Prentice Hall, Englewood Cliffs, New Jersey 07632

Library of Congress Cataloging-in-Publication Data

Robbins, Stephen P.
    Organization theory : structure, design, and applications /
Stephen P. Robbins. -- 3rd ed.
        p.   cm.
    Includes bibliographical references.
    ISBN 0-13-642471-6
    1. Organization. 2. Organizational effectiveness.   I. Title.
HD31.R565   1990
    658.1--dc20   89-39617
                                                            CIP

THIS ONE'S FOR YOU, GRANDMA G

Editorial/production supervision and interior design: Maureen Wilson
Cover design: Karen Stephens
Manufacturing buyer: Laura Crossland

©1990, 1987, 1983 by Prentice-Hall, Inc.
A Paramount Communications Company
Englewood Cliffs, New Jersey 07632

Printed in the United States of America

20 19 18 17 16 15 14 13 12

ISBN 0-13-642471-6

Prentice-Hall International (UK) Limited, *London*
Prentice-Hall of Australia Pty. Limited, *Sydney*
Prentice-Hall Canada Inc., *Toronto*
Prentice-Hall Hispanoamericana, S.A., *Mexico*
Prentice-Hall of India Private Limited, *New Delhi*
Prentice-Hall of Japan, Inc., *Tokyo*
Simon & Schuster Asia Pte. Ltd., *Singapore*
Editora Prentice-Hall do Brasil, Ltda., *Rio de Janeiro*

OVERVIEW

CONTENTS

Preface xxi

PART II   THE DETERMINANTS: WHAT CAUSES STRUCTURE?

5 Strategy   119

6 Organization Size   149

11 Bureaucracy: A Closer Look 308

PREFACE

Organization Theory (OT) is one of the most interesting and relevant subdisciplines within the administrative sciences. For instance, in this book, you'll find answers to such questions as: Are large organizations *more* or *less* efficient than small ones? How do lower-level employees gain power and circumvent their superiors? What will tomorrow's organizations look like? Can managers change their organization's culture if they find that it no longer fits the organization's mission and goals? How is managing in a shrinking organization different from managing in times of growth?

The challenge in writing an OT textbook is to balance rigor and relevance. On the rigor side, you'll find this book provides a comprehensive and up-to-date review of the OT literature. It includes research findings published in recent issues of the *Academy of Management Journal, Academy of Management Review, Administrative Science Quarterly, American Sociological Review, California Management Review, Canadian Journal of Administrative Sciences, Journal of Management, Management Science, Organization Studies, Strategic Management Journal,* and similar journals. In addition to updating the research base, several important changes have been made in this edition. For example, the chapter on strategy has been completely revised to go beyond Chandler and Miles and Snow, to reflect recent contributions by Michael Porter and Danny Miller; and I've included discussions throughout the book on how computers and management information systems are changing organization design.

On the relevance side, I'm proud to say that numerous users have commented about how well-written and practical they've found previous editions of this book. I think you'll find this edition to be even *more* "user friendly." Let me briefly highlight a few of the things that I have done to make it so.

First, each chapter now opens with a real-life vignette. This introduces the topics in that chapter. Second, I've increased the number of "OT Close-Up" boxes by more than 70 percent. These boxes give more detailed insight into relevance of OT concepts. Third, you'll find concepts illustrated by literally hundreds of examples drawn from current periodicals like the *Wall Street Journal, Business Week, Inc., Industry Week, Fortune, Forbes,* and *Time.* A partial list of organizations you'll read about in this book include:

Applied Data Research	IBM
Ballard Medical Products	McDonald's
Celestial Seasonings	Maytag Company
Chrysler Corporation	National Broadcasting
Compaq Computer	Company
Eastman Kodak	New Avanti Corporation
Ford Motor Company	Philip Morris
Fox Broadcasting	Procter & Gamble
General Mills	3M
General Motors	Toyota Motor Co.
GenRad	United Parcel Service
Hewlett-Packard	Western Union

Finally, the cases at the end of the text have been extensively revised. Ten of the sixteen cases are completely new to this edition. As in the past, you'll find familiar names among the case selections: Mrs. Fields' Cookies, Sears, Chrysler Corp., Ford Motor Co., General Motors, the Roman Catholic church, Merck Drugs, Ben & Jerry's Ice Cream, Exxon, Eastman Kodak, AT&T, and the U.S. Employment Service.

A comprehensive instructor's manual is available to text adopters. This manual provides, among other things, sample course outlines, term-paper projects, chapter summaries, comments on discussion questions and cases, a test bank of more than one-thousand examination questions, and a set of transparency masters.

ACKNOWLEDGMENTS

This revision was completed while I was a visiting professor at Southern Illinois University at Edwardsville. I sincerely appreciate the support and collegiality offered me at SIUE by Dean David Ault, and Don Strickland, Ed Harrick, Joe Michlitsch, Stan Frankel, Rick McKinney, Kumar Jain, George Sullivan, Hans Steffen, Dan Thomann, Paul Sultan, John Virgo, and Jim Miller.

The comments of my reviewers were extremely helpful. My thanks to Bernie Hinton (California State University, San Marcos), Danny Miller (École des Hautes Études Commerciales of the University of Montreal and McGill University), and Janet Near (Indiana University, Bloomington). Of course, I accept full responsibility for any errors or omissions.

As I said in the preface to the previous edition, a book is not a book without a publisher. Mine is Prentice Hall. I want to thank all the people at PH who have supported my projects over the years. I particularly want to thank the following people for their assistance on this book: my acquisition editor, Alison Reeves; her editorial assistants, Fran Falk and Lioux Brun; my production editor, Maureen Wilson; college marketing manager, Caroline Ruddle; and PH representatives Mary Adam-Shapiro, Wayne Spohr, and Lisbeth Turgeon.

Stephen P. Robbins
Del Mar, California

1

AN OVERVIEW

AFTER READING THIS CHAPTER, YOU SHOULD BE ABLE TO:

1 Define organization theory.
2 Compare organization theory and organizational behavior.
3 Explain the value in studying organization theory.
4 Describe the systems perspective.
5 Describe the life-cycle perspective.
6 Discuss how systems and life cycles are part of the biological metaphor.

Introduction
THE CELESTIAL SEASONINGS' STORY

If you walk into you local supermarket and find the aisle where coffee and tea products are displayed, odds are you'll see boxes of herbal teas with animated pictures of bears frolicking under waterfalls, chipmunks blowing gold trumpets, and buffalo charging out of the sunset. The teas will have names like Mo's 24, Sleepytime, Red Zinger, Emperor's Choice, Cinnamon Rose, Almond Sunset, and Morning Thunder. The company that brings these teas to your supermarket is Celestial Seasonings, Inc. In 1988 the company had sales in excess of $40 million. It has made its founders—Mo Siegel and John Hay—millionaires. But Celestial Seasonings wasn't always a large, multimillion-dollar organization. In fact, it has grown from the most humble of beginnings.[1]

In the summer of 1971, Mo Siegel and John Hay were in their early

1

twenties and lived in Boulder, Colorado. Both were "free spirits"—more interested in religion, music, and health than the security of an eight-to-five job. But even free spirits have to eat, so Mo and John decided to make and sell herb teas.

Mo and John spent their summer days picking herbs in the canyons surrounding Boulder. Meanwhile, their wives—Peggy Siegel and Beth Hay—sewed bulk tea bags: ten thousand bulk tea bags that first summer! The two couples screened the hundreds of pounds of herbs that the men had collected and mixed them into a concoction that would eventually be called Mo's 24. The mixture would then be crammed into the bulk tea bags and marked. The completed products—which they sold under the brand name of Celestial Seasonings—were sold to natural food stores in the Boulder area.

During the first few years, the people that made up Celestial Seasonings were nothing more than a group of friends and relatives. There were no job descriptions, no production lines, and little specialization of labor. The way the group made decisions was fully in keeping with the values of the founders. Informal meetings were held once a week. It was not unusual for these meetings to last eight hours, while participants dwelled on such topics as the philosophical attributes of tea bags. There were volleyball games during every lunch hour.

But something began to happen in the mid-1970s that changed Celestial Seasonings' structure dramatically. Demand for their herbal teas was exploding. They were moving out of health food stores and into Safeways and A&Ps. More people had to be hired to meet the increased demand. When Celestial Seasonings had been merely two friends and their wives, it could adjust rapidly to new conditions because everyone knew everyone else's job. Communication was easy—they all worked in the same small room. But with more people came the need to develop a more formal structure within which to make and sell their herbal teas. Today Celestial Seasonings employs more than two hundred people who work out of five buildings in the Boulder area. There are departments, production lines, and written job descriptions. The simple days of four people doing everything are gone. Herbs are received in one warehouse and then taken to a highly automated factory for cleaning, milling, and blending. Blending, for instance, is carefully done by specialists to ensure consistency of flavor. On a good day workers will blend eight tons or more of tea into fifteen varieties.

Not surprisingly, Celestial Seasonings has lost a large degree of its "one big happy family" atmosphere. With specialization and departmentalization came the separation of management from workers. Professionals now abound. Executives—many specializing in production, advertising, and distribution—were hired away from Pepsico, General Foods, Quaker Oats, and Procter & Gamble. The company has expanded into the beauty-products field with a natural shampoo/conditioner and is actively looking for new-product opportunities.

Mo Siegel and John Hay created an organization. The means by which four people made a few thousand dollars worth of tea was no longer efficient for making forty different kinds of herbal teas, with herbs imported from thirty-five countries, and generating sales in excess of $40 million a year. This kind of volume requires a coordinated structure of people doing specific work tasks. People doing similar activities had to be grouped together into departments. And increasing layers of management were required to coordinate the departmental activities. Additionally, formal written policies, regulations, and rules had to be introduced to facilitate coordination and to ensure that all employees were treated consistently and fairly.

Celestial Seasonings' success is as much a result of having developed a proper structure of planned and coordinated effort as it is of good marketing. The profitable manufacturing and selling of tea requires obtaining raw materials, running efficient production operations, shipping the finished product on time and to the right place, developing new products, and many other activities. But Celestial Seasonings is not unique. The providing of *any* product or service requires planned coordination. As we'll demonstrate, an understanding of organization theory can help managers effectively coordinate their resources and make for more efficient provision of products or services.

SOME BASIC DEFINITIONS

The Celestial Seasonings story illustrates the creation and growth of an organization. But what precisely do we mean by the term *organization*? Perhaps not as obviously, Mo Siegel and John Hay were also involved with *organization structure, organization design, and organization theory*. Since all four terms are important and are often confused, let's clarify them.

What Is an Organization?

An **organization** is a consciously coordinated social entity, with a relatively identifiable boundary, that functions on a relatively continuōus basis to achieve a common goal or set of goals. That's a mouthful of words, so let us break it down into its more relevant parts.

The words *consciously coordinated* imply management. *Social entity* means that the unit is composed of people or groups of people who interact with each other. The interaction patterns that people follow in an organization do not just emerge; rather, they are premeditated. Therefore, because organizations are social entities, the interaction patterns of their members must be balanced and harmonized to minimize redundancy yet ensure that critical tasks are being completed. The result is that our definition assumes explicitly the need for coordinating the interaction patterns of people.

An organization has a *relatively identifiable boundary.* This boundary can change over time, and it may not always be perfectly clear, but a definable boundary must exist in order to distinguish members from nonmembers. It tends to be achieved by explicit or implicit contracts between members and their organizations. In most employment relationships, there is an implicit contract where work is exchanged for pay. In social or voluntary organizations, members contribute in return for prestige, social interaction, or the satisfaction of helping others. But every organization has a boundary that differentiates who is and who is not part of that organization.

People in an organization have some *continuing bond.* This bond, of course, does not mean lifelong membership. On the contrary, organizations face constant change in their memberships, although while they are members, the people in an organization participate with some degree of regularity. For a salesperson at Sears Roebuck, that may require being at work eight hours a day, five days a week. At the other extreme, someone functioning on a relatively continuous basis as a member of the National Organization for Women may attend only a few meetings a year or merely pay the annual dues.

Finally, organizations exist to achieve something. These "somethings" are *goals,* and they usually are either unattainable by individuals working alone or, if attainable individually, are achieved more efficiently through group effort. While it is not necessary for all members to endorse the organization's goals fully, our definition implies general agreement with the mission of the organization.

Notice how all the parts of our definition align with the entity that Mo Siegel and John Hay created. The goals of Celestial Seasonings are to provide health-related products, at a profit, in an environment that is a good place to work. Mo and John hired people; then they developed a formal set of patterns by which these people were required to interact (including specialized tasks to perform and a hierarchy of managers and workers). Members of Celestial Seasonings are identified as employees, managers, or owners. In return for their work effort, they receive compensation. Finally, the organization's life exists beyond that of any of its members. Employees can quit, but they can be replaced so that the activities they perform can be carried on. In fact, Mo and John were able to sell out their interests in Celestial Seasonings with minimal impact upon the operations of the company.

What Is Organization Structure?

Our definition of *organization* recognizes the need for formally coordinating the interaction patterns of organization members. **Organization structure** defines how task are to be allocated, who reports to whom, and the formal coordinating mechanisms and interaction patterns that will be followed.

We define an organization's structure as having three components: complexity, formalization, and centralization. We review each in detail in Chapter 4.

Complexity considers the extent of differentiation within the organization. This includes the degree of specialization or division of labor, the number of levels in the organization's hierarchy, and the extent to which the organization's units are dispersed geographically. As tasks at Celestial Seasonings became increasingly specialized and more levels were added in the hierarchy, the organization became increasingly complex. Complexity, of course, is a relative term. Celestial Seasonings, for instance, has a long way to go to approach the complexity of a General Electric or an IBM, where there are hundreds of occupational specialties, nearly a dozen levels between production workers and the chief executive officer, and organizational units dispersed in countries throughout the world.

The degree to which an organization relies on rules and procedures to direct the behavior of employees is *formalization*. Some organizations operate with a minimum of such standardized guidelines; others, some of which are even quite small in size, have all kinds of regulations instructing employees as to what they can and cannot do.

Centralization considers where the locus of decision-making authority lies. In some organizations, decision making is highly centralized. Problems flow upward, and the senior executives choose the appropriate action. In other cases, decision making is decentralized. Authority is dispersed downward in the hierarchy. It is important to recognize that, as with complexity and formalization, an organization is not *either* centralized or decentralized. Centralization and decentralization represent two extremes on a continuum. Organizations *tend* to be centralized or *tend* to be decentralized. The placement of the organization on this continuum, however, is one of the major factors in determining what type of structure exists.

What Is Organization Design?

Our third term—organization design—emphasizes the management side of organization theory. **Organization design** is concerned with constructing and changing an organization's structure to achieve the organization's goals. Constructing or changing an organization is not unlike building or remodeling a house. Both begin with an end goal. The designer then creates a means or plan for achieving that goal. In house construction, that plan is a blueprint. In organization building, the analogous document is an organization chart.

As you proceed through this text, you will see a consistent concern with offering prescriptions for how organizations can be *designed* to facilitate the attainment of the organization's goals. This concern should not be surprising, as this book is intended for business students and managers. You are probably more interested in learning how to design organizations than merely knowing how organizations function. You have a managerial perspective, consistently looking for the application potential in concepts. When organization theory is studied from the perspective of the needs of managers and future managers, it is oriented heavily toward organization design.

What Is Organization Theory?

From our previous definitions, it is not too difficult to deduce what we mean by the term **organization theory.** It is the discipline that studies the structure and design of organizations. Organization theory refers to both the descriptive and prescriptive aspects of the discipline. It describes how organizations are actually structured and offers suggestions on how they can be constructed to improve their effectiveness. At the end of this chapter, we introduce a model that identifies explicitly the major subparts that make up this discipline we call organization theory. Chapter 2 presents a brief overview of the evolution of organization theory over time.

Contrasting Organization Theory and Organizational Behavior

Since we're clarifying terminology, it might be helpful in this section to differentiate the subject matter of organization theory (OT) from that of organizational behavior (OB). Many students of management and organizations will take courses in both areas, and a brief comparison of the two should assist you in understanding their different terrains as well as their areas of overlap.

Organizational behavior takes a micro view—emphasizing individuals and small groups. It focuses on behavior *in* organizations and a narrow set of employee performance and attitude variables— employee productivity, absenteeism, turnover, and job satisfaction are those most frequently looked at. Individual behavior topics typically studied in OB include perception, values, learning, motivation, and personality. Group topics include roles, status, leadership, power, communication, and conflict.

In contrast, organization theory takes a macro perspective. Its unit of analysis is the organization itself or its primary subunits. OT focuses on the behavior *of* organizations and uses a broader definition of organizational effectiveness. OT is concerned not only with employee performance and attitudes but with the overall organization's ability to adapt and achieve its goals.

This micro-macro distinction creates some overlap. For instance, structural factors have an impact on employee behavior. So students of OB should consider the structure-behavior relationship. Similarly, some micro topics are relevant to the study of OT. But where micro and macro issues overlap, their emphasis is often different. For instance, the topic of conflict in OB tends to focus on interpersonal and intragroup conflicts that derive from personality differences and poor communication. Conflict, when studied by organization theorists, emphasizes problems of inter-unit coordination. While the student of OB is likely to see all conflicts as "people" problems, the student of OT tends to see the same conflict as resulting from flaws in the organization's design. The issue, of course, is not that one is right and the other is wrong. Rather, OB and OT merely emphasize different levels of organizational analysis.

WHY STUDY ORGANIZATION THEORY?

To this point, we have assumed that you are aware of the value of studying organization theory. This may be an incorrect assumption. Therefore, before we go any further, let us address the question directly: Why study OT?

Organizations are the dominant form of institutions in our society. You were probably born in a hospital, and you will probably be put to rest by a mortuary. Both are organizations. The schools that educate us are organizations, as are the stores where we buy our food, the companies that make our automobiles, and the people who take our income tax, collect our garbage, provide for our military defense, and print our daily newspapers.

Organizations pervade all aspects of contemporary life—society as a whole, the economy, and even our personal lives. It is not unreasonable, then, to expect us to want to understand this phenomenon that is so intertwined in our lives. Even though you may have no desire to apply your knowledge, you may simply seek an answer to why organizations with which you interact (and by which you will probably be employed) are structured the way they are.

At a more sophisticated level, you may want to replace your intuitive theories of organization with ones that have been derived scientifically and systematically. Whether or not you study organizations formally, you carry around with you a set of theories about how organizations operate. You go to the Department of Motor Vehicles to get your driver's license renewed; you make a reservation with an airline; you talk to the loan officer at your bank about arranging a student loan; you order it "your way" at the local fast-food hamburger outlet. You undertake all these activities by using some "theory" about how each of these organizations operates and why its members behave as they do. So the issue is not whether you should use theories for dealing with organizations—reality tells us that we use such theories every day. Doesn't it make sense to use theories that have undergone systematic study?

When we use the phrase *systematic study*, we mean looking at relationships, attempting to attribute causes and effects, and basing our conclusions on scientific evidence; that is, data gathered under controlled conditions and measured and interpreted in a reasonably rigorous manner. The objective is to replace intuition or that "gut feeling" one has as to "why organizations are designed as they are" or "what works best when" with scientifically-based theories.

Probably the most popular reason for studying OT is that you are interested in pursuing a career in management. You want to know how organizations operate, have that knowledge based on some scientific evidence, and then use the knowledge for constructing and changing an organization's structure to achieve the organization's goals. In other words, you expect to practice organization design as a manager, administrator, personnel analyst, organizational specialist, or the like.

The final reason for studying OT may not be very exciting, but it is pragmatic—it may be a requirement for a particular degree or certificate you are seeking. You may perceive yourself as a captive in a required course, believing that studying OT may offer no obvious end that has value to you. If this is the case, then the studying of OT is only a means toward that end. It is hoped that one of the earlier reasons holds more relevance for you.

THE BIOLOGICAL METAPHOR

A metaphor is a popular device for making comparisons. It can be extremely helpful for explaining or providing insight into the workings of two phenomena, one of which you already understand fairly well. In this section, we are going to look at organizations (a phenomenon with which we'll assume you are technically unfamiliar) as if they were living organisms like plants, animals, or human beings (phenomena with which we'll assume you *are* reasonably familiar). We call this comparison the biological metaphor.

One caveat before we proceed. Some scholars have questioned whether the biological metaphor is appropriate for application to organizations.[2] For example, while few would argue that organizations are born, grow, and require continual nourishment for survival, organizations are not predestined to die as all living organisms are. Death may be a part of biological life, but it is not inevitable for organizations. So the metaphor is not perfect. Nevertheless, it has become an increasingly popular conceptual framework for understanding organizations. As you'll see, like living organisms, or-

TEN DIFFERENT WAYS OF LOOKING AT ORGANIZATIONS, OR WHAT YOU SEE IS WHAT YOU GET!

Organizations have been conceptualized in numerous ways.[3] The following represent some of the more frequently used descriptions:

1. *Rational entities in pursuit of goals.* Organizations exist to achieve goals, and the behavior of organizational members can be explained as the rational pursuit of those goals.

2. *Coalitions of powerful constituencies.* Organizations are made up of groups, each of which seeks to satisfy its own self-interest. These groups use their power to influence the distribution of resources within the organization.

3. *Open systems.* Organizations are input-output transformation systems that depend on their environment for survival.

4. *Meaning-producing systems.* Organizations are artificially created entities. Their goals and purposes are symbolically created and maintained by management.

ganizations grow, pass through predictable stages of development, undergo a series of predictable transitions, and deteriorate if the energy they put out isn't replaced by new inputs. Describing organizations as systems and as proceeding through a life cycle should give you new insights into their makeup.

The Systems Perspective

There is wide agreement among organizational theorists that a systems perspective offers important insights into the workings of an organization.[4] The following pages introduce the idea of systems, differentiate *open* from *closed* systems, and demonstrate how an open-systems approach can help you to conceptualize better just what it is that organizations do.

5. *Loosely coupled systems.* Organizations are made up of relatively independent units that can pursue dissimilar or even conflicting goals.

6. *Political systems.* Organizations are composed of internal constituencies that seek control over the decision process in order to enhance their position.

7. *Instruments of domination.* Organizations place members into job "boxes" that constrain what they can do and individuals with whom they can interact. Additionally, they are given a boss who has authority over them.

8. *Information-processing units.* Organizations interpret their environment, coordinate activities, and facilitate decision making by processing information horizontally and vertically through a structural hierarchy.

9. *Psychic prisons.* Organizations constrain members by constructing job descriptions, departments, divisions, and standards of acceptable and unacceptable behaviors. When accepted by members, they become artificial barriers that limit choices.

10. *Social contracts.* Organizations are composed of sets of unwritten agreements whereby members perform certain behaviors in return for compensation.

Definition of a System. A **system** is a set of interrelated and interdependent parts arranged in a manner that produces a unified whole. Societies are systems, and so too are automobiles, plants, and human bodies. They take inputs, transform them, and produce some output. The unique characteristic of the systems viewpoint is the interrelationship of parts within the system. Every system is characterized by two diverse forces: differentiation and integration. In a system, specialized functions are differentiated, which replace diffuse global patterns. In the human body, for instance, the lungs, heart, and liver are all distinct functions. Similarly, organizations have divisions, departments, and like units separated out to perform specialized activities. At the same time, in order to maintain unity among the differentiated parts and form a complete whole, every system has a reciprocal process of integration. In organizations, this integration is typically achieved through devices such as coordinated levels of hierarchy; direct supervision; and rules, procedures, and policies. Every system, therefore, requires differentiation to identify its subparts and integration to ensure that the system doesn't break down into separate elements.

Although organizations are made up of parts or subsystems, they are themselves subsystems within larger systems. Just as the human heart is a subsystem within the body's physiological system, the Graduate School of Business at the University of Texas at Austin is a subsystem within the UT-Austin system. If we focus our attention on UT-Austin as the system, then we also recognize that it functions as part of the larger suprasystem of the University of Texas campuses (which include Austin, Dallas, El Paso, and San Antonio, among others). So not only are there systems but there are subsystems and suprasystems. The classification of these three depends on the unit of analysis. If we focus our attention on the Graduate School of Business and make it the system, then UT-Austin becomes the suprasystem, and departments within the graduate school, such as accounting and management, become the subsystems.

Types of Systems. Systems are classified typically as either closed or open. Closed-system thinking stems primarily from the physical sciences. It views the system as self-contained. Its dominant characteristic is that it essentially ignores the effect of the environment on the system. A perfect **closed system** would be one that receives no energy from an outside source and from which no energy is released to its surroundings. More idealistic than practical, the closed-system perspective has little applicability to the study of organizations.

The **open system** recognizes the dynamic interaction of the system with its environment. A simplified graphic representation of the open system appears in Figure 1–1.

No student of organizations could build much of a defense for viewing organizations as closed systems. Organizations obtain their raw materials and human resources from the environment. They further depend on clients and customers in the environment to absorb their output. Banks take in deposits, convert these deposits into loans and other investments, and use the resulting profits to maintain themselves, to grow, and to pay dividends and taxes. The bank system, therefore, interacts actively with its environment, which is made up of people with savings to invest, other people in need of loans, potential employees looking for work, regulatory agencies, and the like.

Figure 1–2 provides a more complex picture of an open system as it would apply to an industrial organization. We see inputs of

FIGURE 1–1 *Basic Open System*

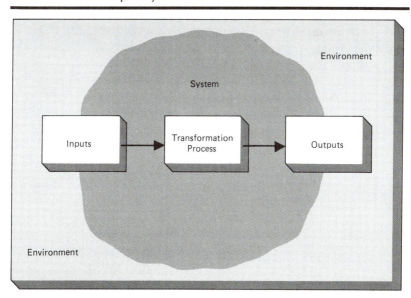

14

FIGURE 1–2 *An Industrial Organization as an Open System*

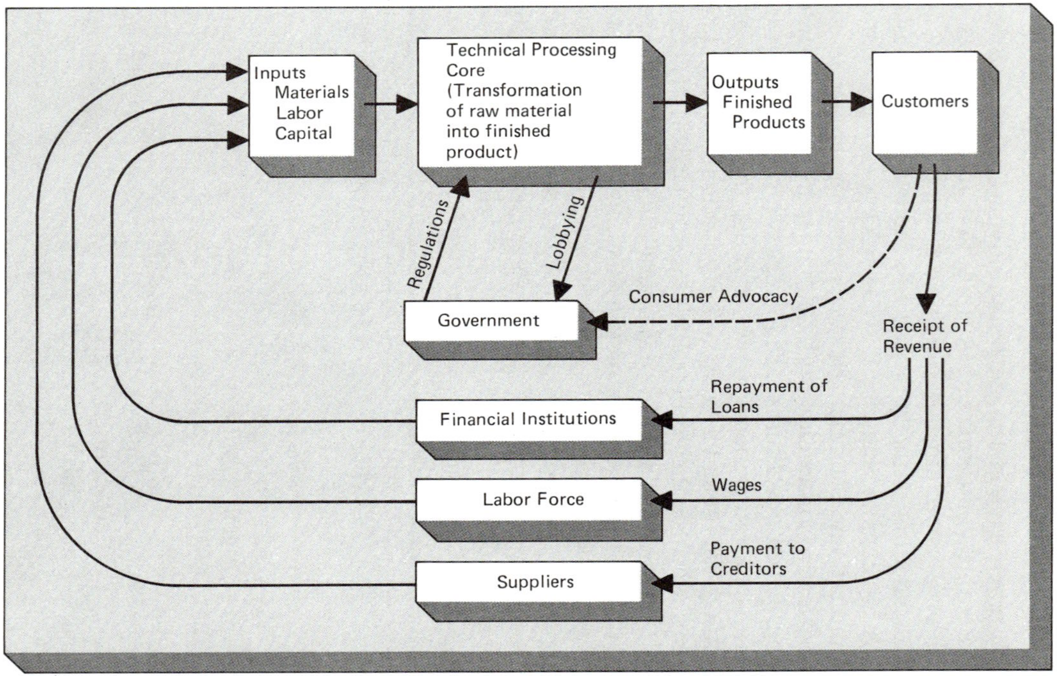

materials, labor, and capital. We see a technological process created for transforming raw materials into finished product. The finished product, in turn, is sold to a customer. Financial institutions, the labor force, suppliers, and customers are all part of the environment, as is government.

If you stop to think about it for a moment, it is difficult to conceive of any system as being fully closed. All systems must have some interaction with their environments if they are to survive. Probably the most relevant way in which to look at the closed-open dichotomy is to consider it as a range rather than as two clearly separate classifications. In this way, we can explain that the degree to which a system is opened or closed varies within systems. An open system, for instance, may become more closed if contact with the environment is reduced over time. The reverse would also be true. General Motors, from its inception through the early 1960s, operated as if it were basically a closed system. Management decided on the products it wanted to sell, produced those products, and offered them to customers. GM assumed that whatever it made would sell, and for decades it was right. Government was generally benign, and consumer-advocate groups were nonexistent or had little influence. GM virtually ignored its environment, for the most part, because its executives saw the environment as having almost no impact on the company's performance. While some critics of GM still attack the firm for being too insulated from its environment, GM has certainly become more open. The actions of consumer groups, stockholders, government regulators, and foreign competition have forced GM to interact with, and be more responsive to, its environment. So while it may not be the model for an open system, GM is more open today than it was thirty years ago.

Characteristics of an Open System. All systems have inputs, transformation processes, and outputs. They take things such as raw materials, energy, information, and human resources and convert them into goods and services, profits, waste materials, and the like. Open systems, however, have some additional characteristics that have relevance to those of us studying organizations.[5]

1. *Environment awareness.* One of the most obvious characteristics of an open system is its recognition of the interdependency between the system and its environment. There is a boundary that separates it from its environment: Changes in the environment affect one or more attributes of the system, and, conversely, changes in the system affect its environment.

Without a boundary there is no system, and the boundary or boundaries determine where systems and subsystems start and stop. Boundaries can be physical, like the clear lines that separate the United States from its neighbors to the north and south. They also can be maintained psychologically through symbols such as titles, uniforms, and indoctrination rituals. At this point, it is sufficient to acknowledge that the concept of boundaries is required for an understanding of systems and that their demarcation for the study of organizations is problematic.

The interdependency of a system and its environment was highly visible in the early 1980s when Chrysler Corporation was fighting to keep its head above water and avoid bankruptcy. Chrysler's dilemma was to a large degree created by its environment—aggressive foreign competition, OPEC nations that had run up the price of gasoline during the 1970s, and the U.S. government's determination to fight inflation by keeping interest rates high. Such environmental forces had hit hard at Chrysler's product line, which, through most of the 1970s, was made up of large, expensive, high-fuel-consuming automobiles. Although General Motors and Ford faced the same environment, they had a larger volume of sales over which to spread the investment of billions of dollars necessary to retool and produce smaller and more efficient cars. GM and Ford also had substantially stronger financial positions. So Chrysler was clearly affected by its environment. But interestingly, the relationship between Chrysler and its environment was two-way. Suppliers, the state of Michigan, the United Automobile Workers union, and the federal government (by way of loan guarantees) were all affected by Chrysler's problems. While few organizations have the impact on their environment of a Chrysler Corporation, the fact remains that all open systems affect their environment to some degree.

2. *Feedback.*   Open systems continually receive information from their environment. This helps the system to adjust and allows it to take corrective actions to rectify deviations from its prescribed course. We call this receipt of environmental information **feedback;** that is, a process that allows a portion of the output to be returned to the system as input (such as information or money) so as to modify succeeding outputs from the system. In the case of Chrysler Corporation, management was able to respond successfully to its problems because it effectively read the feedback it received and adjusted accordingly. The public's favorable response to the fuel-efficient K-cars, attractive convertibles, Caravan wagons, and rigorous quality-control measures all were achieved because Chrysler's management successfully read the feedback it got from its environment.

3. *Cyclical character.* Open systems are cycles of events. The system's outputs furnish the means for new inputs that allow for the repetition of the cycle. This was demonstrated in Figure 1–2; the revenue received by the customers of the industrial firm must be adequate enough to pay creditors and the wages of employees and to repay loans if the cycle is to be perpetuated and the survival of the organization maintained.

4. *Negative entropy.* The term **entropy** refers to the propensity of a system to run down or disintegrate. A closed system, because it does not import energy or new inputs from its environment, will run down over time. In contrast, an open system is characterized by negative entropy—it can repair itself, maintain its structure, avoid death, and even grow because it has the ability to import more energy than it puts out.

5. *Steady state.* The input of energy to arrest entropy maintains some constancy in energy exchange resulting in a relatively steady state. Even though there is a constant flow of new inputs into the system and a steady outflow, on balance the character of the system remains the same. Your body will replace most of its dying cells in any given year, but your physical appearance alters very little. So while an open system is active in processing inputs to outputs, the system tends to maintain itself over time.

6. *Movement toward growth and expansion.* The steady-state characteristic is descriptive of simple or primitive open systems. As the system becomes more complex and moves to counteract entropy, open systems move toward growth and expansion. This is not a contradiction of the steady-state thesis.

To ensure their survival, large and complex systems operate in a way to acquire some margin of safety beyond the immediate level of existence. The many subsystems within the system, to avoid entropy, tend to import more energy than is required for its output.

The result is that the steady state is applicable to simple systems but, at more complex levels, becomes one of preserving the character of the system through growth and expansion. We see this in our bodies as they attempt to store fat. We see it too among large corporations and government bureaucracies that, not satisfied with the status quo, attempt to increase their chances of survival by actively seeking growth and expansion.

A final point on this characteristic needs to be made: The basic system does not change directly as a result of expansion. The most common growth pattern is one in which there is merely a multiplication of the same type of cycles or subsystems. The quantity of the system changes while the quality remains the same. Most colleges and universities, for instance, expand by doing more of the same thing rather than by pursuing new or innovative activities.

7. *Balance of maintenance and adaptive activities.*   Open systems seek to reconcile two, often conflicting, activities. **Maintenance activities** ensure that the various subsystems are in balance and that the total system is in accord with its environment. This, in effect, prevents rapid changes that may unbalance the system. In contrast, **adaptive activities** are necessary so that the system can adjust over time to variations in internal and external demands. So whereas one seeks stability and preservation of the status quo through the purchase, maintenance, and overhaul of machinery; the recruitment and training of employees; and mechanisms such as the provision and enforcement of rules and procedures, the other focuses on change through planning, market research, new-product development, and the like.

Both maintenance and adaptive activities are required if a system is to survive. Stable and well-maintained organizations that do not adapt as conditions change will not endure long. Similarly, the adaptive but unstable organization will be inefficient and unlikely to survive for long.

8. *Equifinality.*   The concept of **equifinality** argues that there are a number of ways to skin a cat. More exactly, it states that a system can reach the same final state from differing initial conditions and by a variety of paths. This means that an organizational system can accomplish its objectives with varied inputs and transformation processes. As we discuss the managerial implications of organization theory, it will be valuable for you to keep the idea of equifinality in mind. It will encourage you to consider a variety of solutions to a given problem rather than to seek some rigid optimal solution.

Importance of the Systems Perspective. The systems point of view is a useful framework for students of management to conceptualize organizations. For managers and future managers, the systems perspective permits seeing the organization as a whole with interdependent parts—a system composed of subsystems. It prevents, or at least deters, lower-level managers from viewing their jobs as managing static, isolated elements of the organization. It encourages all managers to identify and understand the environment in which their system operates. It helps managers to see the organization as stable patterns and actions within boundaries and to gain insights into why organizations are resistant to change. Finally, it directs managers' attention to alternative inputs and processes for reaching their goals.

However, the systems perspective should not be viewed as a panacea. The system's framework has its limitations, the most telling being its abstractness. It is one thing to argue that everything depends on everything else. It is a much different thing to offer suggestions to managers on what precisely will change, and to what degree, if a certain action is taken. Its value, therefore, lies more in its conceptual framework than in its direct applicability to solving managers' organizational problems.

The Life-Cycle Perspective

As noted earlier in this chapter, organizations are born, grow, and eventually die (though it may take a hundred years or more). New organizations are formed daily. At the same time, every day hundreds of organizations close their doors, never to open again. We especially see this birth and death phenomenon among small businesses. They pop up and disappear in every community. In this section, we will build on the biological metaphor of organizations proceeding through life-cycle stages. Like human beings, we will argue, all organizations are born, live, and die. Also, like human beings, some develop faster than others and some do a far better job of aging than others, but the metaphor remains an interesting way to conceptualize the life of an organization.

Definition of a Life Cycle. A **life cycle** refers to a pattern of pre-dictable change. We propose that organizations have life cycles whereby they evolve through a standardized sequence of transitions as they develop over time. By applying the life-cycle metaphor to organizations, we are saying that there are distinct stages through which organizations proceed, that the stages follow a consistent pattern, and that the transitions from one stage to another are predictable rather than random occurrences.

Life-Cycle Stages. The life-cycle concept has received a great deal of attention in the marketing literature. The life cycle is used to show how products move through four stages: birth or formation, growth, maturity, and decline. The implication for management is that the continual introduction of new products is required if the organization is to survive over the long run.

We could use the same four stages in describing organizations, but organizations are not products. Organizations have some unique characteristics, which require some modifications in our description. Research on the organization life cycle leads us to a five-stage model:[6]

1. *Entrepreneurial stage.*   This stage is synonymous with the formation stage in the product life cycle. The organization is in its infancy. Goals tend to be ambiguous. Creativity is high. Progress to the next stage demands acquiring and maintaining a steady supply of resources.

2. *Collectivity stage.*   This stage continues the innovation of the earlier stage, but now the organization's mission is clarified. Communication and structure within the organization remains essentially informal. Members put in long hours and demonstrate high commitment to the organization.

3. *Formalization-and-control stage.*   The structure of the organization stabilizes in the third stage. Formal rules and procedures are imposed. Innovation is deemphasized, while efficiency and stability are emphasized. Decision makers are now more entrenched, with those in senior authority positions in the organization holding power. Decision making also takes on a more conservative posture. At this stage, the organization exists beyond the presence of any one individual. Roles have been clarified so that the departure of members causes no severe threat to the organization.

4. *Elaboration-of-structure stage.* In this stage, the organization diversifies its product or service markets. Management searches for new products and growth opportunities. The organization structure becomes more complex and elaborated. Decision making is decentralized.

5. *Decline stage.* As a result of competition, a shrinking market, or similar forces, the organization in the decline stage finds the demand for its products or services shrinking. Management looks for ways to hold markets and look for new opportunities. Employee turnover, especially among those with the most saleable skills, increases. Conflicts increase within the organization. New people assume leadership in an attempt to arrest the decline. Decision making is centralized in this new leadership.

Do all organizations proceed through the five stages? Not necessarily![7] If possible, management would like to avoid having the organization reach stage five. However, excluding this stage from our model assumes that organizations follow an unending growth curve or at least hold stable. This obviously is an optimistic assumption. No organization, or society for that matter, can endure for eternity. But some can last for a very long time and outlive any of their members. Standard Oil (now Exxon) and U.S. Steel (now USX), for example, are both more than eighty years old. The U.S. government has been around for more than two hundred years. Whether these examples are now in the decline stage is questionable, but certainly our model must recognize decline and even the possibility of death.

Do the life-cycle stages correlate with an organization's chronological age? Not at all! Observation confirms that some organizations have reached stages three and four in less than five years after being formed, while others are forty years old and still in their collectivity stage. In fact, some successful organizations seek to stay in the early stages. For instance, the management of Apple Computer has explicitly stated a commitment to try to remain in stage two as long as it can.[8]

A final question: Can we reconcile our five-stage organization life-cycle model with the more traditional four-stage model of formation, growth, maturity, and decline? The answer is yes. As shown in Figure 1–3, formation and the entrepreneurial stage are synonymous. Collectivity is essentially comparable with growth. Stages three and four in our model—formalization and elaboration—ap-

22

FIGURE 1-3 *Organizational Life Cycle*

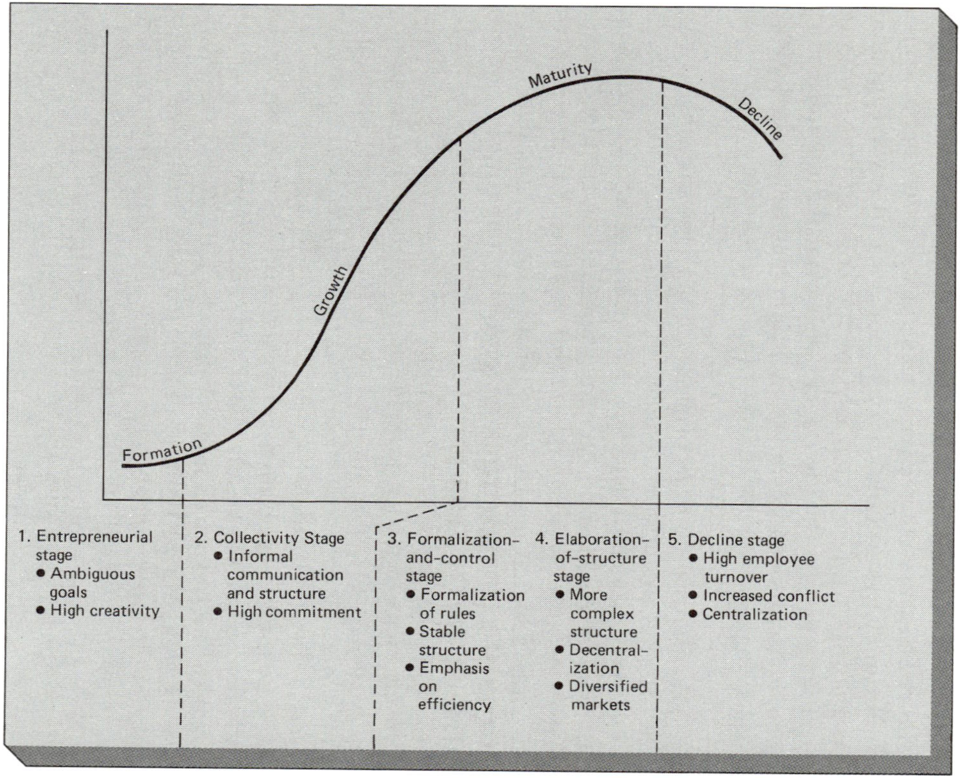

Formation
Growth
Maturity
Decline

1. Entrepreneurial stage
   - Ambiguous goals
   - High creativity

2. Collectivity Stage
   - Informal communication and structure
   - High commitment

3. Formalization-and-control stage
   - Formalization of rules
   - Stable structure
   - Emphasis on efficiency

4. Elaboration-of-structure stage
   - More complex structure
   - Decentralization
   - Diversified markets

5. Decline stage
   - High employee turnover
   - Increased conflict
   - Centralization

pear to align reasonably well with maturity. Finally, of course, decline is consistent in both models.

Importance of the Life-Cycle Perspective. Viewing organizations in a life-cycle perspective offsets the tendency to look at organizations as static entities. Organizations are not snapshots; they are motion pictures. They evolve and change. Using the life-cycle perspective makes us aware when we assess or describe an organization that it hasn't always been the way it is nor will it always be the same in the future.

Additionally, the life-cycle metaphor is valuable when we consider what management can do to make an organization more effective. The actions that are appropriate for a given problem when the organization is growing may be very different if that problem occurs in the decline stage. As a case in point, Chapter 17 will specifically address how managing in a declining organization makes very different demands on a manager than managing during growth.

COMING ATTRACTIONS: THE PLAN OF THIS BOOK

Almost every issue within the field of OT can be cataloged as an answer to one of five questions:

1. How do we know if an organization is successful?
2. What are the components of an organization?
3. What determines the structure of an organization?
4. What options do managers have for designing their organization and when should each be used?
5. How do you apply a knowledge of organization theory to the resolution of current management problems?

Because these five questions are the critical ones in OT, it is only logical that answers to them should be the framework for a textbook on OT. This logic has not been lost on your author. Let us preview the content of this book and demonstrate how it leads to answering the five questions.

The issue of an organization's success is subsumed under the topic of *organizational effectiveness*. This is *the* dependent variable. It is the primary object of our attention. But what constitutes organizational effectiveness is, itself, problematic. In Chapter 3, four approaches to defining and measuring organizational effectiveness are presented. The chapter considers what it is that organizations are trying to do, how various constituencies may define and appraise the same organization's effectiveness differently, and provides guidelines to help you evaluate an organization's effectiveness.

Organization structure has a definite but complicated meaning. As noted previously, the three primary components or *dimensions of an organization* are complexity, formalization, and centralization. They represent the variables that, when combined, create different organizational designs. Chapter 4 takes an in-depth look at each of these dimensions of organization structure.

The most vocal debate in OT surrounds the question of what determines structure. Attention has focused on five determinants: the organization's overall *strategy; size* or the number of people employed by the organization; the degree of routineness in the *technology* used by the organization to transform its inputs into finished products or services; the degree of uncertainty in the organization's *environment;* and the self-serving preferences of those individuals or groups who hold *power and control* in the organization.

The first four of these determinants have been labeled "contingency variables" because their supporters argue that structure will change to reflect changes in these variables.[9] So, for example, if structure is contingent on size, a change in size will result in a change in the organization's structure. The power-control perspective, however, is noncontingent. Its supporters propose that, in all instances, an organization's structure is determined by the interests of those in power and these powerholders will always prefer the structural design that will maximize their control. In Chapters 5 through 9, we review the five determinants and assess under what conditions each can become the major cause of an organization's structure.

If we want to manage an organization's design, we need to know what structural alternatives are at our disposal. And given the various structural types, what are the strengths and weaknesses of each of them. Under what conditions is each preferable? Chapter 10 demonstrates that, by mixing and matching the structural components of complexity, formalization, and centralization, we can develop five basic *organizational design options*. Each is then reviewed and evaluated. Chapters 11 and 12 provide a more in-depth look at two of these options: *bureaucracy* and *adhocracy*. The former is currently the most popular design among large organizations; the latter has increasingly been called "the design of the future."

Certain issues are currently receiving the bulk of attention by organizational theorists as they attempt to offer solutions to organizational problems currently plaguing managers. These include *managing the environment, organizational change, organizational conflict, organizational culture,* and *evolution*. Chapters 13 through 17 look at each of these issues and demonstrate how OT concepts can assist in their management. Following Chapter 17, you'll find a set of cases. They provide additional opportunities to apply OT concepts to the solution of management problems.

Figure 1–4 summarizes the plan of this book and how it has been translated into topics and chapters. Our primary concern is with the impact various structures have on effectiveness. Therefore, we begin with a discussion of organizational effectiveness. Then we define structural components and the determinants of structure. This is followed by a section on the various design options that can be constructed out of the structural components. Attention is continually focused on linking structural designs with effectiveness. That is, after reviewing the various structural options, you should be able to ascertain under what conditions each is preferable. The section on applications demonstrates how OT concepts relate to five current managerial issues.

A final point needs to be made before we proceed to the summary. This point is: OT concepts apply to subunits of an organization as well as to the overall organization. Although we will focus in this book on the structure and design of entire organizations, that is not the only level of analysis to which this book is applicable. The concepts you will be introduced to in the following chapters are relevant to analyzing divisions, departments, and similar subunits within organizations as well as to organizations in their entirety. In fact, most large organizations are too diverse and internally heterogeneous to be treated as a singular structural entity. So when we say that an organization is structured in a certain singular way, in many cases this is a generalization. A closer look typically reveals several different structural forms within most organizations, especially the large and complex ones.

FIGURE 1–4 *Framework for Analyzing Organization Theory*

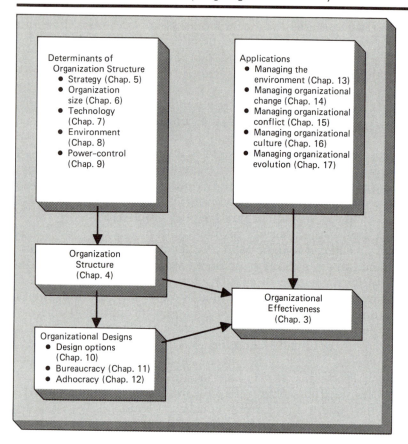

SUMMARY

An organization is a consciously coordinated social entity, with a relatively identifiable boundary, that functions on a relatively continuous basis to achieve a common goal or set of goals. Organization structure is made up of three components: complexity, formalization, and centralization. Organization design is the constructing and changing of structure to achieve the organization's goals. Organization theory is the discipline that studies the structure and design of organizations.

There is no single reason for studying organization theory. It may be merely to understand organization structure. It may be to develop systematic theories of organizations. For many, OT is studied because they expect to be making choices about how organizations will be designed. Realistically, it must also be noted that some study OT not for any direct personal end but rather as a means for fulfilling requirements for a degree or certificate.

The biological metaphor is used to depict organizations as systems that evolve through life-cycle stages. Organizations are described as open systems—made up of interrelated and interdependent parts that produce a unified whole that interacts with its environment. The distinct stages through which organizations evolve are entrepreneurial, collectivity, formalization and control, elaboration of structure, and decline.

FOR REVIEW AND DISCUSSION

1. Are all groups organizations? Discuss.
2. Is a small business, with only two or three employees, an organization?
3. Is OT a prescriptive or a descriptive discipline?
4. How can the systems perspective help you better understand organizations?
5. Compare *open* and *closed* systems.
6. Give an example of (a) negative entropy and (b) equifinality.
7. How can a system be stable yet directed toward growth?
8. Are death rates of public-sector organizations lower than their private-sector counterparts? If so, what does this suggest in terms of organizational life cycles?
9. The birth of a human being is explicitly defined—the emergence of the child from the birth canal. When is an organization born?
10. "An organization is, to some degree, a product of its history." Discuss this statement in light of the life cycle.
11. Is organizational decline inevitable? Defend your position.
12. Contrast organization structure and design.
13. Contrast organizational behavior and organization theory.
14. What is the value of OT for managers? For nonmanagers?
15. For each of the following organizations, identify their inputs, transformation processes, outputs, relevant subsystems, and environment. Be as specific as possible.
    a. the Ford Motor Company
    b. the Roman Catholic church
    c. the Dallas Cowboys football team
    d. U.S. Air Force
    e. St. Joseph's Hospital in Philadelphia
    f. a local drugstore

NOTES

[1] The material on Celestial Seasonings has been adapted from Eric Morgenthaler, "Herb Tea's Pioneer: From Hippie Origins to $16 Million a Year," *Wall Street Journal*, May 7, 1981, p. 1; Nora Gallagher, "We're More Aggressive Than Our Tea," *Across the Board*, July–August 1983, pp. 46–50; "Kraft is Celestial Seasoning's Cup of Tea," *Business Week*, July 28, 1986, p. 73; and "An Herbal Tea Party Gets a Bitter Response," *Business Week*, June 20, 1988, p. 52.

[2] John R. Kimberly, "The Life Cycle Analogy and the Study of Organizations: Introduction," in J. R. Kimberly and R. H. Miles, eds., *The Organizational Life Cycle* (San Francisco: Jossey-Bass, 1980), pp. 6–9.

[3] See, for example, Gareth Morgan, *Images of Organization* (Beverly Hills, Calif.: Sage Publications, 1986).

[4] See Donde P. Ashmos and George P. Huber, "The Systems Paradigm in Organization Theory: Correcting the Record and Suggesting the Future," *Academy of Management Review*, October 1987, pp. 607–21.

[5] This section adapted from Daniel Katz and Robert L. Kahn, *The Social Psychology of Organizations*, 2d ed. (New York: John Wiley, 1978), pp. 23–30.

[6] Adapted from Kim S. Cameron and David A. Whetten, "Models of the Organization Life Cycle: Applications to Higher Education," *Research in Higher Education*, June 1983, pp. 211–24.

[7] James Cook, "Bring On the Wild and Crazy People," *Forbes*, April 28, 1986, pp. 54–56.

[8] Ann M. Morrison, "Apple Bites Back," *Fortune*, February 20, 1984, pp. 86–100.

[9] See, for instance, George Schreyogg, "Continency and Choice in Organization Theory," *Organization Studies*, no. 3, 1980, pp. 305–26; and Henry L. Tosi, Jr., and John W. Slocum, Jr., "Contingency Theory: Some Suggested Directions," *Journal of Management*, Spring 1984, pp. 9–26.

2

THE EVOLUTION OF ORGANIZATION THEORY

AFTER READING THIS CHAPTER, YOU SHOULD BE ABLE TO:

1 Describe the Type 1 through 4 classification framework.
2 Identify Adam Smith's contribution to organization theory.
3 Explain how the Industrial Revolution changed organizations.
4 Define the four principles of scientific management.
5 Describe Henry Fayol's contribution to organization theory.
6 Define Max Weber's bureaucracy.
7 Describe the Hawthorne studies.
8 Contrast Theory X with Theory Y.
9 Identify the major contributors to the contingency approach.
10 Contrast the rational and political perspectives of organizations.

Introduction
UPS: THEY RUN THE TIGHTEST SHIP IN THE SHIPPING BUSINESS

United Parcel Service has been delivering packages for more than eighty years. This privately held company currently has annual revenues in excess of $8 billion and employs 150,000 people to handle between eight and twelve million packages a day. Most of us know little about the company other than it has a lot of funny-looking, dark-brown delivery trucks on the road. But those dark-brown trucks are only part of a well-oiled organization that productivity experts describe as one of the most efficient companies anywhere.[1]

UPS has more than 1000 industrial engineers who use time-study techniques to set standards for every job in the company. For instance, a sorter at one of UPS's one hundred package-sorting hubs is expected to handle 1124 packages an hour and is allowed no more than one mistake per 2500 packages. Drivers of delivery trucks are instructed to walk to a customer's door at the brisk pace of three feet per second, and industrial engineering studies determine the precise time allowances that drivers are permitted for their typical 120 stops per day. UPS also keeps daily worksheets that specify performance goals and work output for every employee and department.

UPS still practices today many of the scientific management principles that, as we'll see, were introduced in the early part of this century by Frederick Taylor.

The current state of organization theory is the result of an evolutionary process. Over a period of many decades, academics and practitioners from diverse backgrounds and with diverse perspectives have studied and analyzed organizations. The purpose of this chapter is to overview these contributions briefly and demonstrate how we got to where we are today. The major theme throughout this review is that current organization theories reflect a cumulative developmental pattern. Theories have been introduced, evaluated, and refined over time; new insights tend to reflect the limitations of earlier theories. So if you want to understand what is happening today in organization theory, you need to look back along the path from which it has come.

DEVELOPING A FRAMEWORK

The real "action" in organization theory has taken place since the turn of the century. There were a few major pre-twentieth-century milestones, which we discuss in the next section. However, the real problem lies in developing a framework that can adequately demonstrate the evolutionary nature of contemporary organization theory. That is, how do you *organize* organization theory?

It has been suggested that there are two underlying dimensions in the evolution of organization theory and that each dimension, in turn, has opposed perspectives.[2] The first dimension reflects that organizations are *systems*. Prior to about 1960, organization theory tended to be dominated by a closed-system perspective. Organizations were seen as essentially autonomous and sealed off from their environment. Beginning around 1960, however, organization theory began to take on a distinctly open-system perspective. Analyses that previously had placed primary focus on the internal characteristics of organization gave way to approaches that emphasized the importance for the organization of events and processes external to it. The second dimension deals with the *ends* of organization structure. Here again are two opposed positions. The rational perspective argues that the structure of an organization is conceived as a vehicle to effectively achieve specified objectives. In contrast, the social perspective emphasizes that structure is primarily the result of the conflicting forces by the organization's constituents who seek power and control. Table 2–1 depicts the evolution of contemporary organization theory along the systems and ends dimensions. The result is four theoretical classifications—labeled Types 1 through 4. The time frame for each is obviously an approximation. In our later discussion, we will introduce a couple of theorists who fall outside these time periods. Overall, however, the data shown in Table 2–1 represent useful guides for understanding the evolution of organization theory.

The early approaches to organization theory in this century conceived of organizations as mechanical devices to achieve goals. As depicted at UPS, attention focused on achieving efficiency in

TABLE 2–1 *Evolution of Contemporary Organization Theory*

APPROXIMATE TIME FRAME	1900–1930	1930–1960	1960–1975	1975–?
Systems perspective	Closed	Closed	Open	Open
Ends perspective	Rational	Social	Rational	Social
Central theme	Mechanical efficiency	People and human relations	Contingency designs	Power and politics
Theoretical classification	Type 1	Type 2	Type 3	Type 4

Based on W. Richard Scott, "Theoretical Perspectives," in Marshall W. Meyer, ed., *Environments and Organizations* (San Francisco: Jossey-Bass Publishers, 1978), p. 22.

internal functions of the organization. We will use the label **Type 1** to describe theorists in this era.

Type 2 theorists operated under closed-system assumptions but emphasized the informal relations and noneconomic motives operating in organizations. Organizations were not well-oiled and perfectly predictable machines. Management could design formal relationships, rules, and the like, but there were informal patterns of communication, status, norms, and friendships created to meet the social needs of organization members.

Rationality returns again in **Type 3**. Theorists during the 1960s and early 1970s saw organizations as the vehicle for achieving goals. They concentrated on size, technology, and environmental uncertainty as the major contingency variables that determined what the right structure for an organization should be. Type 3 theorists argued that properly aligning structure to its contingency variables would facilitate the achievement of the organization's goals. Conversely, implementation of the wrong structure could threaten the organization's survival.

Finally, our current approach to understanding organizations is being strongly influenced by **Type 4** theorists. The social perspective has made a comeback but in an open-system framework. The result is the viewpoint that structure is not the rational effort by managers to create the most effective structure but rather the outcome of the political struggles among coalitions within the organization for control.

We will consider the contributions to organization theory by each type. But first, let's briefly review some of the major contributions that predate the twentieth century.

EARLY CONTRIBUTIONS

Would you believe that organization theory issues were addressed in the Bible? Well they were! For instance, in Exodus, Moses' father-in-law advised Moses:

The thing thou doest is not good. Thou wilt surely wear away, both thou, and this people that is with thee: for this thing is too heavy for thee; thou are not able to perform it thyself alone. Hearken now unto my voice, I will give thee counsel. . . . Moreover thou shalt provide out of all the people able men . . . and place such over them, to be rulers of thousands, and rulers of hundreds, rulers of fifties, and rulers of tens: And let them judge the people at all seasons: and it shall be, that every great matter they shall bring unto thee, but every small matter they shall judge: so shall it be easier for thyself, and they shall bear the burden with thee. If thou shalt do this thing, and God command thee so, then thou shalt be able to endure, and all this people shall also go to their place in peace.[3]

Though the biblical language is a bit antiquated, the message is not: Managers need to delegate authority in large organizations, and only the unusual or exceptional decisions should flow back up the hierarchy for resolution. This brief quotation also provides a simplistic explanation of why diagrams of organization structures have been historically pyramid shaped.

The best structure for an organization is one that promotes effective work effort and minimizes complexity. Such a structure would be both effective and efficient. One of the most enduring and successful models of such a structure is the simple hierarchy of the Roman Catholic church. Its simple, five-level design has proven effective for nearly 2000 years. While the church now has over 400,000 clergy, it still essentially centralizes authority in Rome, with authority moving downward from the pope to cardinals to archbishops to bishops and finally to parish priests.

Most of us are familiar with the advantages of **division of labor**. We know, for instance, that General Motors can produce automobiles at a lower cost by breaking jobs up into a number of smaller tasks. Having employees perform narrow and standardized tasks over and over again as the cars proceed down an assembly line provides significant economies in GM's manufacturing process. But the recognition that there are advantages in the division of labor is not a recent phenomenon. While Henry Ford is widely recognized as having introduced the assembly line to the manufacture of cars in the early years of this century, the advantages of division of labor were recognized and being practiced in Europe more than two centuries ago. For instance, Adam Smith wrote in 1776 about the economic advantages from division of labor in the pin-manufacturing industry.[4] Smith noted that ten individuals, each doing a specialized task, could produce about forty-eight thousand pins a day among them. He proposed, however, that if each were working separately and independently, the ten workers would be lucky to make two hundred, or even ten, pins combined in one day. Smith concluded then what most practicing managers now accept as common sense, that division of labor can bring about significant economic efficiencies.

One of the most important pre-twentieth-century milestones, in terms of its impact on organization theory, was the Industrial Revolution. Begun in the eighteenth century in Great Britain, the revolution had crossed the Atlantic to America by the end of the Civil War. The revolution had two major elements in the United States: Machine power was rapidly replacing human power, and the building of canals and railroads was rapidly changing transportation methods. The result was the widespread creation of factories. Large factories could use steam power to run hundreds of machines efficiently. Finished goods could then be shipped inexpensively by ship or rail throughout the country. The impact on organization design should be obvious. The building of factories required the simultaneous creation of organization structures to facilitate efficient manufacturing processes. Jobs had to be defined, work flows established, departments created, and coordination mechanisms developed. In short, complex organization structures had to be designed.

Let's now turn to contributions made during this century. We will begin with the Type 1 theorists.

TYPE 1 THEORISTS

The Type 1 theorists, also known as the classical school, developed universal principles or models that would apply in all situations. As noted previously, each essentially perceived organizations as closed systems created to achieve goals efficiently.

Frederick Taylor and Scientific Management

The publication in 1911 of Frederick Winslow Taylor's *Principles of Scientific Management* marked the beginning of serious theory building in the field of management and organizations.[5] Taylor was a mechanical engineer by background, employed by Midvale and Bethlehem Steel companies in Pennsylvania. He strongly believed, based on his observation of work methods at the time, that worker output was only about one-third of what was possible. He set out to correct the situation by applying the scientific method to jobs on the shop floor. His desire to find the "one best way" in which each job should be done would be part of what today we would call the issue of work design.

After years of conducting experiments with workers, he proposed four principles of **scientific management,** that, he argued, would result in significant increases in productivity: (1) the replacement of rule-of-thumb methods for determining each element of a worker's job with scientific determination; (2) the scientific selection and training of workers; (3) the cooperation of management and labor to accomplish work objectives, in accordance with the scientific method; and (4) a more equal division of responsibility between managers and workers, with the former doing the planning and supervising, and the latter doing the execution.

In retrospect, we recognize that Taylor offered a limited focus on organizations. He was looking only at organizing work at the lowest level of the organization—appropriate to the managerial job of a supervisor. If you were to take a course today in industrial engineering or production management, you would find that Taylor's work created the foundation for these disciplines. Yet in spite of the fact that he focused on a very limited segment of organizational activity, he revolutionized the manager's job. He explicitly demonstrated that managers should carefully assess the one best way for each job to be done to maximize efficiency. Then it was management's responsibility to explicitly select, train, and motivate workers to ensure that the one best way was followed.

Henri Fayol and Principles of Organization

At about the same time that Taylor was writing up the results of his research on shop management in the United States, the Frenchman Henri Fayol was consolidating his **principles of organization**.[6] Though they were writing at the same time, Fayol's and Taylor's foci were considerably different. Taylor's ideas were based on scientific research whereas Fayol wrote based on his years of experience as a practicing executive. Further, Fayol sought to develop general principles applicable to all managers at all levels of the organization and to describe the functions a manager should perform. Taylor, you will remember, focused on the lowest level in the organization—shop-level management.

Fayol proposed fourteen principles that he argued were universally applicable and could be taught in schools and universities. Many of these organizing principles, though lacking in universality, certainly are widely followed by managers today:

1. *Division of work.* This principle is the same as Adam Smith's "division of labor." Specialization increases output by making employees more efficient.

2. *Authority.* Managers need to be able to give orders. Authority gives them this right. Along with authority, however, goes responsibility. Wherever authority is exercised, responsibility arises. To be effective, a manager's authority must equal his or her responsibility.

3. *Discipline.* Employees need to obey and respect the rules that govern the organization. Good discipline is the result of effective leadership, a clear understanding between management and workers regarding the organization's rules, and the judicious use of penalties for infractions of the rules.

4. *Unity of command.* Every employee should receive orders from only one superior.

5. *Unity of direction.* Each group of organizational activities that have the same objective should be directed by one manager using one plan.

6. *Subordination of individual interests to the general interests.* The interests of any one employee or group of employees should not take precedence over the interests of the organization as a whole.

7. *Remuneration.* Workers must be paid a fair wage for their services.

8. *Centralization.* This refers to the degree to which subordinates are involved in decision making. Whether decision making is centralized (to management) or decentralized (to subordinates) is a question of proper proportion. The problem is to find the optimum degree of centralization for each situation.

9. *Scalar chain.* The line of authority from top management to the lowest ranks represents the scalar chain. Communications should follow this chain. However, if following the chain creates delays, cross communication—a "gangplank"—can be allowed if agreed to by all parties and superiors are kept informed.

10. *Order.* People and materials should be in the right place at the right time.

11. *Equity.* Managers should be kind and fair to their subordinates.

12. *Stability of tenure of personnel.* High employee turnover is inefficient. Management should provide orderly personnel planning and ensure that replacements are available to fill vacancies.

13. *Initiative.* Employees who are allowed to originate and carry out plans will exert high levels of effort.
14. *Esprit de corps.* Promoting team spirit will build harmony and unity within the organization.

Max Weber and Bureaucracy

The third major contribution made by Type 1 theorists was the "ideal-type" organization structure proposed by the German sociologist, Max Weber.[7] Writing in the early part of this century, Weber developed a structural model that, he argued, was the most efficient means by which organizations can achieve their ends. He called this ideal structure **bureaucracy**. It was characterized by division of labor, a clear authority hierarchy, formal selection procedures, detailed rules and regulations, and impersonal relationships. Weber's description of bureaucracy became the design prototype for the structure of most of today's large organizations.

Ralph Davis and Rational Planning

The final contribution of the Type 1 theorists that we will introduce is the **rational-planning** perspective, which proposed that structure was the logical outcome of the organization's objectives. This position was best expressed in the work of Ralph C. Davis.[8]

Davis stated that the primary objective of a business firm is economic service. No business can survive if it doesn't provide economic value. This economic value is generated by the activities members engage in to create the organization's products or services. These activities then link the organization's objectives to its results. It is management's job to group these activities together in such a way as to form the structure of the organization. Davis concluded, therefore, that the structure of the organization is contingent upon the organization's objectives.

The rational-planning perspective offered a simple and straightforward model for designing an organization. Management's formal planning determines the organization's objectives. These objectives, then, in logical fashion, determine the development of structure, the flow of authority, and other relationships.

TYPE 2 THEORISTS

The common theme among Type 2 theorists is recognition of the social nature of organizations. These theorists, who are frequently referred to as forming the human-relations school, view organizations as made up of both tasks and people. Type 2 theorists represent a human counterpoint to Type 1's machine view.

Elton Mayo and the Hawthorne Studies

The second stage in contemporary organization theory began with a set of experiments undertaken at Western Electric Company's Hawthorne Works in Cicero, Illinois, between 1924 and 1927. These **Hawthorne studies**, which would eventually be widely expanded and would carry on through the early 1930s, were initially devised by Western Electric industrial engineers to examine the effect of various illumination levels on worker productivity. Control and experimental groups were established. The experimental group was presented with varying intensity of illumination, while the controlled unit worked under a constant illumination intensity. The engineers had expected individual output to be directly related to the intensity of light. However, there were contradictions in their findings. As the light level was increased in the experimental unit, output rose for each group. To the surprise of the engineers, as the light level was dropped in the experimental group, productivity continued to increase in both. In fact, a productivity decrease was observed in the experimental group only when the light intensity had been reduced to that of moonlight. The engineers concluded that illumination intensity clearly was not directly related to group productivity, but they could not explain the behavior they had witnessed.

The Western Electric engineers turned to Harvard psychologist Elton Mayo and his associates in 1927 to join the study as consultants. This began a relationship that would last through 1932 and encompass numerous experiments covering the redesign of jobs, changes in the length of the workday and workweek, introduction of rest periods, and individual versus group wage plans.[9] For example, in one experiment the researchers sought to evaluate the effect of a group piecework incentive pay system on group productivity. The results indicated that the wage-incentive plan was less of a determining factor on a worker's output than were group pressure and acceptance and the concomitant security. Social norms of the group, therefore, were concluded to be the key determinants of individual work behavior.

It is generally agreed upon by management scholars that the Hawthorne studies had a dramatic impact on the direction of management and organization theory. It ushered in an era of organizational humanism. Managers would no longer consider the issue of organization design without including effects on work groups, employee attitudes, and manager-employee relationships.

Chester Barnard and Cooperative Systems

Merging the ideas of Taylor, Fayol, and Weber with the results from the Hawthorne studies led to the conclusion that organizations are cooperative systems. They are composed of tasks and people that have to be maintained at an equilibrium state. Attention only to technical jobs or the needs of people who do the jobs suboptimizes the system. So managers need to organize around the requirements of the tasks to be done and the needs of the people who will do them.

The notion that an organization is a cooperative system is generally credited to Chester Barnard. He presented his ideas in *The Functions of the Executive*, in which he drew upon his years of experience with American Telephone and Telegraph, including the presidency of New Jersey Bell.[10]

In addition to being one of the first to treat organizations as systems, Barnard also offered other important insights. He challenged the classical view that authority flowed from the top down by arguing that authority should be defined in terms of the response of the subordinate; he introduced the role of the informal organization to organization theory; and he proposed that the manager's major roles were to facilitate communication and to stimulate subordinates to high levels of effort.

Douglas McGregor and Theory X—Theory Y

One of the most frequently mentioned contributions from Type 2 theorists is Douglas McGregor's thesis that there are two distinct views of human beings: one basically negative—**Theory X**—and the other basically positive—**Theory Y**.[11] After reviewing the way managers dealt with employees, McGregor concluded that a manager's view of the nature of human beings is based on a certain grouping of assumptions and that he or she tends to mold his or her behavior toward subordinates according to these assumptions.

Under Theory X, four assumptions are held by managers:

1. Employees inherently dislike work and, whenever possible, will attempt to avoid it.
2. Since employees dislike work, they must be coerced, controlled, or threatened with punishment to achieve desired goals.
3. Employees will shirk responsibilities and seek formal direction whenever possible.
4. Most workers place security above all other factors associated with work and will display little ambition.

In contrast to these negative views of human beings, McGregor listed four other assumptions that he called Theory Y:

1. Employees can view work as being as natural as rest or play.
2. Human beings will exercise self-direction and self-control if they are committed to the objectives.
3. The average person can learn to accept, even seek, responsibility.
4. Creativity—that is, the ability to make good decisions—is widely dispersed throughout the population and is not necessarily the sole province of those in managerial functions.

What are the implications of McGregor's Theory X and Theory Y to organization theory? McGregor argued that Theory Y assumptions were preferable and that they should guide managers in the way they designed their organizations and motivated their employees. Much of the enthusiasm, beginning in the 1960s, for participative decision making, the creation of responsible and challenging jobs for employees, and developing good group relations can be traced to McGregor's advocacy that managers follow Theory Y assumptions.

Warren Bennis and the Death of Bureaucracy

The strong humanistic theme of the Type 2 theorists culminated with a eulogy to the passing of bureaucracy.[12] Warren Bennis, for example, claimed that bureaucracy's centralized decision making, impersonal submission to authority, and narrow division of labor was being replaced by decentralized and democratic structures organized around flexible groups. Influence based on authority was giving way to influence derived from expertise. In the same way that Weber argued that bureaucracy was the ideal organization, Warren Bennis argued the other extreme—conditions now pointed to flexible adhocracies as the ideal organizational form. In fifty years we had essentially moved from one extreme position to another.

TYPE 3 THEORISTS

Neither the mechanistic forces of darkness nor the humanistic forces of light could muster evidence that their solution, and only their solution, was right for all occasions. The conflict between thesis and antithesis led to a synthesis that provided better guidance to managers. That synthesis was a contingency approach.

Herbert Simon and Principles Backlash

The contingency movement gained its momentum in the 1960s; however, Herbert Simon recognized in the 1940s that Type 1 principles would have to give way to a contingency approach. Simon noted that most classical principles were nothing more than proverbs, and many contradicted each other. He argued that organization theory needed to go beyond superficial and oversimplified principles to a study of the conditions under which competing principles were applicable.[13] Still, the 1950s and 1960s tended to be dominated by simplistic principles—of both the mechanistic and humanistic variety. It took approximately twenty years for organization theorists to effectively respond to Simon's challenge.

Katz and Kahn's Environmental Perspective

Daniel Katz and Robert Kahn's book *The Social Psychology of Organizations*, was a major impetus toward promoting the Type 3 open-systems perspective to organization theory.[14] Their book provided a convincing description of the advantages of an open-systems perspective for examining the important relations of an organization with its environment and the need for organizations to adapt to a changing environment if they are to survive.

Since Katz and Kahn's work, numerous theorists have investigated the environment-structure relationship. Various types of environments have been identified, and much research has been conducted to evaluate which structures mesh best with the various environments. No current discussion of organization theory would be complete without a thorough assessment of environment as a major contingency factor influencing the preferred form of structure.

The Case for Technology

Research in the 1960s by Joan Woodward and Charles Perrow, as well as the conceptual framework offered by James Thompson, have made an impressive case for the importance of technology in determining the appropriate structure for an organization.[15] As with environment, no contemporary discussion of organization theory would be complete without consideration of technology and the need for managers to match structure with technology.

The Aston Group and Organization Size

In addition to advocates of environment and technology, the Type 3 theorists include those who advocate organization size as an important factor influencing structure. This position has been most zealously argued by researchers associated with the University of Aston in Great Britain.[16] Large organizations have been shown to have many common structural components. So, too, have small organizations. Maybe most important, the evidence suggests that certain of these components follow an established pattern as organizations expand in size. Such evidence has proven valuable to managers in helping them make organization-design decisions as their organizations grew.

TYPE 4 THEORISTS

The most recent approach to organization theory focuses on the political nature of organizations. The early formation of this position was made by James March and Herbert Simon, but it has been extensively refined by Jeffrey Pfeffer.

March and Simon's Cognitive Limits to Rationality

March and Simon challenged the classical notion of rational or optimum decisions.[17] They argued that most decision makers selected satisfactory alternatives—alternatives that were good enough. Only in exceptional cases would they be concerned with the discovery and selection of optimal alternatives. March and Simon called for a revised model of organization theory—one very different from the rational cooperative-systems view. This revised model would recognize the limits of a decision maker's rationality and acknowledge the presence of conflicting goals.

Pfeffer's Organizations as Political Arenas

Jeffrey Pfeffer has built on March and Simon's work to create a model of organization theory that encompasses power coalitions, inherent conflict over goals, and organizational-design decisions that favor the self-interest of those in power.[18] Pfeffer proposes that control in organizations becomes an end rather than merely a means to rational goals such as efficient production of output. Organizations are coalitions composed of varying groups and individuals with different demands. An organization's design represents the result of the power struggles by these diverse coalitions. Pfeffer argues that if we want to understand how and why organizations are designed the way they are, we need to assess the preferences and interests of those in the organization who have influence over the design decisions. This view is currently very much in vogue.

SUMMARY

Modern organization theory began with the work of the Type 1 theorists. They relied heavily on simplistic and universal principles, developing models of organization that were overly rational and mechanistic. The Type 2 theorists, to a large degree, represented a counterpoint to the rational-mechanistic view. The focus moved away from division of labor and centralized authority toward democratic organizations. The human factor, which tended to be treated as a predictable "given" by the Type 1 theorists, moved to center stage as the core of organization theory in the years between 1930 and 1960.

The current state of organization theory more fully reflects the contributions of the Type 3 and Type 4 theorists. Contingency advocates have taken the insights provided by the earlier theorists and reframed them in a situational context. The contingency view, in addition to underlining the point that there is not "one best way," has made significant strides in identifying those contingency variables that are most important for determining the right structure. The political perspective taken by the Type 4 theorists, which builds on our knowledge of behavioral decision making and political science, has significantly improved our ability to explain organizational phenomena that the contingency advocates' rational assumptions overlooked.

FOR REVIEW AND DISCUSSION

1. Explain how the rational perspective of Type 1 and Type 3 theorists creates a common ground in their viewpoints.
2. Explain how the social perspective of Type 2 and Type 4 theorists creates a common ground in their viewpoint.
3. Are open-systems perspectives superior to the closed variety? Explain.
4. How might theory guide practice?
5. "Adam Smith could be labeled a Type 1 theorist." Do you agree or disagree? Discuss.
6. Contrast Taylor's and Fayol's level of organizational analysis.
7. How valid are Fayol's principles today?
8. "Since most large organizations today are bureaucracies, Weber could be accurately labeled as a Type 4 theorist." Do you agree or disagree? Discuss.
9. What are the implications of the Hawthorne studies to contemporary organization theory?
10. Do you think most managers hold Theory X or Theory Y views of people? How might this view affect their organization-design decisions?

11. What are the key contingency variables that Type 3 theorists have studied?

12. Are the four views in the Type 1–4 classification independent? Defend your position.

NOTES

¹ This example is based on "Behind the UPS Mystique: Puritanism Activity," *Business Week*, June 6, 1983, pp. 66–73; and Daniel Machalaba, "United Parcel Service Gets Deliveries Done by Driving Its Workers," *Wall Street Journal*, April 22, 1986, pp. 1, 26.

² This section is based on W. Richard Scott, "Theoretical Perspectives," in Marshall W. Meyer, ed., *Environments and Organizations* (San Francisco: Jossey-Bass, 1978), pp. 21–28.

³ Exod. 18:17–23.

⁴ Adam Smith, *An Inquiry into the Nature and Causes of the Wealth of Nations* (New York: Modern Library, 1937). Originally published in 1776.

⁵ Frederick W. Taylor, *The Principles of Scientific Management* (New York: Harper & Row, 1911).

⁶ Henri Fayol, *Administration Industrielle et Generale*, (Paris: Dunod, 1916).

⁷ Max Weber, *The Theory of Social and Economic Organizations*, ed., Talcott Parsons, trans. A. M. Henderson and Talcott Parsons (New York: Free Press, 1947).

⁸ See, for example, Ralph C. Davis, *The Principles of Factory Organization and Management* (New York: Harper & Row, 1928); and *The Fundamentals of Top Management* (New York: Harper & Row, 1951).

⁹ Elton Mayo, *The Human Problems of Industrial Civilization* (New York: Macmillan, 1933); and Fritz J. Roethlisberger and William J. Dickson, *Management and the Worker* (Cambridge, Harvard University Press, 1939).

¹⁰ Chester I. Barnard, *The Functions of the Executive* (Cambridge: Harvard University Press, 1938).

¹¹ Douglas McGregor, *The Human Side of Enterprise* (New York: McGraw-Hill, 1960).

¹² Warren G. Bennis, "The Coming Death of Bureaucracy," *Think*, November–December 1966, pp. 30–35.

¹³ Herbert A. Simon, *Administrative Behavior: A Study of Decision-Making Processes in Administrative Organizations* (New York: Macmillan, 1947).

¹⁴ Daniel Katz and Robert L. Kahn, *The Social Psychology of Organizations* (New York: John Wiley, 1966).

¹⁵ Joan Woodward, *Industrial Organization: Theory and Practice* (London: Oxford University Press, 1965); Charles Perrow, "A Framework for the Comparative Analysis of Organizations," *American Sociological Review*,

April 1967, pp. 194–208; and James D. Thompson, *Organizations in Action* (New York: McGraw-Hill, 1967).

[16] See, for example, Derek S. Pugh, David J. Hickson, C. R. Hinings, and C. Turner, "The Context of Organization Structures," *Administrative Science Quarterly*, March 1969, pp. 91–114.

[17] James G. March and Herbert Simon, *Organizations* (New York: John Wiley, 1958).

[18] Jeffrey Pfeffer, *Organizational Design* (Arlington Heights, Ill.: AHM Publishing, 1978); and *Power in Organizations* (Marshfield, Mass.: Pitman Publishing, 1981).

ORGANIZATIONAL EFFECTIVENESS

3

AFTER READING THIS CHAPTER, YOU SHOULD BE ABLE TO:

1 Define four approaches to organizational effectiveness.
2 List the assumptions of each OE approach.
3 Describe how managers can operationalize each approach.
4 Identify key problems with each approach.
5 Explain the value of each approach to practicing managers.
6 Compare the conditions under which each is useful for managers.

Introduction
ARE YOU SURE YOU KNOW WHAT EFFECTIVENESS IS?

On the average, each Toyota employee produces 57.7 vehicles a year. In contrast, Ford gets only 16.1 vehicles from each employee. Similarly, Toyota spends only $630 on labor for each vehicle, whereas Ford spends $2379. Yet, Ford earns $555 per vehicle to only $466 for Toyota.[1] Which company—Ford or Toyota—would you consider more effective?

During the year 1987, Monsanto's sales rose 11 percent over 1986. In contrast, during the same period, Rohm & Haas Chemical's sales rose only 7 percent. Yet, Rohm & Haas' profit increased 41 percent compared to only 1 percent for Monsanto.[2] Which is more effective—Monsanto or Rohm & Haas? And if that's hard to answer, try this: Warner-Lambert's profits declined in 1987, but its return on invested capital that year was a whopping 30.5 percent, far more impressive than Monsanto's 11.2

percent or Rohm & Haas' 17.8 percent.[3] Now, which of these three is more effective?

How do you determine if a college is doing a good job? If all its students get jobs upon graduation, does that tell us the college is effective? Or should we be looking at the percentage increase or decrease in freshmen applications, a statistical report of the number of books checked out from the library by students during the past academic year, a survey asking seniors what they thought of their college experience, the number of publications by faculty members, awards won by graduates, or the average salary of former students twenty years after graduation?

These examples are meant to introduce the problems inherent in defining and measuring organizational effectiveness (OE). As you will see, historically researchers have had considerable difficulty in trying to agree on what the term means. Yet almost all these same researchers are quick to acknowledge that this term—organizational effectiveness—is the central theme in organization theory. In fact, it is difficult to conceive of a theory of organizations that does *not* include the concept of effectiveness.[4]

IMPORTANCE OF ORGANIZATIONAL EFFECTIVENESS

Every discipline in the administrative sciences contributes in some way to helping managers make organizations more effective. Marketing, for instance, guides managers in expanding revenues and market share. Financial concepts assist managers in making the optimum use of funds invested in the organization. Production and operations management concepts offer guidance in designing efficient production processes. Accounting principles assist managers by providing information that can enhance the quality of the decisions they make.

Organization theory presents another answer to the question: What makes an organization effective? That answer is, the proper organization structure! This book will demonstrate that the way we put people and jobs together and define their roles and relationships is an important determinant in whether an organization is successful. As we will demonstrate in later chapters, some structures work better under certain conditions than do others. Importantly, those managers who understand their structural options and the conditions under which each is preferred will have a definite advantage over their less informed counterparts. Organization theory, as a discipline, clarifies which organization structure will lead to, or improve, organizational effectiveness.

Unfortunately, as noted earlier, there is no universal agreement on precisely what organizational effectiveness means. Let's take a look at where we are today in our understanding of OE.

IN SEARCH OF A DEFINITION

The early approach to OE—which probably lasted through the 1950s—was innocently simple. Effectiveness was defined as the degree to which an organization realized its goals.[5] Hidden in this definition, however, were many ambiguities that severely curtailed both research on the subject and practicing managers' ability to grasp and use the concept. For example: Whose goals? Short-term goals or long-term goals? The organization's official goals or actual goals?

Our point may be clearer when we take a goal that most researchers and practitioners agree is a necessary condition for an organization's success: *survival*.[6] If there is anything that an organization seeks to do, it is to survive. But the use of survival as a criterion presumes the ability to identify the death of an organization. Survival is an "alive or dead" evaluation. Unfortunately, organizations don't die as neatly as humans. When a human being dies, we get a certificate that states the precise time of passing and the presumed cause of death. No such equivalent exists for organizations. In fact, most organizations don't die—they're remade. They merge, reorganize, sell off major parts, or move into totally new areas of endeavor. For instance, American Motors no longer exists, but its manufacturing plants, employees, and car designations (i.e., Jeep, Eagle) continue on as part of Chrysler. And International Harvester, which built its reputation in farm equipment, has changed its name to Navistar International and sold its farm machinery business. Navistar is now in the truck-manufacturing business. In the real world, many organizations disappear from the scene or are reformed into another entity—making it difficult to make a survival judgment. Additionally, it would be naive to assume that there are not organizations that survive that are still ineffective or that are effective but purposely not allowed to survive. For some organizations—and favorite targets include government agencies and large corporations—death practically never occurs.[7] They seem to have a life beyond any evaluation as to whether they are doing a good job. Similarly, a week rarely goes by when some management team doesn't conclude that their firm is most effective when it is liquidated, dissolved, or absorbed by some other company. That is, effectiveness is improved by going out of business! Our point should now be obvious: even a goal that almost everyone agrees is important—survival—bogs down under more careful scrutiny.

The 1960s and early 1970s saw a proliferation of OE studies. A review of these studies identified thirty different criteria—all purporting to measure "organizational effectiveness." They are listed in Table 3–1. The fact that few studies used multiple criteria and that the criteria themselves ranged from general measures such as quality and morale to more specific factors such as accident rates and absenteeism certainly leads to the conclusion that organizational effectiveness means different things to different people. Some

TABLE 3–1 *Organizational Effectiveness Criteria*

1. Overall effectiveness	17. Goal consensus
2. Productivity	18. Internalization of organizational goals
3. Efficiency	19. Role and norm congruence
4. Profit	20. Managerial interpersonal
5. Quality	skills
6. Accidents	21. Managerial task skills
7. Growth	22. Information management and
8. Absenteeism	communication
9. Turnover	23. Readiness
10. Job satisfaction	24. Utilization of environment
11. Motivation	25. Evaluations by external entities
12. Morale	26. Stability
13. Control	27. Value of human resources
14. Conflict/cohesion	28. Participation and shared influence
15. Flexibility/adaptation	29. Training and development emphasis
16. Planning and goal setting	30. Achievement emphasis

Source: Drawn from John P. Campbell, "On the Nature of Organizational Effectiveness," in P. S. Goodman, J. M. Pennings, and Associates, eds., *New Perspectives on Organizational Effectiveness* (San Francisco: Jossey-Bass, 1977), pp. 36–41.

of the items in Table 3–1 are even contradictory. Efficiency, for instance, is achieved by using resources to their maximum. It is characterized by an *absence* of slack. In contrast, flexibility/ adaptation can be achieved only by having a surplus; that is, by the *availability* of slack. If absence of slack is a measure of effectiveness, how can a surplus of slack also be a measure of effectiveness?

No doubt part of the length of Table 3–1 is due to the diversity of organizations being evaluated. Additionally, it also reflects the different interests of the evaluators. As we argue later in this chapter, when we consider more specifically how values affect organizational effectiveness, the criteria chosen to define OE may tell more about the person doing the evaluation than about the organization being evaluated. But all thirty criteria cannot be relevant to every organization, and certainly some must be more important than others. The researcher who tabulated these thirty criteria concluded that since an organization can be effective or ineffective on a number of different facets that may be relatively independent of one another, organizational effectiveness has no "operational definition."[8]

This belief that OE defies definition has been widely accepted. From a research perspective, it may be true. On the other hand, a close look at the recent OE literature does see movement toward agreement. Even more important, from a practical standpoint, all of us have and use some operational definition of OE on a regular basis. That is so in spite of a supposed problem by researchers to define it.[9] Let us elaborate on each of these points.

It may have been correct ten years ago to argue that defining OE was equivalent to trying to nail Jello to the wall. A close look at the recent OE literature, however, indicates that scholars may have been focusing for so long on differences that commonalities have been overlooked.[10] As will become evident by the time you finish reading this chapter, there is almost unanimous agreement today that OE requires multiple criteria, that different organizational functions have to be evaluated using different characteristics, and that OE must consider both means (process) and ends (outcomes). If the search was to find a single and universal criterion of OE, then disappointment is understandable. But because organizations do many things and their success depends on adequate performance in a number of areas, the definition of OE must reflect this complexity. The result is that we have to hold our statement of a formal definition to the end of this chapter, after a number of OE concepts have been discussed.

It is occasionally lost on researchers that regardless of whether they can define and label a phenomenon, that phenomenon is still real and continues to function. Gravitation existed for a long time before Newton "discovered" it. While researchers may debate about

OT
CLOSE-UP

A BEST-SELLER'S DEFINITION OF ORGANIZATIONAL EFFECTIVENESS

One of the most successful management books of all times is Tom Peters and Robert Waterman's *In Search of Excellence,* published in 1982.[11] The book has sold more than five million copies!

After studying forty-two companies that Peters and Waterman described as well-managed, highly effective, or "excellent"—these included firms like IBM, Du Pont, 3M, McDonald's, and Procter & Gamble—they found eight common characteristics that these companies had in common. (1) They had a bias for action and getting things accomplished. (2) They stayed close to their customers in order to fully understand their customers' needs. (3) They allowed employees a high degree of autonomy and fostered the entrepreneurial spirit. (4) They sought to increase productivity through employee participation. (5) Their employees knew what the company stands for, and their managers were actively involved in problems at all levels. (6) They stayed close to the businesses they knew and understood. (7) They had organization structures that were elegantly simple, with a minimal number of people in staff support activities. (8) They blended tight, centralized controls for protecting the company's core values with loose controls in other areas to encourage risk-taking and innovation.

While Peters and Waterman's research methods and conclusions have received their share of criticism,[12] it would be naive to ignore the influence that their book has had. For many practicing managers during the middle and late 1980s, *In Search of Excellence* became their managerial Bible. The eight characteristics became similar to commandments, the achievement of which defined organizational effectiveness.

whether or not OE can be defined, the fact is that all of us have a working definition of the term. We all make OE judgments regularly, whenever we buy stock, choose a college, select a bank or car-repair shop, decide which organization will get our donations, and make other, similar decisions. Managers and administrators, of course, also make regular OE determinations when they appraise and compare units or allocate budgets to these units. The point is that evaluating the effectiveness of an organization is a widespread and ongoing activity. From a managerial perspective alone, judgments of OE are going to be made with or without agreement on a formal definition. When managers seek answers to whether things are going well, what needs change, or attempt to compare their organization with others, they are making OE judgments.

The remainder of this chapter is devoted to presenting the diverse approaches that the study of OE has taken. It concludes with an integrative framework that acknowledges the earlier approaches, deals overtly with their differences, and provides a clear but complex definition of organizational effectiveness.

THE GOAL-ATTAINMENT APPROACH

An organization is, by definition, created deliberately to achieve one or more specified goals.[13] It should come as no surprise then to find that goal attainment is probably the most widely used criterion of effectiveness.

The **goal-attainment approach** states that an organization's effectiveness must be appraised in terms of the accomplishment of *ends* rather than means. It is the bottom line that counts. Popular goal-attainment criteria include profit maximization, bringing the enemy to surrender, winning the basketball game, restoring patients to good health, and the like. Their common denominator is that they consider the ends to which the organization was created to achieve.

Assumptions

The goal-attainment approach assumes that organizations are deliberate, rational, goal-seeking entities. As such, successful goal accomplishment becomes an appropriate measure of effectiveness. But the use of goals implies other assumptions that must be valid if goal accomplishment is to be a viable measure. First, organizations must have ultimate goals. Second, these goals must be identified and defined well enough to be understood. Third, these goals must be few enough to be manageable. Fourth, there must be general consensus or agreement on these goals. Finally, progress toward these goals must be measurable.

Making Goals Operative

Given that the assumptions cited are valid, how would managers operationalize the goal-attainment approach? The key decision makers would be the group from which the goals would be obtained. This group would be asked to state the organization's specific goals. Once identified, it would be necessary to develop some measurement device to see how well the goals are being met. If, for instance, the consensus goal were profit maximization, measures such as return on investment, return on sales, or some similar computation would be selected.

The goal-attainment approach is probably most explicit in **management by objectives** (MBO). MBO is a well-known philosophy of management that assesses an organization and its members by how well they achieve specific goals that superiors and subordinates have jointly established. Tangible, verifiable, and measurable goals are developed. The conditions under which they are to be accomplished is specified. The degree to which each goal must be satisfied is also specified. Actual performance is then measured and compared with the goals. Because either an organization accomplishes the specific tasks that it is supposed to or it does not, MBO represents the ultimate in a goal-oriented approach to effectiveness.[14]

Problems

The goal-attainment approach is fraught with a number of problems that make its exclusive use highly questionable. Many of these problems relate directly to the assumptions that we noted earlier.

It is one thing to talk about goals in general, but when you operationalize the goal-attainment approach you have to ask: Whose goals? Top management's? If so, who is included and who is excluded? In some large corporations, just surveying vice presidents and above can include dozens of respondents. It's also possible that some of the decision makers with real power and influence in the organization are not members of senior management. There are cases in which individuals with a number of years of experience or particular expertise in an important area have a significant influence on determining their organization's goals (they are part of the dominant coalition), even though they are not among the senior executive cadre.

What an organization states officially as its goals does not always reflect the organization's actual goals.[15] Official goals tend to be influenced strongly by standards of social desirability. Representative statements such as "to produce quality products at competitive prices," "to be a responsible member of the community," "to ensure that our productive efforts do nothing to damage the environment," "to maintain our reputation for integrity," and "to hire the handicapped and members of minorities" were gleaned from several corporate brochures. These vague "apple pie and flag" official statements may sound good, but rarely do they make any contribution to an understanding of what the organization is actually trying to accomplish. Given the likelihood that official and actual goals will be different, an assessment of an organization's goals should probably include the statements made by the dominant coalition plus an additional listing derived from observations of what members in the organization are actually doing.

An organization's short-term goals are frequently different from its long-term goals. For instance, one firm's primary short-term goal was directed financially—to raise $20 million of working capital within the next twelve months. Its five-year goal, however, was to increase its product market share from 4 to 10 percent. In applying the goal-attainment approach, which goals—short- or long-term—should be used?

The fact that organizations have multiple goals also creates difficulties. They can compete with each other and sometimes are even incompatible. The achievement of "high product quality" and "low unit cost," for example, may be directly at odds with each other. The goal-attainment approach assumes consensus on goals. Given that there are multiple goals and diverse interests within the organization, consensus may not be possible unless goals are stated in such ambiguous and vague terms as to allow the varying interest groups to interpret them in a way favorable to their self-interests. This, in fact, may explain why most official goals in large organizations are traditionally broad and intangible. They act to placate the many different interest groups within the organization.

Multiple goals must be ordered according to importance if they are to have meaning to members. But how do you allocate relative importance to goals that may be incompatible and represent diverse interests? Add to this the fact that, as personnel change and power relationships within the organization change, so will the importance attributed to various goals, and you begin to realize the difficulty that operationalizing the goal-attainment-approach poses.

A last insight should be made before we conclude this section on problems. It just may be that for many organizations, goals do not direct behavior. "The common assertion that goal consensus must occur prior to action obscures the fact that consensus is impossible unless there is something tangible around which it can occur. And this 'something tangible' may well turn out to be actions *already completed.*"[16] In some cases, official goals may merely be rationalizations to explain past actions rather than guides to future actions. Organizations may act first, then later create a "goal" to justify what has happened. If this is true, measuring organizational effectiveness by surveying the dominant coalition should result not in benchmarks against which actual performance can be compared, but rather in formal descriptions of the dominant coalition's perceptions of prior performance.

What does all this mean? It would appear that only the naive would accept the formal statements made by senior management to represent the organization's goals. As one author concluded after finding that corporations issue one set of goals to stockholders, another to customers, a third set to employees, a fourth to the public, and still a fifth set for management itself, formal statements of goals should be treated "as fiction produced by an organization to account for, explain, or rationalize its existence to particular audiences rather than as valid and reliable indications of purpose."[17]

Value to Managers

These problems, while certainly damning, should not be construed as a blanket indictment of goals. Organizations exist to achieve goals—the problems lie in their identification and measurement. The validity of those goals identified can probably be increased significantly by (1) ensuring that input is received from all those having a major influence on formulating the official goals, even if they are not part of senior management; (2) including actual goals obtained by observing the behavior of organization members; (3) recognizing that organizations pursue both short- and long-term goals; (4) insisting on tangible, verifiable, and measurable goals rather than relying on vague statements that merely mirror societal expectations; and (5) viewing goals as dynamic entities that change over time rather than as rigid or fixed statements of purpose.

If managers are willing to confront the complexities inherent in the goal-attainment approach, they *can* obtain reasonably valid information for assessing an organization's effectiveness. But there is more to OE than identifying and measuring specific ends.

SAYING DIFFERENT THINGS TO DIFFERENT AUDIENCES

In October 1979, the management of Chrysler Corporation was attempting to secure a $1.5 billion federal loan guarantee. According to Chrysler's president, Lee Iacocca, based on testimony made to Congress, failure to get this loan guarantee would leave Chrysler with no other option than to file for bankruptcy. However, while Iacocca was in Washington portraying the imminent demise of Chrysler, the company was running full-page advertisements in major magazines and newspapers proclaiming, "We've been around for seventy years and we expect to be around seventy years from now." The intent of these ads, of course, was to encourage prospective customers to buy Chrysler products and to ignore any future concern about the availability of parts, service, and warranty coverage.

In its quest for survival, Chrysler projected itself one way to the public and another way to government officials.

THE SYSTEMS APPROACH

In Chapter 1, we described organizations in a systems framework. Organizations acquire inputs, engage in transformation processes, and generate outputs. It has been argued that defining OE solely in terms of goal-attainment results in only a partial measure of effectiveness. Goals focus on outputs. But an organization should also be judged on its ability to acquire inputs, process these inputs, channel the outputs, and maintain stability and balance. Another way to look at OE, therefore, is through a systems approach.[18]

In the **systems approach,** end goals are not ignored; but they are only one element in a more complex set of criteria. Systems models emphasize criteria that will increase the long-term survival of the organization—such as the organization's ability to *acquire* resources, *maintain* itself internally as a social organism, and *interact* successfully with its external environment. So the systems approach focuses not so much on specific ends as on the means needed for the achievement of those ends.

Assumptions

The assumptions underlying a systems approach to OE are the same that applied in our discussion of systems in Chapter 1. We can elaborate on a few of the more evident ones.

A systems approach to OE implies that organizations are made up of interrelated subparts. If any one of these subparts performs poorly, it will negatively affect the performance of the whole system.

Effectiveness requires awareness and successful interactions with environmental constituencies. Management cannot fail to maintain good relations with customers, suppliers, government agencies, unions, and similar constituencies that have the power to disrupt the stable operation of the organization.

Survival requires a steady replenishment of those resources consumed. Raw materials must be secured, vacancies created by employee resignations and retirements must be filled, declining product lines must be replaced, changes in the economy and the tastes of customers or clients need to be anticipated and reacted to, and so on. Failure to replenish will result in the organization's decline and, possibly, death.

Making Systems Operative

Let us turn now to the issue of how managers can apply the systems approach. First, we look at a sampling of criteria that systems advocates consider relevant; then we consider the various ways in which managers measure these criteria.

The systems view looks at factors such as relations with the environment to assure continued receipt of inputs and favorable acceptance of outputs, flexibility of response to environmental changes, the efficiency with which the organization transforms inputs to outputs, the clarity of internal communications, the level of conflict among groups, and the degree of employee job satisfaction. In contrast to the goal-attainment approach, the systems approach focuses on the means necessary to assure the organization's continued survival. And it should be noted that systems advocates do not negate the importance of specific end goals as a determinant of organizational effectiveness. Rather, they question the validity of the goals selected and the measures used for assessing the progress toward these goals.

It has been suggested that the critical systems interrelationships can be converted into OE variables or ratios.[19] These could include output/input (O/I), transformations/input (T/I), transformations/output (T/O), changes in input/input $(\Delta I/I)$, and so on. Table 3–2 gives some examples of measurement criteria that could be used along with these variables in a business firm, a hospital, and a college.

Another systems approach was used by researchers at the University of Michigan for studying the performance of seventy-five insurance agencies.[20] They used archival records of sales and personnel data to look at ten effectiveness dimensions:

☐ *Business volume.* Number and value of policies sold related to size of agency.
☐ *Production cost.* Cost per unit of sales volume.
☐ *New-member productivity.* Productivity of agents having less than five years' tenure.

TABLE 3–2   *Examples of Effectiveness Measures of Systems for Different Types of Organizations*

SYSTEM VARIABLES	BUSINESS FIRM	HOSPITAL	COLLEGE
O/I	Return on investment	Total number of patients treated	Number of faculty publications
T/I	Inventory turnover	Capital investment in medical technology	Cost of informaiton systems
T/O	Sales volume	Total number of patients treated	Number of students graduated
ΔI/I	Change in working capital	Change in number of patients treated	Change in student enrollment

Adapted from William M. Evan, "Organization Theory and Organizational Effectiveness: An Exploratory Analysis," in S. Lee Spray , ed., *Organizational Effectiveness: Theory, Research, Utilization* (Kent, Ohio: Kent State University Press, 1976), pp. 22–23. With permission.

☐ *Youthfulness of members.* Productivity of members under thirty-five years of age.

☐ *Business mix.* A combination of three conceptually unrelated performance indices, interpreted as reflecting the ability of agencies to achieve high overall performance through any of several strategies.

☐ *Work-force growth.* Relative and absolute change in work-force levels.

☐ *Devotion to management.* Sales commissions earned by agency managers.

☐ *Maintenance cost.* Cost to maintain accounts.

☐ *Member productivity.* Average new-business volume per agent.

☐ *Market penetration.* Proportion of potential market being exploited.

This study considered the key outputs (business volume, member productivity, market penetration). But it is a systems approach because it also considered important means that must be satisfied if the organization is to survive over the long haul. For instance, the inclusion of "new-member productivity" and "youthfulness of members" variables recognizes that successful future sales depend on investing in and developing young talent.

Still another systems application to OE is the management audit.[21] Developed by Jackson Martindell and his American Institute of Management, the **management audit** analyzes the key activities in a business firm, past, present, and future, to ensure that the organization is getting the maximum effort out of its resources. Using a ten-thousand-point analysis sheet, Martindell appraises performance in ten areas: economic function, organization structure, health of earnings, service to stockholders, research and development, board of directors, fiscal policies, production efficiency, sales vigor, and executive evaluation. Although a number of the criteria are relevant to profit-making organizations alone, the concept could be modified for use in the non-profit sector. The ten areas carry various weights, reflecting the importance that Martindell has assigned to each variable in terms of its contribution to the organization's overall performance. Again, it is a systems approach because it recognizes that no organization can reach its performance potential if one or more of its subsystems is performing inadequately.

Problems

The two most telling shortcomings of the systems approach relate to measurement and the issue of whether means really matter.

Measuring specific end goals may be easy compared with trying to measure process variables such as "flexibility of response to environmental changes" or "clarity of internal communications." The problem is that, while the terms may carry a layperson's meaning, the development of valid and reliable measures for tapping their quantity or intensity may not be possible. Whatever measures are used, therefore, may be constantly open to question.

In sports, it is frequently said that "it's *whether* you win or lose that counts, *not* how you play the game!" It can be argued that the same holds true for organizations. If ends are achieved, are means important? The objective is to win, not to get out there and look good losing! The problem with the systems approach, at least according to its critics, is that its focus is on the means necessary to achieve effectiveness rather than on organizational effectiveness itself.

This criticism may take on more substance if we conceptualize both goal-attainment and systems approaches as goal oriented. The first uses *end* goals; the latter uses *means* goals. From this perspective, it may be argued that since both use goals, you might as well use ones that are more meaningful and that (despite their own measurement problems) are easier to quantify; that is, the goal-attainment approach!

Value to Managers

Managers who use a systems approach to OE are less prone to look for immediate results. They are less likely to make decisions that trade off the organization's long-term health and survival for ones that will make them look good in the near term. Additionally, the systems approach increases the managers' awareness of the interdependency of organizational activities. For instance, if management fails to have raw materials on hand when they are needed or if the quality of those raw materials is poor, it will restrict the organization's ability to achieve its end goals.

A final plus for the systems approach is its applicability where end goals either are very vague or defy measurement. Managers of public organizations, for example, frequently use "ability to acquire budget increases" as a measure of effectiveness—substituting an input criterion for an output criterion.

THE STRATEGIC-CONSTITUENCIES APPROACH

A more recent perspective on OE—the **strategic-constituencies approach**—proposes that an effective organization is one that satisfies the demands of those constituencies in its environment from whom it requires support for its continued existence.[22] This approach is similar to the systems view, yet it has a different emphasis. Both consider interdependencies, but the strategic-constituencies view is not concerned with all of the organization's environment. It seeks to appease only those in the environment who can threaten the organization's survival. In this context, most public universities must consider effectiveness in terms of acquiring *students* but need not be concerned with potential *employers* of their graduates. Why? Because the survival of these universities is not influenced by whether their graduates get jobs. On the other hand, private universities, which charge considerably more than their public counterparts, do spend a great deal of time and money in attempting to place their graduates. When parents spend fifty thousand dollars or more to get their son or daughter a bachelor's degree, they expect it to lead to a job or acceptance in a good graduate school. If this does not occur, it will be increasingly difficult for the private school to get freshmen applications. The converse of this example is the university's relations with the legislature in the state within which is operates. Public institutions devote considerable effort to wooing state legislators. Failure to have their cooperation is sure to have adverse budget effects on the public university. The private university's effectiveness, in contrast, is little affected by whether or not it has a favorable relationship with the key people in the state capital.

Assumptions

The goal-attainment approach views organizations as deliberate, rational, and goal-seeking entities. The strategic-constituencies approach views organizations very differently. They are assumed to be political arenas where vested interests compete for control over resources. In such a context, organizational effectiveness becomes an assessment of how successful the organization has been at satisfying those critical constituencies, upon whom the future survival of the organization depends.

The "political arena" metaphor further assumes the organization has a number of constituencies, with different degrees of power, each trying to satisfy its demands. But each constituency also has a unique set of values, so it is unlikely that their preferences will be in agreement. For example, a study of the major tobacco companies found that the public evaluated the companies in terms of not harming smokers' health, while stockholders evaluated the firms' ability to produce cigarettes efficiently and profitably. Not surprisingly—using such diverse criteria—the public rated the tobacco firms as ineffective, and stockholders rated the same firms as highly effective.[23] Effectiveness of a tobacco company, therefore, can be said to be determined by its ability to identify its critical constituencies, assess their preference patterns, and satisfy their demands. Stockholders and consumers might be satisfied with tobacco firms, but if the public, through its legislative representatives, outlaws the sales of cigarettes, then the tobacco companies lose and lose big!

Finally, the strategic-constituencies approach assumes that managers pursue a number of goals and that the goals selected represent a response to those interest groups that control the resources necessary for the organization to survive. No goal or set of goals that management selects is value free. Each implicitly, if not explicitly, will favor some constituency over others. When management gives profits highest priority, for instance, they make the interests of owners paramount. Similarly, adaptability to the environment, customer satisfaction, and a supportive work climate, favor the interests of society, clients, and employees, respectively.

HOW DANIEL LUDWIG LOST $1 BILLION

American Daniel Ludwig became a billionaire in the shipping business. His financial downfall, however, came from his incredibly ambitious Jari project. Ludwig sought to cultivate a supertree for high-grade paper, to mine bauxite, and to build a state-of-the-art paper mill and smelting plant in an area of the Brazilian jungle called Jari.[24] He bought millions of acres of land, hired tens of thousands of people, and spent fifteen years and $1.1 billion developing the Jari project. But it eventually failed. One of the reasons for the failure was that Ludwig didn't understand that the Brazilian government was a strategic constituency

Making Strategic Constituencies Operative

The manager wishing to apply this perspective might begin by asking members of the dominant coalition to identify the constituencies they consider to be critical to the organization's survival. This input can be combined and synthesized to arrive at a list of strategic constituencies.

As an example, a large tire company such as Goodyear Tire and Rubber might have strategic constituencies that include suppliers of critical petroleum products used in the tire-manufacturing process; officers of the United Rubber Workers union; officials at banks where the company has sizable short-term loans; government regulatory agencies that grade tires and inspect facilities for safety violations; security analysts at major brokerage firms who specialize in the tire-and-rubber industry; regional tire jobbers and distributors; and purchasing agents responsible for the acquisition of tires at General Motors, Mack Truck, Caterpillar, and other vehicle manufacturers.

to his enterprise. Without that government's support, his project's effectiveness could be undermined.

Ludwig had long been known for his independence. As he pumped money into his Jari project, he refused to discuss what he was doing with Brazilian government authorities. But even a billionaire can run low on money, and Ludwig had done that by the early 1980s. He asked the Brazilian government for financial assistance but was turned down. His threat to pull out of Jari unless he received government cooperation was seen as heavy-handed and an example of U.S. imperialism. The conflict between Ludwig and the Brazilian government escalated to the point where the government claimed that Ludwig's title to the land at Jari was in doubt. This cutoff any possibility for securing nongovernmental financial aid, and the project collapsed. Ludwig lost more than $1 billion and learned, one would hope, a valuable lesson articulated in the strategic-constituencies approach: Managers must appease those constituencies who have the power to threaten their organization's survival.

This list could then be evaluated to determine the relative power of each. Basically, this means looking at each constituency in terms of how dependent on it our organization is. Does it have considerable power over us? Are there alternatives for what this constituency provides? How do these constituencies compare in the impact they have on the organization's operations?

The third step requires identifying the expectations that these constituencies hold for the organization. What do they want of it? Given that each constituency has its own set of special interests, what goals does each seek to impose on the organization? Stockholders' goals may be in terms of profit or appreciation in the stocks' price; the union's may be in acquiring job security and high wages for its members; whereas the Environmental Protection Agency will want the firm's manufacturing plants to meet all minimum air-, water-, and noise-pollution requirements. Table 3–3 identifies a list of strategic constituencies a business firm might confront and the typical organizational-effectiveness criteria each is likely to use.

The strategic-constituencies approach would conclude by comparing the various expectations, determining common expecta-

TABLE 3–3   *Typical OE Criteria of Selected Strategic Constituencies*

CONSTITUENCY	TYPICAL OE CRITERIA
Owners	Return on investment; growth in earnings.
Employees	Compensation; fringe benefits; satisfaction with working conditions.
Customers	Satisfaction with price, quality, service.
Suppliers	Satisfaction with payments; future sales potential.
Creditors	Ability to pay indebtedness.
Unions	Competitive wages and benefits; satisfactory working conditions; willingness to bargain fairly.
Local community officials	Involvement of organization's members in local affairs; lack of damage to the community's environment.
Government agencies	Compliance with laws; avoidance of penalties and reprimands.

tions and those that are incompatible, assigning relative weights to the various constituencies, and formulating a preference ordering of these various goals for the organization as a whole. This preference order, in effect, represents the relative power of the various strategic constituencies. The organization's effectiveness then would be assessed in terms of its ability to satisfy these goals.

Problems

As with the previous approaches, this one too is not without problems. The task of separating the strategic constituencies from the larger environment is easy to say but difficult to do in practice. Because the environment changes rapidly, what was critical to the organization yesterday may not be so today. Even if the constituencies in the environment can be identified and are assumed to be relatively stable, what separates the strategic constituencies from the "almost" strategic constituencies? Where do you cut the set? And won't the interests of each member in the dominant coalition strongly affect what he or she perceives as strategic? An executive in the accounting function is unlikely to see the world—or the organization's strategic constituencies—in the same way as an executive in the purchasing function. Finally, identifying the expectations that the strategic constituencies hold for the organization presents a problem. How do you tap that information accurately?

Value to Managers

If survival is important for an organization, then it is incumbent upon managers to understand just who it is (in terms of constituencies) that survival is contingent upon. By operationalizing the strategic-constituencies approach, managers decrease the chance that they might ignore or severely upset a group whose power could significantly hinder the organization's operations. If management knows whose support it needs if the organization is to maintain its health, it can modify its preference ordering of goals as necessary to reflect the changing power relationships with its strategic constituencies.

THE COMPETING-VALUES APPROACH

If we are to have a comprehensive understanding of OE, it would seem worthwhile to identify all of the key variables in the domain of effectiveness and then determine how the variables are related. The competing-values approach offers just such an integrative framework.[25]

The main theme underlying the **competing-values approach** is that the criteria you value and use in assessing an organization's effectiveness—return on investment, market share, new-product innovation, job security—depend on who you are and the interests you represent. It is not surprising that stockholders, unions, suppliers, management, or internal specialists in marketing, personnel, production, or accounting may look at the same organization but evaluate its effectiveness entirely differently. You can relate to this fact by thinking about how you evaluate your course instructor. In any class with thirty or more students, you can expect evaluations of the instructor to differ markedly. Probably some students will see the instructor as one of the best they have had. Others will appraise the instructor as one of the worst. The instructor's behavior is a constant; it is the evaluators, with their varied standards of what a "good teacher" is, who create the different ratings. The rating, therefore, probably tells us more about the values of the evaluator (what he or she prefers in terms of an instructor) than it tells us about the teacher's effectiveness.

Assumptions

Before we present the competing-values approach explicitly, the assumptions upon which it was conceived need to be stated.

It begins with the assumption that there is no "best" criterion for evaluating an organization's effectiveness. There is neither a single goal that everyone can agree upon nor a consensus on which goals take precedence over others. Therefore, the concept of OE, itself, is subjective, and the goals that an evaluator chooses are based on his or her personal values, preferences, and interests. This can be seen if we take one organization and look at how OE criteria change to reflect the interests of the evaluator. At Xerox, you might find financial analysts defining OE in terms of high profitability;

production executives focusing on the amount and quality of equipment manufactured; marketing people and competitors looking at the percentage of market that Xerox's various products hold; personnel specialists viewing OE in terms of ability to hire competent workers and absence of strikes; research-and-development scientists keying in on the number of new inventions and products that the company generates; and the city council of Stamford, Connecticut (where Xerox is headquartered), defining OE as a steadily expanding work force.

Competing values goes significantly beyond merely acknowledging diverse preferences. It assumes that these diverse preferences can be consolidated and organized. The competing-values approach argues that there are common elements underlying any comprehensive list of OE criteria and that these elements can be combined in such a way as to create basic sets of competing values. Each one of these sets then defines a unique effectiveness model.

Making Competing Values Operative

To apply this approach, it's necessary to go into more detail of how it evolved. It began with a search for common themes among the thirty OE criteria listed in Table 3–1. What was found were three basic sets of competing values.

The first set is *flexibility* versus *control.* These are essentially two incompatible dimensions of an organization's structure. Flexibility values innovation, adaptation, and change. In contrast, control favors stability, order, and predictability. The flexibility-control dimension is very similar to the adaptation-maintenance dichotomy presented in Chapter 1.

The second set deals with whether emphasis should be placed on the well-being and development of the *people* in the organization or the well-being and development of the *organization* itself. The people-organization dichotomy is another set of essentially incompatible dimensions: the concern for the feelings and needs of the people within the organization versus the concern for productivity and task accomplishment.

The third set of values relates to organizational *means* versus *ends;* the former stressing internal processes and the long term, the latter emphasizing final outcomes and the short term. We saw this dichotomy before when we compared the goal-attainment and systems approaches. Goal attainment focuses on ends, and system emphasizes means.

These three sets of values can be depicted as a three-dimensional diagram. This is shown in Figure 3–1. These values can further be combined to form eight cells or sets of OE criteria. For example, combining people, control, and ends (PCE) creates one cell. Combining organization, flexibility, and means (OFM) creates another. Table 3–4 identifies and describes the eight possible cells formed by combining the three sets of values.

If we plot the eight cells onto the framework established in Figure 3–1, we end up with Figure 3–2. Now we can begin to combine the eight cells into some distinct models. What Figure 3–2 has done is to create four diverse models or definitions of organizational effectiveness. Cells **PFM** and **PFE** are subsumed under the human-relations model. It emphasizes people and flexibility. The **human-relations model** would define OE in terms of a cohesive (as means) and skilled (as ends) work force. The **open-systems model** encompasses the OFM and OFE cells. Effectiveness in this model is defined in terms of flexibility (as means) and the ability to acquire resources (as ends). The **rational-goal model** includes the OCM and OCE cells. The existence of specific plans and goals (as means) and high productivity and efficiency (as ends) is used as evidence of effectiveness. Finally, the PCM and PCE cells form the **internal-process model.** It emphasizes people and control

FIGURE 3–1 *A Three-Dimensional Model of Organizational Effectiveness*

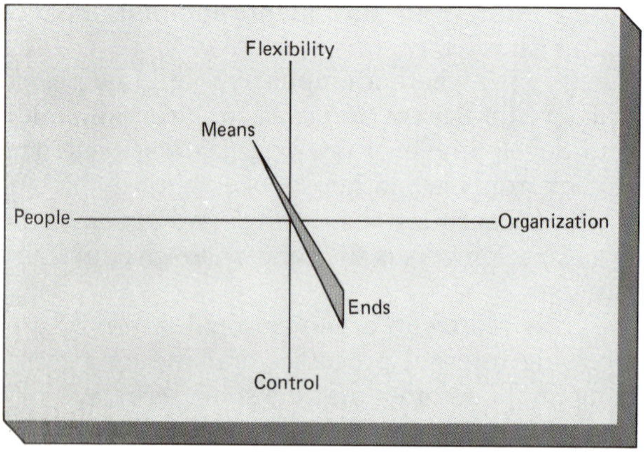

TABLE 3–4   *Eight OE Criteria Cells*

CELLS	DESCRIPTION	DEFINITION
OFM	Flexibility	Able to adjust well to shifts in external conditions and demands.
OFE	Acquisition of resources	Able to increase external support and expand size of work force.
OCM	Planning	Goals are clear and well understood.
OCE	Productivity and efficiency	Volume of output is high; ratio of output to input is high.
PCM	Availability of information	Channels of communication facilitate informing people about things that affect their work.
PCE	Stability	Sense of order, continuity, and smooth functioning of operations.
PFM	Cohesive work force	Employees trust, respect, and work well with each other.
PFE	Skilled work force	Employees have the training, skills, and capacity to do their work properly.

and stresses adequate dissemination of information (as means) and stability and order (as ends) in the assessment of effectiveness.

Note how each model represents a particular set of values and has a polar opposite with contrasting emphasis. "The human relations model with its effectiveness criteria reflecting people and flexibility stands in stark contrast to the rational goal model's value-based stress on organization and stability. The open-systems model, defined by values of organization and flexibility, runs counter to the internal process model, the effectiveness criteria of which reflect a focus on people and stable structures."[26]

Now, given the preceding description of the competing-values approach, how would a manager go about implementing it in his or her organization?

As with strategic constituencies, the first step is to identify the constituencies that the dominant coalition considers critical to the organization's survival. After the strategic constituencies have been isolated, it is necessary to calculate the importance that each constituency places on the eight value sets. This is no simple task because it requires management to put itself in the shoes of each

FIGURE 3–2 *Four Models of Effectiveness Values*

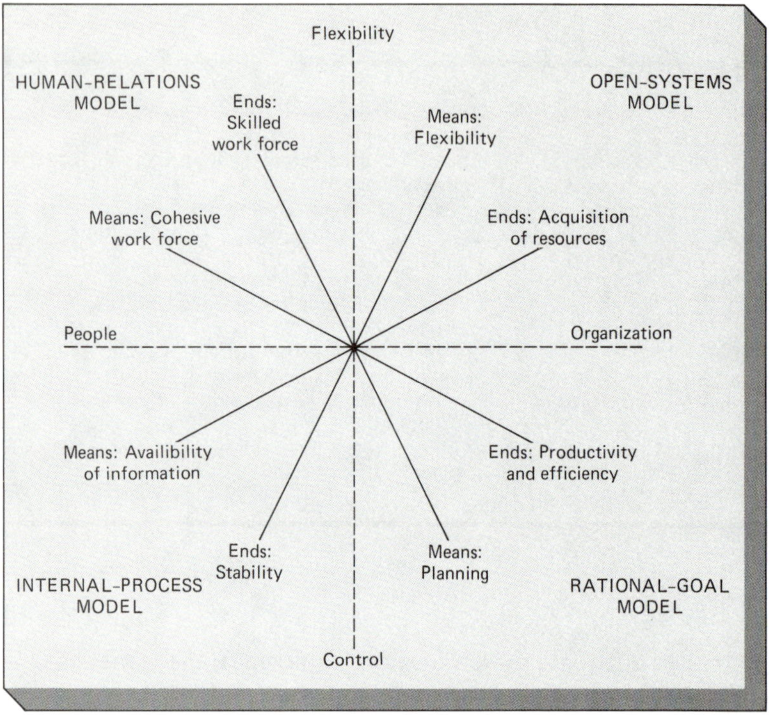

strategic constituency or actually interview constituency members. The questionnaire in Table 3–5 can help with this assessment. It offers questions, the answers to which give a general assessment of how a given constituency perceives an organization's performance on each of the eight effectiveness criteria.

Figure 3–3 illustrates the cumulative results when a group of college students were asked to evaluate two fast-food hamburger chains. We have disguised the companies by referring to them as Alpha and Beta. The Alpha chain is seen as performing quite well except for problems with cohesiveness among workers and concern about the workers' qualifications to do their job properly. On the other hand, the Beta chain seems to be performing well only with regard to flexibility and resource acquisition.

Amoebagrams, such as those illustrated in Figure 3–3, offer insights as to how a constituency or set of constituencies assesses

TABLE 3–5 *Abbreviated Competing-Values Questionnaire*

Rate the organization under study by determining your degree of agreement with each of the following statements:

	DO NOT AGREE	SOMEWHAT AGREE	STRONGLY AGREE
1. (OFM) The organizaiton responds well to changing demands.	1	2	3
2. (OFE) The size of the organization's work force is steadily increasing.	1	2	3
3. (OCM) Employees have a clear understanding of the organization's goals.	1	2	3
4. (OCE) The organization generates a high volume of output.	1	2	3
5. (PCM) Employees are well informed about those things that affect their work.	1	2	3
6. (PCE) The organization's operations function smoothly and in an orderly way.	1	2	3
7. (PFM) Employees work well with each other.	1	2	3
8. (PFE) Employees are well equipped for their jobs.	1	2	3

the organization's performance on the eight effectiveness criteria. It pinpoints areas where strategic constituencies agree and disagree in their evaluations of the organization; it tells management which criteria constituencies perceive as needing improvement; and it focuses management's attention on certain OE models. If a company is undercapitalized and anticipates it will need to approach pension-fund managers to borrow money, then the criteria pension-fund managers use to evaluate the company and their assessment of the company's effectiveness on those criteria are critical. If pension-fund managers emphasize the rational-goal model, management will want to ensure that it looks good against this model's criteria. Similarly, labor-union officials tend to follow the human-relations model. If management's labor contract is coming up for renegotiation, then an assessment of how the union's ne-

FIGURE 3–3 *Comparing the Effectiveness of the Alpha and Beta Companies*

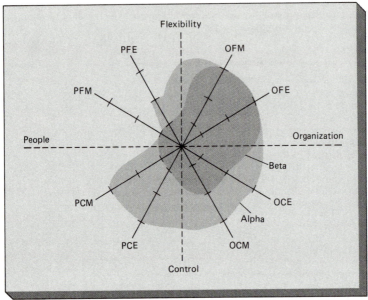

gotiators assess the organization's performance on the human-relations model is important in satisfying this constituency.

It has been proposed that the organization's stage in its life cycle may be an important determinant of which OE model should be emphasized by management.[27] If the organization is to survive and prosper, it is necessary for management to adopt the primary criteria of effectiveness espoused by its strategic constituencies. But strategic constituencies tend to change over time. An important determinant of which constituencies deserve management's greatest attention may be the organization's life-cycle stage. As noted in Chapter 1, we can identify five stages in an organization's life cycle—entrepreneurial, collectivity, formalization and control, elaboration of structure, and decline. Each of these stages makes different demands on management and the organization itself. It seems only logical, therefore, that the organization's strategic constituencies are likely to change from stage to stage to reflect these difficult demands.

In the entrepreneurial stage, the organization is typified by innovation, creativity, and the marshaling of resources. Getting external support is critical. So, too, is being able to demonstrate flexibility. The open-systems model emphasizes these criteria. Therefore, we can expect that banks, venture capitalists, property-leasing agents—typical strategic constituencies in an organization's formative years—will use the open-systems model.

When the organization enters the collectivity stage, strategic constituencies are likely to include unions and employees themselves. Management needs to create a sense of family within the organization and develop high member commitment. This is consistent with pursuit of the criteria articulated in the human-relations model.

In the formalization and control stage, efficiency and orderliness are sought. The organization is becoming mature, and strategic constituencies at this point—employees, lenders, suppliers, customers, and the like—evaluate the organization in terms of its stability and productivity. Such constituencies will look to the internal process and rational-goal models.

At the elaboration-of-structure stage, emphasis is on monitoring the external environment. Strategic constituencies in this stage emphasize the organization's flexibility, ability to acquire resources, and growth rate. These criteria are best met in the open-systems model.

Finally, in the decline stage, the strategic constituencies tend to be similar to those found when the organization is just beginning. The concern again is with the ability of the organization to innovate and acquire resources. So as with the entrepreneurial stage, the open-systems model should dominate in guiding effectiveness evaluations.

The value of linking life-cycle stages, strategic constituencies, and effectiveness models should be obvious. To the degree that our analysis is accurate, management should be able to predict what criteria of success are likely to take precedence, in what sequence, to anticipate the necessary changes, and to decrease the likelihood that any strategic constituencies' concerns are overlooked.

Problems

Since the competing-values model encompasses both ends and means, it overcomes the problems of using merely the goal-attainment or systems approaches. Competing values include strategic constituencies but do nothing to alleviate the problems we pointed out with this approach.

Competing-values methodology results in it being better at assessing a constituencies' perception of how well an organization is doing on the eight criteria than in clarifying which criteria the constituencies are emphasizing.

The use of the life cycle to determine which OE models management should emphasize is interesting, but more research is needed to determine if effectiveness models actually change in predictable ways as organizations develop through their life cycle.

Value to Managers

Competing values acknowledge that multiple criteria and conflicting interests underlie any effort at defining and assessing OE. Additionally, by reducing a large number of effectiveness criteria into four conceptually clear organizational models, the competing-values approach can guide the manager in identifying the appropriateness of different criteria to different constituencies and in different life-cycle stages.

COMPARING THE FOUR APPROACHES

We've presented four different approaches for assessing organizational effectiveness. Each, in its own way, can be a useful model. But under which conditions is each preferred? Table 3–6 summarizes each approach by identifying what it uses to define effectiveness and then notes the conditions under which each is most useful.

SUMMARY

Organizational effectiveness has proven difficult, some even say impossible, to define. Yet as the central theme in organization theory, its meaning and measurement must be confronted. Four approaches have been offered as guides out of the organizational effectiveness "jungle."

The two dominant positions, and frequent antagonists, are the goal-attainment and systems approaches. The former defines OE as the accomplishment of ends. The latter focuses on means—defining OE as the ability

TABLE 3–6 *Comparing the Four OE Approaches*

APPROACH	DEFINITION	WHEN USEFUL
	An organization is effective to the extent that . . .	The approach is preferred when . . .
Goal attainment	it accomplishes its stated goals.	goals are clear, time bound, and measureable.
Systems	it acquires needed resources.	a clear connection exists between inputs and outputs.
Strategic constituencies	all strategic constituencies are at least minimally satisfied.	constituencies have powerful influence on the organization, and the organization must respond to demands.
Competing values	the emphasis of the organization in the four major areas matches constituent preferences.	the organization is unclear about its own emphases, or changes in criteria over time are of interest.

Adapted from Kim S. Cameron, "The Effectiveness of Ineffectiveness," in B. M. Staw and L. L. Cummings, eds., *Research in Organizational Behavior*, vol. 6 (Greenwich, Conn: JAI Press, 1984), p. 276. With permission.

to acquire inputs, process these inputs, channel the outputs, and maintain stability and balance in the system.

A more recent offering is the strategic-constituencies approach. It defines OE as satisfying the demands of those constituencies in the environment from which the organization requires support for its continued existence. Success, then, is the ability to placate those individuals, groups, and institutions upon which the organization depends for its continued operation.

The final perspective is one based on competing values. It has sought to synthesize the large number of OE criteria into four models, each of which is based on a given set of values and each of which, additionally, is preferred depending on where an organization is in its life cycle.

To those who desire a simple definition of organizational effectiveness, this chapter will have proved a disappointment. OE is conceptually complex, and, therefore, so must its definition. **Organizational effectiveness** can be defined as *the degree to which an organization attains its short- (ends) and long-term (means) goals, the selection of which reflects strategic constituencies, the self-interest of the evaluator, and the life stage of the organization.*

FOR REVIEW AND DISCUSSION

1. Why is organizational effectiveness relevant in the study of organization theory?
2. On what factors do almost all definitions of OE agree?
3. "The final test of an organization's effectiveness is survival." Build an argument to support this statement. Then build an argument to refute this statement.
4. Give three examples of OE criteria that are consistent with the goal-attainment approach.
5. "For a business firm, the bottom line is profit. You don't need any other measures of effectiveness." Build an argument to support this statement. Then build an argument to refute this statement.
6. MBO was presented as a goal-attainment approach. Could it also be part of the systems approach? Explain.
7. "Goals are a viable standard against which OE can be measured." Build an argument to support this statement. Then build an argument to refute this statement.
8. Are organizational efficiency and flexibility conflicting goals?
9. Give three examples of OE criteria that are consistent with the systems approach.
10. Why might the administrator of a public agency use "ability to acquire budget increases" as a measure of OE? Could such a measure be dysfunctional?
11. To what degree do specific constituencies use a constant set of OE criteria in evaluating organizations?
12. Compare the strategic-constituencies and competing-values approaches. How are they similar? How are they different?
13. What are the basic values underlying the competing-values approach?
14. How would an organization's life-cycle stage affect the criteria used to evaluate its effectiveness?
15. Select three or four organizations familiar to you and members of your class. How have you, *historically*, evaluated their effectiveness? How would you now assess their effectiveness using the goal-attainment, systems, and strategic-constituencies approaches?

NOTES

[1] Cited in Thomas Moore, "Make-Or-Break Time for General Motors," *Fortune*, February 15, 1988, p. 35.

[2] "1987's Surprise: Many Happy Returns," *Business Week*, March 14, 1988, p. 127.

[3] Ibid., p. 130.

[4] Paul S. Goodman and Johannes M. Pennings, "Perspectives and Issues: An Introduction," in P. S. Goodman, J. M. Pennings, and Associates, eds., *New Perspectives on Organizational Effectiveness* (San Francisco: Jossey-Bass, 1977), p. 2.

[5] Amitai Etzioni, *Modern Organizations* (Englewood Cliffs, N.J.: Prentice Hall, 1964), p. 8.

[6] John R. Kimberly, "Issues in the Creation of Organizations: Initiation, Innovation, and Institutionalization," *Academy of Management Journal*, September 1979, p. 438.

[7] Jeffrey Pfeffer, "Usefulness of the Concept," in Goodman et al., *Organizational Effectiveness*, p. 139; and H. Kaufman, *Are Government Organizations Immortal?* (Washington, D.C.: Brookings Institution, 1976).

[8] John P. Campbell, "On the Nature of Organizational Effectiveness," in Goodman, et al., *Organizational Effectiveness*, p. 15.

[9] Kim S. Cameron, "A Study of Organizational Effectiveness and Its Predictors," *Management Science*, January 1986, p. 88.

[10] Kim S. Cameron, "Effectiveness as Paradox: Consensus and Conflict in Conceptions of Organizational Effectiveness," *Management Science*, May 1986, pp. 539–53.

[11] Thomas J. Peters and Robert H. Waterman, *In Search of Excellence* (New York: Harper & Row, 1982).

[12] See, for instance, "Who's Excellent Now?," *Business Week*, November 5, 1984, pp. 76–78; Kenneth E. Aupperle, William Acar, and David E. Booth, "An Empirical Critique of *In Search of Excellence:* How Excellent Are the Excellent Companies?," *Journal of Management*, Winter 1986, pp. 499–512; and Michael A. Hitt and R. Duane Ireland, "Peters and Waterman Revisited: The Unended Quest for Excellence," *Academy of Management Executive*, May 1987, pp. 91–98.

[13] Charles Perrow, "The Analysis of Goals in Complex Organizations," *American Sociological Review*, December 1961, pp. 854–66.

[14] Campbell, "On the Nature of Organizational Effectiveness," p. 26.

[15] Charles K. Warriner, "The Problem of Organizational Purpose," *Sociological Quarterly*, Spring 1965, pp. 139–46.

[16] Karl Weick, *The Social Psychology of Organizing* (Reading, Mass.: Addison-Wesley, 1969), p. 8 (author's emphasis).

[17] Warriner, "Problem of Organizational Purpose," p. 140.

[18] Ephraim Yuchtman and Stanley E. Seashore, "A Systems Resource Approach to Organizational Effectiveness," *American Sociological Review*, December 1967, pp. 891–903.

[19] William M. Evan, "Organization Theory and Organizational Effectiveness: An Exploratory Analysis," in S. Lee Spray, ed., *Organizational Effectiveness: Theory, Research, Utilization* (Kent, Ohio: Kent State University Press, 1976), pp. 21–24.

[20] Stanley E. Seashore and Ephraim Yuchtman, "Factorial Analysis of Organizational Performance," *Administrative Science Quarterly*, December 1967, pp. 377–95.

[21] Jackson Martindell, *The Scientific Appraisal of Management* (New York: Harper & Row, 1962).

[22] Jeffrey Pfeffer and Gerald Salancik, *The External Control of Organizations* (New York: Harper & Row, 1978).

[23] Robert H. Miles, *Coffin Nails and Corporate Strategies* (Englewood Cliffs, N.J.: Prentice Hall, 1982).

[24] Based on "Anatomy of a Failure," *Newsweek*, January 25, 1982, p. 45; and "Two Giant U.S. Business Efforts That Failed in Brazil," *Forbes*, October 19, 1987, pp. 18–19.

[25] See, for example, Robert E. Quinn and John Rohrbaugh, "A Competing Values Approach to Organizational Effectiveness," *Public Productivity Review*, no. 5, 1981, pp. 122–40; and Robert E. Quinn and John Rohrbaugh, "A Spatial Model of Effectiveness Criteria: Towards a Competing Values Approach to Organizational Analysis," *Management Science*, March 1983, pp. 363–77.

[26] Quinn and Rohrbaugh, "A Competing Values Approach to Organizational Effectiveness," p. 138.

[27] Kim S. Cameron and David A. Whetten, "Perceptions of Organizational Effectiveness Over Organizational Life Cycles," *Administrative Science Quarterly*, December 1981, pp. 525–44; and Robert E. Quinn and Kim S. Cameron, "Organizational Life Cycles and Shifting Criteria of Effectiveness: Some Preliminary Evidence," *Management Science*, January 1983, pp. 33–51.

DIMENSIONS OF ORGANIZATION STRUCTURE

AFTER READING THIS CHAPTER, YOU SHOULD BE ABLE TO:

1 Describe the three components comprising complexity.
2 Compare functional with social specialization.
3 Identify the benefits that accrue from formalization.
4 Define socialization.
5 List the most popular formalization techniques.
6 Describe the relationships between complexity, formalization, and centralization.
7 Identify why organizations might practice decentralization.
8 Discuss how MIS effects structural dimensions.

Introduction

CORPORATE AMERICA IS RESTRUCTURING!

The article's headline reads, "IBM Unveils a Sweeping Restructuring in Bid to Decentralize Decision Making."[1] But IBM isn't alone. In the last couple of years, the names of firms that have restructured their organization read like a Who's Who of corporate America—AT&T, Apple Computer, Black & Decker, General Electric, General Motors, Kraft, Philip Morris, Pillsbury, RJR Nabisco, Texaco, and Walt Disney Productions. In fact, it's difficult nowadays to find a well-managed organization that *hasn't* recently restructured to cut costs, become more responsive to customers and competitors, or achieve some similar aim. But what is it that these organizations are *restructuring?*

Our answer to this question is complexity, formalization, and centralization. Acceptance of these three components as the core dimensions of organizational structure, while generally widespread today, is not universal.[2] Before we begin to discuss these three core dimensions, it is worthwhile to list a dozen or so of the more popular variables used to define structural dimensions. Notice, if you will, how several of these variables have been defined differently by various theorists:

☐ *Administrative component.* The number of line supervisors, managers, and staff personnel relative to the total number of employees.[3]

☐ *Autonomy.* The extent to which top management has to refer certain typical decisions to a higher level of authority.[4]

☐ *Centralization.* The proportion of jobs whose occupants participate in decision making and the number of areas in which they participate,[5] or concentration of power arrangements,[6] or an index reflecting the locus of decision making with respect to major and specific policies, the degree of information sharing between levels, and the degree of participation in long-range planning.[7]

☐ *Complexity.* The number of occupational specialties, the professional activity, and the professional training of employees.[8]

☐ *Delegation of authority.* The ratio of the number of specific management decisions the chief executive has delegated to the number he or she has the authority to make.[9]

☐ *Differentiation.* The number of specialty functions represented in a firm[10] or the difference in cognitive and emotional orientation among managers in different departments.[11]

☐ *Formalization.* The extent to which an employee's role is defined by formal documentation.[12]

☐ *Integration.* The quality of the state of collaboration that exists among departments that are required to achieve unity of effort[13] or plans or feedback used for coordination between organizational units.[14]

☐ *Professionalization.* The degree to which employees use a professional organization as a major reference, belief in service to the public, belief in self-regulation, dedication to one's field, and autonomy.[15]

☐ *Span of control.* The number of subordinates that an individual manager can and should supervise.[16]

☐ *Specialization.* The number of occupational specialties and the length of training required by each[17] or the degree to which highly specialized requirements are spelled out in formal job descriptions for various functions.[18]

☐ *Standardization.* The range of variation that is tolerated within the rules defining the jobs.[19]

☐ *Vertical span.* The number of levels in the authority hierarchy from the bottom to the top.[20]

This listing is meant to indicate that there is by no means complete agreement among theorists as to what makes up the term *organization structure.* As you proceed through this chapter, you will find that almost all the dimensions cited are considered directly or indirectly. So a more accurate conclusion may be that theorists generally agree on the dimensions of organization structure but disagree on operational definitions and whether a dimension is primary or subsumed under some larger dimension.

With acknowledgment made to the divergent labels and definitions given to structure, let us proceed to construct an in-depth understanding of the term by looking at the first of our dimensions—complexity.

COMPLEXITY

What do we mean by the term *complexity?* Why is complexity important? The purpose of this section is to answer these two questions.

Definition

Complexity refers to the degree of differentiation that exists within an organization.[21] *Horizontal differentiation* considers the degree of horizontal separation between units. *Vertical differentiation* refers to the depth of the organizational hierarchy. *Spatial differentiation* encompasses the degree to which the location of an organization's facilities and personnel are dispersed geographically. An increase in any one of these three factors will increase an organization's complexity.

Horizontal Differentiation. **Horizontal differentiation** refers to the degree of differentiation between units based on the orientation of members, the nature of the tasks they perform, and their education and training. We can state that the larger number of different occupations within an organization that require specialized knowledge and skills, the more complex that organization is. Why? Because diverse orientations make it more difficult for organizational members to communicate and more difficult for management to coordinate their activities. For instance, when organizations create specialized groups or expand departmental designations, they differentiate groups from each other, making interactions between those groups more complex. If the organization is staffed by people who have similar backgrounds, skills, and training, they are likely to see the world in more similar terms. Conversely, diversity increases the likelihood that they will have different goal emphases, time orientations, and even a different work vocabulary. Job specialization reinforces differences—the chemical engineer's job is clearly different from that of the personnel recruitment interviewer. Their training is different. The language that they use on their respective jobs is different. They are typically assigned to different departments, which further reinforces their divergent orientations.

The most visible evidence in organizations of horizontal differentiation is specialization and departmentation. As we will show, the two are interrelated. But let us begin by looking at specialization.

Specialization refers to the particular grouping of activities performed by an individual. It can be achieved in one of two ways. The most well known form of specialization is through **functional specialization**—in which jobs are broken down into simple and repetitive tasks. Also known as **division of labor,** functional specialization creates high substitutability among employees and facilitates their easy replacement by management. If *individuals* are specialized, rather than their *work*, we have **social specialization.** Social specialization is achieved by hiring professionals who hold skills that cannot be readily routinized. The work typically done by civil engineers, nuclear physicists, and registered nurses is specialized, but the activities they perform vary by situation.

An increase in either form of specialization results in increased complexity within the organization. Why? Because an increase in specialization requires more sophisticated and expensive methods for coordination and control. Later in this chapter—in our discussion of formalization—we'll analyze social specialization. However, because most organizations rely so heavily on functional specialization, we should elaborate on the efficiencies inherent in division of labor.[22]

In Chapter 2, we briefly mentioned Adam Smith's discourse in his *Wealth of Nations* on how functional specialization worked in the manufacturing of straight pins. Even though Adam Smith wrote more than two hundred years ago, most organizations still rely heavily on division of labor today.

But why does division of labor still work? First, in highly sophisticated and complex jobs, no one person can perform all the tasks, owing to physical limitations. If one person had to build a complete Chevrolet alone, even possessing the hundreds of skills necessary, it would take months of full-time effort. Second, limitations of knowledge act as a constraint. Some tasks require highly developed skills; others can be performed by the untrained. If many of the tasks require a large amount of skill, it may be impossible to find people capable of performing all the tasks involved. Further, if all employees are engaged in each step of, say, an organization's manufacturing process, all must have the skills necessary to perform both the most demanding and the least demanding tasks. The result would be that except when performing the most skilled or highly sophisticated task, employees would be working below their skill level. Since skilled workers are paid more than unskilled, and their wages should reflect their highest level of skill, it represents poor usage of resources to pay individuals for their ability to do complex and difficult tasks while requiring them to do easy ones.

Another element in favor of division of labor is efficiency. One's skill at performing a task increases through repetition. Efficiency is also exhibited in reducing time spent in changing tasks; the time spent in putting away one's tools and equipment from a prior step in the work process and getting ready for another are eliminated through functional specialization. Additionally, training for functional specialization is more efficient from the organization's perspective. It is easier and less costly to train workers to do a specific and repetitive task than to train them for difficult and complex activities. Finally, division of labor increases efficiency and productivity by encouraging the creation of special inventions and machinery.

Division of labor creates groups of specialists. The way in which we group these specialists is called **departmentation.** Departmentation is, therefore, the way in which organizations typically coordinate activities that have been horizontally differentiated. Departments can be created on the basis of simple numbers, function, product or service, client, geography, or process. Most large corporations will use all six. For instance, the basic segmentation may be by function (e.g., finance, manufacturing, sales, personnel). Sales, in turn, may be segmented by geography, manufacturing by product, individual production plants by process, and so forth. On the other hand, in a very small organization, simple numbers represent an informal and highly effective method by which people can be grouped.

DIVISION OF LABOR HELPS WIN WORLD WAR II

In 1940, the standard time to build a 10,400-ton Liberty Ship was six months. The demands of World War II, however, required a major breakthrough in shipbuilding. That breakthrough was provided by Henry J. Kaiser.

Kaiser was a builder of bridges, dams, and pipelines. When he signed his initial contract to build thirty cargo vessels, neither he nor his principal assistants had ever built a ship. But that was to prove no handicap. They might not have known anything about mass-producing ships, but no one else did either. At least his bridge and pipeline builders didn't have to unlearn the procedures for custom building ships one at a time. Using division-of-labor and mass-production techniques, Kaiser succeeded in cutting the time to build Liberty Ships, from keel laying to launching, down to thirty-six days. At the peak of the wartime effort, workers constructed one ship in eighty hours and thirty minutes!

Kaiser coordinated delivery and distribution of supplies, which had been unheard of in shipbuilding. He also had major parts of the ship—like its hull and superstructure—built simultaneously. But his biggest success was in building parts of vessels in scattered locations around his shipyards by workers doing routine and repetitive tasks, then piecing their work together into ships. By the use of interchangeable parts, ships could be put together like refrigerators.

Kaiser's results were awesome. By 1943, his three shipyards were launching three ships every four days.

Vertical Differentiation. **Vertical differentiation** refers to the depth in the structure. Differentiation increases, and hence complexity, as the number of hierarchical levels in the organization increases. The more levels that exist between top management and operatives, the greater the potential of communication distortion, the more difficult it is to coordinate the decisions of managerial personnel, and the more difficult it is for top management to oversee the actions of operatives.

Vertical and horizontal differentiation should not be construed as independent of each other. Vertical differentiation may be understood best as a response to an increase in horizontal differentiation. As specialization expands, it becomes increasingly necessary to coordinate tasks. Since high horizontal differentiation means that members will have diverse training and background, it may be difficult for the individual units to see how their tasks fit into the greater whole. A company specializing in road construction will employ surveyors, grading architects, bridge designers, clerical personnel, asphalt tenders, cement masons, truck drivers, and heavy-duty-equipment operators. But someone must supervise each of these occupational groups to ensure that the work is done according to plan and on time. The result is a need for increased coordination, which shows itself in the development of vertical differentiation.

Organizations with the same number of employees need not have the same degrees of vertical differentiation. Organizations can be tall, with many layers of hierarchy, or flat, with few levels. The determining factor is the span of control.

The **span of control** defines the number of subordinates that a manager can direct effectively. If this span is wide, managers will have a number of subordinates reporting to them. If it is narrow, managers will have few underlings. All things being equal, the smaller the span, the taller the organization. This point is important and requires elaboration.

Simple arithmetic will show that the difference between an average management span of, say, four, and one of eight in a company of four thousand nonmanagerial employees can make a difference of two entire levels of management and of nearly eight hundred managers.[23]

This statement is illustrated in Figure 4–1. You will note that each of the operative (lowest) levels contains 4096 employees. All

FIGURE 4–1 *Contrasting Spans of Control*

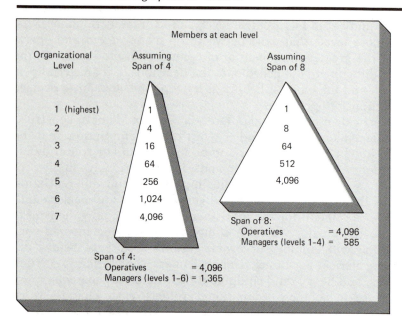

the other levels represent management positions: 1365 managers (levels 1–6) with a span of 4; 585 managers (levels 1–4) with a span of 8. The narrower span (4) creates high vertical differentiation and a tall organization. The wider span creates a flatter organization.

The evidence is clouded on whether the tall or flat organization is more effective. Tall structures provide closer supervision and tighter "boss-oriented" controls, and coordination and communication become complicated because of the increased number of layers through which directives must go. Flat structures have a shorter and simpler communication chain, less opportunity for supervision since each manager has more people reporting to him or her, and reduced promotion opportunities as a result of fewer levels of management.

An early study at Sears, Roebuck lent support for the flat organization, or low vertical-differentiation case.[24] Two groups of Sears' stores, having between 150 and 175 employees, were the subject of the investigation. One group had only two levels of management: the store manager and approximately thirty department managers. The second group, in contrast, had three levels: a store manager, group managers, and merchandise managers. The conclusions drawn from this investigation were that among the stores studied, the two-level organizations outperformed the three-level stores on sales volume, profit, and morale criteria.

It would be simplistic to conclude that wider spans lead to higher organizational performance. A more recent study, for instance, found no support for the general thesis that flat organizations are preferable.[25] The evidence suggested that the larger the organization, the less effective the flat organizations. Increased size brings with it complexity and more demands on every manager's time. Tall structures, with their narrow spans, reduce the manager's day-to-day supervisory responsibilities and give more time for involvement with the manager's own boss. Further evidence indicates that, in addition to the size of the organization, type of job and the individual characteristics of the job holder will moderate the span-organizational effectiveness relationship.[26] Certain jobs require more direction, whereas others require less, and individuals, depending on their education, skills, and personal characteristics, vary in the degree of freedom or control they prefer.

Spatial Differentiation. An organization can perform the same activities with the same degree of horizontal differentiation and hierarchical arrangement in multiple locations. Yet this existence of multiple locations increases complexity. Therefore, the third element in complexity is **spatial differentiation,** which refers to the degree to which the location of an organization's offices, plants, and personnel are dispersed geographically.

Spatial differentiation can be thought of as an extended dimension to horizontal and vertical differentiation. That is, it is possible to separate tasks and power centers geographically. This separation includes dispersion by both number and distance. Several examples may make this clearer.

A manufacturing company differentiates horizontally when it separates marketing functions from production. Yet if essentially identical marketing activities are carried on in six geographically dispersed sales offices—Seattle, Los Angeles, Atlanta, New York, Toronto, and Brussels—while all production is done in a large factory in Cleveland, this organization is more complex than if both the marketing and production activities were performed at the same facility in Cleveland. Similarly, consider two banks. Both have assets of $300 million. But one operates in a branch-banking state—for example, California—while the other is in a unit-banking state—for example, Illinois—that legally forbids branch offices. The California bank might have a dozen branch offices in a dozen different cities to do the same amount of volume that the Illinois bank does under one roof. It's only logical that communication, coordination, and control are made easier for management in the Illinois bank where spatial differentiation is low.

The spatial concept also applies with vertical differentiation. While tall structures are more complex than flat ones, a tall or-

OT
CLOSE-UP

PETERS' PRACTICAL PROPOSAL: MAKE EVERY ORGANIZATION FLATTER!

In spite of the evidence indicating that wider spans are not universally applicable, management consultant and writer Tom Peters (of *In Search of Excellence* fame) argues strongly that *all* organizations should radically increase their spans of control.[27]

Peters believes that North American organizations have too many vertical layers and too many middle managers. To support his case, he cites research showing that supervisors in U.S. organizations average spans of ten, while Japanese organizations have one hundred or even two hundred.[28] Peters proposes that no organization needs more than five layers at the maximum.[29] As he notes, the Catholic church, with 800 million members, has achieved and maintained a position of world leadership and power for more than 1500 years with only five layers—pope, cardinal, archbishop, bishop, and parish priest.

Peters' solution to making all North American organization structures more effective includes setting five-layer limits on the most complex organizations (with three levels preferred) and minimum spans of control at the supervisory level of twenty-five to seventy-five. He admits his solution is a radical response to making organizations more flexible and responsive. But his advice should not be ignored because, if for no other reason, more and more practicing managers are looking to Tom Peters for advice on how to make their organizations more competitive in today's changing world.

ganization in which different levels of authority are dispersed geographically is more complex than is its counterpart whose management is physically concentrated. If senior executives reside in one city, middle managers in half a dozen cities, and lower-level managers in a hundred different company offices around the world, complexity is increased. Even though computer technology has dramatically improved the ability for these separated decision makers to retrieve information and communicate with each other, complexity has still increased.

Finally, the spatial-differentiation element considers distance as well as numbers. If the state of Delaware has two regional welfare offices—one in Dover and another in Wilmington—they will be approximately forty-five miles apart. Even though the state of Alaska also has only two comparably sized offices—in Anchorage and Fairbanks, which are separated by 350 miles—the Delaware welfare organization is less complex.

In summary, spatial differentiation is the third element in defining complexity. It tells us that even if horizontal and vertical differentiation were to remain the same across spatially separated units, the physical separation itself would increase complexity.

Do the Three Come as a Package? What, if any, relationship is there among the three elements of horizontal, vertical, and spatial differentiation? At the extreme ranges of organization size, you would expect a high intercorrelation. Exxon, Polaroid, General Mills, the U.S. Postal System, and most of the diversified industrial or government organizations with which you are familiar rate high on all three elements. Moe's Dry Cleaning, a small shop made up of only Moe and his wife, is low on all three. Can we generalize, however, beyond the extreme cases?

The answer is No! The three elements do not have to come as a package. It's been noted, for instance, that colleges usually have a low degree of vertical differentiation and little or no spatial differentiation, but a high degree of horizontal differentiation.[30] On the other hand, an army battalion is characterized by high vertical differentiation and little horizontal differentiation.[31]

A closer look at organizations tells us that the various elements may differ significantly within a given organization. This is particularly evident with horizontal differentiation. The work that employees have to do is most repetitive at the lowest levels in the organization, particularly at the operating core. This would include production and clerical activities. We would expect these types of jobs to have high horizontal differentiation. The manager's job, because of its varied activities, is not likely to be heavily horizontally differentiated.

Why Is Complexity Important?

We have identified the key elements in complexity. It would not be inappropriate now to inquire: So what? What does it mean for managers if their organization is high or low in complexity?

Organizations contain subsystems that require communication, coordination, and control if they are to be effective. The more complex an organization, the greater the need for effective communication, coordination, and control devices. In other words, as complexity increases, so do the demands on management to ensure that differentiated and dispersed activities are working smoothly and together toward achieving the organization's goals. The need for devices such as committees, computerized information systems, and formal policy manuals is reduced for organizations that are low in complexity. It is when there are a number of employees each doing a very small part of the activities that the organization needs to have done (most of these employees having little idea of exactly what others in the organization do every day), an elaborate hierarchy of management positions, and facilities and personnel spread over a large geographical area that it becomes clear that these communication and coordinating devices are absolutely necessary. So one way of answering the "What does complexity mean to managers?" question is to say that it creates different demands and requirements on managers' time. The higher the complexity, the greater amount of attention they must pay to dealing with problems of communication, coordination, and control.

This has been described as a paradox in the analysis of organizations.[32] Management's decision to increase differentiation is made typically in the interests of economy and efficiency. But these decisions create cross-pressures to add managerial personnel to facilitate control, coordination, and conflict reduction. So the economies that complexity creates may be counterbalanced by the increased burden of keeping the organization together. In fact, there may be a built-in automatic process in organizations that fosters increased complexity. Placed in a systems perspective, we know that organizations have a natural propensity to grow to survive. Over time, therefore, those organizations that survive will tend to become more complex as their own activities and the environment around them become more complex. We can add, then, that an understanding of complexity is important, for it is a characteristic that managers should look for and expect if their organization is healthy.

FORMALIZATION

The second component of organization structure is formalization. In this section, we define the term, explain its importance, introduce the two general ways in which management can achieve it, demonstrate the more popular formalization techniques, and compare formalization with complexity.

Definition

Formalization refers to the degree to which jobs within the organization are standardized. If a job is highly formalized, the job incumbent has a minimum amount of discretion over what is to be done, when it is to be done, and how he or she should do it. Employees can be expected to always handle the same input in exactly the same way, resulting in a consistent and uniform output. There are explicit job descriptions, lots of organizational rules, and clearly defined procedures covering work processes in organizations where there is high formalization. Where formalization is low, employees' behavior would be relatively nonprogrammed. Such jobs would offer employees a great deal of freedom to exercise discretion in their work. So formalization is a measure of standardization. Since an individual's discretion on the job is inversely related to the amount of behavior that is preprogrammed by the organization, the greater the standardization, the less input the employee has into how his or her work is to be done. This standardization not only eliminates employees' engaging in alternative behaviors but also removes the need for employees to consider alternatives.

Does It Have to Be in Writing? There is some debate as to whether the rules and procedures of formalization have to be in writing or whether the standardization of behavior created by tradition and unwritten regulations should also be included in the definition.

For instance, formalization has been defined as "the extent to which rules, procedures, instructions, and communications are written."[33] Following this definition, formalization would be measured by determining if the organization has a policies-and-procedures manual, assessing the number and specificity of its regulations, reviewing job descriptions to determine the extent of elaborateness and detail, and looking at other similar official documents of the organization.

An alternative approach argues that formalization applies to both written and unwritten regulations.[34] Perceptions, then, are as important as reality. For measurement purposes, formalization would be calculated by considering, in addition to official documents of the organization, *attitudes* of employees as to the degree to which job procedures were spelled out and rules were enforced.

Of this debate, you might ask: Who cares? While the differences between these two positions might appear minor, that is not the case. When both approaches have been used, they obtain different results.[35] Although originally thought to be merely two separate ways of measuring the same construct—one measuring hard data and the other hard data and attitudes—research indicates otherwise. So the issue of whether formalization considers only the organization's written documents is critical to its definition.

Our position is to recognize that formalization can be explicit or implicit, the latter including both written records *and* employee perceptions. But for clarity purposes, we'll use the explicit definition throughout this book. That is, unless noted otherwise, when we talk about formalization, we'll be referring to the organization's *written* regulations.

Range of Formalization. It's important to recognize that the degree of formalization can vary widely among and within organizations. Certain jobs are well known to have little formalization. College book salespeople—the people from various publishers who call on professors to discuss their companies' new publications—have a great deal of freedom in their jobs. They have no standard sales pitch, and the extent of rules and procedures governing their behavior may be little more than requiring the submission of a weekly sales report and some suggestions on what to emphasize for the various new titles. At the other extreme, on other jobs (for example, the clerical and editorial positions in the same publishing houses for which the college book salespeople work), employees are required to "clock in" at their work station by 8 A.M. or be docked a half-hour's pay and, once at that work station, are required to follow a set of precise procedures dictated by management.

It is generally true that the narrowest of unskilled jobs—those that are simplest and most repetitive—are most amenable to high degrees of formalization. The greater the professionalization of a job, the less likely it is to be highly formalized. Yet there are obvious exceptions. Public accountants and consultants, for instance, are required to keep detailed records of their hour-by-hour activities so that their companies can bill clients appropriately for their services. In general, however, the relationship holds. The jobs of lawyers, engineers, social workers, librarians, and like professionals tend to rate low on formalization.

Formalization differs not only with whether the jobs are unskilled or professional but also by level in the organization and by functional department. Employees higher in the organization are increasingly involved in activities that are less repetitive and require unique solutions. The discretion that managers have increases as they move up the hierarchy. So formalization tends to be inversely related to level in the organization. Additionally, the kind of work in which people are engaged influences the degree of formalization. Jobs in production are typically more formalized than are those in sales or research. Why? Because production tends to be concerned with stable and repetitive activities. Such jobs lend themselves to standardization. In contrast, the sales department must be flexible to respond to changing needs of customers, while research must be flexible if it is to be innovative.[36]

Why Is Formalization Important?

Organizations use formalization because of the benefits that accrue from regulating employees' behavior. Standardizing behavior reduces variability. McDonald's, for example, can be confident that a Big Mac will look and taste the same whether it is made at an outlet in Portland, Maine; Biloxi, Mississippi; Fairbanks, Alaska; or Amsterdam, Holland. McDonald's, in fact, attributes its corporate success to its product consistency and uniformity. The company's operating manual has 385 pages describing the most minute activities in each outlet. No cigarette, candy, or pinball machines are allowed. Strict standards of employee grooming are specified. The manual states that the basic hamburger patty must be 1.6 ounces of pure beef, with no more than 19 percent fat content. Hamburger buns must have 13.3 percent sugar in them. French fries are to be kept under the warming light for no more than seven minutes. Specifically designed scoops are to be used to ensure that the precise number of fries goes into each pouch. Even the exact procedure for greeting customers and taking orders is standardized.[37] Is there any doubt why the food at McDonald's, regardless of where in the world it is purchased, always looks and tastes the same? As the above description demonstrates, it isn't by chance!

Standardization also promotes coordination. Football coaches spend dozens of house introducing a complex set of procedures for their players. When the quarterback calls "wing-right-44-on-3," each team member knows exactly what task is to be performed. Formalization allows automobiles to flow smoothly down the assembly line, as each worker on the line performs a highly standardized set of repetitive activities. It also prevents members of a paramedic unit from standing around at the scene of an accident and arguing about who is to do what. If you watch the behaviors of the medical staff in the operating room on a rerun of the TV series "M.A.S.H.," you will observe a highly coordinated group of organizational members performing a precise set of standardized procedures.

The economics of formalization also should not be overlooked. The greater the formalization, the less discretion required from a job incumbent. This is relevant because discretion costs money. Jobs that are low on formalization demand greater judgment. Given that sound judgment is a scarce quality, organizations have to pay more (in terms of wages, salaries, and benefits) to acquire the services of individuals who possess this ability. To secure the services of a plant purchasing agent who can perform purchasing duties effectively and efficiently *with no formal directives* might cost an organization fifty thousand dollars a year. However, if the purchasing agent's job is highly formalized to the point that a comprehensive manual is available to resolve nearly any question or problem that might occur, this job may be done just as competently by someone with far less experience and education—for twenty thousand dollars a year!

This explains, incidentally, why many large organizations have accounting manuals, personnel manuals, and purchasing manuals, occasionally running to several thousand pages in length. These organizations have chosen to formalize jobs wherever possible so as to get the most effective performance from employees at the lowest cost.

The "Make or Buy" Decision

We noted earlier the difference between unskilled and professional employees and indicated a relationship between each classification and the propensity to formalize jobs. In this section, we propose that formalization can take place on the job or off. When it's done on the job, we use the term *externalized* behavior. This means that the formalization is external to the employee; that is, the rules, procedures, and regulations governing the individual's work activity are specifically defined, codified, and enforced through direct management supervision. This characterizes the formalization of unskilled employees. It is also what is typically meant by the term *formalization*. Professionalization is another alternative—it creates *internalized* behavior through social specialization. Professionals are socialized before entering the organization. So while formalization can take place in the organization, we will show how others are hired preprogrammed, with their rules already built in. When it comes to formalization, therefore, organizations can choose to "make or buy" the behaviors they desire.[38]

Socialization refers to an adaptation process by which individuals learn the values, norms, and expected behavior patterns for the job and the organization of which they will be a part. All employees will receive at least some molding and shaping on the job, but for certain members, the socialization process will be substantially accomplished *before* they join the organization. This is specifically true of professionals.

Professionals undergo many years of education and training before they practice their craft. Engineers, for instance, must spend four or more years studying before they can be certified. This education process gives the engineer a common body of knowledge that can be called upon in performing the job. It is often overlooked, however, that this training also includes molding the person to think and act like an engineer. In a similar vein, it can be argued that one of the main tasks of a business school is to socialize students to the attitudes and behaviors that business firms want. If business executives believe that successful employees value the profit ethic, are loyal, work hard, desire to achieve, and willingly accept directives from their superiors, they can hire individuals out of business schools who have been premolded in this pattern.

So management has two decisions. First, what degree of standardization of behavior is desired? Second, will the standardization desired be "made" in house or "bought" outside? The in-house variety is emphasized with unskilled employees, although all members will get some of this if only to fine tune the member to the unique culture of the particular organization. For the most part, unskilled jobs are highly differentiated—both horizontally and vertically—and formalization by way of rules, work-flow procedures, and training is used to coordinate and control the behavior of people performing these jobs. In contrast, when management hires professionals, it is "buying" individuals whose prior training has included internalizing their job descriptions, procedures, and rules. One scholar has described the professional (in rich, although clearly sexist, terms) as "the ultimate eunuch, capable of doing everything well in the harem except what he should not do—and in this case that is to mess around with the goals of the organization or the assumptions that determine to what ends he will use his professional skills."[39]

Direct on-the-job formalization and professionalization are basically substitutes for each other. "The organization can either control [employee behavior] directly through its own procedures and rules, or else it can achieve indirect control by hiring duly trained professionals."[40] We can expect to find that as the level of professionalization increases in an organization, the level of formalization decreases.

Formalization Techniques

Managers have at their disposal a number of techniques by which they can bring about the standardization of employee behavior. In this section, we review the most popular of these techniques.

Selection.   Organizations do not choose employees at random. Job applicants are processed through a series of hurdles designed to differentiate individuals likely to be successful job performers from those likely to be unsuccessful. These hurdles typically include completion of application blanks, employment tests, interviews, and background investigations. Applicants can and do get rejected at each of these steps.

An effective selection process will be designed to determine if job candidates "fit" into the organization.[41] A "good" employee is defined as one who will perform his or her job in a satisfactory manner and also whose personality, work habits, and attitudes align with what the organization desires. If the selection process does anything, it tries to prevent the employment of misfits; that is, individuals who do not accept the norms of the organization. A recruiter for an executive search firm once confided that he believed the secret to the successful placement of middle- and top-level managers was attaining a reading of the organization's personality or culture and then screening applicants for compatibility. He noted that it was rarely difficult to find candidates with the experience and abilities to fill a vacancy. The problem was finding the right chemistry between a candidate and the people who were doing the hiring. The recruiter said he spent considerable time just talking with executives in the client company. This was done in the belief that certain "types" of people were more likely than others to fit into the company.

Selection should be recognized as one of the most widely used techniques by which organizations control employee discretion. Whether the hiring covers unskilled or professional employees, organizations use the selection process to screen in the right people and screen out those who think and act in ways that management considers undesirable. The selection of professionals may be done with greater latitude than the selection of unskilled employees— the former's prior professionalization reducing the need for the organization to identify misfits. Part of this task was assumed by the universities and associations that conferred the professional's certification. However, all new members must meet the organization's minimum requirements of an acceptable employee, and the selection process provides one of the most popular mechanisms for achieving this end.

Role Requirements.   Individuals in organizations fulfill roles. Every job carries with it expectations on how the role incumbent is supposed to behave. Job analysis, for instance, defines the jobs that need to be done in the organization and outlines what employee behaviors are necessary to perform the jobs. This analysis develops the information from which job descriptions are created. The fact that organizations identify jobs to be done and the desirable role behaviors that go with those jobs means that role expectations play a major part in regulating employee behavior.

Role expectations may be explicit and defined narrowly. In such cases, the degree of formalization is high. Of course, the role expectations attributed to a given job by management and members of a role set can traverse the spectrum from explicit and narrow to very loose. The latter, for instance, allows employees freedom to react to situations in unique ways. It puts minimum constraints on the role incumbent. So organizations that develop exacting and complicated job descriptions go a long way toward defining the expectations of how a particular role is to be played. By loosening or tightening role expectations, organizations are actually loosening or tightening the degree of formalization.

Rules, Procedures and Policies. **Rules** are explicit statements that tell an employee what he or she ought or ought not to do. Procedures are a series of interrelated sequential steps that employees follow in the accomplishment of their job tasks. Policies are guidelines that set constraints on decisions that employees make. Each of these represents techniques that organizations use to regulate the behavior of members.

Sales clerks are told that no checks can be accepted unless the customer has three pieces of identification. All level 3 managers are instructed that expenditures over five hundred dollars require approval by a superior. Employees are required to submit expense-reimbursement reports, typed, on form B-446, in duplicate, within thirty days of the outlay. Each of these examples represents the imposition of rules on employees. Their identifying characteristic is that they tell employees explicitly what they can do, how they are to do it, and when they are to do it. Rules leave no room for employee judgment or discretion. They state a particular and specific required behavior pattern.

Procedures are established to ensure standardization of work processes. The same input is processed in the same way, and the output is the same each day. If one were to ask an accounts-payable clerk what his or her job involved, the answer would probably correspond closely with the procedurized description of his or her activities. Rather than have the clerk, through trial and error, develop an individualized way of handling the accounts payable (which might include some critical deviations from the pattern that management wants the clerk to follow), the organization has provided a procedure. For example, when invoices are received daily, they are stamped in, alphabetized, and merged with purchase orders; then tabulations are checked and vouchers are prepared. Vouchers are to be completed as follows: use preprinted voucher tags, place voucher number in top right corner, place date in top left corner, write in appropriate accounts to be charged, check to ensure total of accounts equals invoice amount, initial in bottom right corner. These steps follow a specific standardized sequence that results in a uniform output.

Policies provide greater leeway than rules do. Rather than specifying a particular and specific behavior, policies allow employees to use discretion but within limited boundaries. The discretion is created by including judgmental terms (such as "best," "satisfied," "competitive"), which the employee is left to interpret. The statement from the personnel manual at a major midwestern hospital that it will "pay competitive wages" illustrates a policy. This policy does not tell the wage and salary administrator what should be paid, but it does provide parameters for wage decisions to be made. The term *competitive* requires interpretation, yet it sets discretionary limits. If other local hospitals pay between $5.75 and $6.40 an hour for an inexperienced orderly, hourly rates of $5.20 or $7.25 would clearly not be within the guidelines set by the policy.

Policies need not be written to control discretion. Employees pick up on an organization's implied policies merely by observing the actions of members around them. An employment interviewer in the personnel department of the hospital just described may never find in writing a policy that the hospital gives hiring preference to relatives of current employees, but nepotism may be an observable practice. The interviewer can be expected to be socialized to this implied policy, and its influence on the interviewer's behavior will be just as strong as if it were printed in boldface type in the personnel policy manual.

Training. Many organizations provide training to employees. This includes the on-the-job variety where understudy assignments, coaching, and apprenticeship methods are used to teach employees preferred job skills, knowledge, and attitudes. It also includes off-the-job training such as classroom lectures, films, demonstrations, simulation exercises, and programmed instruction. Again, the intent is to instill in employees preferred work behaviors and attitudes.

New employees are often required to undergo a brief orientation program in which they are familiarized with the organization's objectives, history, philosophy, and rules as well as relevant personnel policies, such as hours of work, pay procedures, overtime requirements, and benefit programs. In many cases, this is followed by specific job training. For instance, new computer programmers at one bank undergo several days of training to learn the organization's system. Counter help at McDonald's is required to read the company's operating manual, after which they undergo several weeks of on-the-job training, during which their job behaviors receive close scrutiny by the operating managers. The recent liberal arts graduate who is hired by a New York book publisher to be a production editor may understudy a seasoned veteran for three to six months before being set free on his or her own.

Rituals. Rituals are used as a formalization technique with members who will have a strong and enduring impact on the organization. That certainly includes individuals who aspire to senior-level management positions as well as pledges seeking active status in a fraternity or faculty members vying for tenure. The common threat underlying rituals is that members must prove that they can be trusted and are loyal to the organization before they can be "knighted," the "proving process" being the ritual.

Business firms that promote from within do not put new employees into top management positions. The typical reason cited would be that they lack relevant experience. Given the fact that many promotions place employees in situations very unlike their previous jobs, it is probably correct to conclude that experience is only part of the explanation. Another part is that top management positions are held out as rewards to those in the company who prove by their abilities, length of service, and loyalty that they are committed to the goals and norms of the firm. Managers are, after all, "the guardians of the organization's ideology."[42] Senior managers are the *primary* gatekeepers. Thus, the organization has a heavy stake in ensuring that managers have proven themselves before they are promoted to influential senior positions. Even among firms that may fill their senior positions from outside the organization, great care is taken to assure that the candidate has paid his or her "dues" on earlier jobs and, based on personality tests and extensive interviews with top executives, appears likely to fit in.

Relationship between Formalization and Complexity

There is considerable evidence to support a strong association among specialization, standardization, and formalization.[43] Where employees perform narrow, repetitive, and specialized tasks, their routines tend to be standardized, and a large number of rules and regulations govern their behavior. Assembly-line workers have highly specialized jobs with standardized routines and a wealth of formal rules and procedures to follow.

On the other hand, we find cases of high complexity being linked with low formalization.[44] For instance, the highly trained specialist or professional does not require a great number of rules and regulations. High formalization in such activities would only impose redundant controls.

The preceding findings are not contradictory. They acknowledge the important difference between functional and social specialization and the fact that the two types of specialization have different effects on the need for formalization. High horizontal differentiation, when achieved through division of labor, typically means hiring unskilled personnel to perform routine and repetitive tasks. Division of labor, then, tends to be associated with a high degree of formalization to facilitate coordination and control. Where high horizontal differentiation is achieved by hiring specialists and professionals, formalization will tend to be low. These people do nonroutine tasks. Their previous socialization will have instilled internal standards of control, so high formalization is not necessary. Our conclusion, therefore, is that the key to understanding the complexity-formalization relationship is to focus on the degree of horizontal differentiation and the way it is achieved.

CENTRALIZATION

Where are decisions made in the organization: up on top by senior management or down low where the decision makers are closest to the action? This question introduces the last of the components that make up organization structure. The subject of this section is centralization and its counterpart, decentralization.

Definition

Centralization is the most problematic of the three components. Most theorists concur that the term refers to the degree to which decision making is concentrated at a single point in the organization. A high concentration implies high centralization, whereas a low concentration indicates low centralization or what may be called **decentralization.** There is also agreement that it is distinctly different from spatial differentiation. Centralization is concerned with the dispersion of authority to make decisions within the organization, not geographic dispersion. However, beyond these points, the water quickly becomes muddy. The following questions suggest the breadth of the problem.

1. *Do we look only at formal authority?* **Authority** refers to the formal rights inherent in a managerial position to give orders and expect the orders to be obeyed. There is no doubt that centralization of decision making encompasses those with formal authority in the organization. But what about those people who have informal influence over decisions? Jim Miller is a $6.80-an-hour metal handler at a large steel company, but his fiancée's father is vice president for manufacturing at the firm. The future father-in-law frequently asks for and follows the advice provided by Jim. At a major television network, Barbara Harris is a staff research specialist in the programming department. Her job is to identify characteristics that differentiate successful from unsuccessful prime-time programs. She prepares the reports on her findings, but she has no formal authority. Yet the director of programming has her attend meetings informally where decisions for future programming are made. Additionally, he rarely makes a major programming decision without checking out Barbara's opinion. Jim and

Barbara have no formal authority in their positions, but they do affect decisions. Is this consistent with high centralization or low?

2. *Can policies override decentralization?*   Many organizations push the making of decisions down to lower levels, but then the decision makers are bound by policies. Because decision choices are constrained by policies, do these low-level decision makers actually have discretion or is it artificial? In other words, has decentralization really occurred if policies force the decisions to conform with what they would be if top management made them themselves? One could argue that, even though employees low in the organization are making many decisions, if those decisions are programmed by organizational policies, a high degree of centralization exists.

3. *What does "concentration at a single point" mean?*   There may be agreement that centralization refers to concentration at a single point, but exactly what that means is not clear. Does a "single point" mean an individual, a unit, or a level in the organization? Most people think of centralized decisions as being made high in the organization, but this may not be true if the single point is a low-level manager. Does it matter to operative employees whether decisions are made one level above them or six? Either way, they are allowed little input into their work. If operative employees are not permitted to participate in decisions about their work, isn't decision making centralized regardless of whether it is concentrated at the next level up or at the very top of the organization?

4. *Does an information-processing system that closely monitors decentralized decisions maintain centralized control?* Advanced information technology, via computers, facilitates decentralization. But that same technology allows top managers to learn of the consequences of any decision rapidly and to take corrective action if the decision is not to top management's liking.

If discretion is delegated downward but closely monitored by those above, is it real decentralization? In such cases, there is no real sharing of control in the organization. One could argue that there is only the appearance of decentralization, and top management maintains effective centralized control.

5. *Does the control of information by lower-level members result in the decentralization of what appears to be centralized decisions?*   Managers rely on those beneath them to provide the information from which decisions are made. Information is passed upward, but of course it is filtered. If it were not screened and filtered, top management would be inundated with information. But this filtering requires subordinates to make judgments and interpretations of what information should be transmitted. Thus, the filtering process gives subordinates power to pass on to top management only that information that they want top management to have. Further, they can structure that information in such a way so as to get the decisions made that the lower-level members want. As such, even though it may appear that decision making is centralized with top management, is it not really decentralized, since the decision inputs, and hence eventually the decisions, are controlled by lower-level personnel?

These questions were not introduced to confuse you. They are meant to dramatize our position that centralization is a tough concept to nail down. Yet our pragmatic approach demands that we develop a definition that can resolve these issues. Toward that end, **centralization** can be described more specifically as *the degree to which the formal authority to make discretionary choices is concentrated in an individual, unit, or level (usually high in the organization), thus permitting employees (usually low in the organization) minimum input into their work.*

This more elaborate definition answers the questions posed earlier. (1) Centralization is concerned only with the formal structure, not the informal organization. It applies only to formal authority. (2) Centralization looks at decision discretion. Where decisions are delegated downward but extensive policies exist to constrain the discretion of lower-level members, there is increased centralization. Policies can, therefore, act to override decentralization. (3) Concentration at a single point can refer to an individual, unit, or level, but the single point *implies* concentration at a high level. (4) Information processing can improve top management control, but the decision choice is still with the low-level member. Thus, an information-processing system that closely monitors decentralized decisions does not maintain centralized control. (5) The transference of all information requires interpretation. The filtering that occurs as information passes through vertical levels is a fact of life. The top managers are free to verify the information they receive and to hold subordinates accountable in their choices of what they filter out, but control of information input is a form of de facto decentralization. Management decisions are centralized if concentrated at the top, but the more the information input to those decisions is filtered through others, the less concentrated and controlled the decision is.

SOPHISTICATED INFORMATION SYSTEMS WILL BE CHANGING ORGANIZATION STRUCTURES

Sophisticated information systems—specifically the widespread use by management personnel of personal computers that can tap into large centralized data bases and that are linked together as part of a larger computer network—will be changing the way we look at organization structures.[45]

For example, when managers have direct access to data, they can handle more subordinates. Why? Because computer control can substitute for personal supervision. The result can be wider spans of control, fewer levels in the organization, and organizations that are lower in complexity.

Information systems may also lead to less formalization and more decentralized organizations. Again, the reason is that management information systems can substitute computer control for rules and decision discretion. Computer technology rapidly apprises top managers of the consequences of any decision and allows them to take corrective action if the decision is not to their liking. Information systems should lead to the appearance of more decentralization with no commensurate loss of control by top management. Of course, sophisticated management information systems might also lead to more *centralized* organizations. Top managers will have the capability of bypassing middle management and directly accessing data from the operating floor, thus decreasing senior management's dependence on lower-level managers (who can hoard or distort information) and allowing the former to make almost all key operational decisions (or at least closely monitor them).

Decision Making and Centralization

Managers—regardless of where they are in the organization—make decisions. The typical manager must make choices about goals, budget allocations, personnel, the ways in which work is to be done, and ways to improve his or her unit's effectiveness. As critical as a knowledge of authority and the chain of command are to the understanding of centralization, of equal importance is the awareness of the decision-making process. The degree of control one holds over the full decision-making process is, itself, a measure of centralization.

Decision making is presented traditionally as the making of choices. After developing and evaluating at least two alternatives, the decision maker chooses a preferred alternative. From the perspective of individual decision making, this is an adequate presentation. But from an organizational perspective, the making of a choice is only one step in a larger process.[46]

Figure 4–2 depicts this larger process. Information must be gathered. This input establishes the parameters of what can be done. The information gathered goes a long way toward controlling what should and will be done. As noted earlier, the fact that top-level managers rely on information fed to them from individuals lower in the vertical hierarchy gives those subordinates the opportunity to communicate the information they want to. Once the information is gathered, it must be interpreted. The interpretations are then transmitted as advice to the decision maker as to what should be done. The third step is acting on the advice to make the choice. Much of the choosing, of course, has been done previously when that information was selectively screened and interpreted. The decision choice establishes what the decision maker desires or intends to have done. Wishes, unfortunately, do not always become actions. The decision must be authorized and conveyed before it can be executed. Where there are many layers in the vertical hierarchy, the final execution may differ from the intention. Breakdowns in communication can result in a divergence between intentions and actions. So, too, can the interests of those who initiate action. President John Kennedy found this out in 1962 when on several occasions he ordered his secretary of state to see that U.S. missiles in Turkey were removed because he thought that they might precipitate war with Russia.[47] Despite his formal orders and impassioned personal pleas, State Department officials in Turkey

FIGURE 4–2 *Organization Decision-Making Process*

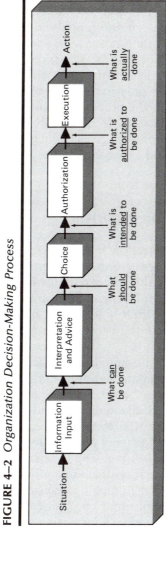

Based on T. T. Paterson, *Management Theory* (London: Business Publications, 1969), p. 150.

saw such action as having harmful effects on Turkish public opinion, so they did nothing.

Referring to Figure 4–2, it can be said that decision making is most centralized when the decision maker controls all the steps: "He collects his own information, analyzes it himself, makes the choice, needs seek no authorization of it, and executes it himself."[48] As others gain control over these steps, the process becomes decentralized. Therefore, decentralization will be greatest when the decision maker controls only the making of the choice; this is the least that one can do in the process and still be a decision maker. So viewing the organizational decision process as more than merely choosing between alternatives gives us insight into the intricacies involved in defining and assessing the degree of centralization in an organization.

Why Is Centralization Important?

The heading for this section may mislead you. That it implies centralization, in contrast to decentralization, is important. The term *centralization* in this context is meant to be viewed in the same way complexity and formalization are viewed in this chapter. It represents a range—from high to low. It may be clearer, therefore, if we ask: Why is the centralization-decentralization issue important?

As described, in addition to being collections of people, organizations are decision-making and information-processing systems. Organizations facilitate the achievement of goals through coordination of group effort; decision making and information processing are central for coordination to take place. Yet—and this point is often overlooked by students of decision-making and organization theory—information itself is not the scarce resource in organizations. Advanced information technology provides managers with bundles of data to assist in making decisions. We live in a world that drenches us with information. The scarce resource is the processing capacity to attend to information.[49]

Managers are limited in their ability to give attention to data they receive. Every manager has some limit to the amount of information that he or she can process. After that limit is reached, further input results in information overload. To avoid reaching the point where a manager's capacity is exceeded, some of the decisions can be given to others. The concentration of decision making at a single point can be dispersed. This dispersion or transfer is decentralization.

There are other reasons why organizations might decentralize. Organizations need to respond rapidly to changing conditions at the point at which the change is taking place. Decentralization facilitates speedy action because it avoids the need to process the information through the vertical hierarchy. It can be acted upon by those closest to the issue. This explains why marketing activities tend to be decentralized. Marketing personnel must be able to react quickly to the needs of customers and actions of competitors.

In addition to speed, decentralization can provide more detailed input into the decision. If those most familiar with an issue make a decision, more of the specific facts relevant to that issue will be available. The sales people at a company's facilities in Rio de Janeiro are much more likely to know the relevant facts for making pricing decisions on the company's products in Brazil than would a sales executive five thousand miles north in New York.

Decentralizing decision making can provide motivation to employees by allowing them to participate in the decision-making process. Professionals and skilled employees are particularly sensitive to having a say in those decisions that will affect how they do their jobs. If management holds humanistic values, the firm is likely to favor decentralization. If certain groups are likely to hold humanistic values, they are the professionals and the skilled. Because these people desire to share in the decision-making process, the opportunity to do so should be motivating. On the other hand, if management holds autocratic values and centralizes authority, employee motivation can be predicted to be low.

A final plus for decentralization is the training opportunity that it creates for low-level managers. By delegating authority, top management permits less experienced managers to learn by doing. By making decisions in areas where impact is less critical, low-level managers get decision-making practice with the potential for minimum damage. This prepares them for assuming greater authority as they rise in the organization.

Of course, the goal of decentralization is not always desirable. There are conditions under which centralization is preferred. When a comprehensive perspective is needed in a decision or where concentration provides significant economies, centralization offers distinct advantages. Top-level managers are obviously in a better position to see the big picture. This provides them with advantages in choosing actions that will be consistent with the best interests of the whole organization rather than merely benefiting some special-interest group. Further, certain activities are clearly done more efficiently when centralized. This explains, for instance, why financial and legal decisions tend to be centralized. Both functions permeate activities throughout the organization, and there are distinct economies to centralizing this expertise.

This discussion leads to the conclusion that either high or low centralization may be desirable. Situational factors will determine the "right" amount. But *all* organizations process information so that managers can make decisions. As such, attention must be given to identifying the most effective way in which to organize where those decisions should be made.

Relationship of Centralization, Complexity, and Formalization

As we close this chapter on structural components, it is important to attempt to identify what relationships there are, if any, between centralization and complexity and between centralization and formalization.

Centralization and Complexity.   The evidence strongly supports an inverse relationship between centralization and complexity.[50] Decentralization is associated with high complexity. For example, an increase in the number of occupational specialties means an increase in the expertise and ability necessary to make decisions. Similarly, the more that employees have undergone professional training, the more likely they are to participate in decision making. Conversely, the evidence finds that the greater the centralization of work decisions, the less professional training is likely to be exhibited by employees. We expect, therefore, to find high complexity associated with decentralization when we examine the structure of organizations.

Centralization and Formalization.   The centralization-formalization relationship is as ambiguous as the centralization-complexity relationship is clear. A review of the evidence is marked by inconsistent results.

The early work found no strong relationships between centralization and formalization.[51] Later research reported a strong negative relationship between the two components; that is, organizations were both highly formalized and decentralized.[52] One follow-up effort, attempting to reconcile the controversy, yielded inconclusive results.[53] The most recent efforts support the high formalization-decentralization hypothesis.[54] Obviously, the relationship is complex. Given this caveat, however, we can suggest a tentative analysis.

High formalization can be found coupled with either a centralized or decentralized structure. Where employees in the organization are predominantly unskilled, you can expect lots of rules and regulations to guide these people. Autocratic assumptions also tend to dominate, so management keeps authority centralized. Control is exercised through both formalization and concentration of decision making in top management.

With professional employees, on the other hand, you might predict both low formalization and decentralization. Research confirms this alignment.[55] Yet the type of decision moderates this relationship. Professionals expect decentralization of decisions that affect their work directly, but this does not necessarily apply to personnel issues (i.e., salary and performance-appraisal procedures) or strategic organization decisions. Professionals want the predictability that comes with standardization of personnel matters, so you might expect to find decentralization paired with extensive rules and regulations. Additionally, professionals' interest is in their technical work, not in strategic decision making. This can result in low formalization and centralization. Centralization, however, is confined to strategic rather than to operative decisions, the former having little impact on the work activities of the professional.

SUMMARY

This chapter defines and describes the three main components of organization structure—complexity, formalization, and centralization.

Complexity refers to the degree of differentiation that exists within an organization. Horizontal differentiation considers the degree to which jobs are dispersed geographically. It is measured by the number of horizontal separation between units. It is measured by calculating the number of occupational specialties and the average length of training required by each. Vertical differentiation refers to the depth of the organization and is measured by counting the number of hierarchical levels separating the chief executive from the employees working on the organization's output. Spatial differentiation encompasses the degree to which jobs are dispersed geographically. It is measured by the number of separate locations, the average distance of these sites from headquarters, and the proportion of the organization's personnel located at these separate units.

The greater the horizontal differentiation, holding the span of control constant, the taller the hierarchy; the more geographically dispersed the organizational units, the more complex the organization. And the more complex the organization, the greater the difficulties of communication, coordination, and control.

Formalization refers to the degree to which jobs within the organization are standardized. The higher the formalization, the more regulated the behavior of the employee. Formalization can be achieved on the job. In such cases, the organization would make use of rules and procedures to regulate what employees do. But a pseudoformalization process can occur off the job in the training the employees received prior to joining the organization. This characterizes professional employees. The professionalization they have undergone has socialized them to think and behave in accordance with the norms of their profession.

The most popular formalization techniques are the selection process (for identifying individuals who will fit into the organization); role requirements; rules, procedures, and policies; training; and having employees undergo rituals to prove their loyalty and commitment to the organization.

Centralization is the most problematic of the three components. It is defined as the degree to which the formal authority to make discretionary choices is concentrated in an individual, unit, or level (usually high in the organization), thus permitting employees (usually low in the organization) minimum input into their work.

The degree of control that an individual holds over the full decision-making process can be used as a measure of centralization. The five steps in this process are (1) collecting information to pass on to the decision maker about what can be done, (2) processing and interpreting that information to present advice to the decision maker about what should be done, (3) making the choice as to what is intended to be done, (4) authorizing elsewhere what is intended to be done, and (5) executing or doing it. Decision making is most centralized when the decision maker controls all these steps.

Decentralization reduces the probability of information overload, facilitates rapid response to new information, provides more detailed input into a decision, instills motivation, and represents a potential vehicle for training managers in developing good judgment. On the other hand, centralization adds a comprehensive perspective to decisions and can provide significant efficiencies.

FOR REVIEW AND DISCUSSION

1. What are the advantages and disadvantages to division of labor?
2. From a management perspective, is a tall or flat structure preferred? Explain.
3. Are the three complexity measures intercorrelated? Discuss.
4. How might a manager's job differ in an organization low in complexity compared with his or her counterpart managing a highly complex organization?
5. "Management would probably prefer high formalization." Do you agree or disagree? Discuss.
6. "Employees would probably prefer high formalization." Do you agree or disagree? Discuss.
7. Compare the formalization of unskilled workers with that of professionals.
8. What can management do to increase formalization?
9. "An organization that is high in complexity will be high in formalization." Do you agree or disagree? Discuss.
10. How might the systems framework better help you to understand the concept of formalization?
11. Reconcile the following two statements: (a) Where decisions are delegated downward but extensive policies exist to constrain the discretion of lower-level members, there is increased centralization. (b) An information-processing system that monitors decentralized decisions does not maintain centralized control.
12. What is authority? How is it related to centralization?
13. Describe the organizational decision-making process. Is it different from the individual decision-making process? Discuss.
14. Discuss the advantages and disadvantages to centralization.
15. You are evaluating an organization's structure. You find that production activities are highly formalized, whereas the level of formalization for research-design personnel is low. Similarly, you find legal decisions are highly centralized, but marketing decisions are decentralized. How do you arrive at *organizationwide* measures of organization structure if units within the organization are not homogeneous on each component?

NOTES

[1] Michael W. Miller and Paul B. Carroll, "IBM Unveils a Sweeping Restructuring in Bid to Decentralize Decision Making," *Wall Street Journal*, January 29, 1988, p. 3.

[2] For a critique of the methodology by which complexity, formalization, and centralization have come to dominate the definitions of major structural dimensions and for presentation of an alternative approach, see Richard Blackburn and Larry L. Cummings, "Cognitions of Work Unit Structure," *Academy of Management Journal*, December 1982, pp. 836–54.

[3] Bernard C. Reimann, "Dimensions of Structure in Effective Organizations: Some Empirical Evidence," *Academy of Management Journal*, December 1974, pp. 693–708.

[4] Ibid.

[5] Jerald Hage, "An Axiomatic Theory of Organizations," *Administrative Science Quarterly*, December 1965, pp. 289–320.

[6] James D. Thompson, *Organizations in Action* (New York: McGraw-Hill, 1967).

[7] Reimann, "Dimensions of Structure."

[8] Jerald Hage and Michael Aiken, "Relationship of Centralization to Other Structural Properties," *Administrative Science Quarterly*, June 1967, pp. 79–80.

[9] Reimann, "Dimensions of Structure."

[10] Max Weber, *The Theory of Social and Economic Organizations*, ed. Talcott Parsons, and trans. A. M. Henderson and Talcott Parsons (New York: Free Press, 1947).

[11] Paul R. Lawrence and Jay W. Lorsch, *Organization and Environment* (Boston: Division of Research, Graduate School of Business Administration, Harvard University, 1967).

[12] Reimann, "Dimensions of Structure."

[13] Lawrence and Lorsch, *Organization and Environment*.

[14] Charles Perrow, *Organizational Analysis: A Sociological View* (Belmont, Calif.: Wadsworth, 1970).

[15] Richard H. Hall, "Professionalization and Bureaucratization," *American Sociological Review*, February 1968, pp. 92–104.

[16] William G. Ouchi and John B. Dowling, "Defining the Span of Control," *Administrative Science Quarterly*, September 1974, pp. 357–65.

[17] Hage, "Axiomatic Theory of Organizations."

[18] Reimann, "Dimensions of Structure."

[19] Hage, "Axiomatic Theory of Organizations."

[20] Reimann, "Dimensions of Structure."

[21] See, for example, James L. Price and Charles W. Mueller, *Handbook of Organizational Measurement* (Marshfield, Mass.: Pitman Publishing, 1986), pp. 100–105.

[22] For a recent review of the division of labor literature, see Nancy M. Carter and Thomas L. Keon," The Rise and Fall of the Division of Labour, the Past 25 Years," *Organization Studies*, no. 1, 1986, pp. 57–74.

[23] Harold Koontz, "Making Theory Operational: The Span of Management," *Journal of Management Studies*, October 1966, p. 229.

[24] James C. Worthy, "Organization Structure and Employee Morale," *American Sociological Review*, April 1950, pp. 169–79.

[25] Lyman W. Porter and E. E. Lawler, III, "Properties of Organization Structure in Relation to Job Attitudes and Job Behavior," *Psychological Bulletin*, July 1965, pp. 23–51.

[26] John M. Ivancevich and James H. Donnelly, Jr., "Relation of Organization and Structure to Job Satisfaction, Anxiety-Stress, and Performance," *Administrative Science Quarterly*, June 1975, pp. 272–80.

[27] Tom Peters, *Thriving on Chaos* (New York: Knopf, 1988), pp. 354–65.

[28] Ibid., p. 356.

[29] Ibid., p. 359.

[30] Richard H. Hall, *Organizations: Structure and Process*, 3d ed. (Englewood Cliffs, N.J.: Prentice Hall, 1982), p. 84.

[31] Ibid.

[32] Ibid., p. 90.

[33] D. S. Pugh, D. J. Hickson, C. R. Hinings, and C. Turner, "Dimensions of Organization Structure," *Administrative Science Quarterly*, June 1968, p. 75.

[34] Hage and Aiken, "Relationship of Centralization to Other Structural Properties," p. 79.

[35] Johannes Pennings, "Measures of Organization Structure: A Methodological Note," *American Journal of Sociology*, November 1973, pp. 686–704; and Eric J. Walton, "The Comparison of Measures of Organization Structure," *Academy of Management Review*, January 1981, pp. 155–160.

[36] Henry Mintzberg, *The Structuring of Organizations* (Englewood Cliffs, N.J.: Prentice Hall, 1979), pp. 91–92.

[37] As reported in Richard L. Daft, *Organization Theory and Design*, 2d ed. (St. Paul, Minn.: West Publishing Co., 1986), p. 178.

[38] Charles Perrow, *Complex Organizations: A Critical Essay* (Glenview, Ill.: Scott, Foresman, 1972), p. 27.

[39] Charles Perrow, "Is Business Really Changing?," *Organizational Dynamics*, Summer 1973, p. 40.

[40] Perrow, *Complex Organizations*, p. 101.

[41] Benjamin Schneider, "The People Make the Place," *Personnel Psychology*, Autumn 1987, pp. 437–52.

[42] Perrow, *Complex Organizations*, p. 100.

[43] See, for example, Pugh et al. "Dimensions of Organization Structure," pp. 65–105; Christopher R. Hinings and Gloria L. Lee, "Dimensions of Organization Structure and Their Context: A Replication," *Sociology*, January 1971, pp. 83–93; John Child, "Organization Structure and Strategies of Control: A Replication of the Aston Study," *Administrative Science Quarterly*, March 1972, pp. 163–77; and Lex Donaldson and Malcolm Warner, "Structure of Organizations in Occupational Interest Associations," *Human Relations*, July 1974, pp. 721–38.

[44] See, for example, Jerald Hage, "Axiomatic Theory of Organizations," pp. 289–320.

[45] See, for example, Richard Leifer, "Matching Computer-Based Information Systems With Organizational Structures," *MIS Quarterly*, March 1988, pp. 63–72.

[46] T. T. Paterson, *Management Theory* (London: Business Publications, 1969), p. 150.

[47] Graham T. Allison, *Essence of Decision: Explaining the Cuban Missile Crisis* (Boston: Little, Brown, 1971), pp. 141–42.

[48] Henry Mintzberg, *The Structuring of Organizations*, p. 187.

[49] Herbert A. Simon, *Administrative Behavior*, 3d ed. (New York: Free Press, 1976), p. 294.

[50] See, for example, Hage and Aiken, "Relationship of Centralization to Other Structural Properties," pp. 72–91; and Child, "Organization Structure and Strategies of Control," pp. 163–177.

[51] Pugh et al. "Dimensions of Organization Structure," pp. 65–105.

[52] Child, "Organization Structure and Strategies of Control."

[53] Lex Donaldson, John Child, and Howard Aldrich, "The Aston Findings on Centralization: Further Discussion," *Administrative Science Quarterly*, September 1975, pp. 453–60.

[54] Peter H. Grinyer and Masoud Yasai-Ardekani, "Dimensions of Organizational Structure: A Critical Replication," *Academy of Management Journal*, September 1980, pp. 405–21.

[55] Hage and Aiken, "Relationship of Centralization to Other Structural Properties."

5

STRATEGY

AFTER READING THIS CHAPTER, YOU SHOULD BE ABLE TO:

1 Define strategy.
2 Compare business-level with corporate-level strategy.
3 Describe Chandler's "structure-follows-strategy" thesis.
4 List and define Miles and Snow's four strategic types.
5 Explain the structural implications from Porter's competitive strategies.
6 Describe Miller's integrative strategy-structure framework.
7 Explain the industry-structure relationship.

Introduction
STRATEGY AT HEWLETT-PACKARD

Hewlett-Packard is the world's largest manufacturer of test and measurement instruments as well as a major producer of electronic calculators and computers.[1] From its very beginning, H-P has pursued a strategy that brings the products of scientific research into industrial application while maintaining the collegial atmosphere of a university laboratory. The firm has concentrated on advanced technology and offers mostly state-of-the-art products to a variety of industrial and consumer markets. H-P's strategy is to pursue actively a given product line and market as long as the company has a distinctive technological or design advantage. But when products reach the stage where success depends primarily on low costs and highly competitive prices, H-P typically moves out of that market and turns its attention to a new design or an entirely new product.

Hewlett-Packard's strategy of technological innovation is supported by a highly flexible organization structure. It is organized around integrated, self-contained, product divisions that are given a great deal of independence. New divisions arise when a particular product line becomes large enough to support its continued growth out of the profit it generates. New divisions also tend to be created when single divisions get to about two thousand people. H-P has found that above this number, people start to lose identification with the product line.

A lot of factors go into the success of any company. In Hewlett-Packard's case, it has undoubtedly been very effective at identifying profitable markets, hiring competent scientists and engineers, and creating a corporate culture that fosters innovation and high performance. But a large part of H-P's success—as typified by annual sales in excess of $10 billion and profits of more than $830 million—has been the development of a flexible structure that facilitates the company's innovation strategy. That is, H-P has found the right fit between its corporate strategy and its organization structure.

If you had studied organization theory thirty years ago, the subject of this chapter (but certainly not its current content) would have been the only variable considered as *causing* structure. That is, in those days there was a single answer to the question, What determines structure? That answer was "the organization's goals and strategies."

A lot has happened in the last three decades. Researchers have identified a number of variables as determinants, some looking a great deal more promising than others. Strategy is now just one in that set of variables. In this chapter, we review the current state of the strategy **imperative** (an imperative *dictates* something; in our usage that "something" is structure). Chapters 6 through 9 consider four alternative variables.

The early acceptance of goals and strategy as determinants of an organization's structure was founded on assumptions inherent in classical economic theory. These included the following:

1. The organization has a goal or goals toward which it drives.
2. It moves toward its goals in a "rational" manner.
3. The organization exists to transform economic inputs to outputs.
4. The environment within which the organization operates is a given.[2]

If these assumptions are valid, an organization's structure can be interpreted as the outcome of a rational process. As Peter Drucker has noted, "Structure is a means for attaining the objectives and goals of an institution. Any work on structure must therefore start with objectives and strategy."[3]

Notice that this approach takes a closed-systems perspective. The environment is given. Another author expresses it this way: "Once the goals of the organization have been determined, or specified, then the development of structure, the flow of authority, and the other relationships clearly follow in a logical fashion."[4] Structure is seen as just a rational means by which inputs are translated to outputs.

WHAT IS STRATEGY?

The preceding paragraphs have used the terms *goals* and *strategy* as if they meant the same thing. However, they are interrelated but are not the same.

Goals refer to ends. Strategy refers to both means and ends. As such, goals are part of an organization's strategy. We discussed goals in Chapter 3, so let us clarify the concept of strategy:

Strategy can be defined as the determination of the basic long-term goals and objectives of an enterprise, and the adoption of courses of action and the allocation of resources necessary for carrying out these goals. Decisions to expand the volume of activities, to set up distant plants and offices, to move into new economic functions, or to become diversified along many lines of business involve the defining of new basic goals. New courses of action must be devised and resources allocated and reallocated in order to achieve these goals and to maintain and expand the firm's activities in the new areas in response to shifting demands, changing sources of supply, fluctuating economic conditions, new technological developments, and the actions of competitors.[5]

This definition does not tell us whether strategy has to be premeditated or whether it can just emerge. These, in fact, represent two views on strategy and deserve expanded attention.[6]

One view can be called a **planning mode.** This view describes strategy as a plan or explicit set of guidelines developed in advance. Managers identify where they want to go; then they develop a systematic and structured plan to get there. Until recently this viewpoint dominated the OT literature.

A more current perspective is what we can call an **evolutionary mode.** Strategy is not necessarily a well-thought-out and systematic plan. Rather, it evolves over time as a pattern in a stream of significant decisions. Many a business firm has found itself following the evolutionary mode. A manufacturer of women's clothing, for instance, bought a local hotel because it was priced right and generated a high rate of return. This purchase was followed by the acquisition of more hotels. Success in the hotel business led to the acquisition of a restaurant chain. Today the company is essentially in the hospitality and fast-food business, with less than 10 percent of its revenues coming from the manufacture of women's wear. While the company's executives never developed a formal strategy to pursue opportunities in hotels and fast food, it evolved as if it had been planned ahead of time.

Just as goals can be seen as something that are preestablished and guide subsequent behavior or as explanations developed after the behavior to justify or rationalize it, strategy can be viewed as premeditated or as something that can become clear only over time. The early writers looking at the strategy-structure relationship assumed the planning mode to be the proper way in which to view strategy. As we have noted, the broader evolutionary perspective has been gaining acceptance in recent years. Its major advantage lies in being able to cope with both static and dynamic strategies. If there is a strategy imperative, then strategy should predict structure. Also, as strategy changes—whether explicitly planned or implicitly evolving—structure should follow.

In summary, strategy considers both means and ends. The goals and decisions making up an organization's strategy may be planned ahead of time or may just evolve as a pattern in a stream of significant decisions. Either way, those advocates of the "strategy determines structure" position perceive decision makers as *choosing* the structure they have. It may be true, as we shall see in later chapters, that the organization's transformation processes, environment, and other factors are major determinants of structure, but these are one step removed from the actual change process. This process is shown in Figure 5–1. As we will demonstrate in Chapter 9, even if an organization's transformation processes and environment determine structure, they are not givens. They are chosen by the organization's dominant decision makers.

FIGURE 5–1 *The Strategy Imperative*

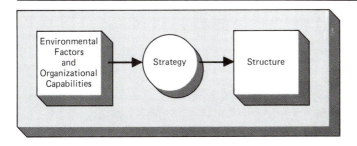

TYPES OF STRATEGY

If all organizations produced a single product or service, the management of any organization could develop a single strategy that encompassed everything it did. But many organizations are in diverse lines of businesses, many of which are only vaguely related. A firm like General Electric, for instance, makes multimillion dollar power systems for hydroelectric dams as well as consumer products like microwave ovens and light bulbs. Organizations that are in multiple businesses, therefore, need to develop different strategies for different levels of activities. Thus it is necessary to differentiate between corporate-level and business-level strategies. (See Figure 5–2.)

If an organization is in more than one line of business, it will need a **corporate-level strategy.** This strategy seeks to answer the question, In what set of businesses should we be? Corporate-level strategy determines the roles that each business in the organization will play. At a company like Paramount Communications Corp. (formerly Gulf & Western), top management's corporate-level strategy integrates the business-level strategies for its entertainment, publishing, and other divisions.

Business-level strategy seeks to answer the question, How should we compete in each of our businesses? For the small organization in only one line of business or the large organization that has avoided diversification, business-level strategy is typically the same as corporate strategy. But for organizations in

FIGURE 5–2 *Levels of Strategy*

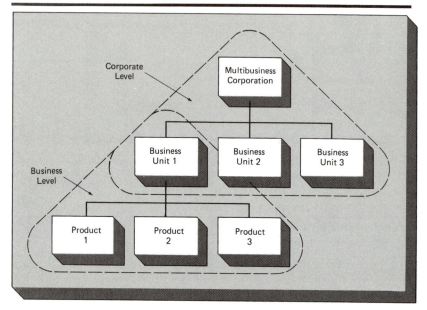

multiple businesses, each division will have its own strategy that defines the products or services that it will offer, the customers it wants to reach, and the like. So Paramount Communications' publishing division would have its own unique business strategy that encompasses its trade, educational, and other publication products.

Most contemporary strategy-structure theories we discuss focus on business-level strategies. But the original research on this topic began by looking at the corporate-level strategies of such companies as DuPont and Sears, Roebuck. To the degree that strategy actually determines structure, strategy level is an important point to keep in mind. Why? For small organizations in only one line of business or nondiversified large organizations, business and corporate strategy will be the same, and the organization should have a relatively uniform organization structure. But organizations with diverse business strategies should be expected to have a variety of structural configurations; that is, management will design structures to fit with the different strategies.

CLASSIFYING STRATEGIC DIMENSIONS

For the most part, research on the strategy-structure relationship has focused on a rather narrow aspect of strategy—the degree of product diversification. But as noted in our definition at the beginning of this chapter, strategy encompasses a lot more than whether an organization chooses to diversify and, if so, the number and types of diversified products or services the organization decides to offer. For instance, the decision by owners of a private family business to take their organization public by selling stock to the public and then listing it on a major stock exchange is clearly a significant change in strategy.[7] Top management will now have to disclose more information to external constituencies (i.e., stock-exchange officials, brokerage firms, stockholders) and more decisions will require board member approval. Research indicates that the strategic action of becoming a public organization tends to lead to more centralized decision making and an increase in formalization.[8]

In recent years, researchers have developed a richer and more complete analysis of the content of corporate strategies.[9] While the following four dimensions are not assumed to depict comprehensively all the complex aspects of strategy, they do encompass the dimensions of strategic content that have received the most attention. At this point, we present them to demonstrate the diversity in strategic dimensions. However, later in this chapter we come back to these four dimensions and consider each's implications on organization structure.

Innovation. To what degree does an organization introduce major new products or services? An **innovation strategy** does not mean a strategy merely for simple or cosmetic changes from previous offerings but rather one for meaningful and unique innovations. Obviously, not all firms pursue innovation. This strategy may appropriately characterize 3M Co. or Apple Computer, but it certainly is not a strategy pursued by Reader's Digest.

Marketing Differentiation. The **marketing differentiation strategy** strives to create customer loyalty by uniquely meeting a particular need. It doesn't necessarily mean the organization is producing a higher-quality or more up-to-date product. The organization seeks to create a favorable image for its product through advertising, market segmentation, and prestige pricing. This would describe the strategy used by premium beer producers and designer-label apparel manufacturers.

Breadth. The **breadth strategy** refers to the scope of the market to which the business caters: the variety of customers, their geographic range, and the number of products. Some grocery chains, for instance, have chosen to operate only in a given community. Others, however, extend their operations to the regional, national, or even international level.

Cost Control. Finally, the **cost-control strategy** considers the extent to which the organization tightly controls costs, refrains from incurring unnecessary innovation or marketing expenses, and cuts prices in selling a basic product. This would describe the strategy pursued by Wal-Mart or generic grocery products.

CHANDLER'S STRATEGY-STRUCTURE THESIS

The classic work on the relationship between an organization strategy and its structure was done by Harvard historian Alfred Chandler and published in the early 1960s.[10] All the current work on the strategy-structure relationship has been clearly influenced by Chandler's research.

Chandler studied close to a hundred of America's largest firms. Tracing the development of these organizations from 1909 to 1959, which included extensive case histories of such companies as Du Pont, General Motors, Standard Oil of New Jersey, and Sears, Chandler concluded that changes in corporate strategy preceded and led to changes in an organization's structure. As Chandler put it, "A new strategy required a new or at least refashioned structure if the enlarged enterprise was to be operated efficiently . . . unless structure follows strategy, inefficiency results."[11]

Chandler found that the companies he studied began as centralized structures. This reflected the fact that they offered limited product lines. As demand for their products grew, the companies expanded. They increased their product lines and had to develop different structures to cope with their changing strategies. For instance, they integrated vertically by purchasing many of their own sources of supply. This reduced their dependency on suppliers. To produce a greater variety of products more efficiently, they created separate product groups within the organization. The result was structures that were fundamentally different. Growth and diversification gave rise to the need for an autonomous multidivisional structure. The highly centralized structure became inefficient and impractical for dealing with the significantly greater complexity. As Chandler summarized the situation, "Unless new structures are developed to meet new administrative needs which result from an expansion of a firm's activities into new areas, functions, or product lines, the technological, financial, and personnel economies of growth and size cannot be realized."[12]

Chandler essentially argued that organizations typically begin with a single product or line. They do only one thing—such as manufacturing, sales or warehousing. The simplicity of this strategy is compatible with a loose or simple structure. Decisions can be centralized in the hands of a single senior manager. Because the organization's strategy is narrowly focused, the structure to execute it can be low in both complexity and formalization. So, Chandler concluded, the efficient structure for an organization with a single product strategy is one that is simple—high centralization, low formalization, and low complexity.

As organizations seek to grow, their strategies become more ambitious and elaborate. From the single-product line, companies typically expand activities within their same industry. This vertical integration strategy makes for increased interdependence among organizational units and creates the need for a more complex coordinative device. This desired complexity is achieved by redesigning the structure to form specialized units based on functions performed.

Finally, if growth proceeds further, into product diversification, again structure must be adjusted if efficiency is to be achieved. A product-diversification strategy demands a structural form that allows for the efficient allocation of resources, accountability for performance, and coordination between units. This can best be achieved through the creation of a multiple set of independent

FIGURE 5–3 *Chandler's Thesis*

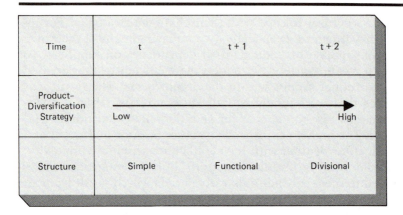

divisions, each responsible for a specified product line. This evolution is depicted in Figure 5–3.

Following Chandler's theory, successful organizations that diversify should have a different structure from that of successful firms that follow a single-product strategy. General Motors, for instance, adopted a product-diversification strategy and followed with a multidivisional form. In contrast, Alcoa maintained a vertical integration strategy and has matched it with a functional structure. Both GM and Alcoa have been successful with different structures, but, Chandler would argue, that is because they are following different strategies.

The Research

Is Chandler right? Does structure follow strategy? Limitations inherent in Chandler's research plus additional studies that have tried to duplicate and extend his work suggest that the theory has some validity but some distinct restrictions as well.

First, let's look at Chandler's sample of organizations. His companies were not a cross section of organizations in general. He looked only at very large and powerful industrial business firms. Whether his findings would be applicable to small- and medium-sized organizations, service companies, or those in the public sector could not be answered from this sample.

Next, a careful review of Chandler's work reveals that when he used the term strategy, he really meant *growth* strategy. Growth was his major concern, not profitability. In organizational-effectiveness terms, a proper strategy-structure fit à la Chandler is more likely to lead to growth than increased profitability.[13]

These caveats should not be taken as permanently damning. Within the parameters set by Chandler, several studies have confirmed his conclusions, specifically relating to a strong relationship between product diversification and the multidivisional form.[14] One researcher essentially supported Chandler's findings, although he used a different classification scheme for defining strategy.[15] Organizational strategies were labeled as single business (no diversification), dominant business (70 to 95 percent of sales coming from one business or a vertically integrated chain), related business (diversified in related areas, with no one business accounting for more than 70 percent of sales), and unrelated business (diversified in unrelated areas, with no one business accounting for more than 70 percent of sales). The researcher found that the related and unrelated business strategies were associated with multidivisional structures, while single-business strategies were linked with functional structures. No single structure was found consistently in the dominant-business category.

Conclusions

Chandler's claim that strategy influences structure seems well supported, but this generalization is constrained by the limitations and definitions inherent in Chandler's work. He looked only at large, profit-making organizations. He focused on growth as a measure of effectiveness rather than profitability. Additionally, his definition of strategy is far from all-inclusive. Strategy can, for instance, also include concern with market segmentation, financial strengths and leverage opportunities, actions of competitors, assessment of the organization's comparative advantage vis-à-vis its competition, and the like. Nevertheless, "there appears to be little question that strategy influences structure at the top levels of business firms. The evidence on this point is overwhelming."[16]

CONTEMPORARY STRATEGY-STRUCTURE THEORY

As we noted previously, strategy is a broad concept and can be dissected along a number of dimensions. Since Chandler's work in the early 1960s, the most important research on the strategy-structure relationship has been undertaken by Miles and Snow. Additionally, the landmark work of Michael Porter on competitive strategies has direct relevance to the strategy-structure relationship. Finally, Danny Miller has developed an integrative framework that can help us to synthesize strategy terminology and assess its impact on structural design. In this section, we review each of these three contributions.

Miles and Snow's Four Strategic Types

Raymond Miles and Charles Snow classify organizations—based on the rate at which they change their products or markets—into one of four strategic types: defenders, prospectors, analyzers, and reactors.[17] While their discussion centers on business firms, the categories they use probably have their counterpart in nonprofit organizations as well.

Defenders seek stability by producing only a limited set of products directed at a narrow segment of the total potential market. Within this limited niche, or domain, defenders strive aggressively to prevent competitors from entering their "turf." Organizations do this through standard economic actions such as competitive pricing or production of high-quality products. But defenders tend to ignore developments and trends outside their domains, choosing instead to grow through market penetration and perhaps some limited product development. There is little or no scanning of the environment to find new areas of opportunity, but there is intensive planning oriented toward cost and other efficiency issues. The result is a structure made up of high horizontal differentiation, centralized control, and an elaborate formal hierarchy for communications. Over time, true defenders are able to carve out and maintain small niches within their industries that are difficult for competitors to penetrate. An example of a defender strategy is the manufacturer of Soft-Soap. The company has chosen a narrow domain—the liquid hand-and-body soap market—and hopes to fend off competitors such as Procter & Gamble by promoting aggressively and developing a narrow range of similar products.

Prospectors are almost the opposite of defenders. Their strength is finding and exploiting new-product and market opportunities. Innovation may be more important than high profitability. This describes, for instance, several magazine publishers who introduce new magazine titles almost monthly, constantly attempting to identify new market segments. It would also be the appropriate label for an organization like 3M.[18] That company has built its reputation and long-term profitability on developing innovative products, getting quickly to the market with those products, exploiting opportunities while they are still innovative, and then getting out.

The prospector's success depends on developing and maintaining the capacity to survey a wide range of environmental conditions, trends, and events. Therefore, prospectors invest heavily in personnel who scan the environment for potential opportunities. Since flexibility is critical to prospectors, the structure will also be flexible. It will rely on multiple technologies that have a low degree of routinization and mechanization. There will be numerous decentralized units. The structure will be low in formalization, have decentralized control, with lateral as well as vertical communications. "In short, the prospector is effective—it can respond to the demands of tomorrow's world. To the extent that the world of tomorrow is similar to that of today, the prospector cannot maximize profitability because of its inherent inefficiency."[19]

Analyzers try to capitalize on the best of both the preceding types. They seek to minimize risk and maximize opportunity for profit. Their strategy is to move into new products or new markets only after viability has been proved by prospectors. Analyzers live by imitation. They take the successful ideas of prospectors and copy them. Manufacturers of mass-marketed fashion goods that are rip-offs of designer styles follow the analyzer strategy. This label also probably characterizes such well-known firms as Digital Equipment Corporation, IBM, and Caterpillar.[20] They essentially follow their smaller and more innovative competitors with superior products, but only after their competitors have demonstrated that the market is there.

Analyzers must have the ability to respond to the lead of key prospectors, yet at the same time maintain operating efficiency in their stable product and market areas. Analyzers will tend to have smaller profit margins in the products and services that they sell than will prospectors, but they are more efficient. Prospectors have to have high margins to justify the risks that they take and their productive inefficiencies.

Analyzers seek both flexibility and stability. They respond to these goals by developing a structure made up of dual components. Parts of these organizations have high levels of standardization, routinization, and mechanization for efficiency. Other parts are adaptive, to enhance flexibility. In this way, they seek structures that can accommodate both stable and dynamic areas of operation. But in this compromise there can be costs. If situations change rapidly, demanding that organizations move fully in either direction, their ability to take such action is severely limited.

Reactors represent a residual strategy. The label is meant to describe the inconsistent and unstable patterns that arise when one of the other three strategies is pursued improperly. In general, reactors respond inappropriately, perform poorly, and as a result are reluctant to commit themselves aggressively to a specific strategy for the future. What can cause this? Top management may have failed to make the organization's strategy clear. Management may not have fully shaped the organization's structure to fit the chosen strategy. Management may have maintained its current strategy-structure relationship despite overwhelming changes in environmental conditions. Whatever the reason, however, the outcome is the same. The organization lacks a set of response mechanisms with which to face a changing environment.

Table 5–1 summarizes the Miles and Snow strategic typologies. It shows the goal(s) of each, the type of environment that each faces, and the structural mechanisms that management would choose to achieve their goal(s). The reactor strategy is omitted for the obvious reason that it results in ineffective performance.

The key element in Miles and Snow's strategy-structure theory is management's assessment of environmental uncertainty. If management selects a defender strategy, for instance, it suggests that it perceives the environment as stable. Of course, perceptions of environmental uncertainty are not objective interpretations. Managers in two organizations can face exactly the same environment and perceive it very differently. This is precisely what happened in the tire industry in the early 1980s.[21] Goodyear assessed its environment and saw increased demand for replacement tires. In

TABLE 5–1   *Miles and Snow's Strategic Typologies*

STRATEGY	GOAL(S)	ENVIRONMENT	STRUCTURAL CHARACTERISTICS
Defender	Stability and efficiency	Stable	Tight control; extensive division of labor; high degree of formalization; centralized.
Analyzer	Stability and flexibility	Changing	Moderately centralized control; tight control over current activities; looser controls for new undertakings.
Prospector	Flexibility	Dynamic	Loose structure; low division of labor; low degree of formalization; decentralized.

Adapted from Raymond E. Miles, Charles C. Snow, Alan D. Meyer, and Henry J. Coleman, Jr., "Organizational Strategy, Structure, and Process," *Academy of Management Review,* July 1978, pp. 552–56.

spite of high prices for gasoline, Goodyear's management predicted that more fuel-efficient cars would stimulate more driving. Also, the rise of two-income families would require more driving. Goodyear, therefore, took a prospector strategy and invested several hundred million dollars in new tire plants. In contrast, Firestone saw the same environment but interpreted it quite differently. It forecasted significantly less driving, and hence demand for replacement tires, owing to the increased cost of driving each mile, the replacement of the automobile by airlines for intercity travel, and a significantly expanded use of car pools and public transportation for day-to-day travel. Based on its interpretation, Firestone's strategy was that of defender. It shelved plans to build new factories and actually closed down a number of its plants. The result was that Firestone reduced its U.S. tire capacity by one-third.

Figure 5–4 describes Miles and Snow's four strategies as falling along a continuum that ranges from low to high in terms of environmental change and uncertainty. Following the logic of this theory, the more uncertainty and change that management fore-

FIGURE 5–4 *Environment-Strategy Continuum*

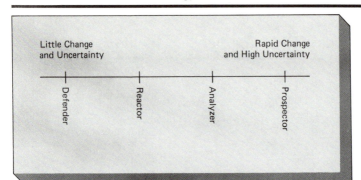

OT
CLOSE-UP

APPLYING THE MILES AND SNOW FRAMEWORK TO THE TOBACCO INDUSTRY

The tobacco industry provides some excellent examples of Miles and Snow's strategies in practice.[22] Beginning in the early 1950s with a report that linked cigarette smoking to heart and lung diseases, tobacco firms have faced consistent levels of high environmental uncertainty. They have been the target of health and consumer-action groups. A series of government regulations have restricted their ability to do business. Their access to the public broadcast media has been significantly limited. The current warnings printed on every pack of cigarettes is obviously not placed there voluntarily by the tobacco companies. The interesting thing is that the major tobacco firms chose very different strategies in response to their environment.

Philip Morris chose the prospector route. For example, it was the first to design products specifically to bring women into the smoking market and has been a pioneer in product packaging.

R.J. Reynolds (now part of RJR Nabisco) was the analyzer. Its strategy has been to become an early adopter of the successful incasts, the more it would move to the right along the continuum in Figure 5–4. Similarly, as strategies move to the right along the continuum, the organization's structure should be modified or redesigned to be increasingly flexible and adaptive.

Management perceives little or no change and uncertainty in the environment under the defender strategy. The successful structure, under such conditions, should be designed for optimum efficiency. This efficiency can best be achieved through high division of labor, standardization of operations, high formalization, and centralized decision making.

Organizations following a reactor strategy respond to change reluctantly. Management perceives some change and uncertainty, but they are not likely to make any substantial adjustments until

novations of others. As an analyzer, it operated—and it still does—in two product-market spheres simultaneously—one relatively stable and the other changing. In its stable sphere (established brand names), Reynolds has routine operations. In its more turbulent sphere, top managers watch competitors for new ideas and then rapidly adopt those that look most promising.

American Brands was the defender. In an environment of rapid change, American focused on a narrow product-market segment and lost market share badly.

Liggett & Myers represented the reactor strategy. Top management consistently perceived change and uncertainty in its product markets but was unable to respond effectively. In contrast to its competitors, Liggett demonstrated substantially less internal consistency. It has generally been too late with too little.

Given the common dynamic environment the tobacco firms faced, Miles and Snow's theory would suggest the greatest success would be achieved by analyzers and prospectors, with defenders and reactors bringing up the rear. And that's precisely what has happened. Between 1950 and 1975, Reynolds (the analyzer), Philip Morris (the prospector), American (the defender), and Liggett (the reactor) generated respective compounded growth rates in earnings per share of 9.16, 8.35, 5.61, and .75 percent. More recently, between 1986 and 1988, Reynolds and Philip Morris changed places, but American and Liggett were still significantly behind the two leaders.

forced to by environmental pressures. So this structure is likely to look very much like the one described for defenders.

Managers pursuing an analyzer strategy perceive a considerable degree of change and uncertainty but wait until competitors develop a viable response, and then they quickly adopt it. As for structure, analyzers try to combine the best of both worlds by tightly structuring their current and more stable activities while developing flexible structures for new activities that face greater uncertainties.

Finally, prospector strategies require the greatest degree of structural flexibility. There is a lot of change and uncertainty, so structures should be highly adaptive. This would translate into low complexity, low formalization, and decentralized decision making.

Porter's Competitive Strategies

Michael Porter of the Harvard Graduate School of Business argues that no firm can successfully perform at an above-average level by trying to be all things to all people. He proposes that management must select a strategy that will give its organization a competitive advantage. Management can choose from among three strategies: cost leadership, differentiation, and focus.[23] Which one management chooses depends on the organization's strengths and competitor's weaknesses. Management should avoid a position in which it has to slug it out with everybody in the industry. Rather, the organization should put its strength where the competition isn't.

When an organization sets out to be the low-cost producer in its industry, it is following a **cost-leadership strategy.** Success with this strategy requires that the organization be *the* cost leader and not merely one of the contenders for that position. Additionally, the product or service being offered must be perceived as comparable to that offered by rivals, or at least acceptable to buyers.

How does a firm gain such a cost advantage? Typical means include efficiency of operations, economies of scale, technological innovation, low-cost labor, or preferential access to raw materials. Examples of firms that have used this strategy include MCI, Gallo wines, and Hyundai automobiles.

The firm that seeks to be unique in its industry in ways that are widely valued by buyers is following a **differentiation strategy.** It might emphasize high-quality, extraordinary service, innovative design, technological capability, or an unusual, positive brand image. The key is that the attribute chosen must be different from those offered by rivals and significant enough to justify a price premium that exceeds the cost of differentiation.

There is no shortage of firms that have found at least one attribute that allows them to differentiate themselves from competitors: Cray Research (supercomputer technology), Toyota (reliability), IBM (superiorly trained personnel), Häagen Dazs (quality ingredients in ice cream), or Ferrari (performance).

The first two strategies sought a competitive advantage in a broad range of industry segments. The **focus strategy** aims at a cost advantage (cost focus) or differentiation advantage (differentiation focus) in a narrow segment. That is, management will select a segment or group of segments in an industry (such as product variety, type of end buyer, distribution channel, or geographic location of buyers) and tailor the strategy to serve them to the exclusion of others. The goal is to exploit a narrow segment of a market. Of course, whether a focus strategy is feasible or not depends on the size of a segment and whether it can support the additional cost of focusing. Stouffer's used a cost-focus strategy in its Lean Cuisine line to reach calorie-conscious consumers seeking both high-quality products and convenience. Similarly, colleges that appeal to working students by offering only night classes hope to gain a competitive advantage over their rivals by following a differentiation-focus strategy.

Porter uses the term **stuck in the middle** to describe organizations that are unable to gain a competitive advantage by one of the previous strategies. Such organizations will find it very difficult to achieve long-term success. When they do, according to Porter, it is usually a result of competing in a highly favorable industry or having all their rivals similarly stuck in the middle.

Porter notes that successful organizations frequently get themselves into trouble by reaching beyond their competitive advantage and ending up stuck in the middle. Laker Airways provides such a case. It began, in 1977, by offering no-frills flights between London and New York at rock-bottom prices. This cost-leadership strategy resulted in a resounding success. In 1979, however, the firm began to add new routes and offer upscale services. This blurred the public's image of Laker, allowed the competition to make significant inroads, and led to Laker's declaration of bankruptcy in 1982.

What's the structural implications from these four strategies? First, no predictions are made for the stuck-in-the-middle strategy. Like the reactor strategy described by Miles and Snow, it is not recommended as a desirable route to success. Second, predictions have generally excluded the focus strategy for the simple reason that it is merely a derivative of one of the other two. So let's look at the two that are left: cost leadership and differentiation.

The goal of cost leadership is to achieve efficiencies through tight controls, minimization of overhead, and economies of scale. The best structure for achieving this end would be one that is high in complexity, high in formalization, and centralized. In contrast, a differentiation strategy relies essentially on the development of unique products. This demands a high degree of flexibility, which can best be achieved through low complexity, low formalization, and decentralized decision making.[24]

Miller's Integrative Framework

Danny Miller of École des Hautes Études Commerciales (at the University of Montreal) and McGill University developed the four strategy dimensions of innovation, marketing differentiation, breadth, and cost-control introduced earlier in this chapter. These four categories do an excellent job of tapping the concepts that Chandler, Miles and Snow, and Porter addressed. For example, breadth encompasses Chandler's concept of product diversification; market differentiation is consistent with Miles and Snow's prospector strategy; and cost-control aligns with Porter's cost leadership.

Table 5–2 summarizes Miller's framework and predicted structural characteristics. Note that this categorization scheme dissects Porter's differentiation into two dimensions: *marketing* differentiation; and innovation, which deals with *product* differentiation. Notice, too, that Miller assumes that breadth can be achieved two ways—moving into a market segment by doing more *innovation* or moving into more *stable* and placid settings.

Miller's research, for the most part, confirms the predicted structural characteristics in Table 5–2.[25] The exception are those predictions made for the breadth-stability dimension. Miller has

TABLE 5–2 *Miller's Integrative Framework*

STRATEGIC DIMENSION	CHALLENGE	PREDICTED STRUCTURAL CHARACTERISTICS
Innovation	To understand and manage more products, customer types, technologies, and markets	Scanning of markets to discern customer requirements; low formalization; decentralization; extensive use of coordinative committees and task forces
Market differentiation	To understand and cater to consumer preferences	Moderate to high complexity; extensive scanning and analysis of customers' reactions and competitor strategies; moderate to high formalization; moderate decentralization
Breadth Breadth-innovation	To select the right range of products, services, customers, and territory	High complexity; low formalization; decentralization
Breadth-stability		High complexity; high formalization; high centralization
Cost control	To produce standardized products efficiently	High formalization; high centralization

Based on Danny Miller, "The Structural and Environmental Correlates of Business Strategy," *Strategic Management Journal*, January–February 1987, pp. 55–76.

no compelling explanation for this finding. However, in spite of this one inconsistency, Table 5–2 offers a generally valid guide for summarizing the strategy-structure relationship. Moreover, it is interesting how closely Miller's results align with Miles and Snow's recommendations. Innovation and breadth-innovation generally require the same flexible structures as described by Miles and Snow for their prospectors. Cost control requires stability and structural characteristics consistent with Miles and Snow's defenders. Finally, marketing differentiation blends the need for flexible marketing and stable production, which suggests structural characteristics that Miles and Snow attributed to their analyzers.

LIMITATIONS TO
THE STRATEGY IMPERATIVE

We have presented the positive case for strategy determining structure. Not surprisingly, as with many issues in organization theory, there is another side in the debate.

No one argues that strategy *cannot* determine structure. That possibility does exist. Attacks on the strategy imperative lie basically in questioning the degree of discretionary latitude that managers actually have. For instance, it seems logical that the impact of strategy would be greater in the early development period of an organization. Once personnel are hired, equipment purchased, and procedures and policies established, they are a whole lot tougher to change. When the organization is in its infancy, vested interests have yet to be solidified. But once the die is cast, managers may be severely restricted in their discretion. Similarly, it is logical that the capital-to-labor ratio in an organization will affect the impact of strategy on structure. If the ratio is low (i.e., labor intensive), then managers have much more flexibility, and hence discretion, to exercise change and influence structure.

Another challenge to the strategy imperative deals with the lag factor. When management implements a new strategy, there is often no immediate change in structure. Does this suggest that structure does not follow strategy? Advocates of a strong strategy-structure relationship say "no." They point out that there is often a lag—structures respond to changes in strategy, but slowly. At the extreme, this lag argument can be considered a "cop-out."[26] If researchers fail to find a strategy-structure relationship in the study of an organization, they can always claim that there is a lag, and structure just hasn't caught up yet. More realistically, however, we find that this lag is not purely a random phenomenon. Some organizations are slower to adapt their structures to changes in strategy than are others. The major factor affecting response is the degree of competitive pressure. The less competition an organization faces, the less rapid its structural response.[27] Without competition, the concern for efficiency is reduced. So we would conclude that where an organization faces minimal competition, there is likely to be a significant lag between changes in strategy and modifications in structure.

TABLE 5–3   *Propositions Regarding the Effects of Structure
on the Strategic Decision Process*

COMPLEXITY

As the level of *complexity* increases, so does the probability that
1. Members initially exposed to the decision stimulus will not recognize it as being strategic or will ignore it because of parochial preferences;
2. A decision must satisfy a large constraint set, which decreases the likelihood that decisions will be made to achieve organization-level goals;
3. Strategic action will be the result of an internal process of political bargaining, and moves will be incremental; and
4. Biases induced by members' parochial perceptions will be the primary constraint on the comprehensiveness of the strategic decision process. In general, the integration of decisions will be low.

FORMALIZATION

As the level of *formalization* increases, so does the probability that
1. The strategic decision process will be initiated only in response to problems or crises that appear in variables monitored by the formal system;
2. Decisions will be made to achieve precise, yet remedial, goals, and means will displace ends;
3. Strategic action will be the result of standardized organizational processes, and moves will be incremental; and
4. The level of detail achieved in the standardized organizational processes will be the primary constraint on the comprehensiveness of the strategic decision process. The integration of decisions will be intermediate.

CENTRALIZATION

As the level of *centralization* increases, so does the probability that
1. The strategic decision process will be initiated only by the dominant few, and it will be the result of proactive, opportunity-seeking behavior;
2. The decision process will be oriented toward achieving "positive" goals (i.e., intended future domains) that will persist in spite of significant changes in means;
3. Strategic action will be the result of intendedly rational choices, and moves will be major departures from the existing strategy; and
4. Top management's cognitive limitations will be the primary constraint on the comprehensiveness of the strategic process. The integration of decisions will be relatively high.

Source: Adapted from James W. Fredrickson, "The Strategic Decision Process and Organzational Structure," *Academy of Management Review,* April 1986, p. 284.

COULD STRATEGY FOLLOW STRUCTURE?

Is it possible that strategy and structure are positively related but that the causal arrow is opposite from what we've assumed? Maybe structure determines strategy! One author acknowledges at least the logical possibility, "as when a multidivisional structure is installed because everyone else is doing it and then an acquisition strategy is developed to make the structure viable."[28]

A little thought would certainly suggest that structure can influence strategy. Structure can motivate or impede strategic activity as well as simply constrain strategic choices. For instance, strategic decisions made in a centralized structure are typically going to have less diversity of ideas and are more likely to be consistent over time than in a decentralized organization, where input is likely to be diverse and the people providing that input change, depending on the situation. Table 5–3 offers a set of propositions regarding the effect that our three structural dimensions of complexity, formalization, and centralization might have on the strategic decision process.

Should the propositions in Table 5–3 be accepted as valid? That's difficult to answer. However, the notion that structure determines strategy has some preliminary support. A study of 110 large manufacturing firms found that strategy followed structure.[29] Another study of 54 firms listed among the top half of *Fortune's* 500 found that structure influences and constrains strategy rather than the other way around.[30] If further research were to support these conclusions, we could state that as a structural determinant, strategy is of limited importance.

THE INDUSTRY-STRUCTURE RELATIONSHIP

Closely related to the issue of strategy's impact on structure is the role of industry as a determinant of structure. There are distinguishing characteristics of industries that affect the strategies they will choose.[31] Therefore, as shown in Figure 5–5, strategy may merely be an intermediate step between the unique characteristics of the industry in which the organization operates and the structure it implements to achieve alignment.

FIGURE 5–5 *Industry-Structure Relationship*

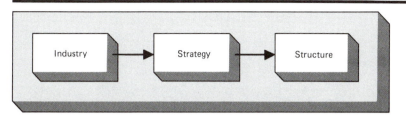

Industries differ in terms of growth possibilities, regulatory constraints, barriers to entry and mobility, and numerous other factors. "Simply knowing the industry in which an organization operates allows one to know something about product life cycles, required capital investments, long-term prospects, types of production technologies, regulatory requirements, and so forth."[32] Public utilities, for example, face little competition and can have more tightly controlled structures. Similarly, if a firm is in the automobile industry and seeks to competitively produce cars to sell in the $10,000 to $15,000 range, it will need to be extremely large in size and utilize standardized operations. In some industries, strategic options are relatively few. The major-home-appliance industry, as a case in point, is rapidly becoming the exclusive province of companies that compete only on a high-volume, low-cost basis. On the other hand, the tobacco industry supports a much broader range of strategic options—competing on manufacturing, marketing, or product-innovation bases.

To illustrate how industry can effect structure, let's take two variables that tend to differ by industry category—capital requirements for entry and product-innovation rates. Figure 5–6 shows four industry categories with examples for each. Type A industries rate high on both variables, while type C industries are high on capital requirements and low on product innovation. The high capital requirements tend to result in large organizations and a limited number of competitors. Firms in type A and C industries will be highly structured and standardized, with the type Cs being more decentralized to facilitate rapid response to innovations introduced by competitors. Type B and D industries, because of low capital requirements, tend to be made up of a large number of small firms. Type D, however, will likely have more division of

FIGURE 5–6 *Two Variable Analyses of Industries*

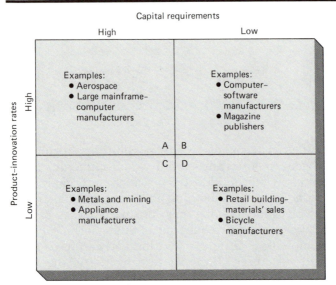

labor and more formalization than type Bs because low product innovation allows for greater standardization. In the same way that capital requirements influence organizational size and number of competitors, we should expect high product-innovation rates to result in less formalization and more decentralization of decision making.

The preceding analysis argues that industry categories *do* influence structure. Although there are certainly intraindustry differences—Revlon and Mary Kay are both in personal-care products but use very different marketing channels—there is a high degree of similarities within industry categories. These similarities lead to strategies that tend to have largely common elements—which results in structural characteristics that are very similar.

SUMMARY

The early position on "what determines structure" was the organization's goals and strategies. Structure was seen as just a rational means to facilitate the attainment of goals. More recently, strategy has been offered as but one of a number of variables vying for the crown of "major determinant of structure."

Strategy was defined as including both the long-term goals of an organization plus a course of action that will provide the means toward their attainment. To some it is seen as planned in advance; others view it as evolving over time as a pattern in a stream of significant decisions.

Chandler studied nearly one hundred of America's largest business firms and concluded that "structure follows strategy." While there is considerable support for this thesis, the limitations in his research restrict any wide generalization of his findings.

Miles and Snow offered a four-category strategy-structure typology that allowed for specific structural predictions. Analysis of major firms in the tobacco industry confirmed this typology's predictive capability.

Porter proposed that organizations can pursue one of four strategies: cost leadership, differentiation, focus, and stuck-in-the-middle. Specific structural predictions could be made for the first two strategies.

Miller introduced a strategy framework composed of four dimensions—innovation, marketing differentiation, breadth, and cost control—that integrates the work of Chandler, Miles and Snow, and Porter.

Attacks on the strategy imperative have generally focused on three points: (1) managerial discretion over changes in strategy may be considerably less than suggested; (2) where competition is low, the lag may make the interaction between strategy and structure appear almost unrelated; and (3) structure may determine strategy rather than vice versa.

The industry in which organizations operate was introduced as an important factor influencing strategy and, hence, structure. Industries differ in terms of growth possibilities, regulatory constraints, barriers to entry, and so forth. Most firms within a given industry share these characteristics. The result is that firms within industry categories tend to have similar organization structures.

FOR REVIEW AND DISCUSSION

1. What is an "imperative"?
2. "The strategy imperative is based on classical economic assumptions." Build an argument to support this statement.
3. Contrast planning and evolutionary modes. Which dominates the management-theory literature?
4. What is Chandler's thesis? What evidence does he present to support this thesis?
5. What criticisms can you direct at Chandler's research?
6. Does Chandler's thesis have any application to small-business management?
7. If structures are relatively stable over time, does this imply that strategies don't change?

8. Using Miles and Snow's typology, describe the structure that would align with each strategy type.

9. Using Miller's integrative framework, attempt as best you can to reconcile Chandler, Miles and Snow, and Porter's strategy-structure theories.

10. Under what conditions might you expect strategy to exert a significant influence on structure?

11. "Strategy follows structure rather than vice versa." Build an argument to support this statement. Then build an argument to refute this statement.

12. Relate the structure-follows-strategy thesis to the systems framework.

13. Do you think there is any relationship between an organization's life-cycle stage and organizational strategies? Explain.

14. How are strategy and industry categories related?

15. Using Figure 5–6 as a guide, select examples of firms that you believe fit into each of the four boxes. Do these firms' structures align with the predictions made for each box?

NOTES

[1] Based on Raymond E. Miles and Charles C. Snow, "Fit, Failure, and the Hall of Fame," *California Management Review*, Spring 1984, p. 21.

[2] Joseph McGuire, *Theories of Business Behavior* (Englewood Cliffs, N.J.: Prentice Hall, 1964), p. 47.

[3] Peter F. Drucker, *Management: Tasks, Responsibilities, Practices* (New York: Harper & Row, 1974), pp. 523–24.

[4] Henry L. Tosi, *Theories of Organization*, 2nd ed. (New York: John Wiley, 1984), p. 39.

[5] Alfred D. Chandler, Jr., *Strategy and Structure: Chapters in the History of the Industrial Enterprise* (Cambridge, Mass.: MIT Press, 1962), p. 13.

[6] Henry Mintzberg, "Research in Strategy-Making," *Proceedings of the Academy of Management*, 32nd meeting (Minneapolis, 1972), pp. 90–94.

[7] Lex Donaldson, *In Defence of Organization Theory: A Reply to the Critics* (Cambridge, England: Cambridge University Press, 1985), p. 159.

[8] D. S. Pugh, "The Context of Organization Structures," *Administrative Science Quarterly*, March 1969, pp. 91–114.

[9] This section is based on Danny Miller, "The Structural and Environmental Correlates of Business Strategy," *Strategic Management Journal*, January–February 1987, pp. 55–76. See also Danny Miller, "Configurations of Strategy and Structure," *Strategic Management Journal*, May–June 1986, pp. 233–49.

[10] Chandler, *Strategy and Structure*.

[11] Ibid., p. 15.

[12] Ibid., p. 16.

[13] See, for instance, John M. Stopford, "Growth and Organizational Change in the Multinational Firm," D.B.A. dissertation, Harvard Business School, 1968; and Peter H. Grinyer, Masoud Yasai-Ardekani, and Shawki Al-Bazzaz, "Strategy, Structure, the Environment, and Financial Performance in 48 United Kingdom Companies," *Academy of Management Journal*, June 1980, pp. 193–226.

[14] Stopford, "Growth and Organizational Change"; and Richard P. Rumelt, "Strategy, Structure, and Economic Performance," Graduate School of Business Administration, Harvard University, 1974.

[15] Leonard Wrigley, "Divisional Autonomy and Diversification," D.B.A. dissertation, Harvard Business School, 1970.

[16] John B. Miner, *Theories of Organizational Structure and Process* (Chicago: Dryden Press, 1982), p. 315.

[17] Raymond E. Miles and Charles C. Snow, *Organizational Strategy, Structure, and Process* (New York: McGraw-Hill, 1978).

[18] Russell Mitchell, "Masters of Innovation, How 3M Keeps Its New Products Coming," *Business Week*, April 10, 1989, pp. 58–63.

[19] Raymond E. Miles, Charles C. Snow, Alan D. Meyer, and Henry J. Coleman, Jr., "Organizational Strategy, Structure, and Process," *Academy of Management Review*, July 1978, p. 553.

[20] Thomas J. Peters and Robert H. Waterman, Jr., *In Search of Excellence* (New York: Harper & Row, 1982), pp. 178–79.

[21] Ralph E. Winter, "Goodyear, Firestone Split on Future Demand for Tires," *Wall Street Journal*, February 23, 1981, p. 21; and "Firestone after the Turnaround: Where Next?" *Business Week*, April 23, 1984, pp. 58–60.

[22] The following discussion is based on Robert H. Miles, *Coffin Nails and Corporate Strategies* (Englewood Cliffs, N.J.: Prentice Hall, 1982), pp. 102–13; and "How the Producers Rank," *Business Week*, January 23, 1989, p. 59.

[23] Michael E. Porter, *Competitive Strategy: Techniques for Analyzing Industries and Competitors* (New York: Free Press, 1980); and *Competitive Advantage: Creating and Sustaining Superior Performance* (New York: Free Press, 1985).

[24] See, for example, Vijay Govindarajan, "Decentralization, Strategy, and Effectiveness of Strategic Business Units in Multibusiness Organizations," *Academy of Management Review*, October 1986, pp. 844–56; and Danny Miller, "Relating Porter's Business Strategies to Environment and Structure: Analysis and Performance Implications," *Academy of Management Journal*, June 1988, pp. 280–308.

[25] Danny Miller, "Structural and Environmental Correlates."

[26] Miner, *Organizational Structure and Process*, p. 316.

[27] Gareth P. Dyas and Heinz T. Thanheiser, *The Emerging European Enterprise: Strategy and Structure in French and German Industry* (Boulder, Colo.: Westview Press, 1976); and Lawrence G. Franko, *The European Multinationals: A Renewed Challenge to American and British Big Business* (Stamford, Conn.: Greylock, 1976).

[28] Miner, *Organizational Structure and Process*, p. 315.

[29] Barbara W. Keats and Michael Hitt, "A Causal Model of Linkages Among Environmental Dimensions, Macro Organizational Characteristics, and Performance," *Academy of Management Journal*, September 1988, pp. 570–98.

[30] Robert A. Pitts, "The Strategy-Structure Relationship: An Exploration into Causality." Working paper, Pennsylvania State University, 1979.

[31] Raymond E. Miles and Charles C. Snow, "Toward a Synthesis in Organization Theory," in M. Jelinek, J. A. Litterer, and R. E. Miles, eds., *Organizations by Design: Theory and Practice* (Plano, Texas: Business Publications, 1981), pp. 548–50.

[32] Ibid., p. 549.

6

ORGANIZATION SIZE

AFTER READING THIS CHAPTER, YOU SHOULD BE ABLE TO:

1 Define organization size.
2 List the pros and cons of large size.
3 Summarize the conclusions from the Aston Group's research.
4 Describe the effect of size on complexity, formalization, and centralization.
5 Explain the effect of size on the administrative component.
6 List which OT issues are of greater and lesser importance to small-business managers.

Introduction
DO YOU GET THE PICTURE?

Eastman Kodak has sales in excess of $13 billion a year and employs 125,000 people. These employees obviously cannot fit neatly into one building or into several departments supervised by a couple of managers. It's hard to envision these 125,000 people being organized in any manner other than one that would be labeled as high in complexity. On the other hand, a local one-hour-photo-processing firm that employs six people and generates less than $200,000 a year in sales is not likely to need decentralized decision making or extensive written documentation defining company policies and regulations. Comparing these two photography-related firms suggests that an organization's size influences its structure.

The conclusion that size influences structure can also be arrived at through a more sophisticated reasoning process. As an organization hires more operative employees, it will attempt to take advantage of the economic benefits from specialization. The result will be increased horizontal differentiation. Grouping like functions together will facilitate intragroup efficiencies but at the expense of intergroup relations, which will suffer as each performs its different activities. Management, therefore, will need to increase vertical differentiation to coordinate the horizontally differentiated units. This expansion in size is also likely to result in spatial differentiation. All this increase in complexity will reduce top management's ability to supervise directly the activities within the organization. The control achieved through direct surveillance, therefore, will be replaced by the implementation of formal rules and regulations. This increase in formalization may also be accompanied by still greater vertical differentiation as management creates new units to coordinate the expanding and diverse activities of organizational members. Finally, with top management further removed from the operating level, it becomes difficult for senior executives to make rapid and informative decisions. The solution is to substitute decentralized decision making for centralization. Following this reasoning, we see changes in size leading to major structural changes.

While the preceding description is logical enough, does it actually happen this way in practice? This chapter, after addressing the issue of defining size, reviews the evidence on the size-structure relationship and attempts to test the validity of our logical scenario.

DEFINING ORGANIZATION SIZE

There is wide agreement by OT researchers on how an organization's size is defined. Over 80 percent of studies using **organization size** as a variable define it as the total number of employees.[1] This is consistent with the assumption that since it is people and their interactions that are structured, their number should be more closely associated with structure than with any other size measure. However, just because there is high agreement among researchers on what constitutes an organization's size is no assurance that they are right!

For example, the total number of employees may be an adequate measure for organizations composed solely of full-time employees. But what if the organization has a large number of part-time workers? How are they to be counted? Or what if the business is seasonal? It's not unusual for retail stores to increase their sales staff by 50 percent during the Christmas holiday season. How should these seasonal workers be assessed? Counting the total number of employees also doesn't distinguish among different types of industries. A small beauty parlor may have three employees; while one with fifty employees would be quite large. On the other hand, a steel plant with two hundred employees is small in an industry where average plants employ several thousand workers. Should the measure of an organization's size—and the subsequent assessment of whether it is small or large—be qualified to reflect industry norms? Finally, it's been noted that using a count of the total number of employees as the measure of organizational size inherently mixes size with efficiency.[2] If one organization requires one hundred people to carry out the same activities performed by fifty people in another organization, is the first twice as large or merely half as efficient? The answers to these questions are not easy.

Although it can be argued that different measures of size are not interchangeable,[3] most of the evidence suggests that counting the total number of employees is as good as many other measures, the reason being that total number is highly related to other measures of size. For instance, one study found the correlation between number of employees and the organization's net assets to be .78.[4] Number of employees also appears valid in hospitals and colleges. The correlation between total hospital labor force and average daily patient load was found to exceed .96,[5] whereas size of full-time and part-time faculty correlates with student enrollment at above .94.[6] One can conclude from these studies that the total number of employees appears to be highly related to other popular gauges of size. As such, it should be a fairly accurate measure across organizations.

ADVOCATES OF THE SIZE IMPERATIVE

One of the strongest arguments for the importance of size as a determinant of structure has been made by Peter Blau. Based on studies of government agencies, universities, and department stores, he concluded that "size is the most important condition affecting the structure of organizations."[7] For instance, in one of Blau's most cited studies, he looked at fifty-three autonomous state and territorial employment-security agencies whose responsibilities included administering unemployment insurance and providing employment services. In addition, his analysis included the structure of over twelve hundred local agency branches and three hundred and fifty headquarters divisions.[8] What Blau found was that increasing size promotes structural differentiation but at a decreasing rate. Increases in organization size are accompanied by initially rapid and subsequently more gradual increases in the number of local branches into which the agency is spatially dispersed, the number of official occupational positions expressing division of labor, the number of vertical levels in the hierarchy, the number of functional divisions at the headquarters, and the number of sections per division. Blau's conclusions are visually depicted in Figure 6–1. An increase of, say, five hundred employees when an organization has only three hundred members, has a significantly larger impact on structural differentiation than a similar addition of five hundred employees to an organization that already employs twenty-three hundred. That is, the difference between X' and Y' is smaller than the difference between X and Y.

Research at the University of Aston in Great Britain also found size to be the major determinant of structure.[9] For example, the **Aston Group** looked at forty-six organizations and found that increased size was associated with greater specialization and formalization. They concluded that "an increased scale of operation increases the frequency of recurrent events and the repetition of decisions," which makes standardization preferable.[10]

One researcher's efforts to replicate the Aston findings resulted in supportive evidence.[11] He found that organizational size was related positively to specialization, formalization, and vertical span and negatively to centralization. In further comparing his results with Blau, he concluded that "larger organizations are more specialized, have more rules, more documentation, more extended

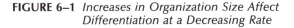

FIGURE 6–1 *Increases in Organization Size Affect Differentiation at a Decreasing Rate*

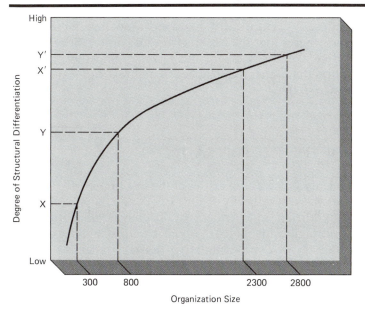

hierarchies, and a greater decentralization of decision making further down such hierarchies."[12] He also agreed with Blau that the impact of size on these dimensions expanded at a decreasing rate as size increased. That is, as size increased, specialization, formalization, and vertical span also increased but at a declining rate, whereas centralization decreased but at a declining rate as size increased.

One of the strongest cases for the size imperative has been made by Meyer.[13] Acknowledging that a relationship between size and structural dimensions does not imply causation, he designed a research project that allowed for causal inferences. He created a longitudinal study of 194 city, county, and state departments of finance in the United States. He compared them over a five-year period. He argued that only by comparing organizations over time would it be possible to determine the time ordering of variables. That is, even if size and structure were found to be related among a set of organizations at a specific time, only a longitudinal analysis would permit the elimination of the counterhypothesis that structure causes size. Meyer's findings led him to conclude that "one cannot underestimate the impact of size on other characteristics of organizations."[14] Specifically, he found that the effects of size showed everywhere; that the relationship was unidirectional (that is, size caused structure but not the reverse); and the impact of other variables that appeared to affect structure disappeared when size was controlled.

CRITICS OF THE SIZE IMPERATIVE

There has been no shortage of critics of the size imperative. Attacks have been launched specifically against Blau's and the Aston Group's research. In addition, independent studies have demonstrated no impact or minimal impact of size upon structure. Finally, there is some preliminary evidence indicating that size affects structure only in organizations that have professional managers—not among those that are owner controlled.

Chris Argyris analyzed Blau's data, questioned his measures, and argued that civil-service organizations are unique.[15] On this last point, he noted that civil-service organizations have budget limitations, distinct geographical boundaries, predetermined staff sizes, and are influenced primarily by regulations. He also acknowledged the role of managerial discretion. Managers in government bureaus follow traditional management theories regarding task specialization, unity of command, span of control, and so forth. Thus, you would expect to find that an increase in the number of employees was accompanied by an increase in differentiation because managers believe in the appropriateness of management theories and are able to act on their beliefs. Size may be related to structure, Argyris concluded, but you cannot say that it causes it.

Blau's size imperative was also challenged by Mayhew and his associates.[16] Using a computer program that determined the degrees of differentiation possible for each level of size, they concluded that Blau's findings of a relationship between size and complexity were a mathematical certainty when equal probabilities were assigned to all possible structural combinations.

The Aston Group's research has had its share of critics, too.

Aldrich reanalyzed the Aston data and proposed several alternative and equally plausible interpretations.[17] For example, size is the *result*, not the cause: technology determines structure, which in turn determines size. Aldrich said that the firms that were high in complexity and formalization simply needed to employ a larger work force than less structured firms did.

Even some of the Aston researchers have questioned the group's original position after an abbreviated replication.[18] They used fourteen of the organizations that had been included previously. Since some time had gone by between the original study and the replication, there was an opportunity to do a partial longitudinal test of Aston's original findings. The data, however, showed that although size generally decreased over the time period, the measure of structure dimension increased. This was counter to the original findings.

A general attack on the size imperative has come from Hall and his associates. They studied seventy-five highly diverse organizations. They ranged in size from six employees to over nine thousand and included business, governmental, religious, educational, and penal organizations. Hall believed that if size and the structural dimensions of complexity and formalization were related, this diverse set of organizations would allow that relationship to surface. Their results were mixed. The researchers concluded that "neither complexity nor formalization can be implied from organizational size." Even though some relationships were statistically significant, enough deviant cases existed to question seriously the assumption that large organizations are necessarily more complex than small ones. Hall sided with Aldrich's structure-causes-size thesis when he concluded, "If a decision is made to enlarge the number of functions or activities carried out in an organization, it then becomes necessary to add more members to staff the new functional areas."[19] However, in terms of objectivity, it must be noted that the evidence was more inconsistent than damning. Hall and his associates, therefore, may question the size-structure relationship, but their research has certainly not demonstrated that the two are unrelated.

A final consideration relates to the status of the management in the organization. A study of 142 small- and medium-sized businesses found that changes in size were related to changes in structure among those firms that were run by professional managers but that no such relationship appeared among the businesses that were controlled by owner-managers.[20] Specifically, it was found that increases in size were associated with more horizontal differ-

HAVE ECONOMIES OF SCALE BEEN OVERSOLD?

Organizational theorists have long assumed that there was a positive relationship between organizational size and economies of scale. As one author put it, it has been believed "that big is good; bigger is better; [and] biggest is best."[21]

But look around. The big guys today don't seem to always be winning against their smaller competitors. In fact, more often than not, the Davids are clearly defeating the Goliaths. Today, for instance, about the only American steel plants making any money are minimills run by firms like Nucor Corp. and Chaparral Steel. They are significantly more efficient than the huge plants run by USX and Bethlehem. Similarly, General Motors' size and its dependence on vertical integration puts it at a distinct disadvantage against the likes of a Chrysler. Why? Flexibility! Chrysler purchases 70 percent of its components outside the firm and can find the lowest-cost supplier, whereas GM is able to go outside for only 30 percent of its components.[22]

These results are not aberrations. A review of more than thirty studies, which covered a wide range of organizational types and assessed the size-efficiency relationship, found no economy-of-scale effects.[23] But how can that be? Why isn't bigger more efficient? Why might the long-held assumption of economies of scale no longer be accurate? Well, certainly there have always been diseconomies associated with large size. But they didn't tend to matter much in more stable times. Foreign competition, deregulation, corporate raiders, and similar forces are putting a premium on flexibility and change. And in such times, large size can be a liability.[24] Additionally, many of the traditional advantages of size, such as access to low-cost capital markets and internal manufacturing efficiencies, can now be achieved by midsize organizations through issuance of junk bonds, subcontracting out of manufacturing and services, participation in joint ventures, use of franchising, and similar strategies.

entiation, more formalization, and more delegation of decision making only in firms controlled by professional managers. While it is dangerous to generalize from a single study, this research may help to explain some of the diverse findings in previous studies where there have been a large number of business firms in the sample but no control for the type of ownership. If, for example, owner-managers are unwilling to dilute their personal power over their organizations by decentralizing decision making—even though this unwillingness reduces their organization's effectiveness—we should expect the relationship between a business organization's size and its structure to be moderated by the kind of management the firm has.

CONCLUSIONS ON THE SIZE-STRUCTURE RELATIONSHIP

In overview terms, the relationship between size and structure is not clear.[25] Although some have found a strong relationship and argue for its causal nature, others have challenged these findings on methodological grounds or have argued that size is a consequence rather than a cause of structure. But when we look at the research in more specific terms, a clearer pattern seems to evolve. We will demonstrate that size certainly does not dictate all of an organization's structure but that it is important in predicting some dimensions of structure.

Size and Complexity

Blau found that the impact of size on complexity was at a decreasing rate. As noted by Argyris, this conclusion may apply only to government-type agencies that had the unique characteristics of the unemployment offices studied. Meyer's findings certainly cannot be ignored. Although also restricted to government offices, he demonstrated strong evidence in favor of the size imperative. We might conclude tentatively that size affects complexity, but at a decreasing rate, in government organizations. Whether this also holds in business firms is questionable. It may well be that in business organizations, where managers have greater discretion, structure causes size. Consistent with the strategy imperative, if managers have discretion, they may choose to make their structures more complex (consistent with management theory) as more activities and personnel are added. Neither can it be ruled out that the size-structure relationship is circular. There is evidence indicating that size generates differentiation and that increasing differentiation also generates increasing size.[26]

The strongest case can be made for the effect of size on vertical differentiation.[27] In fact, one study found that size alone was the dominant predictor of vertical differentiation, explaining between 50 and 59 percent of the variance.[28] A less strong but certainly solid case can be made for the size-horizontal differentiation relationship. That is, the larger the organization, the more pronounced (at declining rates) the division of labor within it, the same being true for the functional differentiation of the organization into divisions.[29]

The size-spatial differentiation relationship is problematic. Blau's high correlations are almost certainly attributable to the kind of organizations he studied. Other efforts to assess this relationship have failed to generate Blau's strong positive relationship; however, still other investigations support Blau.[30] Further research covering diverse types of organizations is needed before conclusions of any substance can be drawn.

What about the criticism of the Aston Group's work and Hall's research? Our position is that they have not demonstrated the impotence of size. More longitudinal studies are needed to clarify the size-structure causation. But in the interim, we propose that the critics have pointed out methodological problems with several of the important studies confirming the impact of size on complexity and have suggested potential alternative hypotheses, although they certainly have not demonstrated size to be irrelevant. Even Hall noted that six of his eleven measures of complexity were significantly related to size.[31]

Size and Formalization

The Aston findings supported the view that size affects formalization. Hall's conclusion was that formalization could not be implied from knowledge of organization size, but he also acknowledged that it could not be ignored either. A recent comprehensive review of twenty-seven studies covering more than one thousand organizations concluded that the relationship between size and formalization was high, positive, and statistically significant.[32]

There would appear to be a logical connection between an increase in size and an increase in formalization. Management seeks to control the behavior of employees. Two popular methods are direct surveillance and the use of formalized regulations. Although not perfect substitutes for each other, as one increases, the need for the other should decrease. Because surveillance costs should increase very rapidly as organizations expand in size, it seems reasonable to propose that there would be economies if management substituted formalization for direct surveillance as size increased. The evidence supports this contention.[33] Rules and surveillance are both aspects of control. The former is impersonal; the latter requires such activities as supervising work closely and inspecting the quantity and quality of work. In small organizations, control through surveillance may be achieved relatively easily through informal face-to-face relationships. But as the organization grows, there are more subordinates to supervise, so that it becomes increasingly efficient to rely more on rules and regulations for exerting control. We can expect, therefore, to find an increase in formal rules and regulations within an organization as that organization increases in size.

After reviewing the size-formalization literature, one author proposed boldly that "the larger the organization, the more formalized its behavior."[34] His explanation, however, emphasized that larger organizations formalize those activities that have a propensity to recur often. The larger the organization, the more that behaviors repeat themselves, and hence management is motivated to handle them more efficiently through standardization. With increased size comes greater internal confusion. Given managements' general desires to minimize this confusion, they seek means to make behavior at lower levels in the hierarchy more predictable. Management turns to rules, procedures, job descriptions, and other formalization techniques to bring about this predictability.

A final point on the size-formalization relationship should be noted: We cannot ignore whether the organization is independent or is a subsidiary of a larger organization.[35] Parent firms often impose rules and regulations to maintain financial and reporting consistencies that would be unnecessary if the small firm were independent. So a moderating factor on size's effect on formalization would be whether the organization was a subsidiary of a larger firm. If so, expect the former to have higher formalization than its size alone would dictate.

Size and Centralization

"It is only common sense that it is impossible to control large organizations from the top: because much more is happening than an individual or set of individuals can comprehend, there is inevitable delegation."[36] But is that the way the evidence stacks? As we concluded, formalization increases with size. These rules and regulations *allow* top management to delegate decision making while at the same time ensure that the decisions are made in accordance with the desires of top management. But the research is mixed in demonstrating that size leads to decentralization.[37] In fact, one comprehensive review concluded that the relationship between size and centralization is not significantly different from zero.[38] Precisely why this occurs is not clear. One possibility is that these studies combine professionally managed and owner-managed business enterprises. The desire to maintain control by the owner-manager is likely to override the loss in organizational effectiveness, with the result being no move toward decentralized decision making as size increases.

A CRITICAL QUESTION: HOW BIG IS BIG?

Throughout this chapter we have tried to assess what effect, if any, changes in an organization's size have on its structure. One interesting finding has been that size's influence seems to dissipate as the number of employees expands. Once an organization becomes large in size, it tends to be high in complexity, high in formalization, and decentralized. That is, once an organization becomes big, increases in the number of employees have no noticeable further influence on structure. This conclusion, then, begs the question: How big is big? Put another way, at what point do additional employees become irrelevant in determining an organization's structure?

Our answer can only be an approximation. However, most estimates tend to fall in the range of fifteen hundred to two thousand employees.[39] Organizations with fewer than fifteen hundred employees tend to be labeled as "small." On the other hand, when an organization or any of its subunits gets to around two thousand employees, it becomes increasingly difficult to coordinate without differentiating units, creating formalized rules and regulations, or delegating decision making downward. So we'll define a **large organization** as one having approximately two thousand or more employees.

OT
CLOSE-UP

KEEPING IT SMALL

Among organizations that purposely seek to keep their organizational units small in order to maintain flexibility and responsiveness to change, there is no clear consensus on when a unit has become too big. For instance, compare Hewlett-Packard and Magna International's solution to the problem.

Both of these highly successful firms pride themselves on keeping units small. Hewlett-Packard, on one hand, tends to use about two thousand employees as a cutoff. When plants get permanently beyond that number, H-P builds a new facility to absorb future growth. On the other hand, Magna International is a diversified Canadian auto-parts manufacturer with more than ten thousand employees and almost $1 billion (Canadian) in annual sales. It uses two hundred people as its cutoff. Magna is made up of more than one hundred separate enterprises; each operates under its own name and has exactly one factory. When a plant gets more work than it can handle, Magna does not add to it; rather, it "clones" the facility and starts a new operation. Magna's CEO believes small units encourage entrepreneurship and focus responsibility squarely with the plant manager.[40]

The preceding definition now allows us to make two important statements. First, adding employees to an organization once it has approximately two thousand members should have a minimal impact on its structure. Second, a change in size will have its greatest impact on structure when the organization is *small*. The big organization, with five or ten thousand employees, can double its size and you're not likely to see any significant changes in its structure. But if an organization with five hundred employees doubles its size, you should expect that it will be followed by significant structural changes.

SPECIAL ISSUES RELATING TO ORGANIZATION SIZE

In this section we address two issues related to size. First, as the number of operative personnel increases, what effect does it have on the number of administrators and supporting staff? Second, is organization theory applicable to small organizations?

The Administrative-Component Debate

Most of us have heard of **Parkinson's Law.** Writing partly in jest and partly in truth, Parkinson declared that "work expands so as to fill the time available for its completion." He argued that, in government at least, "there need be little or no relationship between the work to be done and the size of the staff to which it may be assigned."[41] According to Parkinson, the number of officials in an organization and the quantity of work to be done are not related to each other at all. To "prove" his law, he trotted out figures on the British Royal Navy. As shown in Table 6–1, between 1914 and 1928, the number of warships commissioned declined by nearly 68 percent. Total personnel in the Navy declined by approximately 32 percent. But that apparently had no bearing on the administrative staff, whose purpose it was to manage the ships and personnel. The number of on-shore officials and clerks rose by 40 percent over the fourteen-year period, and the officer corps increased by a startling 78 percent!

Parkinson's insight initiated a wealth of research into what is

TABLE 6–1   *Comparative Data on the British Royal Navy,
1914 versus 1928*

CATEGORY	1914	1928	% INCREASE OR DECREASE
Ships in commission	62	20	−67.74
Total navy personnel	146,000	100,000	−31.50
Dockyard workers	57,000	62,439	+9.54
Dockyard officials and clerks	3,249	4,558	+40.28
Admiralty officers	2,000	3,569	+78.45

From *Parkinson's Law* by C. Northcote Parkinson. Copyright © 1957 by C. Northcote Parkinson. Reprinted by permission of Houghton Mifflin Company.

now referred to as the **administrative component.** It has been stated, in fact, that probably more studies have been conducted on the relationship between organizational size and the administrative component than on any other aspect of organization structure.[42] But what exactly does this term *administrative component* mean?

As with so many concepts to which you have been introduced in this book, the administrative component has no universally agreed-upon definition. Some examples include the ratio between managers and employees; the proportion of line managers and their support staff to operating or production personnel; staff versus line, with the staff composing the administrative component; and all the personnel in an organization who engage in "support" activities.[43] Although there is no general agreement on one of these definitions, we will use the last one. It can be used in various types of organizations and attempts to identify administrative overhead. "Thus, custodial workers, some drivers, cafeteria employees, clerical help, and so on, are included in the administrative component, regardless of whether they are directly employed in 'staff' or 'general administrative' divisions."[44] Those persons who contribute indirectly to the attainment of the organization's goals, whether operatives or managers, become part of the administrative component. This, then, is our working definition. However, keep in mind that researchers have used various definitions, and that may explain some of the diversity in the findings we will report.

The Positive-Correlation Argument. Parkinson's thesis says basically that there would be a positive relationship between organizational size and the administrative component. As organizations increased in size, the relative size of the administrative component would increase disproportionately. Can this relationship be defended intuitively? The basic explanation would be that administrators and staff are responsible for providing coordination, and because coordination becomes increasingly difficult as more employees who contribute directly to the organization's goals are added, the administrative component can be expected to increase out of proportion to increases in size. Some studies support this positive relationship. For instance, a study of over four hundred

OT
CLOSE-UP

U.S. SCHOOLS APPEAR TOP-HEAVY WITH ADMINISTRATORS

Maybe one of the reasons why American students aren't performing as well as their counterparts in other countries, in spite of the tremendous amount of money spent in the United States on elementary and secondary education, is that the money isn't going into teaching but into the administrative component.[46]

A recent study shows that between 1960 and 1984, the number of U.S. teachers grew by 57 percent and the number of principals and supervisors by 79 percent. During that same period, the ranks of other staffers, from curriculum specialists to guidance counselors, skyrocketed—nearly 500 percent. Although teachers still outnumber non-classroom personnel by a seven-to-one margin, since 1970 the portion of spending devoted to teacher salaries has dropped, from 50 to 41 percent.

Educators attribute some of the growth in the administrative component to expanding social needs in order to serve more poor, disadvantaged, and minority students whose personal problems—if left unattended—can severely hinder learning. In Chicago, for instance, the number of classroom teachers dropped by 7 percent between 1976 and 1986, whereas the number of school psychologists rose by nearly 21 percent and the ranks of social workers grew by 64 percent.

California school districts found that the administrative compo-nent—superintendent, assistants, principals, business managers, and other support staff—increased as the size of the school district increased.[45] But there are far more studies showing the size-ad-ministrative component relationship to be either negative or cur-vilinear.

The Negative-Correlation Argument. Exclusive of any empirical data, it seems more reasonable to expect the administrative component to decline as size increases. We are not arguing that the absolute number of supportive personnel would decline but rather that it should decline as a *proportion* as size increases. This conclusion is based on the assumption of efficiencies from economies of scale. As organizations expand, they of course require more managers and staff to facilitate coordination. But not in the same proportion as size increases. A manufacturing firm that does $5 million a year in sales and employs sixty people may require the services of a full-time purchasing agent. If sales doubled, it's unlikely that the firm would need two purchasing agents. Similarly, a typical hos-pital can increase its patient load by 10 percent with little or no addition in accounting personnel, dietitians, and the like. Both examples illustrate economies of scale that suggest that as an or-ganization grows, there should be a decrease in the proportion of personnel allocated to indirect activities. The logic of this argu-ment has received substantial empirical support.

A study of Veteran's Administration hospitals found the ad-ministrative component to decrease as the organizations increased in size.[47] An investigation of five sets of organizations—including package delivery services, automobile dealerships, volunteer fire companies, labor-union locals, and political associations—also found a negative relationship.[48] In each of the sets of organizations, as the size of the organizations increased, the administrative com-ponent declined. Census information by industry was used by an-other investigator to test the size-administrative component re-lationship.[49] While a negative relationship was found, it was concluded that this could be explained better as due to the loss of control across hierarchical levels than to economies of scale with large size. Moreover, owner-managed organizations and partner-ships were found to be less likely to add administrators than in-corporated firms were because to do so would result in dilution of the owners' personal power. So while this research confirms the negative correlation, it suggests that maintenance of control may be a primary motivator for owners of firms to keep the number of administrators and support staff in check as the size of the organization increases.

The Curvilinear Argument. There is also evidence to suggest that the size-administrative component relationship is not linear.[50] Rather, it is curvilinear—the administrative component is greater for smaller and larger organizations than for those of moderate size. As organizations move out of the small category, they enjoy the benefits from economies of scale. But as they become large, they lose these benefits and become so complex as to require significant increases in the administrative component to facilitate coordination and control.

Conclusions. Trying to draw practical conclusions from the research on the administrative component may be impossible. No consistent patterns emerge. Whether this is due to the fact that *any* relationship found between size and the administrative component is purely spurious or due to inconsistencies in the way that the administrative component is measured can be answered only through more research. It's possible, for example, that the dominant determinant of the administrative component is not size at all. Arguments have been made that better predictors include complexity,[51] technology and environment,[52] and whether the organization is declining or growing.[53] On this last determinant, for instance, several investigations have found that the process of decline in organizations does not have the opposite effect on the administrative component as does growth. The administrative component tends to increase on the upswings but the decreases on the downswings are not as great, suggesting that management may be reluctant to let members of the administrative component go during periods of decline. We will discuss the different problems associated with growth versus decline at length in Chapter 17.

So where does all this leave us? First, there are economies of scale operating to reduce the relative size of the administrative component as the organization's size increases. But these economies do not exist *regardless* of the increase in size. At some point, the diseconomies of size offset the economies, and more support staff is required to coordinate the organization's activities. Just where this "point" is, however, is unclear. It undoubtedly varies by industry or type of organization, reflecting different technologies and environments.

Second, size is not the only factor that influences the administrative component. Other factors undoubtedly include the type of organization, environment and technology, complexity, and whether the organization is undergoing growth or decline.

Finally, maybe Parkinson was right given the "animal" he chose to observe—the British Royal Navy. The navy was probably operating in the diseconomy zone, where increases in size were accompanied by comparable or large increases in the administrative component. Also, government employees in organizations such as the military and public school systems have little motivation to keep the administrative component in check as we might expect in owner-dominated business firms. Maybe what Parkinson discovered is that "in the absence of direct performance measures, managers build empires."[54] However, Parkinson's observation is undoubtedly not a "law"; rather, he has given us an accurate description of what occurs under certain specific conditions.

Organization Theory and Small Businesses

We live in a society dominated by large organizations. It is true that more than 30 percent of all U.S. organizations have three or fewer employees, but they employ less than one-half of 1 percent of the work force.[55] In contrast, organizations with a thousand or more employees may not be many in number—only about eight thousand of the four million organizations in the United States fall in this category—but they employ nearly 25 percent of the entire work force! While there may be a great number of small organizations, large organizations have the greatest impact on our society.

These considerations have not been lost on those who study organization theory. Studies are made up almost exclusively of medium-sized and large organizations, those with hundreds of employees or more. Even textbook authors fall prey to this bias—you'll find lots of references in this book to large school districts and government agencies or firms the size of General Motors, Sears, and IBM but rarely a mention of the small business, particularly the owner-managed firm. As such, it may be appropriate to ask: Does the organization theory being described in this book have any application to those who manage or expect to manage a small business?

The answer is a resounding Yes! The right structural design is critical if a small business is to succeed. An important point, however, is that small businesses face different problems than large organizations; therefore, we should expect a different priority to be assigned to OT issues by the small business manager.

Issues of Reduced Importance. All the structural variables take on lesser importance to the small business manager because the range of variation in small businesses is typically limited. Small businesses tend to have a minimal degree of horizontal, vertical, and spatial differentiation; and most are characterized by low formalization and high centralization. There is less internal specialization. When specialized expertise is needed, it is typically purchased from outside. For instance, instead of having full-time accountants and lawyers on staff, these services can be bought as they're needed. Vertical differentiation in small businesses is usually low for the obvious reason that these structures tend to be flat. Similarly, spatial differentiation is usually low because small businesses don't spread their activities widely. Even separate units, such as in a chain of small, retail, women's wear stores, tend to be geographically close in most small businesses. You'll also find little formalization in small businesses. The small-business manager achieves control but not usually through high formalization. Some of that control is achieved by holding on to the decision-making machinery; that is, you can expect most small businesses to be characterized by centralized decision making.

In addition to these structural issues, there are other concerns that take on reduced importance in small business organizations. These include stimulating innovation, managing conflict, and changing the organization's culture. The topic of stimulating innovation, discussed in Chapter 14, has reduced importance to small business. The concern of organization theorists with innovation is largely a response to the constraints that high complexity and formalization impose on an organization's creative juices. These constraints don't exist in most small businesses. Managing conflict—the topic of Chapter 15—should be of lesser importance for the small-business manager because small size facilitates communication, allows for all members to have a clear sense of the organization's mission, and reduces the likelihood of goal incompatibility. Finally, organizational culture (discussed in Chapter 16) presents less of a problem for small businesses. Small organizations tend to be young in age. As a result, they have less sense of history and fewer traditions. Because their cultures are younger and less entrenched, they are less likely to require change. And when change *is* required, it's easier to implement.

Issues of Increased Importance. The OT issues that take on greater importance for small business include control and accountability, efficiency, and environmental dependence.

The small-business owner is often willing to settle for lesser monetary reward in return for personal control and accountability. In place of formalization, he tends to control through direct supervision and observation. Small-business managers are strong advocates of "management by walking around."

Achieving high efficiency is typically more important in the small business than in the large for the simple reason that large organizations have more slack resources. Slack resources act as shock absorbers to reduce the impact of mistakes. The fact that small organizations have less tolerance for inefficiency than established large organizations do places an increased importance on ensuring that the right structural design is chosen. Therefore, the structural-design problem, discussed in Chapters 10 through 12, may be more critical to the small business manager.

Last, we suggest that the environment that confronts the small business is often very different from the one facing its larger counterpart. The larger an organization is, the more it is able to use its power to control its environment and reduce its dependence on such constituencies as material suppliers, competitors, and financial sources. Small businesses rarely have much influence over their environment. This places an increased importance on the organization's environmental monitoring system. The effective small business must have a structural design that facilitates rapid and accurate assessment of its environment and allows for this information to be acted upon promptly.

Conclusions. Small businesses are different from their larger counterparts. They have different concerns and priorities. Some issues presented in this book have limited relevance to the small organization while others take on much greater importance.

In addition to the different OT agenda that small businesses have, we have argued that their managers have a more limited set of structural options. If there is any message in this section, it may be for the small-business manager to guard against what can be called Generalmotorsitis—the desire to build a complex and sophisticated organization design regardless of whether it is appropriate. The small business has unique problems that require unique structural solutions. The appropriate structural design for a small business is not merely a scaled-down version of the design used by its industry's giants.

SUMMARY

Organizational size is defined as the total number of employees. Strong arguments have been proposed indicating that size is the major determinant of structure, but there has been no shortage of critics to this position.

A review of the evidence indicates that size has a significant influence on vertical differentiation. The effect of size on spatial differentiation is unclear. Increases in formalization appear to be related closely to increases in organizational size. Finally, although common sense suggests that size and centralization would be inversely related, research demonstrates mixed findings.

More studies have probably been conducted on the relationship between organization size and the administrative component than any other aspect of organization structure. We defined the administrative component as all the personnel in an organization who engage in supportive activities. Our literature review led us to conclude that the relationship between size and the administrative component is curvilinear and that other factors—the type of organization, environment and technology, complexity, and whether the organization is growing or declining—in addition to size influence the administrative component.

Finally, we noted that OT is based on studies made up almost exclusively of medium-sized and large organizations. Small businesses face different problems and have a different priority in terms of importance of OT concepts. In addition to the fact that small businesses have a different OT agenda, their managers have a more limited set of structural options.

FOR REVIEW AND DISCUSSION

1. American College has 100 full-time faculty, 10 part-time faculty, and 1,500 full-time students. National College has 30 full-time faculty, 150 part-time faculty, and 2000 full-time students. Continental College has 50 full-time faculty, 30 part-time faculty, and 2500 students. Assuming

that each has a support staff of 75 and no part-time students, which organization is the largest in size? Explain.

2. "One of the strongest cases for the size imperative has been made by Meyer." What is the support for this statement?

3. "Size is the major determinant of structure." Build an argument to support this statement. Then build an argument to refute this statement.

4. How does ownership moderate the size-structure relationship?.

5. What is the relationship between size and complexity?

6. What is the relationship between size and formalization?

7. What is the relationship between size and centralization?

8. At what point in an organization's growth do additions to size have relatively little further impact on structure?

9. When will size have its greatest impact on structure?

10. What is the administrative component? Why is it an important issue in OT?

11. "Size and the administrative component should be correlated positively." Build an argument to support this statement. Then build an argument to refute this statement.

12. Relate (a) the administrative component, (b) economies of scale, and (c) coordination.

13. Which dominates in our society—small or large organizations? Which type of organization dominates OT research? Is there a discrepancy here? Explain.

14. What are some of the problems unique to the small-business manager?

15. Which OT issues take on increased importance for the small-business manager? Reduced importance?

NOTES

[1] J. R. Kimberly, "Organizational Size and the Structuralist Perspective: A Review, Critique, and Proposal," *Administrative Science Quarterly*, December 1976, pp. 571–97.

[2] Nina Gupta, "Some Alternative Definitions of Size," *Academy of Management Journal*, December 1980, p. 761.

[3] Ibid., pp. 759–66; and Richard Z. Gooding and John A. Wagner III, "A Meta-Analytic Review of the Relationship Between Size and Performance: The Productivity and Efficiency of Organizations and Their Subunits," *Administrative Science Quarterly*, December 1985, pp. 462–81.

[4] D. S. Pugh, D. J. Hickson, C. R. Hinings, and C. Turner, "The Context of Organization Structures," *Administrative Science Quarterly*, March 1969, pp. 91–114.

[5] Theodore Anderson and Seymour Warkov, "Organization Size and Functional Complexity: A Study of Administration in Hospitals," *American Sociological Review*, February 1961, p. 25.

[6] Amos Hawley, Walter Boland, and Margaret Boland, "Population Size and Administration in Institutions of Higher Education," *American Sociological Review*, April 1965, p. 253.

[7] Peter M. Blau and Richard A. Schoenherr, *The Structure of Organizations* (New York: Basic Books, 1971).

[8] Peter M. Blau, "A Formal Theory of Differentiation in Organizations," *American Sociological Review*, April 1970, pp. 201–18.

[9] See, for example, Pugh et al., "The Context of Organization Structures"; and D. J. Hickson, D. S. Pugh, and D. C. Pheysey, "Operations Technology and Organization Structure: An Empirical Reappraisal," *Administrative Science Quarterly*, September 1969, pp. 378–97.

[10] Pugh et al., "The Context of Organization Structures," p. 112.

[11] John Child and Roger Mansfield, "Technology, Size, and Organization Structure," *Sociology*, September 1972, pp. 369–93.

[12] John Child, "Predicting and Understanding Organization Structure," *Administrative Science Quarterly*, June 1973, p. 171.

[13] Marshall W. Meyer, "Size and the Structure of Organizations: A Causal Analysis," *American Sociological Review*, August 1972, pp. 434–41.

[14] Ibid., p. 440.

[15] Chris Argyris, *The Applicability of Organizational Sociology* (London: Cambridge University Press, 1972), pp. 1–19.

[16] B. H. Mayhew, R. L. Levinger, J. M. McPherson, and T. F. James, "System Size and Structural Differentiation in Formal Organizations: A Baseline Generator for Two Major Theoretical Propositions," *American Sociological Review*, October 1972, pp. 629–33.

[17] Howard E. Aldrich, "Technology and Organization Structure: A Reexamination of the Findings of the Aston Group," *Administrative Science Quarterly*, March 1972, pp. 26–43.

[18] J. H. K. Inkson, D. S. Pugh, and D. J. Hickson, "Organizational Context and Structure: An Abbreviated Replication," *Administrative Science Quarterly*, September 1970, pp. 318–29.

[19] Quotes in this paragraph are from Richard H. Hall, J. Eugene Haas, and Norman J. Johnson, "Organizational Size, Complexity, and Formalization," *American Sociological Review*, December 1967, pp. 903–12.

[20] Guy Geeraerts, "The Effect of Ownership on the Organization Structure in Small Firms," *Administrative Science Quarterly*, June 1984, pp. 232–37.

[21] Tom Peters, *Thriving on Chaos* (New York: Knopf, 1988), p. 20.

[22] Ibid., pp. 17–18.

[23] Richard Z. Gooding and John A. Wagner III, "Meta-Analytic Review."

[24] Walter Adams and James W. Brock, *The Bigness Complex* (New York: Pantheon, 1986).

[25] Jeffrey D. Ford and John W. Slocum, Jr., "Size, Technology, Environment

and the Structure of Organizations," *Academy of Management Review*, October 1977, p. 566.

[26] N. P. Hummon, P. Doriean, and K. Teuter, "A Structural Control Model of Organizational Change," *American Sociological Review*, December 1975, pp. 813–24.

[27] Dennis S. Mileti, David F. Gillespie, and J. Eugene Haas, "Size and Structure in Complex Organizations," *Social Forces*, September 1977, pp. 208–17; and Lex Donaldson and J. Angus Robertson, "A Meta-Analysis of Size and Hierarchy: Universal Generalization Moderated by Routineness and Managerial Capitalism." Paper presented at Annual Academy of Management Conference; Chicago, August 1986.

[28] John R. Montanari, *An Expanded Theory of Structural Determination: An Empirical Investigation of the Impact of Managerial Discretion on Organization Structure*. Unpublished doctoral dissertation, University of Colorado, Boulder, 1976.

[29] See, for example, Mileti, Gillespie, and Haas, "Size and Structure in Complex Organizations," pp. 213–14; George A. Miller and Joseph Conaty, "Differentiation in Organizations: Replication and Cumulation," *Social Forces*, September 1980, pp. 265–74; and George A. Miller, "Meta-analysis and the Culture-free Hypothesis," *Organization Studies*, no. 4, 1987, pp. 309–25.

[30] Mileti, Gillespie, and Haas, "Size and Structure of Complex Organizations," p. 214.

[31] Hall, Haas, and Johnson, "Organizational Size," pp. 903–12.

[32] George A. Miller, "Meta-analysis and the Culture-free Hypothesis."

[33] William A. Rushing, "Organizational Size, Rules, and Surveillance," in Joseph A. Litterer, ed., *Organizations: Structure and Behavior*, 3rd ed. (New York: John Wiley, 1980), pp. 396–405; and Y. Samuel and B. F. Mannheim, "A Multidimensional Approach Toward a Typology of Bureaucracy," *Administrative Science Quarterly*, June 1970, pp. 216–28.

[34] Henry Mintzberg, *The Structuring of Organizations* (Englewood Cliffs, N.J.: Prentice Hall, 1979), p. 233.

[35] Lex Donaldson, *In Defense of Organization Theory: A Reply to the Critics* (Cambridge: Cambridge University Press, 1985), p. 158.

[36] Richard H. Hall, *Organizations: Structure, and Process*, 2d ed. (Englewood Cliffs, N.J.: Prentice Hall, 1977), p. 184.

[37] Blau and Schoenherr, *The Structure of Organizations*; Child and Mansfield, "Technology, Size and Organization Structure"; Pradip N. Khandwalla, "Mass Output Orientation of Operations Technology and Organization Structure," *Administrative Science Quarterly*, March 1974, pp. 74–97; and George A. Miller, "Meta-analysis and the Culture-free Hypothesis."

[38] George A. Miller, "Meta-analysis and the Culture-free Hypothesis."

[39] See for example, Daniel Robey, *Designing Organizations*, 2nd ed. (Homewood, Ill.: Richard D. Irwin, 1986), p. 121; and Richard L. Daft, *Organization Theory and Design*, 2nd ed. (St. Paul: West Publishing, 1986), p. 196.

[40] John Case, "How to Grow Without Getting Big," *INC.*, December 1986, pp. 108–12.

[41] C. Northcote Parkinson, *Parkinson's Law* (Boston: Houghton Mifflin, 1957), p. 33.

[42] John Child, "Parkinson's Progress: Accounting for the Number of Specialists in Organizations," *Administrative Science Quarterly*, September 1973, pp. 328–46.

[43] Ibid., p. 329.

[44] Hall, *Organizations*, p. 110.

[45] Frederic W. Terrien and Donald L. Mills, "The Effect of Changing Size upon the Internal Structure of Organizations," *American Sociological Review*, February 1955, pp. 11–14.

[46] This section is based on "Beating Back the Education 'Blob,'" *U.S. News & World Report*, April 27, 1987, p. 67.

[47] Anderson and Warkov, "Organizational Size and Functional Complexity," pp. 23–28.

[48] Bernard P. Indik, "The Relationship between Organization Size and Supervision Ratio," *Administrative Science Quarterly*, December 1964, pp. 310–12.

[49] Louis R. Pondy, "Effects of Size, Complexity, and Ownership on Administrative Intensity," *Administrative Science Quarterly*, March 1969, pp. 47–60.

[50] See, for example, John E. Tsouderos, "Organizational Change in Terms of a Series of Selected Variables," *American Sociological Review*, April 1955, pp. 206–10; J. Eugene Haas, Richard H. Hall, and Norman Johnson, "The Size of the Supportive Component in Organizations: A Multi-Organizational Analysis," *Social Forces*, October 1963, pp. 9–17; and Hawley, Boland, and Boland, "Population Size and Administration."

[51] William A. Rushing, "The Effects of Industry Size and Division of Labor on Administration," *Administrative Science Quarterly*, September 1967, pp. 273–95; and Sheila R. Klatzky, "Relationship of Organizational Size to Complexity and Coordination," *Administrative Science Quarterly*, December 1970, pp. 428–38.

[52] John H. Freeman, "Environment, Technology, and the Administrative Intensity of Manufacturing Organizations," *American Sociological Review*, December 1973, pp. 750–63.

[53] Gerry E. Hendershot and Thomas F. James, "Size and Growth as Determinants of Administrative-Production Ratios in Organizations," *American Sociological Review*, April 1972, pp. 149–53; John H. Freeman and Michael T. Hannan, "Growth and Decline Processes in Organizations," *American Sociological Review*, April 1975, pp. 215–28.

[54] Mintzberg, *The Structuring of Organizations*, p. 240.

[55] U.S. Department of Labor, Bureau of Labor Statistics, *Employment and Wages, First Quarter 1976* (Springfield, Va.: National Technical Information Service, 1979), pp. 548–49.

7

TECHNOLOGY

AFTER READING THIS CHAPTER, YOU SHOULD BE ABLE TO:

1   Define technology.
2   Describe the contributions of Woodward, Perrow, and Thompson.
3   Explain the moderating influence of industry and size on the technology-structure relationship.
4   Summarize how the concept of routineness runs through most studies on technology.
5   Identify the influence of level of analysis on the technology-structure relationship.
6   Describe the effect of technology on complexity, formalization, and centralization.

Introduction
FORD VERSUS AVANTI

The Ford Motor Company and the New Avanti Corp. both produce automobiles. You know about Ford. It builds about three million cars a year, worldwide, on an assembly-line basis. A typical Ford production line turns out fifty to sixty cars per hour. In contrast, you may not have heard of Avanti. Operating out of a former steel mill in Youngstown, Ohio, it makes high-performance luxury cars based on a twenty-five-year-old Studebaker design. Avanti hand-builds each car to order, one at a time, and its 130 production employees produce two cars a day. While both companies are in the automobile-manufacturing industry, they use dramatically different technologies to build their vehicles. Forgetting for a moment that Ford's size overwhelms Avanti—the former making more cars in twenty minutes worldwide than the latter produces in a year—you would expect these differences to effect the structures of their respective organizations. For instance, the tasks that employees do—highly routine and specialized at Ford and quite loose, flexible, and interchanging at Avanti—should have a significant influence on each one's structure. And, of course, it does.

The preceding example illustrates that the way in which an organization converts its inputs to outputs has some bearing on structure. Is it *the* dominant determinant of a structure or is it merely *a* determinant? By the time you finish reading this chapter, you will find that it can be both. As usual, however, let us begin by clarifying what we mean by the term. As with so many concepts in OT, the way in which it is defined and measured has a great deal to do with the consistency of the research surrounding it and the confidence we have in generalizing from this research. There is probably no construct in OT where diversity of measurement has produced more incompatible findings and confusion than the research on technology.

DEFINING TECHNOLOGY

As long as we stay at a relatively abstract level, there is general agreement among OT researchers that **technology** refers to the information, equipment, techniques, and processes required to transform inputs into outputs in the organization. That is, technology looks at *how* the inputs are converted to outputs. There is also agreement that the concept of technology, despite its mechanical or manufacturing connotation, is applicable to all types and kinds of organizations. As discussed in Chapter 1, all organizations turn inputs into outputs. Regardless of whether the organization is a manufacturing firm, a bank, a hospital, a social service agency, a research laboratory, a newspaper, or a military squadron, it will use a technology of some sort to produce its product or service.

The problems begin when we move from the abstract to the specific. At issue is basically the question, How does one measure technology? Researchers have used a number of technology classifications. A partial list would include operations techniques used in work-flow activities; characteristics of the materials used in the work flow; varying complexities in the knowledge system used in the work flow; the degree of continuous, fixed-sequence operations; the extent of automation; and the degree of interdependence between work systems. Each of these measures of technology is a bit different, and you would expect them to obtain different results even if they were applied to the same organization.

But this introduces several additional problems: varying types and sizes of organizations and different levels of analysis. Some studies have been limited to manufacturing firms. Others have included only very large organizations. Still others have been directed at the organizational level, yet the researchers attempt to compare their findings with studies conducted at the work unit or job level. Not surprisingly, these efforts to compare apples with oranges, under the guise of fruit, or generalizing to all organizations from samples that are highly limited, might be expected to end up producing conflicting results. And that is exactly what has happened.

Where does this leave us? To minimize confusion, we will restrict our discussion to only the landmark contributions to the technology-structure debate. We present the three paradigms cited most frequently and evaluate the research undertaken to test their validity. The three take very different perspectives on technology, but they will give you the basics for understanding what we know about how technology affects structure. After reviewing these three positions, we tie them together, ascertain where we stand today on the technological imperative, and determine what specific statements we can make accurately as to the impact of technology on structure.

THE INITIAL THRUST: WOODWARD'S RESEARCH

The initial interest in technology as a determinant of structure can be traced to the mid-1960s and the work of Joan Woodward.[1] Her research, which focused on production technology, was the first major attempt to view organization structure from a technological perspective.

Background

Woodward chose approximately one hundred manufacturing firms in the south of England. These firms ranged in size from fewer than two hundred and fifty employees to more than one thousand. She gathered data that allowed her to compute various measures of structure: the number of hierarchical levels, the span of control, the administrative component, the extent of formalization, and the like. She also gathered financial data on each firm (profitability, sales, market share, and so on) which allowed her to classify the companies as above average, average, or below average in terms of success or organizational effectiveness. Her objective was straightforward: Is there a correlation between structural form and effectiveness? Her hypothesis, derived from the classical prescriptions of management theorists, was that there is one optimum form of organizational structure that leads to organizational effectiveness.

Her efforts to link common structures with effectiveness were a dismal failure. The structural diversity among the firms in each of her effectiveness categories was so great that it was impossible to establish any relationship or draw any valid conclusions between what was regarded as sound organizational structure and effectiveness. It was only after Woodward grouped the firms according to their typical mode of production technology that relationships between structure and effectiveness became apparent.

Woodward categorized the firms into one of three types of technologies: **unit, mass,** or **process production.** She treated these categories as a scale with increasing degrees of technological complexity, with unit being the least complex and process the most complex. Unit producers would manufacture custom-made products such as tailor-made suits, turbines for hydroelectric dams, or Avanti cars. Mass producers would make large-batch or mass-produced products such as refrigerators or Ford automobiles. The third category, process production, included heavily automated continuous-process producers such as oil and chemical refiners.

Conclusions

Woodward found that there were (1) distinct relationships between these technology classifications and the subsequent structure of the firms, and (2) the effectiveness of the organizations were related to the "fit" between technology and structure.

For example, the degree of vertical differentiation increased with technical complexity. The median levels for firms in the unit, mass, and process categories were three, four, and six. More important, from an effectiveness standpoint, the above-average firms in each category tended to cluster around the median for their production group.

Woodward also found that the administrative component varied directly with type of technology; that is, as technological complexity increased, so did the proportion of administrative and supportive staff personnel. But not all the relationships were linear. For instance, the mass-production firms had the smallest proportion of skilled workers, and the mass-production firms scored high in terms of overall complexity and formalization, whereas the unit and process firms tended to rate low on these structural dimensions.

A careful analysis of her findings led Woodward to conclude that for each category on the technology scale (unit, mass, process) and for each structural component there was an optimal range around the median point that encompassed the positions of the more effective firms. That is, within each technological category, the firms that conformed most nearly to the median figures for each structural component were the most effective. (See Table 7–1). The mass-production technology firms were highly differentiated, relied on extensive formalization and did relatively little to delegate authority. Both the unit and process technologies, in contrast, were structured more loosely. Flexibility was achieved through less vertical differentiation, less division of labor and more group activities, more widely defined role responsibilities, and decentralized decision making. High formalization and centralized control apparently was not feasible with unit production's custommade, nonroutine technology and not necessary in the heavily automated, inherently tightly controlled, continuous-process technology.

Woodward's investigation demonstrated a link between tech-

TABLE 7–1   *Summary of Woodward's Findings on the Relationship between Technological Complexity and Structure*

STRUCTURAL CHARACTERISTIC	LOW ←	TECHNOLOGY	→ HIGH
	UNIT PRODUCTION	MASS PRODUCTION	PROCESS PRODUCTION
Number of vertical levels	3	4	6
Supervisor's span of control	24	48	14
Manager/total employee ratio	1:23	1:16	1:8
Proportion of skilled workers	High	Low	High
Overall complexity	Low	High	Low
Formalization	Low	High	Low
Centralization	Low	High	Low

nology, structure, and effectiveness. Firms that most nearly approximated the typical structure for their technology were most effective. Firms that deviated in either direction from their ideal structure were less successful. Therefore, Woodward argued that effectiveness was a function of an appropriate technology-structure fit. Organizations that developed structures that conformed to their technologies were more successful than those that did not.

Woodward was also able to explain the disparity between her findings and the classical prescriptions of management theorists—these principles must have been based on these theorists' experiences with organizations that used mass-production technologies. The mass-production firms had clear lines of authority, high formalization, a low proportion of skilled workers achieved through a high division of labor, wide spans of control at the supervisory level, and centralized decision making. But since all organizations don't use mass-production technology, these principles lacked generalizability. So Woodward's research spelled the beginning of the end for the view that there were universal principles of management and organization. Her work was to represent the initial transition by OT scholars from a principles perspective to a contingency theory of organizations.

Evaluation

Several follow-up studies have supported Woodward's findings, but she has also had her share of criticism. Let us review what others have had to say about Woodward's research.

Edward Harvey was an early advocate of Woodward.[2] He believed that the underlying foundation of Woodward's scale was technical specificity. That is, he assumed that more specific technologies present fewer problems that require new or innovative solutions than do more diffuse or complex technologies. So he took forty-three different industrial organizations and rated them as technically diffuse (which closely paralleled Woodward's unit production), technically intermediate (akin to mass production), and technically specific (similar to Woodward's process production). These categories were based on the number of major product changes that the sample firms had experienced in the ten years prior to the study. Harvey found, consistent with Woodward's technological imperative, a relationship between technical specificity and structure. Basically, organizations with specific technologies had more specialized subunits, more authority levels, and higher ratios of managers to total personnel than did those with diffuse technologies.

Woodward's findings were also supported in another study of manufacturing firms.[3] The researcher found, as Woodward did, no evidence that there was such a thing as a universally optimum structural form. His data constituted strong evidence to confirm Woodward's claim that unit, mass, and process production result in different structural forms and that proper fit within categories increased the likelihood that the organization would be successful.

Woodward's research and analysis by no means developed a tightly sealed argument for the technological imperative. Attacks have been made at a number of levels.[4] Her measure of technology has been criticized as unreliable. Her methodology, since it relied primarily on subjective observations and interviews, is open to interpretational bias. Woodward implies causation, yet her methodology can allow her to claim only association. Her measures of organizational success are open to attack as lacking rigor. Finally, since her firms were all British companies engaged almost exclusively in manufacturing, any generalizations to all organizations, or even to manufacturing firms outside Great Britain, must be guarded.

KNOWLEDGE-BASED TECHNOLOGY: PERROW'S CONTRIBUTION

One of the major limitations of Woodward's perspective on technology was its manufacturing base. Since manufacturing firms represent less than half of all organizations, technology needs to be operationalized in a more general way if the concept is to have meaning across all organizations. Charles Perrow has proposed such an alternative.[5]

Background

Perrow looked at knowledge technology rather than at production technology. He defined technology as "the action that an individual performs upon an object, with or without the aid of tools or mechanical devices, in order to make some change in that object."[6] Perrow then proceeded to identify what he believed to be the two underlying dimensions of knowledge technology.

The first dimension considers the number of exceptions encountered in one's work. Labeled **task variability,** these exceptions will be few in number if the job is high in routineness. Jobs that normally have few exceptions in their day-to-day practice include those on an automobile assembly line or as a fry cook at McDonald's. At the other end of the spectrum, if a job has a great deal of variety, a large number of exceptions can be expected. Typically, this characterizes top management positions, consulting jobs, or the work of those who make a living by putting out fires on offshore oil platforms. So task variability appraises work by evaluating it along a variety-routineness continuum.

The second dimension assesses the type of search procedures followed to find successful methods for responding adequately to task exceptions. The search can, at one extreme, be described as well defined. An individual can use logical and analytical reasoning in search for a solution. If you are basically a high-B student and you suddenly fail the first exam given in a course, you logically analyze the problem and find a solution. Did you spend enough time studying for the exam? Did you study the right material? Was the exam fair? How did other good students do? Using this kind of logic, you can find the source of the problem and rectify it.

In contrast, the other extreme would be ill-defined problems. If you are an architect assigned to design a building to conform to standards and constraints that you have never read about or encountered before, you will not have any formal search technique to use. You will have to rely on your prior experience, judgment, and intuition to find a solution. Through guess work and trial and error you might find an acceptable choice. Perrow called this second dimension **problem analyzability,** ranging from well defined to ill defined. Table 7–2 represents a ten-item questionnaire that measures these two dimensions.

These two dimensions—task variability and problem analyzability—can be used to construct a two-by-two matrix. This is shown in Figure 7–1. The four cells in this matrix represent four types of technology: routine, engineering, craft, and nonroutine.

Routine technologies (cell 1) have few exceptions and easy-to-

---

TABLE 7–2 *Measuring Technology*

Task variability and problem analyzability can be measured in an organizational unit by having employees answer the following ten questions. Scores are normally derived from responses scored on a one-to-seven scale for each question.

Task variability
1. How many of these tasks are the same from day to day?
2. To what extent would you say your work is routine?
3. People in this unit do about the same job in the same way most of the time.
4. Basically, unit members perform repetitive activities in doing their jobs.
5. How repetitive are your duties?

Problem analyzability
1. To what extent is there a clearly known way to do the major types of work you normally encounter?
2. To what extent is there a clearly defined body of knowledge of subject matter which can guide you in doing your work?
3. To what extent is there an understandable sequence of steps that can be followed in doing your work?
4. To do you work, to what extent can you actually rely on established procedures and practices?
5. To what extent is there an understandable sequence of steps that can be followed in carrying out your work?

Michael Withey, Richard L. Daft, and William H. Cooper, "Measures of Perrow's Work Unit Technology: An Empirical Assessment and a New Scale," *Academy of Management Journal,* March 1983, p. 59.

FIGURE 7–1 *Perrow's Technology Classification*

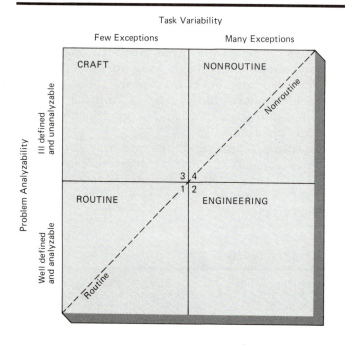

analyze problems. The mass-production processes used to make steel or automobiles or to refine petroleum belong in this category. A bank teller's job is also an example of activities subsumed under routine technology. **Engineering technologies** (cell 2) have a large number of exceptions, but they can be handled in a rational and systematic manner. The construction of office buildings would fall in this cell, as would the activities performed by tax accountants. **Craft technologies** (cell 3) deal with relatively difficult problems but with a limited set of exceptions. This would include shoemaking, furniture restoring, or the work of performing artists. Finally, **nonroutine technologies** (cell 4) are characterized by many exceptions and difficult-to-analyze problems. Examples of nonroutine technologies would be strategic planning and basic research activities. In summary, Perrow argued that if problems can be studied systematically, using logical and rational analysis, cells 1 or 2 would be appropriate. Problems that can be handled only by intuition, guesswork, or unanalyzed experience require the technology of cells 3 or 4. Similarly, if new, unusual, or unfamiliar problems appear regularly, they would be in either cells 2 or 4. If problems are familiar, then cells 1 or 3 are appropriate.

Perrow also proposed that task variability and problem analyzability were positively correlated. By that he meant that it would be unusual to find instances where tasks had very few exceptions and search was clearly unanalyzable or where tasks had a great many exceptions and search was well defined and easily analyzable. So the four technologies can be combined into a single routine-nonroutine dimension. This is shown in Figure 7–1 as a diagonal line.

Conclusions

Perrow argued that control and coordination methods should vary with technology type. The more routine the technology, the more highly structured the organization should be. Conversely, nonroutine technologies require greater structural flexibility. Perrow then identified the key aspects of structure that could be modified to the technology: (1) the amount of *discretion* that can be exercised for completing tasks, (2) the *power* of groups to control the unit's goals and basic strategies, (3) the extent of *interdependence* between these groups, and (4) the extent to which these groups engage in *coordination* of their work using either feedback or the planning of others.

What does all this mean? Simply that the most routine technology (cell 1) can be accomplished best through standardized coordination and control. These technologies should be aligned with structures that are high in both formalization and centralization. At the other extreme, nonroutine technologies (cell 4) demand flexibility. Basically, they would be decentralized, have high interaction among all members, and be characterized as having a minimum degree of formalization. In between, craft technology (cell 3) requires that problem solving be done by those with the greatest knowledge and experience. That means decentralization. And engineering technology (cell 2), because it has many exceptions but analyzable search processes, should have decisions centralized but should maintain flexibility through low formalization. Table 7–3 summarizes Perrow's predictions.

TABLE 7–3 *Perrow's Technology-Structure Predictions*

CELL	TECHNOLOGY	STRUCTURAL CHARACTERISTIC			
		FORMALIZATION	CENTRALIZATION	SPAN OF CONTROL	COORDINATION AND CONTROL
1	Routine	High	High	Wide	Planning and rigid rules
2	Engineering	Low	High	Moderate	Reports and meetings
3	Craft	Moderate	Low	Moderate-wide	Training and meetings
4	Nonroutine	Low	Low	Moderate-narrow	Group norms and group meetings

Evaluation

The two-by-two matrix of technologies and the predictions of what structural dimensions are most compatible with these technologies were not examined empirically by Perrow. But others have tested the theory.

One study of fourteen medium-sized manufacturing firms that looked only at the two extreme cells—routine and nonroutine technologies—found support for Perrow's predictions.[7] Another, covering sixteen health and welfare agencies, confirmed (1) that organizations do have diverse technologies and (2) that the more routine the work, the more likely decision making will be centralized.[8]

State employment-service agencies were the set of organizations analyzed in yet another test of Perrow's theory.[9] In this study, technology was operationalized at the unit rather than the organizational level, in the belief that if routineness of technology actually affects structure, this effect should be greatest at the unit level. Again, the results proved consistent with Perrow's predictions: work that was high in routineness was associated with high formalization.

In summary, there appears to be considerable support for Perrow's conclusions. Organizations and organizational subunits with routine technologies tend to have greater formalization and centralization than do their counterparts with nonroutine technologies.

One note of caution before we move on. Perrow's original theory went somewhat beyond what we have presented here. He predicted, for instance, relationships between the type of technology and structural aspects such as hierarchical discretion levels and types of coordination. These other relationships have found limited support by way of empirical studies.[10] We point this out to acknowledge that Perrow has his critics and that there is ammunition available for attacking his matrix theory. But at the general level—and by that we mean the issues of whether technologies can be differentiated on the basis of routineness and whether more routine technologies are associated with higher degrees of formalization and centralization—the evidence is largely supportive.

TECHNOLOGICAL UNCERTAINTY: THOMPSON'S CONTRIBUTION

The third major contribution to the technology-structure literature has been made by James Thompson.[11] In contrast to Woodward and Perrow, Thompson is not a member of the technological-imperative school. Rather, as will be shown, Thompson's contribution lies in demonstrating that technology determines the selection of a strategy for reducing uncertainty and that specific structural arrangements can facilitate uncertainty reduction.

Background

Thompson sought to create a classification scheme that was general enough to deal with the range of technologies found in complex organizations. He proposed three types that are differentiated by the tasks that an organizational unit performs.

Long-linked Technology. If tasks or operations are sequentially interdependent, Thompson called them long-linked. This technology is characterized by a fixed sequence of repetitive steps, as shown in Figure 7–2A. That is, activity A must be performed before activity B, activity B before activity C, and so forth. Examples of **long-linked technology** include mass-production assembly lines and most school cafeterias.

Because long-linked technologies require efficiency and coordination among activities, owing to sequential interdependencies, the major uncertainties facing management lie on the input and output sides of the organization. Acquiring raw materials, for instance, and disposing of finished goods become major areas of concern. As a result, management tends to respond to this uncertainty by controlling inputs and outputs. One of the best means for achieving this end is to integrate vertically—forward, backward, or both. This allows the organization to encompass important sources of uncertainty within its boundaries. Reynolds Metals, for example, has large plants for manufacturing aluminum foil. It integrates backward by controlling its input, operating aluminum mines and reduction mills that provide the raw materials to the foil plants. It integrates forward by controlling its output, mar-

FIGURE 7–2 *Thompson's Technology Classification*

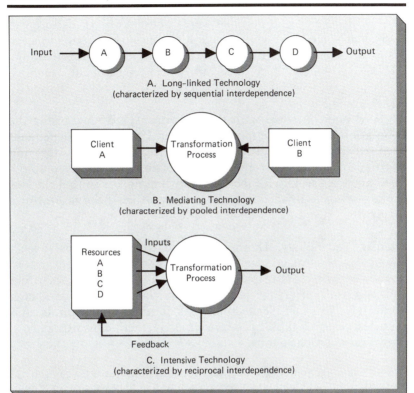

A. Long-linked Technology
(characterized by sequential interdependence)

B. Mediating Technology
(characterized by pooled interdependence)

C. Intensive Technology
(characterized by reciprocal interdependence)

keting much of its foil through supermarkets under the name of Reynolds Wrap.

Mediating Technology. Thompson identified **mediating technology** as one that links clients on both the input and output side of the organization. Banks, telephone utilities, most large retail stores, computer-dating services, employment and welfare agencies, and post offices are examples. As shown in Figure 7–2B, mediators perform an interchange function linking units that are otherwise independent. The linking unit responds with standardizing the organization's transactions and establishing conformity in clients' behavior. Banks, for instance, bring together those who want to save (depositors) with those who want to borrow. They don't know each other, but the bank's success depends on attracting both. A bank with money and no borrowers cannot succeed. Failure can also occur when borrowers are plentiful but no one wants to leave his or her money with the bank. As a result, the managers of mediating technologies face uncertainty as a result of the organization's potential dependency on clients and the risks inherent in client transactions.

How does one deal with this uncertainty? By increasing the populations served. The more clients one has, the less dependent one is upon any single client. So banks seek many depositors and attempt to develop a diversified loan portfolio. Similarly, employment agencies seek to fill jobs for many employers so that the loss of one or two major accounts will not jeopardize the organization's survival.

Intensive Technology.   Thompson's third category—**intensive technology**—represents a customized response to a diverse set of contingencies. The exact response depends on the nature of the problem and the variety of problems, which cannot be predicted accurately. This includes technologies dominant in hospitals, universities, research labs, full-service management-consulting firms, or military combat teams.

The intensive technology is most dramatically illustrated by the general hospital. At any moment an emergency admission may require some combination of dietary, X-ray, laboratory, and housekeeping or hotel services, together with the various medical specialties, pharmaceutical services, occupational therapies, social work services, and spiritual or religious services. Which of these, and when, can be determined only from evidence about the state of the patient.[12]

Figure 7–2C demonstrates that intensive technology achieves coordination through mutual adjustment. A number of multiple resources are available to the organization, but only a limited combination is used at a given time depending on the situation. The selection, combination, and ordering of these resources are determined by feedback from the object itself. Because of this need for flexibility of response, the major uncertainty that managers confront is the problem itself. So managers respond by ensuring the availability of a variety of resources to prepare for any contingency.

As in our hospital example, the organization has a wealth of specialized services and skills available with which it can respond to a variety of situations.

Conclusions

The structural implications from Thompson's framework are less straightforward than are those derived from the work of Woodward and Perrow. Basically, each technology creates a type of interdependence. Long-linked technology is accompanied by **sequential interdependence**—the procedures are highly standardized and must be performed in a specified serial order. Mediating technology has **pooled interdependence**—two or more units each contribute separately to a larger unit. Intensive technology creates **reciprocal interdependence**—the outputs of units influence each other in a reciprocal fashion. Each of these interdependencies, in turn, demands a certain type of coordination that will facilitate organizational effectiveness yet minimize costs.

In general terms, we can translate Thompson's insights into structural terminology. He argued that the demands placed on decision making and communication as a result of technology increased from mediating (low) to long-linked (medium) to intensive (high). Mediating technology is coordinated most effectively through rules and procedures. Long-linked should be accompanied by planning and scheduling. Intensive technology requires mutual adjustment. This suggests that

> Mediating technology = low complexity and high formalization
> Long-linked technology = moderate complexity and formalization
> Intensive technology = high complexity and low formalization

Let us look at the research to evaluate empirically the validity of Thompson's predictions.

Evaluation

There is, unfortunately, a shortage of data against which Thompson's predictions can be judged. The only study of consequence using Thompson's dimensions measured not structure but rather the technology-organizational effectiveness relationship.[13] Analyzing 297 subunits from seventeen business and industrial firms, investigators were able to support part of Thompson's model. Long-linked and mediating technologies were associated closely with the use of standardization, rules, and advanced planning, whereas intensive technologies were characterized by mutual adjustments to other units. They concluded that the criterion of effectiveness varies with the type of technology used by the organizational unit.

The lack of data makes it impossible to conclude whether Thompson's framework is valid or invalid. It is interesting and it allows for comparing a wide range of varying organizations. Its value, however, may lie far more in offering a rich and descriptive technology classification than in providing insights into the relationship between technology and structure.

TYING IT TOGETHER: WHAT DOES IT ALL MEAN?

In this section, we integrate what we know about technology and draw some meaningful generalizations from what is clearly a highly heterogeneous body of research. We can begin by looking at two variables that may confound the technology-structure relationship.

Influence of Industry and Size

Technology and structure are both multidimensional concepts. As a result, it is possible that technology may be related to structure although not in any simple, straightforward manner. There are, in fact, some logical arguments to support the idea that the industry within which the organization operates and the organization's size confound a clear causal relationship between technology and structure.

Industry. In Chapter 5, we discussed industry as a determinant of structure by way of its impact on strategy. Here we again discuss industry but in terms of its interrelationship with technology.

Organizations within any given industry may have to adopt the conventional core technology to be competitive. Just as industry often influences the efficient operating size of an organization, its degree of competition, or extent of government regulation, it can also limit the viable set of technology options.[14] For example, a consumer's purchase of videocassette blank tapes is a decision based substantially on price. Sales volume favors the low-cost manufacturer, which essentially demands that firms in this industry use a technology along the lines of mass production. Similarly, supermarket chains have little choice but to implement a standardized and routine technology in their core operations.

Obviously, an organization's industry—and the niche within the industry that the organization has chosen—does not *dictate* a given technology. You could, for example, build a huge, 80,000-square-foot supermarket in a suburban shopping mall with an engineering type of technology. You could have all the merchandise behind counters, put four or five dozen clerks behind the counters, and have the clerks gather each customer's order by selecting items one by one off the shelf. Why don't supermarkets do this? Because it's inefficient! In some large cities there are one or two grocery stores that offer such specialized service. Note, however, that they operate in a unique niche (usually gourmet foods) and their prices are almost always a lot higher than those found at the popular serve-yourself supermarkets.

Size. The strongest attacks against the technological imperative has come from those who argue that organizational size is the critical determinant of structure.[15] For instance, several of the Aston Group studies failed to find an association between technology and organization structure.[16] Rather, size was found to have a more dominant influence on structure.

In one case, the Aston Group was able to support Woodward's conclusions concerning technology and structure, but again the explanation for the association was based on size.[17] If technology has an influence on structure, the Aston Group reasoned, it is most likely to affect those activities closest to the technology itself. Therefore, the larger the size of the organization, the smaller the role technology is likely to play. Conversely, the smaller the organization, the more likely it is that the whole organization will be impinged upon by the production work flow or operating core. They then noted that the firms Woodward sampled were basically small in size and thus more likely to be influenced by their technology. Their conclusion: in smaller organizations the structure of operations is likely to be dominated by the primary transformation process, but in large organizations the impact of technology is not likely to be so powerful. And where is technology's influence the greatest? On those organizational units immediately impinged upon by the operating core.

The preceding discussion suggests that an organization's size moderates the impact of technology on structure. In small organizations, divisions of large organizations, or organizational activities most closely related to the operating core, technology should explain more of the resultant structure.

Summary. Figure 7–3 illustrates an integration of the industry-size-technology-structure relationship. Industry constrains technology options. But organizations need to reach a particular size before advantages can be obtained from the benefits offered by the more complex technologies. The decision to adopt a complex technology is unlikely to be made until the organization has reached a large enough size to capitalize on economies of scale. So size determines technology. Yet, as Figure 7–3 demonstrates, the causal arrow can also go the other way—from technology to size. The decision, for example, to use mass-production technology may lead to the decision to increase the organization's size so as to enable it to better utilize the technology more efficiently. Discount stock brokerage firms use a routine technology but require a sizable operation with reasonably high volume in order to operate profitably.

FIGURE 7–3 *Industry-Size Integrative Model*

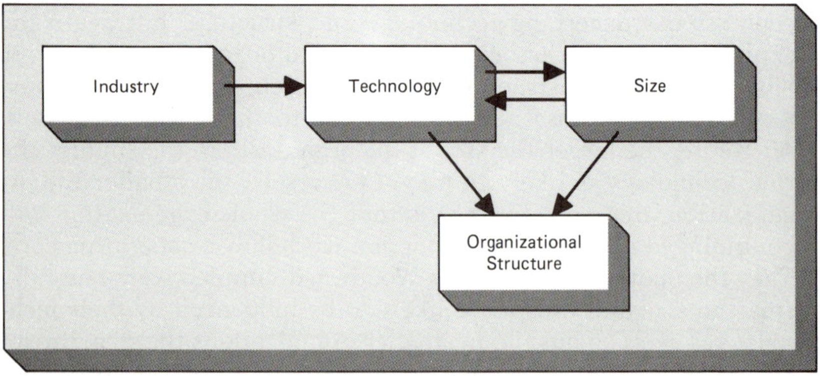

The Common Denominator: Routineness

The common theme throughout this chapter, sometimes more explicitly evident than others, is that the processes or methods that transform inputs into outputs differ by their degree of routineness.[18]

Woodward identified three types of technology—unit, mass, and process—each representing, respectively, an increased degree of technological complexity. At the extremes, unit technology deals with custom or nonroutine activities; process technology describes automated and standardized activities. Her mass technology is basically routine in nature. Perrow, too, presented two extremes—routine and nonroutine technologies. His "in-between" technologies—engineering and craft—also differ on routineness, the former more standardized than the latter. Finally, Thompson's categories include two technologies that are relatively routine (long-linked and mediating) and one that is nonroutine (intensive). Table 7–4 summarizes these observations.

The research on technology has gone a number of different ways, yet there is a common underlying theme. Of course, the technology paradigms of Woodward, Perrow, Thompson, and others are not substitutable for each other. But this is not a book for researchers. Our intention is to provide some insights into organization theory for use by managers. Given this less demanding objective, conceptualizing technology as differing by degrees of routineness should be adequate for our analysis, included at the end of this chapter, which evaluates technology's impact on our three structural components.

TABLE 7–4 *Cataloging Technologies as Routine or Nonroutine*

	TECHNOLOGY	
CONTRIBUTOR	ROUTINE	NONROUTINE
Woodward	Mass, Process	Unit
Perrow	Routine, Engineering	Craft, Nonroutine
Thompson	Long-linked, Mediating	Intensive

TECHNOLOGY AND THE COLLEGE CLASSROOM

How many different instruction technologies are there to teach college students? There is the ever-popular formal lecture method, but there are other ways to transform the uninformed into the enlightened. These would include the case analysis method, the laboratory method, the group discussion method, the experiential exercise method, and the programmed learning method.

The most effective technology is clearly constrained by class size. A decision to teach introductory psychology in class sections of five hundred students almost precludes case study and discussion methods. Large size dictates a routine technology. Why? Because an instructor can't effectively manage a classroom with hundreds of students if each student requires a great deal of special attention. Moderating factors like the availability of graduate assistants or the use of true-false and multiple-choice examinations can allow faculty members to effectively reach a large number of students, but we should still expect to find routine technologies with large class sizes.

Students who desire the special attention of a nonroutine technology are not without options. The small, private college fits this niche in the higher education market. But providing nonroutine technology is expensive. Colleges that have average class sizes of eight or ten students also typically have average tuition fees at or above eight to ten thousand dollars a year.

Work-Unit Level Versus Organizational Level

Organizations and their components are rarely homogeneous, but some studies seem to have overlooked this reality. If differentiation is a characteristic of complex organizations, then shouldn't subunits within these organizations typically be diverse?

Any basketball fan would be quick to point out that a team comprised of one seven-foot-three-inch-ball player, two at six feet eight inches, and two at six feet two has a very different mix from one with five players who are each six feet seven inches. Their averages are the same, but those averages are deceiving. Why?

Because averages alone ignore variations. What's true for basketball teams is also true for organizations with diverse technologies. Almost all large organizations and many of moderate size have multiple technologies. Averaging these subunits to arrive at a composite measure or simply identifying a singular technology from among several and calling it the dominant technology ends up misrepresenting the true state of affairs. We should expect that studies assessing the technology-structure relationship at the organizational level of analysis, where there is a great deal of variation in technology between subunits, would result in aggregate measures that are likely to be meaningless. As we'll see, this is precisely what happens.

Technology research has been undertaken at the organizational and work unit levels. Both view technology as the means by which tasks are accomplished, but one considers the organization as the unit of analysis, and the other considers the work unit as the primary unit. Organizational-level analysis starts with the major product or service offered, which leads it to focus on the dominant conversion technology. Work-unit-level analysis starts with the tasks performed by individual employees, leading it to consider the methods by which they are accomplished.

When these two types of studies are combined, it is difficult if not impossible to draw useful conclusions. However, when they are separated, a clear pattern emerges. The organizational-level studies still are mixed, with few consistent relationships appearing between technology and structure. But the work-unit-level studies provide a completely different picture. In evaluating the relationship between technology and a set of structural variables in eight work-unit-level studies, at least half the correlations were found to be significant, and all were in the same direction.[19]

Why do work-level studies support the technological imperative, whereas those at the organizational level do not? Several explanations have been offered.[20] First, work-unit level studies have far fewer conceptual and methodological problems. They hold a unified concept of technology, and homogeneity is greater. The other reason for the high technology-structure correlation at the work-unit level is undoubtedly related to size. Work-unit-level studies are looking at technology at the operating core. If there is a technological imperative, this is where it should be most evident because technology's impact should be greatest closest to the core. The fact that organizational-level studies are conceptually and methodologically heterogeneous, plus the realization that technology at this level should have a lesser effect on structure, suggest that a reasonable doubt must remain concerning the demise of the technological imperative. And if there is such an imperative, it may exist only with small organizations or those with homogeneous technologies throughout.

Manufacturing Versus Service Technologies

In addition to causing problems by mixing studies using varied levels of analysis, researchers have also been guilty of mixing manufacturing and service organizations. Summaries of studies assessing the relationship between technology and structure indicate that nearly 80 percent of those that looked at *only* manufacturing organizations or service organizations supported the relationship. But when data from manufacturing and service settings were combined, only about 14 percent achieved supportive results.[21] This suggests that there may be real differences between the dominant technologies in the two types of organizations. Moreover, when the researchers combine the two types of organizations, they may wash out underlying relationships. So research studies that combine manufacturing and service organizations are less likely to find a significant relationship between technology and structure.

Conclusions

The technology-structure relationship is not at all clear. Technology has, in most studies, been presented in a narrow and singular view. That is, firm X uses technology Y and has a structure described as Z. In reality, firm X undoubtedly employs several technologies. Since organizations do diverse things, most use different methods with different activities. Even accepting the simplified single-technology perspective, technology's impact on structure is not *all-pervasive*. It is more likely applicable to structural dimensions at or near the organization's operating core and to smaller more than larger organizations. Consistent with selectivity, it also affects some structural dimensions more than others. Its varying impact on these structural dimensions is the subject of our next section.

TECHNOLOGY AND STRUCTURE

As we have done with strategy and size, we now want to review the literature to determine the relationship of technology to the three structural dimensions of complexity, formalization, and centralization. Despite all the qualifications stated in the previous section, there are some important findings.

Technology and Complexity

The evidence, while not overwhelming, indicates that routine technology is positively associated with low complexity. The greater the routineness, the fewer the number of occupational groups and the less training possessed by professionals.[22] This relationship is more likely to hold for the structural activities in or near the operating core—such as the proportion of maintenance employees and the span of control of first-line supervisors.

The reverse also holds; that is, nonroutine technology is likely to lead to high complexity. As the work becomes more sophisticated and customized, the span of control narrows and vertical differentiation increases.[23] This, of course, is intuitively logical. Customized responses require a greater use of specialists, and managers require a smaller span of control because the problems that they confront are mostly of the nonprogrammed variety.

Technology and Formalization

A review of five major technology studies found routine technology to be positively related with formalization. While only one of the sample correlations was statistically significant, all were positive, which has a one-in-one-thousand occurrence due to chance.[24] However, when size was controlled for, the relationship vanished. Another study also supported the routineness-formalization relationship.[25] Routineness was significantly associated with the presence of a rules manual, presence of job descriptions, and the degree to which job descriptions were specified. Routine technologies permit management to implement rules and other formalized regulations because how to do the job is well understood, and the job is repetitive enough to justify the cost to develop such formalized systems. Nonroutine technologies require control systems that permit greater discretion and flexibility.

These studies suggest that care must be taken in generalizing about technology's impact on formalization. That they are related is undoubtedly true. But when controlled for size, most of this association disappears. We propose, therefore, that the relationship holds for small organizations and activities at or near the operating core. As the operating core becomes more routine, the operating work becomes more predictable. In such situations, high formalization is an efficient coordination device.

Technology and Centralization

The technology-centralization relationship generates inconsistent results. The logical argument would be that routine technologies would be associated with a centralized structure, whereas the nonroutine technology, which would rely more heavily on the knowledge of the specialist, would be characterized by delegated decision authority. This position has met with some support.[26]

A more generalizable conclusion is that the technology-centralization relationship is moderated by the degree of formalization.[27] Both formal regulations and centralized decision making are control mechanisms, and management can substitute them for one another. Routine technologies should be associated with centralized control if there is a minimum of rules and regulations. However, if formalization is high, routine technology can be accompanied by decentralization. So we would predict routine technology to lead to centralization but only if formalization is low.

SUMMARY

Technology refers to the processes and methods that transform inputs into outputs in the organization. The three landmark contributions to understanding technology were presented by Joan Woodward, Charles Perrow, and James Thompson.

Woodward proposed three types of production technology: unit, mass, and process. Her major contribution lay in identifying distinct relationships among these technology classes and the subsequent structure of the firms, and in indicating that the effectiveness of the firms was related to the "fit" between technology and structure.

Perrow proposed a broader view of technology by looking at knowledge. He identified two underlying dimensions of knowledge technology: task variability and problem analyzability. These combine to create four types of technology: routine, engineering, craft, and nonroutine. Perrow concluded that the more routine the technology, the more highly structured the organization should be.

Thompson demonstrated that the interdependency created by a technology is important in determining an organization's structure. Specifically, he identified long-linked, mediating, and intensive technologies; noted the unique interdependency of each; determined how each dealt with the uncertainty it faced; and predicted the structural coordination devices that were most economical for each.

We concluded that the technological imperative, if it exists, is supported best by job-level research, is most likely to apply only to small organizations and to those structural arrangements at or near the operating core, and that "routineness" is the common denominator underlying most of the research on technology.

Finally, evidence indicates that routine technology is positively associated with low complexity and high formalization. Routine technology is positively correlated with centralization but only if formalization is low.

FOR REVIEW AND DISCUSSION

1. What does the term *technology* mean?
2. What are the main contributions to OT made by Joan Woodward? Charles Perrow? James Thompson?
3. Describe the various technologies that might be used in
   a. a plumbing-repair firm
   b. the admissions office at a highly selective college
   c. a firm that manufactures wristwatches
4. Clarify how "routineness" reconciles the more specific technology classifications.
5. How are technology and interdependence related, if at all?
6. Differentiate between work-unit-level and organizational-level analyses of technology. Which has proven to be more valuable in explaining organization structures? Why?
7. "Technology is really part of strategy." What does this mean?
8. Under what conditions is technology likely to be a major determinant of structure?
9. What is the relationship between technology, size, industry, and structure?
10. How does technology influence a classroom's structure? Is size a stronger determinant? Explain.

11. In what ways might a service organization's technology be different from a manufacturing organization's?
12. How would you measure an organization's technology?
13. If you were analyzing an organization's technology and found there were four different types—ranging from routine to nonroutine—how would you assess the impact of technology on this organization's structure?
14. What is an organization's *dominant* technology?
15. Where do top-level management positions fall on Perrow's two-by-two matrix? Why? Does your answer suggest that management can be taught? Explain.

NOTES

[1] Joan Woodward, *Industrial Organization: Theory and Practice* (London: Oxford University Press, 1965).

[2] Edward Harvey, "Technology and the Structure of Organizations," *American Sociological Review*, April 1968, pp. 247–59.

[3] William L. Zwerman, *New Perspectives on Organization Theory* (Westport, Conn.: Greenwood Publishing, 1970).

[4] See, for example, Lex Donaldson, "Woodward Technology, Organizational Structure, and Performance—A Critique of the Universal Generalization," *Journal of Management Studies*, October 1976, pp. 255–73.

[5] Charles Perrow, "A Framework for the Comparative Analysis of Organizations," *American Sociological Review*, April 1967, pp. 194–208.

[6] Ibid.

[7] Karl Magnusen, "Technology and Organizational Differentiation: A Field Study of Manufacturing Corporations." Doctoral dissertation, University of Wisconsin, Madison, 1970.

[8] Jerald Hage and Michael Aiken, "Routine Technology, Social Structure, and Organizational Goals," *Administrative Science Quarterly*, September 1969, pp. 366–77.

[9] Andrew H. Van de Ven and André L. Delbecq, "A Task Contingent Model of Work-Unit Structure," *Administrative Science Quarterly*, June 1974, pp. 183–97.

[10] See, for example, Lawrence Mohr, "Operations Technology and Organizational Structure," *Administrative Science Quarterly*, December 1971, pp. 444–59.

[11] James D. Thompson, *Organizations in Action* (New York: McGraw-Hill, 1967).

[12] Ibid., p. 17.

[13] Thomas A. Mahoney and Peter J. Frost, "The Role of Technology in Models of Organizational Effectiveness," *Organizational Behavior and Human Performance*, February 1974, pp. 122–38.

[14] Raymond E. Miles and Charles C. Snow, "Toward a Synthesis in Organization Theory," in M. Jelinek, J. A. Litterer, and R. E. Miles, *Organizations by Design: Theory and Practice* (Plano, Tex.: Business Publications, 1981), pp. 549–51.

[15] It is interesting that a careful review of a recent study that proposes to give renewed support to the technological imperative (see Robert M. Marsh and Hiroshi Mannari, "Technology and Size as Determinants of the Organizational Structure of Japanese Factories," *Administrative Science Quarterly*, March 1981, pp. 33–57) finds that complexity and formalization are a function of size and that centralization varies randomly in relation to both technology and size.

[16] David J. Hickson, D. S. Pugh, and Diana C. Pheysey, "Operations Technology and Organization Structure: An Empirical Reappraisal," *Administrative Science Quarterly*, September 1979, pp. 378–97; and D. S. Pugh, D. J. Hickson, C. R. Hinings, and C. Turner, "The Context of Organization Structures," *Administrative Science Quarterly*, March 1969, pp. 91–114.

[17] Hickson, et al., "Operations Technology."

[18] See Donald Gerwin, "Relationships between Structure and Technology at the Organizational and Job Levels," *Journal of Management Studies*, February 1979, p. 71; and James L. Price and Charles W. Mueller, *Handbook of Organizational Measurement* (Marshfield, Mass.: Pitman, 1986), pp. 209–14.

[19] Donald Gerwin, "Relationships between Structure and Technology."

[20] Ibid; and Louis W. Fry, "Technology-Structure Research: Three Critical Issues," *Academy of Management Journal*, September 1982, pp. 532–52.

[21] Peter Mills and Dennis J. Moberg, "Perspectives on the Technology of Service Organizations," *Academy of Management Review*, July 1982, pp. 467–78.

[22] Hage and Aiken, "Routine Technology," pp. 366–77.

[22] See, for example, Stanley H. Udy, Jr., *Organization of Work* (New Haven, Conn.: HRAF Press, 1959); Hickson et al., "Operations Technology," and Raymond G. Hunt, "Technology and Organization," *Academy of Management Journal*, September 1970, pp. 235–52.

[24] Gerwin, "Relationships between Structure and Technology."

[25] Hage and Aiken, "Routine Technology."

[26] Andrew Van de Ven, André Delbecq, and Richard Koenig, Jr., "Determinants of Coordination Modes within Organizations," *American Sociological Review*, April 1976, pp. 322–38.

[27] Jerald Hage and Michael Aiken, "Relationship of Centralization to Other Structural Properties," *Administrative Science Quarterly*, June 1967, pp. 72–92.

8

ENVIRONMENT

AFTER READING THIS CHAPTER, YOU SHOULD BE ABLE TO:

1 Define environment.
2 Differentiate the specific from the general environment.
3 Explain the key dimensions of environmental uncertainty.
4 Describe the contributions of Burns and Stalker, Emery and Trist, and Lawrence and Lorsch.
5 Review the three-stage process of change in the population-ecology model.
6 Contrast mechanistic and organic structures.
7 Describe the effect of environmental uncertainty on complexity, formalization, and centralization.

Introduction
THINGS ARE CHANGING
AT PROCTER & GAMBLE

For decades, Procter & Gamble was *the* dominant force in the soap and packaged-food industry.[1] Its large bureaucratic structure—with autonomous divisions and centralized decision making—worked efficiently because P&G was the dominant player in almost every market in which it competed. The practice of high centralization—for example, the decision on whether the company's new decaffeinated instant Folger's coffee should have a green or gold cap went up to P&G's CEO—worked because the company faced a stable environment. P&G didn't introduce many new

204

products because it didn't have to. And when new products were developed, they went through long and thorough test-marketing before actual launching. P&G prided itself on following a low-risk approach to its business.

In recent years, however, P&G's most respected and long-dominant brand names have found themselves up against vigorous competition. Long-time competitors were no longer content to live in P&G's shadow. For example, Crest was losing market share to Colgate and new rival liquid detergents were eroding some of Tide's market. P&G has responded with some dramatic structural changes. Interdivisional teams have been created to coordinate projects across divisional lines. Top management has begun to loosen its stranglehold on decision making; business teams have been created that can make decisions on everything from product development to cost-cutting. And production employees are making most day-to-day operating decisions. As a result of these changes, P&G has become a more aggressive and responsive force in its markets. It is now developing more products than ever before and getting them to the marketplace much quicker.

In Chapter 1, we discussed organizations in an open-systems framework. The key to understanding organizations as open systems, we said, was the recognition that organizations interact with their environment. But since that introduction, we have said little about the environment and its impact on the organization. In this chapter, that omission will be rectified.

A common theme in organization theory is that organizations must adapt to their environments if they are to maintain or increase their effectiveness. In open-systems terms, we can think of organizations as developing monitoring and feedback mechanisms to identify and follow their environments, sense changes in those environments, and make appropriate adjustments as necessary. At Procter & Gamble, management realized that its environment had changed—competitors had become more aggressive—which required P&G to adapt if it were to continue to be the dominant force in its industry.

In this chapter, we clarify what we mean by the term *environment* and assess the relationship between environment and structure. A central point throughout this chapter is that different organizations face different degrees of environmental uncertainty. Because managers do not like uncertainty, they try to eliminate it or, at least, minimize its impact on their organization. We demonstrate that structural design is a major tool that managers have for controlling environmental uncertainty.

DEFINING ENVIRONMENT

There is no shortage of definitions for environment. Their common thread is consideration of factors outside the organization itself. For instance, the most popular definition identifies the **environment** as everything outside an organization's boundaries. One author has proposed that ascertaining an organization's environment appears simple enough. "Just take the universe, subtract from it the subset that represents the organization, and the remainder is environment."[2] We agree with this writer when he adds that, unfortunately, it really isn't that simple. First, let us differentiate between an organization's general and its specific environment.

General Versus Specific Environment

An organization's environment and general environment are essentially the same. The latter includes everything, such as economic factors, political conditions, the social milieu, the legal structure, the ecological situation, and cultural conditions. The **general environment** encompasses conditions that *may* have an impact on the organization, but their relevance is not overtly clear. Consider genetic engineering, which is in the general environment for drug firms. Though there is little current applicability of genetic engineering to products offered by most drug companies, it is very likely that breakthroughs in this area will totally reshape the products that drug manufacturers will be marketing in the 21st century. The management at drug firms such as Merck, Schering, and Bristol-Myers must recognize that advances in genetic engineering will undoubtedly have a far-reaching impact on their organizations' future growth and profitability. But the impact of genetic engineering on drug firms is only potentially relevant. As a result, organizations give the bulk of their attention to their specific environment.

The **specific environment** is that part of the environment that is directly relevant to the organization in achieving its goals. At any given moment, it is the part of the environment with which management will be concerned because it is made up of those critical constituencies that can positively or negatively influence the organization's effectiveness. It is unique to each organization and it changes with conditions. Typically, it will include clients or customers, suppliers of inputs, competitors, government regulatory agencies, labor unions, trade associations, and public pressure groups (see Figure 8–1). The United Steelworkers' Union is in the specific environment of Inland Steel but in the general environment of Mary Kay cosmetics. An appliance manufacturer, who had never sold to Sears, Roebuck, recently signed a three-year contract to sell 40 percent of its output of washing machines to Sears to be sold under the retailer's Kenmore brand. This action moved Sears from the manufacturer's general environment to its specific environment.

An organization's specific environment will vary depending on the domain it has chosen. **Domain** refers to the claim that the organization stakes out for itself with respect to the range of products or services offered and markets served. It identifies the organization's niche. Volkswagen and Mercedes are both German firms that manufacture automobiles, but they operate in distinctly

FIGURE 8–1 *The Organization and Its Specific Environment*

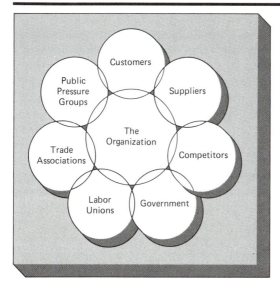

different domains. Similarly, Miami-Dade Junior College and the University of Michigan are both public institutions of higher education, but they do substantially different things and appeal to different segments of the higher-education market. These two colleges have identified different domains.

Why is the concept of domain important? It is because the domain of an organization determines the points at which it is dependent upon its specific environment.[3] Change the domain and you will change the specific environment.

Actual Versus Perceived Environment

Any attempt to define environment requires making a distinction between the objective or actual environment and the one that managers perceive. Evidence indicates that measures of the actual characteristics of the environment and measures of perceived characteristics are not highly correlated.[4] What you see depends on where you sit! Further, it is perceptions—not reality—that lead to the decisions that managers make regarding organization design.

Unfortunately, an organization's environment is not like a thousand-pound gorilla. You cannot miss the latter, but environments are not readily spotted and clearly demarcated. The same environment that one organization perceives as unpredictable and complex may be seen as static and easily understood by another organization.[5] People low in an organization may select parts of that something "out there" and call it the specific environment whereas people higher up in that same organization see something else to be the firm's specific environment. You can also expect differences based on background, education, and functional area within which individuals work. Even senior managers in the same firm are likely to see the environment dissimilarly. This suggests that organizations construct or invent their environments and that the environment created depends on perception.

It should not be lost that it is the perceived environment that counts. Managers respond to what they see. As we proceed in our discussion, keep in mind that the structural decisions that managers make to better align their organization with the degree of uncertainty in their specific environment depends on the managers' perception of what makes up the specific environment and their assessment of uncertainty.

Environmental Uncertainty

From our perspective, the environment is important because not all environments are the same. They differ by what we call **environmental uncertainty.** Some organizations face relatively static environments: few forces in their specific environment are chang-

OT
CLOSE-UP

THE VALUE OF INSIDE INFORMATION FOR DEFENSE CONTRACTORS

In the mid-1980s, most of us were astounded to read regularly about the Pentagon paying $400 for a standard ballpeen hammer or $700 for regulation toilet seats. Congress responded by reviewing the defense procurement process. One of the conclusions concerning the ludicrous prices was that a lack of competitive bidding existed on the more than $160 billion a year in defense contracts. The Pentagon was essentially bestowing monopolies on most major suppliers by awarding sole-source contracts.

To correct this situation, the Reagan administration instituted competitive bidding for a majority of defense jobs. Interestingly, this change created a new monster that threatened the entire procurement system—consultants dealing in inside information.[6]

By making the procurement process competitive, the Pentagon succeeded in saving money, but, at the same time, they made inside information far more valuable than it had been in the past. Under the revised system, defense contractors like McDonnell-Douglas struggled to learn in advance what the services wanted in future systems. And, once the bidding began, they scrambled to find out what their rivals were proposing. Suddenly there was high environmental uncertainty. In order to reduce that uncertainty, these defense contractors hired consultants, who were playing both sides of the table. They would buy proprietary information from military-service employees for $5000, for instance, and then sell it to a defense contractor for $50,000. Ironically, by making the bidding process competitive, the Pentagon had substituted one problem (contractors illegally trading on inside information) for another (paying too much for defense contracts).

ing. There are no new competitors, no new technological break-throughs by current competitors, little activity by public pressure groups to influence the organizations, or such. Other organizations face very dynamic environments: rapidly changing government regulations affecting their business, new competitors, difficulties in acquiring raw materials, continually changing product prefer-ences by customers, and so on. Static environments create signif-icantly less uncertainty for managers than do dynamic ones. And since uncertainty is a threat to an organization's effectiveness, management will try to minimize it.[7] In this chapter, we show that management's concern is with reducing environmental uncer-tainty and that this can be accomplished through manipulation of the organization's structure.

LANDMARK CONTRIBUTIONS

Undoubtedly you are not interested in reviewing the dozens of studies that contribute to the body of literature on organizational environments. But several are so important in influencing the cur-rent way we look at the environment that we would be derelict in not reviewing them briefly. In the following pages, we have sum-marized the landmark work of Burns and Stalker, Emery and Trist, and Lawrence and Lorsch.

Burns and Stalker

Tom Burns and G. M. Stalker studied twenty English and Scottish industrial firms to determine how their organizational structure and managerial practice might differ based on different environ-mental conditions.[8] Using interviews with managers and their own observations, they evaluated the firms' environmental conditions in terms of the rate of change in their scientific technology and their relevant product markets. What they found was that the type of structure that existed in rapidly changing and dynamic envi-ronments was significantly different from that in organizations with stable environments. Burns and Stalker labeled the two struc-tures as organic and mechanistic, respectively.

Mechanistic structures were characterized by high complexity, formalization, and centralization. They performed routine tasks, relied heavily on programmed behaviors, and were relatively slow in responding to the unfamiliar. **Organic structures** were relatively flexible and adaptive, with emphasis on lateral rather than on vertical communication, influence based on expertise and knowledge rather than on authority of position, loosely defined responsibilities rather than rigid job definitions, and emphasis on exchanging information rather than on giving directions. (See Table 8–1.)

Burns and Stalker believed that the most effective structure is one that adjusts to the requirements of the environment, which means using a mechanistic design in a stable, certain environment and an organic form in a turbulent environment. However, they recognized that the mechanistic and organic forms were ideal types defining two ends of a continuum. No organization is purely mechanistic or purely organic but, rather, moves toward one or the other. Moreover, they emphasized that one was not preferred over the other. The nature of the organization's environment determined which structure was superior.

Efforts to test Burns and Stalker's conclusions have met with general support.[9] For instance, NASA must deal with an endless series of unpredictable problems.[10] It requires a structure that can allow the organization to respond and adapt to continual change. It should not be surprising, therefore, to find that NASA's structure closely follows the characteristics of an organic form.

TABLE 8–1   *Comparing Mechanistic and Organic Structures*

CHARACTERISTIC	MECHANISTIC	ORGANIC
Task Definition	Rigid	Flexible
Communication	Vertical	Lateral
Formalization	High	Low
Influence	Authority	Expertise
Control	Centralized	Diverse

Emery and Trist

Fred Emery and Eric Trist proposed a more sophisticated view by offering a model that identified four kinds of environment that an organization might confront: (1) *placid-randomized,* (2) *placid-clustered,* (3) *disturbed-reactive,* and (4) *turbulent field.*[11] Emery and Trist described each as increasingly more complex than the previous one.

1. The **placid-randomized environment** is relatively unchanging, therefore posing the least threat to an organization. Demands are distributed randomly, and changes take place slowly over time. When changes do occur, they are not predictable. The placid-randomized environment has been described as analogous to the economist's state of pure competition in which there are enough buyers to absorb the organization's product, and nothing the organization does affects the market. As such, uncertainty is low. Additionally, because change is slow and random, managerial decision making is not likely to give much consideration to the environment.

While not many organizations are fortunate enough to find themselves in a placid-randomized environment, a state worker's compensation agency in many respects enjoys this type of environment. Its environment is relatively stable, and no single client can have any significant impact on the agency's operation.

2. The **placid-clustered environment** also changes slowly, but threats to the organization are clustered rather than random. That means that forces in the environment are linked to one another. For example, input suppliers or output distributors may join forces to form a powerful coalition. So it is more important for organizations facing a placid-clustered environment to know their environment than when threats were random.

The placid-clustered environment would describe public utilities that have nuclear power plants. If the utility attempts to deal with an element in its environment unilaterally (such as the Nuclear Regulatory Commission) without adequate regard for the potential impact on other organized environmental elements (such as environmental protection groups), it opens the potential for a unified reaction. So organizations in a placid-clustered environment are motivated to engage in long-range planning, and their structures will tend to be centralized.

3. The **disturbed-reactive environment** is much more complex

than the previous two. There are many competitors seeking similar ends. One or more organizations in the environment may be large enough to exert influence over their own environment and over other organizations. Two or three large companies in an industry can dominate. A couple of large firms, for instance, can exert price leadership in such industries as steel, aluminum, automobiles, tobacco, and soft drinks. Bethlehem or Armco Steel cannot afford to ignore the future plans and current actions of USX Corp. Similarly, when 7-Up began to actively market their soda by emphasizing its caffeine-free contents, the other major soft-drink firms—notably Coca-Cola and PepsiCo—quickly introduced caffeine-free products.

Organizations facing a disturbed-reactive environment develop planned series of tactical initiatives, calculate reactions by others, and evolve counteractions. This competition requires flexibility to survive, and the structure of these organizations tends toward decentralization.

4. The **turbulent-field environment** is the most dynamic and has the highest uncertainty. Change is ever present, and elements in the environment are increasingly interrelated. By shifting together, elements in the environment create a compounded change effect on the organization. Because change is dramatic and cannot be predicted, management's efforts to anticipate it through planning will have little positive value.

Many experts, arguing along the lines of *Future Shock*,[12] believe that this environment became more and more evident in the 1970s and that it may have become the dominant one for the 1980s and 1990s. In a turbulent-field environment, the organization may be required to develop new products or services on a continuing basis to survive. Also, it may have to reevaluate its relationship to government agencies, customers, and suppliers continually. This environment characterized personal-computer manufacturers in the late 1980s.

Before we relate Emery and Trist's classifications to preferred structural arrangements, we should spend a moment to elaborate on our statement that many experts believe that the turbulent-field environment may be the dominant one for the 1980s and 1990s. This position results from assessing the rapid changes that we have undergone in North America in the past several decades. A few of these changes are listed in Table 8–2.

The argument can be made that organizations today face far

TABLE 8–2   *Major Environment Changes in Recent Years*

Technological
   Introduction of microcomputers
   Telecommunication satellites
   Worldwide telephone direct dialing
Social
   Women's movement
   Concern for physical fitness
   Resurgence of urban centers for commercial and residential development
Economic
   Deregulation of the airline and trucking industries
   Rapid rise, then fall, of oil prices
   Decline in the inflation rate
Political
   End of military draft
   Election of conservative candidates
   Shift of government powers from the federal to state levels

more dynamic and turbulent environments than in previous times. Certainly the environment is more turbulent for some organizations than for others, but we may have entered an era in which the turbulent field is the rule rather than the exception.

Although Emery and Trist offered no specific suggestions as to the type of structure suited best to each environment, their classifications are not difficult to reconcile with Burns and Stalker's terminology. Emery and Trist's first two environments will be responded to with more mechanistic structures, whereas the dynamic environments will require a structure that offers the advantages of the organic form. Regardless of the terms used, the theme underlying Emery and Trist's four-environment model is also compatible with the research findings on technology; that is, the less routine the technology, the greater the uncertainty, the less effective the mechanistic qualities, and the more important it is to use flexible structural forms. Routine technology is associated with stability, and it is handled best by structures that have well-coordinated and highly structured forms. Uncertainty means instability and the potential for major and rapid changes. Only a flexible structure can respond promptly to such changes.

Lawrence and Lorsch

Paul Lawrence and Jay Lorsch, both of the Harvard Business School, went beyond the work of Burns and Stalker and Emery and Trist in search of more information about the relationship between environmental differences and effective organization structures.[13] They chose ten firms in three industries—plastics, food, and containers—in which to carry out their research.

Lawrence and Lorsch deliberately chose these three industries because they appeared to be the most diverse—in terms of environmental uncertainty—they could find. The plastics industry was highly competitive. The life cycle of any product was historically short, and firms were characterized by considerable new-product and process development. The container industry, on the other hand, was quite different. There had been no significant new products in two decades. Sales growth had kept pace with population growth but nothing more. Lawrence and Lorsch described the container firms as operating in a relatively certain environment, with no real threats to consider. The food industry was midway between the two. There had been heavy innovation, but new-product generation and sales growth had been less than plastics and more than containers.

Lawrence and Lorsch sought to match up the internal environments of these firms with their respective external environments. They hypothesized that the more successful firms within each industry would have better matches than the less successful firms would. Their measure of the *external* environment sought to tap the degree of uncertainty. This measurement included the rate of change in the environment over time, the clarity of information that management held about the environment, and the length of time it took for management to get feedback from the environment on actions taken by the organization. But what constituted an organization's *internal* environment? Lawrence and Lorsch looked at two separate dimensions: *differentiation* and *integration.*

The term **differentiation** as used by Lawrence and Lorsch closely parallels our definition of horizontal differentiation, But, in addition to task segmentation, Lawrence and Lorsch argued that managers in various departments can be expected to hold different attitudes and behave differently in terms of their goal perspective, time frame, and interpersonal orientation. Different interests and differing points of view mean that members in each department often find it difficult to see things the same way or to agree on integrated plans of action. Therefore, the degree of differentiation becomes a measure of complexity and indicates greater complications and more rapid changes. The other dimension that interested Lawrence and Lorsch was **integration,** the quality of collaboration that exists among interdependent units or departments that are required to achieve unity of effort. Integration devices that organizations typically use include rules and procedures, formal plans, the authority hierarchy, and decision-making committees.

The unique, and probably the most important, part of Lawrence and Lorsch's study was that they did not assume the organization or the environment to be uniform and singular. In contrast to previous researchers, they perceived both the organization and the environment as having subsets; that is, that *parts* of the organization deal with *parts* of the environment. They were proposing what was patently obvious, except that no one had said it before: that an organization's internal structure could be expected to differ, from department to department, reflecting the characteristics of the subenvironment with which it interacts. They postulated that a basic reason for differentiating into departments or subsystems was to deal more effectively with subenvironments. For example, in each of the ten organizations that Lawrence and Lorsch studied, the researchers were able to identify market, technical-economic, and scientific subenvironments. These three subenvironments corresponded to the sales, production, and research-and-development functions within the organizations.

Lawrence and Lorsch postulated that the more turbulent, complex, and diverse the external environment facing an organization, the greater the degree of differentiation among its subparts. If the external environment were very diverse and the internal environment were highly differentiated, they further reasoned there would be a need for an elaborate internal integration mechanism to avoid having units going in different directions. The need for increased integration to accommodate increases in differentiation related to the different goals of departmental managers. In all three industries, the researchers found manufacturing people to be most concerned with cost efficiency and production matters. Research and engineering people emphasized scientific matters. Marketing people's orientation was toward the marketplace.

In reference to their three industries, Lawrence and Lorsch

hypothesized that the plastics firms would be the most differentiated, followed by food and container firms, in that order. And this is precisely what they found. When they divided the firms within each industry into high, moderate, and low performers, they found that the high-performing firms had a structure that best fit their environmental demands. In diverse environments, subunits were more differentiated than in homogeneous environments. In the turbulent plastics industry, this meant high differentiation. The production units had relatively routine activities, in contrast to sales and research and engineering. Where the greatest standardization existed, in the container industry, there was the least differentiation. Departments within the container firms generally had similar structures. The food firms, as postulated, were in the middle ground. Additionally, the most successful firms in all three industries had a higher degree of integration than their low-performing counterparts.

What does all this mean? First, there are multiple specific environments with different degrees of uncertainty. Second, successful organizations' subunits meet the demands of their subenvironments. Since differentiation and integration represent opposing forces, the key is to match the two appropriately, creating differentiation between departments to deal with specific problems and tasks facing the organization and getting people to integrate and work as a cohesive team toward the organizations' goals. Successful organizations have more nearly solved the dilemma of providing both differentiation and integration by matching their internal subunits to the demands of the subenvironment. Finally, Lawrence and Lorsch present evidence to confirm that the environment in which an organization functions—specifically in terms of the level of uncertainty present—is of foremost importance in selecting the structure appropriate for achieving organizational effectiveness.

Before we leave Lawrence and Lorsch, it should be mentioned that they have been criticized sharply for their use of perceptual measures of environmental uncertainty.[14] As noted earlier, actual and perceived degrees of uncertainty are likely to differ. Attempts to replicate Lawrence and Lorsch's work using objective measures of uncertainty have often failed, suggesting that their results may be a function of their measure.[15] From a research standpoint, this criticism is valid. However, from the practicing manager's perspective, it is his or her perceptions that count. So while you should recognize that Lawrence and Lorsch have used perceptual measures and that defining the environment in terms of certainty-uncertainty criteria is by no means simple, you should also recognize that the findings of Lawrence and Lorsch represent an important contribution to our understanding of the impact of the environment on organization structure.

A SYNTHESIS:
DEFINING THE ENVIRONMENT
AND ENVIRONMENTAL UNCERTAINTY

In this section, we look for common threads among the studies on the environment. Since our goal is integration and clarity rather than merely the presentation of many diverse research findings, we think it is important to seek some common ground in the environmental literature. Toward that end, recent research suggests that there are three key dimensions to any organization's environment. They are labeled: capacity, volatility, and complexity.[16] As you will see, these three dimensions synthesize much of the literature previously discussed.

The **capacity** of an environment refers to the degree to which it can support growth. Rich and growing environments generate excess resources, which can buffer the organization in times of relative scarcity. Abundant capacity, for example, leaves room for an organization to make mistakes, while scarce capacity does not. In the late 1980s, firms operating in the cellular-telephone business had relatively abundant environments, whereas those in the petroleum-refining industry faced relative scarcity.

The degree of instability in an environment is captured in the **volatility** dimension. Where there is a high degree of unpredictable change, the environment is dynamic. This makes it difficult for management to predict accurately the probabilities associated with various decision alternatives. At the other extreme is a stable environment. The change in procurement procedures in the defense industry that was described earlier in this chapter has resulted in the environment of aerospace firms like McDonnell-Douglas, General Dynamics, and Northrop moving from relatively stable to dynamic.

Finally, the environment needs to be assessed in terms of **com-**

plexity; that is, the degree of heterogeneity and concentration among environmental elements. Simple environments are homogeneous and concentrated. This might describe the tobacco industry, since there are relatively few players. Its easy for firms in this industry to keep a close eye on the competition. In contrast, environments characterized by heterogeneity and dispersion are called complex. This is essentially the current environment in the computer software business. Everyday there is another "new kid on the block" with whom established software firms have to deal.

Figure 8–2 summarizes our definition of the environment along its three dimensions. The arrows in this figure are meant to indicate movement toward higher uncertainty. So organizations that operate in environments characterized as scarce, dynamic, and complex face the greatest degree of uncertainty. Why? Because they have little room for error, high unpredictability, and a diverse set of elements in the environment to constantly monitor.

Given this three-dimensional definition of environment, we can offer some general conclusions. There is evidence that relates the degrees of environmental uncertainty to different structural arrangements. Specifically, the more scarce, dynamic, and complex the environment, the more organic a structure should be. The more abundant, stable, and simple the environment, the more the mechanistic structure will be preferred.

FIGURE 8–2 *Three-Dimensional Model of the Environment*

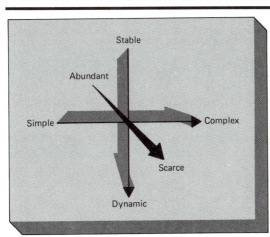

Note how the preceding conclusions align with our discussion of technology and structure in the previous chapter. Routine technologies operate in relative certainty, whereas nonroutine technologies imply relative uncertainty. High environmental uncertainty or technology of a nonroutine nature both require organic-type structures. Similarly, low environmental uncertainty or routine technology can be managed more effectively in mechanistic structures.

THE ENVIRONMENTAL IMPERATIVE

As a result of our previous analysis, you should now have a reasonable understanding of what environment is and what some scholars have found in their efforts to better understand the environment-structure relationship. You now have the background to interpret more fully the cases for and against the environmental imperative.

The Case For

The case for the theory that environment determines structure has been made by Burns and Stalker, Emery and Trist, and Lawrence and Lorsch. Basically, they believe that environmental pressures generate task demands that are met by appropriate technical structures. A more elaborate defense can be built using the systems perspective.

Organizations are dependent on acquiring inputs and disposing of outputs if they are to operate and survive. These flow from and to the environment. In a closed system, the most effective organization would be one that was technologically efficient. Since you assume no interactions or problems with the environment in a closed system, success depends on internal efficiencies. The structural design, therefore, would be one that handled the transformation process most efficiently. But organizations cannot ignore their environments. It's true that some organizations need to pay much closer attention than do others and that some subunits within an organization must monitor their subenvironments more closely than other subunits, but no organization is so autonomous that it can insulate itself completely from its environment.

Because all organizations are dependent, in some degree, on their environments, that dependency creates uncertainty for managers. Those things that management cannot control directly create uncertainties. But managers do not like making decisions under conditions of high uncertainty. Since they cannot eliminate uncertainty, they look to options within their control that can reduce it. One of those options is designing the organization so as to be able to respond best to the uncertainty. If uncertainty is high, therefore, the organization will be designed along flexible lines to adapt to rapid changes. If uncertainty is low, management will opt for a structure that is most efficient and offers the highest degree of managerial control, which is the mechanistic form.

THE IMPACT OF UNIONS ON ORGANIZATION STRUCTURE

Many of the employees of organizations such as General Motors, Bethlehem Steel, National Van Lines, and the City of New York are unionized. So for the managements of these organizations, the United Auto Workers, Steelworkers, Teamsters, American Federation of State, County, and Municipal Employees, or similar labor groups are part of their specific environment. Question: Does the existence of these unions significantly affect the structure of the employing organization? The answer, not surprisingly, is Yes.[17]

A review of the evidence finds that unionized organizations *are* structured differently from nonunion ones. In contrast to nonunionized organizations, union workplaces are run more by rules and there is greater rigidity in the scheduling of work and hours. More specifically, unionized locations appear to use seniority as a factor in promotions more strictly and independently of performance on the job and utilize more structured forms of training. Besides being more formalized, the structure in unionized organizations also is more highly differentiated. Work is divided into highly specialized and narrowly defined jobs, and there are more job classifications and wage grades for classifying workers.

In summary, where unions exist, organizations tend toward mechanistic structures.

The Case Against

If there is an environmental imperative, it may be limited only to those subunits at the boundary of the organization—those that interact directly with the environment. For instance, the structure of purchasing and marketing functions may be a direct response to their dependency on the environment. Yet it may have little or

WHO SAYS THAT THE TIMES ARE CHANGING?

Take a look at the names of the fifteen largest U.S. industrial corporations (as measured by assets) in 1929. How many of them would you expect still to be in the top fifteen in 1988? How many would have been able to maintain their top-fifteen ranking through the Great Depression, World War II, the jet age, the cold-war era, the Vietnam war, and the dramatic changes these and other events have wrought on U.S. society? Two? Three? Maybe four? Would you believe eleven? That's the correct answer!

For those who want tangible evidence that the past sixty years have *not* really been characterized by rapid change, look at the following rankings:

1929 RANKING	COMPANY (SUCCESSOR COMPANY)	1988 RANKING
1.	U.S. Steel (USX Corp.)	—
2.	Standard Oil/New Jersey (Exxon)	4
3.	General Motors	1
4.	Standard Oil/Indiana (Amoco)	11
5.	Bethlehem Steel	—

no impact on production, R&D, accounting, and similarly insulated activities. It may also be, since environments are perceived, that environments are created to reflect the structures from which they are seen.[18] If environments are creations, then it is possible that differentiated structures will perceive a heterogeneous environment or that decentralized structures will perceive more environmental uncertainty as a consequence of their structural ar-

1929 RANKING	COMPANY (SUCCESSOR COMPANY)	1988 RANKING
6.	Ford Motor Co.	2
7.	Socony Mobil (Mobil Oil)	7
8.	Anaconda (Atlantic Richfield)	—
9.	Texaco	14
10.	Standard Oil/California (Chevron)	9
11.	General Electric	3
12.	Du Pont	10
13.	Shell Oil	12
14.	Armour & Co. (Greyhound)	—
15.	Gulf Oil (Chevron)	9

Source: Based on data in *Fortune*, April 28, 1986, p. 182; and *Fortune*, April 24, 1989, p. 354.

In 1988, U.S. Steel, Bethlehem, Anaconda and Armour had dropped out of the top fifteen (although USX was eighteenth and Atlantic Richfield was sixteenth). They were replaced by IBM (5), Chrysler (6), Philip Morris (8), Xerox (13), and Eastman Kodak (15).

These rankings provide very strong evidence that in spite of all the talk about high-technology industries, entrepreneurship, and the growth of small organizations, there has been very little shake-up among the major industrial institutions in the United States.

rangement. This may, in fact, explain Lawrence and Lorsch's findings. A stronger case, however, may be built around the argument that the environment is relatively impotent in its effect on structure.

A major contention of the environmental imperative supporters is that organizations structure themselves to minimize the impact of uncertainty; that is, events that the organization cannot forecast. As noted earlier in our discussion of the specific environment, not all uncertainty in the environment may have consequences for the organization. Uncertainty, therefore, is relevant only when it occurs along with dependence.[19] Moreover, uncertainty is *unplanned* variation. "Mere change, or rate of change, is no guarantee that the situation is uncertain. Change, variation, and a dynamic environment may all be capable of being predicted, in which case, there is no uncertainty."[20] For instance, the twentieth century can be characterized as a period of constant and unrelenting change, accelerating in recent years.

Today's businesses are not only affected by more forces than ever before, but the forces themselves are more volatile, quickly changing, and unpredictable than ever before. The forces operating in earlier times were not only fewer in number but easier to understand and more stable and longer lasting.[21]

Of course, from a different perspective, we might argue that instead of reflecting increasing change, what may be occurring is only management's reduced ability to forecast. The past is no longer a prologue to the future. There may be no more dynamic changes going on in the 1980s and 1990s than occurred in the 1940s, 1950s, or 1960s. Only back in those days, the direction and degree of change were easier to predict. We have entered an age of discontinuity, which makes our forecasts of the future highly prone to error. So change may be a constant; it is only our reduced ability to predict it that may have *created* turbulent environments.

To take an even more extreme position, it can be argued that the claim that today's organizations face far more dynamic and turbulent environments than in previous times is just completely erroneous. As Nobellaureate Herbert Simon has noted, the years of real environmental uncertainty took place between the Civil War and World War I. The world changed from a rural, agricultural, horse-powered society to an urban, industrialized world with railroads, telegraphs, steamships, electric lights, automobiles, and airplanes. Dramatic technological breakthroughs were coming from all directions. Simon argues that nothing in the past seventy years, "with the possible exception of The Bomb, has so changed the basic terms of human existence as those new technologies did."[22] In relative terms, today's managers may be facing a far less dynamic environment than were their counterparts of three generations ago.

Finally, it has been said that the environmental imperative is just not in agreement with observed reality.[23] Not only do organizations that operate in ostensibly similar environments have different structures, they often show no significant difference in effectiveness. Further, many organizations have similar structures and very diverse environments. This latter point is consistent with your author's observation that the mechanistic form of structure is dominant in America today. Look around you. Schools, businesses, governmental agencies, hospitals, athletic teams, and even social clubs essentially fit the mechanistic model. If the environment is actually turbulent, shouldn't organic structures be in the majority?

The Population-Ecology View

The last decade has seen the growth and development of what certainly stands as an extreme environmental-imperative position. This position—which has been labeled the natural selection or **population-ecology** view[24]—argues that the environment selects certain types of organizations to survive and others to perish based on the fit between their structural characteristics and the characteristics of their environment. Population ecologists argue that organizational forms must either fit their environmental niches or fail.

Population ecology relies heavily on biology's survival-of-the-fittest doctrine. This doctrine argues that there is a natural selection process that allows the strongest and most adaptable species to survive over time. Population ecology applies the same kind of thinking to organizations. The environment "naturally" selects "in" some organizations and selects "out" others. Those selected "in" are the survivors, while those selected "out" perish. More specifically, population ecologists would argue that organizations that survive have resources and structural dimensions that the casualties didn't.

Assumptions of Population Ecology. The population-ecology perspective has some distinct assumptions, which need articulating. First, it focuses on groups or populations of organizations, not on individual organizations. It's designed to explain, for example, that the retail grocery business in the late 1940s tended to be split about evenly between small "mom and pop" stores and supermarkets, but that the environment selected out almost all of the former because they were inefficient. Second, population ecology defines organizational effectiveness as simply survival. At any time, the organizations that operate in any industry are defined as effective because they are among the survivors. Third, population ecologists assume that the environment is totally determining. In direct contrast to the theme in Chapter 5, where strategy was described as determining structure, the population-ecology view assumes that management—at least in the short or intermediate term—has little impact on an organization's survival. Managers are perceived as impotent observers. If there is a shift in the environmental niche that the organization occupies, there is little that management can do. Survival is determined solely by how well the environment supports the organization. Success, therefore, is a result of luck or chance. Organizations that survive are merely in the right place at the right time, and that positioning has nothing to do with managerial choice. If you're a home builder producing for the lower segment of the market and interest rates drop drastically, the demand for the homes you build will go up and you'll be able to build and sell a large number. But if interest rates rise rapidly, you're not likely to sell many houses. In this case, interest rates—which exist in the environment—determine whether you survive, not managerial action. A fourth assumption of population ecology is that the carrying capacity of the environment is limited. There are only so many hospitals, for instance, that a given community's size can absorb. This sets up a competitive arena where some organizations will succeed and others will fail. Finally, population ecology assumes the existence of a three-stage process that explains how organizations, operating in similar environmental niches, end up having common structural dimensions. The process proposes that forces of change generate in the environment rather than from managerial action. This three-stage process is described in the next section.

Organizational Change Process. How do organizations change to better fit with the environment they face? The answer can be found in a three-stage process of change that recognizes *variations* within and between organizations, the *selection* of those variations that are best suited to their environments, and a *retention* mechanism that sustains and reproduces those variations that are positively selected (see Figure 8–3).

Within any population of organizations—for example, fast-food restaurants, chemical firms, general hospitals, and private colleges—there will be variations in organizational forms. These can be planned or random variations; but the key point is that there will be diversity. Some of these variations, however, are better suited to their environments than others. Those that are well suited survive, while the others fall out of the set and perish. Organizations that have a form that fit their environment are positively selected and survive, while others either fail or change to match their environmental requirements. This finally leads to the retention of those variations that are positively selected. Over time, selected organizational forms tend to develop in populations that share common size requirements for efficiency, technologies, and control systems.

Following the above process, we should expect to find common organizational practices and structural characteristics within common populations. The reason is that those organizations that were different were less able to compete. There are not enough resources in any environment to support an unlimited number of organizations, so there is a natural selection process that reproduces

FIGURE 8–3 *Population-Ecology View of the Change Process*

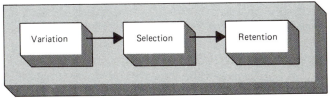

organizational structures that best fit with their environment. Over the very long run, of course, even the positively selected variations are likely to be selected "out" because environments change and, in so doing, favor a different set of variations.

Every industry is made up of sets of organizations that can be divided into populations with common resources and technologies. But there is only so much money and so many people, market segments, and other resources available in the environment. Organizations can define a niche for themselves—for example, emphasizing low cost, quality, convenience of location, hours of service, or the like—but there is still competition. The survivors will be those that have best adjusted their internal resources to their environment.

What happened to the afternoon daily newspapers? In most major cities they have gone the way of the horse and buggy. Their failure had little to do with the quality of their management. Rather, the environment changed—the evening news on television could provide the same information in a more timely manner. Those newspapers that have survived in metropolitan areas have tended to be the large morning papers.

The airline industry also offers an illustration of what happens when the environment changes. Deregulation changed the rules so that the most efficient airlines survived, whereas the high-cost and less efficient—such as Braniff and Frontier—failed. Adjustments have been made and continue to be made within the airline industry as a result of deregulation. We can expect that "airlines under conditions of deregulation will probably become more efficient, more price competitive, less unionized, and less middle-sized. But they may also be less safe; offer fewer, more crowded flights; and be less humanistic."[25]

Limitations to Population-Ecology View. Population ecology is not a general theory to explain why and how organizations survive. As its critics have shown, it has clear limitations.[26]

The theory ignores managerial motives and abilities. But management is not always impotent. It may not be all powerful, as it is often depicted in management textbooks; however, neither is it irrelevant. Management can choose the domains or niches it wants to compete in and, especially in the long-term, change its domain.

Population ecology appears to have limited application to large and powerful organizations. The reason is that these organizations can often insulate themselves against failure. They have strong constituencies in government that will protect them. For example, the U.S. steel industry, when pounded by Japanese and other competitors, found strong support in Congress for foreign-import quotas. Additionally, as we show in Chapter 13, large organizations can control their environments because many elements in their environment—suppliers, customers, labor unions, and the like—are dependent upon them and accede to their demands. And among public-sector organizations, efficiency and adaptation are not effectiveness criteria—we simply do not let public schools, county libraries, and city garbage collectors go out of business.[27] So population ecology may best be described as a special theory applicable to small and powerless business organizations. Reality tells us that most large business organizations, as well as almost all those organizations in the public sector, tend to be relatively immune to threats from the environment and are rarely selected "out."

Implications. Population ecology provides an explanation for why organizations in common populations tend to have common structural characteristics and why certain types of organizations survive while others die. It can explain why small organizations so often fail, why the divisional structure became popular in the 1960s, and why organic structures flourished in the 1980s among high-tech firms. Maybe most important of all, it can explain the rise and proliferation of the bureaucratic form and why most organizations today are primarily bureaucracies.[28]

Population ecology also tells us that survival will be significantly influenced by the capacity and stability of the organization's environment. Is the capacity of the environment rich or lean? The richer the environment, the more organizations that will survive. In the mid-1980s, the environment facing the farm-equipment industry was considerably leaner than that in which manufacturers of word processors operated. Additionally, the more stable the environment, the harder it is for new organizations to enter and compete. Stable, certain environments tend to retain large organizations with high market shares.

For OT researchers, population ecology's contribution includes calling into question traditional research methods. OT researchers have traditionally looked at different structural relationships and sought to relate them to varying degrees of organizational effectiveness. Population ecologists have correctly noted that such research is biased. It doesn't survey *all* organizations; merely the survivors. The truly "ineffective" organizations are not studied because they died too soon. So the value of OT research is likely to be improved if researchers look at organizations that have failed as well as those that have survived.

Acceptance of population ecology as a mainstream theory, at least among students of management and business, is not likely to occur. Why? Because it runs counter to the doctrine of rational attribution. Outcomes that are random—which can be attributed to luck or chance—cannot, by definition, be managed. A view that organizational success is pure happenstance is not likely to be widely accepted in schools of business and management whose survival is based on a proactive view of managers.

The population-ecology perspective is, in fact, OT's equivalent of financial investment's efficient market theory (EMT). EMT states that stock prices always tend to reflect everything known about the prospects of individual companies and the economy as a whole. If all current information is already embedded in the price of any stock, research and analysis cannot improve your performance in making stock portfolio decisions. According to EMT, because stock prices are the result of a perfectly efficient market, anyone who outperforms the market has done so on luck. EMT, like population ecology, assumes that success is a matter of luck or being in the right place at the right time. Stock market researchers obviously take a dim view of EMT. Similarly, students of management are not likely to embrace population ecology's extreme environmental determinism.

THE ENVIRONMENT-STRUCTURE RELATIONSHIP

It is time to attempt some specific formulations on the environment-structure relationship. As in the previous chapters, we look at the effect on complexity, formalization, and centralization. However, before we make these formulations, several general predictions about the environment-structure relationship are offered.

Every organization depends on its environment to some degree, but we cannot ignore the obvious, namely, that some organizations are much more dependent on the environment and on certain subenvironments than others are. The environment's effect on an organization, therefore, is a function of its vulnerability, which in turn is a function of dependence.[29] In the late 1980s, American Airlines was less vulnerable to economic fluctuations than was Air Wisconsin. Firms such as Safeway Stores and Revlon are more vulnerable to consumer advocate groups than, say, manufacturers of cement. Organizations whose employees are unionized are more vulnerable to union activity, and their effectiveness is more dependent on maintaining good relations with the union's leadership than nonunionized organizations are.

The evidence demonstrates that a dynamic environment has more influence on structure than a static environment does.[30] A dynamic environment will push an organization toward an organic form, even if large size or routine technology suggests a mechanistic structure. However, a static environment will not override the influence of size and technology. This evidence, when linked with our observation of the dearth of organic structures, implies that (1) dynamic environments are not, in actuality, that prevalent; (2) managers may not recognize dynamic environments when they see them; or (3) organizations have devised ways in which to reduce their dependencies when facing dynamic environments.

Environment and Complexity

Environmental uncertainty and complexity are directly related. That is, high environmental uncertainty tends to lead to greater complexity. In order to respond to a dynamic and more complex environment, organizations become more differentiated. An organization faced with a volatile environment will need to monitor that environment more closely than one that is stable. That is typically accomplished by creating differentiated units. Similarly, a complex environment requires the organization to buffer itself with a greater number of departments and specialists.

Environment and Formalization

We predict that stable environments should lead to high formalization because stable environments create a minimal need for rapid response, and economies exist for organizations that standardize their activities. But, we caution against assuming that a dynamic environment must lead to low formalization throughout the organization. Management's preference will undoubtedly be toward insulating operating activities from uncertainty. If successful, a dynamic environment is likely to lead to low formalization of boundary activities while maintaining relatively high formalization within other functions.

Environment and Centralization

The more complex the environment, the more decentralized the structure.[31] Regardless of the stable-dynamic dimension, if a large number of dissimilar factors and components exist in the environment, the organization can best meet the uncertainties that this causes through decentralization. It is difficult for management to comprehend a highly complex *environment* (note that this is different from a complex *structure*). Management information-processing capacity becomes overloaded, so decisions are carved up into subsets and are delegated to others.

Disparities in the environment are responded to through decentralization.[32] When different responses are needed to different subenvironments, the organization creates decentralized subunits to deal with them. So we can expect organizations to decentralize selectively. This can explain why, even in organizations that are generally highly centralized, marketing activities are typically decentralized. This is a response to a disparity in the environment; that is, even though the environment is generally static, the market subenvironment tends toward being dynamic.

Finally, the evidence confirms that extreme hostility in the environment drives organizations to, at least temporarily, centralize their structures.[33] A wildcat strike by the union, an antitrust suit by the government, or the sudden loss of a major customer all represent severe threats to the organization, and top management responds by centralizing control. When survival is in question, top management wants to oversee decision making directly. Of course, you may note that this appears to contradict an earlier prediction. You would expect this dynamic environment to be met with decentralization. What appears to happen is that two opposing forces are at work, with centralization the winner. The need for innovation and responsiveness (via decentralization) is overpowered by top management's fear that the wrong decisions may be made.

SUMMARY

The theme of this chapter has been that different organizations face different degrees of environmental uncertainty and that structural design is a major tool that managers can use to eliminate or minimize the impact of environmental uncertainty.

The environment was defined as everything outside an organization's boundaries. Our concern, however, is with the specific environment—that part most relevant to the organization. Management desires to reduce uncertainty created by this specific environment.

Three landmark contributions were cited. Burns and Stalker argued that an organization's structure should be mechanistic in a stable, certain environment and organic when the environment is turbulent. Emery and Trist identified four kinds of environments—placid-randomized, placid-clustered, disturbed-reactive, and turbulent field—the inference being that different environments require different structural arrangements. Lawrence and Lorsch's major contributions included the recognition that there are multiple specific environments with different degrees of uncertainty, that successful organizations' subunits meet the demands of their subenvironments, and that the degree of environmental uncertainty is of utmost importance in the selection of the right structure. We synthesized the studies into three dimensions: capacity (abundant-scarce), volatility (stable-dynamic), and complexity (simple-complex).

The environment-structure relationship is complicated, but we concluded that (1) the environment's effect on an organization is a function of dependence, (2) a dynamic environment has more influence on structure than does a static one, (3) complexity and environmental uncertainty are directly related, (4) formalization and environmental uncertainty are inversely related, (5) the more complex the environment, the greater the decentralization, and (6) extreme hostility in the environment leads to temporary centralization.

FOR REVIEW AND DISCUSSION

1. "Environmental states are objective." Do you agree or disagree with this statement? Discuss.
2. What is the difference between an organization's general environment and its specific environment?
3. Why do managers dislike environmental uncertainty? What can they do to reduce it?
4. Describe the technology and environment that fit best with (a) mechanistic and (b) organic structures.
5. Why would an organic structure be inefficient in a stable environment?

6. "Turbulent field best describes the environment that most organizations face today." Build an argument to support this statement. Then build an argument to refute your previous position.

7. What was Lawrence and Lorsch's main contribution to OT?

8. "Differentiation and integration are opposing forces." Do you agree or disagree? Discuss.

9. Define each of the following environmental dimensions: (a) capacity, (b) volatility, and (c) complexity.

10. Under what conditions is environment likely to be a major determinant of structure?

11. What is the argument for an environmental imperative?

12. According to the population-ecology view, how do organizations change?

13. Why is a limited carrying capacity within the environment critical to the population-ecology view?

14. If the population ecologists are right, what can management do to make their organizations more effective?

15. Why is the population-ecology perspective not likely to gain a strong following in business schools?

NOTES

[1] Jolie B. Solomon and John Bussey, "Pressed By Its Rivals, Procter & Gamble Company Is Altering Its Ways," *Wall Street Journal*, May 20, 1985, p. 1.

[2] Robert H. Miles, *Macro Organizational Behavior* (Santa Monica, Calif.: Goodyear Publishing, 1980), p. 195.

[3] James D. Thompson, *Organizations in Action* (New York: McGraw-Hill, 1967), p. 27.

[4] H. Kirk Downey, Don Hellriegel, and John W. Slocum, Jr., "Environmental Uncertainty: The Construct and Its Application," *Administrative Science Quarterly*, December 1975, pp. 613–29.

[5] William H. Starbuck, "Organizations and Their Environments," in Marvin D. Dunnette, ed., *Handbook of Industrial and Organizational Psychology* (Chicago: Rand McNally, 1976), p. 1080.

[6] Tim Carrington and Edward T. Pound, "Pushing Defense Firms To Compete, Pentagon Harms Buying System," *Wall Street Journal*, June 22, 1988, p. 1.

[7] William R. Dill, "Environment as an Influence on Managerial Autonomy," *Administrative Science Quarterly*, March 1958, pp. 409–43.

[8] Tom Burns and G. M. Stalker, *The Management of Innovation* (London: Tavistock, 1961).

[9] See Henry Mintzberg, *The Structuring of Organizations* (Englewood Cliffs, N.J.: Prentice Hall, 1979), pp. 270–72.

[10] Margaret K. Chandler and Leonard R. Sayles, *Managing Large Systems* (New York: Harper & Row, 1971), p. 180.

[11] Fred E. Emery and Eric L. Trist, "The Causal Texture of Organizational Environments," *Human Relations*, February 1965, pp. 21–32.

[12] Alvin Toffler, *Future Shock* (New York: Bantam, 1970).

[13] Paul Lawrence and Jay W. Lorsch, *Organization and Environment: Managing Differentiation and Integration* (Boston: Division of Research, Harvard Business School, 1967).

[14] See, for example, Henry L. Tosi, Ramon J. Aldag, and Ronald G. Storey, "On the Measurement of the Environment: An Assessment of the Lawrence and Lorsch Environmental Subscale," *Administrative Science Quarterly*, March 1973, pp. 27–36; and H. Kirk Downey and John W. Slocum, Jr., "Uncertainty: Measures, Research, and Sources of Variation," *Academy of Management Journal*, September 1975, pp. 562–78.

[15] Ramon J. Aldag and Ronald G. Storey, "Environmental Uncertainty: Comments on Objective and Perceptual Indices," in Arthur G. Bedeian, A. A. Armenakis, W. H. Holley, Jr., and H. S. Feild, Jr., eds., *Proceedings of the Annual Meeting of the Academy of Management* (Auburn, Alabama:Academy of Management, 1975), pp. 203–5.

[16] Gregory G. Dess and Donald W. Beard, "Dimensions of Organizational Task Environments," *Administrative Science Quarterly*, March 1984, pp. 52–73.

[17] This section is based on Anil Verma, "Union Status as a Context Variable: The Impact of Unions on Organizational Structure." Paper presented at the Western Academy of Management Conference, Hollywood, Calif., April 1987.

[18] Karl E. Weick, *The Social Psychology of Organizing* (Reading, Mass.: Addison-Wesley, 1969).

[19] Jeffrey Pfeffer, *Organizational Design* (Arlington Heights, Ill.: AHM Publishing, 1978), p. 133.

[20] Ibid.

[21] Ian I. Mitroff and Ralph H. Kilmann, "Corporate Taboos as the Key to Unlocking Culture," in R. H. Kilmann, Mary J. Saxton, Roy Serpa, and Associates, *Gaining Control of the Corporate Culture* (San Francisco: Jossey-Bass, 1985), p. 191.

[22] Herbert A. Simon, *The New Science of Management Decision*, rev. ed. (Englewood Cliffs, N.J.: Prentice-Hall, 1977), pp. 100–101.

[23] John Child, "Organizational Structure, Environment, and Performance: The Role of Strategic Choice," *Sociology*, January 1972, pp. 1–22.

[24] Michael T. Hannan and John H. Freeman, "The Population Ecology of Organizations," *American Journal of Sociology*, March 1977, pp. 929–64; Howard E. Aldrich, *Organizations and Environments* (Englewood Cliffs, N.J.: Prentice Hall, 1979); Douglas R. Wholey and Jack W. Brittain, "Organizational Ecology: Findings and Implications," *Academy of Management Review*, July 1986, pp. 513–33; and Dave Ulrich, "The Population

Perspective: Review, Critique, and Relevance," *Human Relations*, March 1987, pp. 137–52.

[25] Howard Aldrich, Bill McKelvey, and Dave Ulrich, "Design Strategy from the Population Perspective," *Journal of Management*, Spring 1984, p. 71.

[26] Charles Perrow, *Complex Organizations: A Critical Essay*, 3rd ed. (Glenview, Ill.: Scott, Foresman, 1986), pp. 211–16; Andrew H. Van de Ven, "Review of *Organizations and Environments* by H. E. Aldrich," *Administrative Science Quarterly*, June 1979, pp. 320–26; Wai Fong Foo, John C. Oliga, and Anthony G. Puxty, "The Population Ecology Model and Management Action," *Journal of Enterprise Management*, June 1981, pp. 317–25; and Amos H. Hawley, "Human Ecology: Persistence and Change," *American Behavioral Scientist*, January–February 1981, pp. 423–44.

[27] Charles Perrow, *Complex Organizations*, p. 213.

[28] John Langston, "The Ecological Theory of Bureaucracy: The Case of Josiah Wedgwood and the British Pottery Industry," *Administrative Science Quarterly*, September 1984, pp. 330–54.

[29] David Jacobs, "Dependency and Vulnerability: An Exchange Approach to the Control of Organizations," *Administrative Science Quarterly*, March 1974, pp. 45–59.

[30] Mintzberg, *Structuring of Organizations*, p. 272.

[31] Ibid., pp. 273–76.

[32] Ibid., pp. 282–85; and Edward F. McDonough III and Richard Leifer, "Using Simultaneous Structures to Cope with Uncertainty," *Academy of Management Journal*, December 1983, pp. 727–35.

[33] Mintzberg, *Structuring of Organizations*, pp. 281–82.

9

POWER-CONTROL

AFTER READING THIS CHAPTER, YOU SHOULD BE ABLE TO:

1 Describe the strategic choice argument.
2 Present the case against strategic choice.
3 Identify the power-control assumptions about organizational decision making.
4 Distinguish between power and authority.
5 Describe how an individual or group gains power.
6 Define politics.
7 Explain the power-control model of how structures emerge.
8 Describe the power-control interpretation of technology and environment's role on structure.
9 Explain the power-control view of structural change.
10 Predict the degree of complexity, formalization, and centralization that those in power prefer.

Introduction
GAINING POWER AT THE NETWORK

The following story is told about one executive's rise at a major television network in New York City. We'll call him Dave.[1]

Dave's job at the network was to make merchandising tie-ups for the network shows. For example, he'd arrange to market toys and games as tie-ins to successful Saturday morning children's programs and popular game shows. When he got the job, he worked out of a small office in a leased part of an old hotel, down the street from corporate headquarters, with just a couple of employees. But Dave had big ambitions and decided the best way to make a name for himself at the network was to expand his operation. He began taking over room after room, suite after suite, until he had a whole floor at the hotel. He set up merchandising racks and display rooms, hired specialists to develop new toys and games, and created an international licensing department. At the same time that Dave was creating his little dynasty, his network was erecting a big new corporate headquarters. And Dave had it all figured out. When the new building was finished, he moved his department in. Instead of one small office, he now oversaw an operation that consumed half a floor of office space with display rooms, conference rooms, and executive offices. Moreover, Dave had increased his department's visibility by making sure that all executives in the company got an ample complimentary supply of all of his department's toys and games. Over the prior two-year period, every senior executive was supplied with an unlimited wealth of free goodies to distribute as birthday presents and Christmas gifts.

Interestingly, when a new computer system was installed, Dave's department was found to be a big money loser. But top management couldn't cut out a department that now employed hundreds of people and that allowed executives in the company to be Santa Claus to every kid they knew. All the company did was promote Dave and put a financial person in under him. Dave's operation continued to expand, although it still didn't make any money. All the while, of course, Dave had become a senior executive at the network, with a nice six-figure salary.

Dave's story introduces another perspective on how organization structures evolve. Organizational members, looking to satisfy their self-interests, seek to gain power and then use that power to create structures that work to their benefit.

In the previous four chapters we looked at strategy, size, technology, and environment as independent determinants of structure. We found that none of these four contingency variables was *the* determinant of structure. Each contributed by explaining a part, but only a part. Is it possible that the problem is that the variables interrelate; that is, by combining them, could we get a whole greater than the sum of the parts? Efforts in this direction suggest that (1) there is an interaction among the variables so that by combining them we can explain more of the variance,[2] but (2) at best, these four factors explain only 50 to 60 percent of the variability in structure.[3] It may be that these contingency variables, either individually or in combination, are not as powerful as originally thought. Another possibility is that these variables are more potent than the evidence indicates, but the fault resides in the weaknesses of the research techniques used to measure these variables.

The power-control viewpoint proposes still another answer: A major piece of the puzzle remains missing. This viewpoint suggests that power and control can explain a good portion of the residual variance.

In this chapter, we'll step outside the confines of rationality and maximizing organizational effectiveness into the world of organizational power and politics. We'll introduce the **power-control** view that an organization's structure, at any given time, is to a large extent the result of those in power selecting a structure that will, to the maximum degree possible, maintain and enhance their control.

A MAJOR ATTACK: STRATEGIC CHOICE

A substantive attack against those arguing for the dominance of technological, environmental, or other forces as structural imperatives was developed by John Child in the early 1970s.[4] Child's work, which essentially is an expansion of the strategy-structure thesis presented in Chapter 5, sought to demonstrate that managers have considerable latitude in making strategic choices.

The Logic of Strategic Choice

Child's **strategic choice** argument is that while there are constraints on managerial-decision discretion, managers still have significant latitude for making choices. Just as they choose objectives, personnel, or control techniques, managers also choose the organization's structural design. Environmental factors such as competitors, unions, and government agencies are part of the constraints, but rather than impinging directly on an organization's structure, these factors are mediated by managerial choice. Similarly, technology can control structure only to the degree that managers choose a technology that demands certain structural dimensions. So environment and technology are *constraints* on managers rather than imperatives. Child's argument can be condensed basically into four points.[5]

1. *Decision makers have more autonomy than that inferred by those arguing for the dominance of environmental, technological, or other forces.* Managers can select from among a wide range of viable alternatives compatible with the domain they occupy, or they can choose to enter a new domain. Businesses enter and leave markets regularly, whereas schools make decisions as to what curricula to offer, hospitals choose what type of patients to serve, and so forth. In choosing a given domain, management simultaneously determines its patterns of interdependence with its environment. When a large hotel chain chooses to operate a hotel and casino in Atlantic City, it voluntarily adds the New Jersey Gaming Commission to its specific environment. Organizations are *not* constrained to do what they have done in the past. Given the fact that environmental domains are fairly broad, there may be a variety of organizational forms that are viable, rather than a single one.

The same logic holds true for technology. The selection of a domain determines the activities the organization will engage in, and hence technology is also chosen. If an organization decides to offer consulting advice tailored to the unique needs of its clients, it is not likely to use long-linked technology. Similarly, the fact that Honda of America chose to build a manufacturing facility in Ohio that could produce at least six hundred cars a day, which would retail in the $10,000 to $15,000 range, pretty well eliminated any technology other than mass production. Had Honda of America decided to produce only six cars a day at that plant and to charge $100,000 or more for each car (which describes more accurately the production facility at Rolls Royce), then mass production might not at all be appropriate. The point is that the choice of domain and its complementary activities and tasks are chosen by management. Technology does not dictate structure. Management dictates structure by its choice of domain.

2. *Organizational effectiveness should be construed as a range instead of a point.* Organizational effectiveness is not an optimum point of achievement. It is a range. This is important because managers don't optimize in their decision making. They "satisfice," seeking outcomes that are satisfactory and sufficient.[6] In other words, they make choices that are good enough. Rather than seeking a structure that would result in *high* effectiveness, managers select structures that merely satisfy the minimal requirements of effectiveness. They might, for instance, trade off an optimum profit for greater power or autonomy, stability, or other objectives. This means that decision makers may be content with varying levels of organizational effectiveness, so long as they all meet or exceed the minimally satisfactory level. The range between maximizing and "good enough" creates an area in which managers can utilize their discretion.

3. *Organizations occasionally have the power to manipulate and control their environments.* Organizations are not always pawns being acted upon by their environments. Managers of large companies are able to create demand for their products and control their competitive environments. Large and small organizations alike can enter into informal relationships with competitors to limit the severity, scope, and danger posed by the competition. Other actions can include mergers, joint ventures, vertical integration, or even lobbying for government regulation. The merger of Gulf Oil into Chevron produced a new organization more powerful in controlling its environment. The Kinney Shoe Company expanded its control when it integrated vertically—from the manufacturing of shoes to both the manufacturing and the retailing of its shoes. An extensive study of the pharmaceutical industry demonstrates a successful case where organizations manipulate and control environmental forces.[7]

The pharmaceutical industry has been extremely effective in shaping its environment, particularly in the areas of pricing and distribution of products, patent and copyright law, and the cooptation of external opinion leaders. After World War II, the pharmaceutical industry turned to government legislation to protect itself against the growing number of companies producing products chemically equivalent to brand-name prescription drugs. The large manufacturers formed the National Pharmaceutical Council, which lobbied before state boards of pharmacy to make it illegal for a pharmacist to substitute a chemically equivalent generic drug for a brand name called for on a prescription. This council was enormously successful. Within eight years, thirty-eight state boards of pharmacy had enacted the council's antigeneric position. The result, of course, was to bolster the profits of the brand names and substantially increase the costs of entry into the industry for new firms.

Until the pharmaceutical firms brought pressure on the U.S. Patent Office to relax its traditional interpretation of the law, no "naturally occurring" substances were patentable, including antibiotics. Competition was fierce as new firms sought to produce standard antibiotics. The price of penicillin in 1955, for instance, was only 6 percent of what it had been in 1945. Industry representatives lobbied for patent protection under the guise that it was necessary if firms were to be economically motivated to develop new drugs. The lobbying effort was successful, allowing firms to patent nearly two thousand variations of antibiotics between 1950 and 1958. The results on profits were sizable: the patented antibiotics generated a gross profit 75 percent above that from the unpatented antibiotics.

The pharmaceutical firms were also very successful in coopting institutional gatekeepers, particularly the American Medical Association (AMA). Pharmaceutical firms and the AMA moved from an adversarial relationship in the 1940s to the complete cooptation of the AMA by the drug companies in the 1960s. During the 1950s, the AMA dropped its strict stand on drug advertising in its journals and permitted any drug approved by the Federal Drug Administration to be listed by brand name. The AMA's Council on Drugs was replaced by a committee with more lenient standards. The result was that between 1953 and 1960 the income of the AMA from journal advertisements tripled. During this same period, revenues from membership dues and subscriptions increased only 20 percent.

4. *Perceptions and evaluations of events are an important intervening link between environments and the actions of organizations.* There is a difference between objective characteristics of the environment and the perception and evaluation of these characteristics by organization members. People do not always perceive environmental characteristics accurately. Their interpretations will show themselves in the decisions they choose. Their strategic choices, in other words, are likely to exert a significant influence on structural design, regardless of the actual characteristics of the environment. Decision makers evaluate the organization's environment, make interpretations based on their experience, and use this information to influence the design of the internal structure.

The Case Against Strategic Choice

The generalizability of the strategic-choice argument is restricted by two facts: (1) Commitments often lock an organization into a limited domain and (2) there are barriers to entry in many markets. Both of these forces can constrain managers from doing much with their discretionary latitude.

Physical and human-resource commitments often lock organizations into a narrow domain for a long time. Once management spends $100 million constructing a state-of-the-art plant to build television sets, it restricts its options in getting out of the television-manufacturing business and getting into magazine publishing. Similarly, personnel are not totally variable costs. Laws make it increasingly difficult to fire employees at will. If an organization's personnel were hired and trained to operate a soft-drink-bottling plant, management just can't—with the wave of a magic wand—make its employees electrical engineers and move into the computer memory-disk business.

Barriers to market entry include economies of scale, absolute costs, and product differentiation.[8] Economies of scale favor those organizations that are already in a market and command substantial market share. The high concentration in industries that produce automobiles, steel, and major appliances is not by chance. It is a reflection of the economies of scale and the difficulties that new firms—with small market shares—would have in competing against the "biggies." There are also absolute cost differences that may be lower for existing organizations because of knowledge or technology not available to new entrants. 3M's knowledge of adhesive technology allows it to produce its adhesive products at a lower cost than a new competitor could. Finally, product differentiation clearly favors existing organizations that have achieved high visibility and whose brands have gained wide recognition. In 1975, for instance, it was pretty easy for someone with a little money and a few good ideas to get into the athletic-shoe-manufacturing business. That is no longer true as Reebok, Nike, and L.A. Gear have grown to dominate the market.

These entry constraints mean that strategic choice is most applicable in domains where entry is relatively easy. That means that managerial latitude is going to be greater in industries like consulting or residental real estate sales. On the other hand, strategic choice is not likely to have much relevance in the dry breakfast cereal business, where competitors would have to come up against the likes of Kellogg, General Mills, and Post.

Summary

Strategic choice reaffirms that organizational decision makers have a degree of discretionary latitude in choosing their strategies and market domains. Even though critics have argued that discretion may be limited, the strategic-choice position nevertheless opened

OT
CLOSE-UP

THE INFLUENCE OF THE CEO'S PERSONALITY ON STRUCTURE

Would you be surprised to find out that chief executive officers with a thirst for power delegate very little authority, that CEO's who are suspicious of others erect elaborate information systems so they can closely monitor what's going on, or that CEO's with strong creative and technical interests often set up substantial research departments? Probably not! This has led to the conclusion, consistent with the strategic-choice perspective, that the personality of an organization's CEO might be a decisive influence on determining structure.

Recent research offers confirming evidence.[9] Specifically, it has been found that a CEO's need to achieve (*nAch*)—that is, the degree to which he or she strives to continually do things better—strongly influences structure. In what way? The more achievement-oriented the CEO, the more he or she centralizes power and imposes high formalization. This structural form allows the CEO to take major credit the door to thinking in terms of discretion on the part of the decision maker to *choose* an organization's structure. Additionally, it called into question the assumption that decision makers would seek an organizational structure that would optimize organizational effectiveness. The ideas presented in the remainder of this chapter owe a debt to the insights offered by John Child in his strategic-choice thesis.

FURTHER CHALLENGES TO THE CONTINGENCY PERSPECTIVE

The contingency perspective—which states that structure will change to reflect changes in strategy, size, technology, and environment—makes a number of implicit assumptions about organizational de-

for, and to carefully monitor and control, the performance of his or her organization.

Does this conclusion apply to all organizations? The evidence indicates that the relationship between *nAch* and formalization is significantly stronger in small than in large organizations and in young than in old organizations. However, the preference for centralization by high achievers seems to be evident regardless of the size or age of the organization.

A final question: Is the CEO's personality a more powerful determinant than the traditional contingency variables of size, technology, and environmental uncertainty? Yes and no! On the no side, size was found to be a significant determinant. Consistent with the research studies discussed in Chapter 6, large organizations tend to be more decentralized and formalized. On the yes side, however, is the evidence that the *nAch* of the CEO seems to be a more powerful determinant of structure than the organization's technology or its environment. But, according to this research, this impact of the CEO's preference is probably more potent in small organizations than in large ones.

cision making. It implies, for instance, that decision makers follow the traditional decision-making process as proposed in management theory. Additionally, it assumes rationality, that top management is the dominant coalition in the organization, and that goal consensus exists. We'll look at each of these assumptions and then argue the power-control viewpoint that these assumptions really don't accurately describe organizational decision making.

Organizational decision making was briefly mentioned in Chapter 4. Here we want to discuss how management theory proposes that individuals make decisions. Management theory argues that the decision-making process begins by determining that a problem exists; that is, that there is an unsatisfactory condition. Frequently this is expressed as a disparity between what is and what should be. Once the need for a decision has been determined, the decision maker identifies all the decision criteria. These are the factors that are important in making the decision. They are selected based on the interests of the organization. Then these factors are weighted to reflect their relative importance. After the criteria have been identified and weighted, the decision maker lists all the alternatives that might solve the problem and meet the criteria requirements. Once listed, the alternatives are evaluated against the criteria. The strengths and weaknesses of each are assessed, and based on this evaluation, the best alternative is chosen.

This traditional decision-making process is simple and clear but, unfortunately, not a very accurate telling of how real decision makers in organizations make choices.

In further accordance with almost all of management theory, the contingency perspective is committed to **rationality.** Rational decisions, in contrast to irrational ones, are consistent with the organization's goals and directed toward maximizing them. As one author succinctly put it, rational decision making presumes "that thinking should precede action; that action should serve a purpose; that purpose should be defined in terms of a consistent set of pre-existent goals; and that choice should be based on a consistent theory of the relation between actions and its consequences."[10]

The **dominant coalition** refers to that group within an organization with the power to influence the outcomes of decisions. In the contingency perspective, the dominant coalition and top management are assumed to be one and the same. This is important because it ignores the possibility that others in the organization, besides management, might have the power to influence structural decisions.

A final assumption of the contingency perspective is that decision makers share a common purpose and that purpose is to serve the interests of the organization. Self-interests are sublimated for the good of the organization. Should a decision maker find difficulty in choosing between alternatives that would benefit the organization and those that would benefit him or her personally, the contingency perspective implies that the interests of the organization will predominate.

If these four assumptions were accurate, we should expect contingency variables—such as technology and environment—to explain fully why structures are designed the way they are in the real world. But, power-control advocates argue, these assumptions *aren't* accurate! Decision makers don't follow the traditional decision-making process. Their decisions are neither consistent nor value maximizing; hence, they don't meet the definition of rational. The actual structural decision in an organization will be made by those members with power; that is, the dominant coalition. This group may or may not be synonymous with those who hold formal authority in top management positions. Lastly, the dominant coalition is typically made up of individuals with divergent interests, thus making goal consensus difficult if not impossible.

Power-control supporters are offering another set of assumptions about organizational decision making. They are proposing a process characterized by nonrationality, divergent interests, dominant coalitions, and power. These are strong assertions and require some elaboration. The following attempts to provide evidence and explanation in support of their position.

Nonrationality

Two separate arguments can be made against rational decision making in organizations. First, individual decision makers aren't able to be totally rational. Second, even if individuals could be rational, organizations can't!

Decision makers are human beings and thus have human frailties. They seldom have a consistent ordering of goals; they do not always pursue systematically the goals they hold; they make choices with incomplete information; and they seldom conduct an exhaustive search for alternatives.[11] More realistically, decision makers recognize only a limited number of decision criteria. They propose only a limited number of alternatives. Their choice of criteria and the weights they give them, and their choice of alternatives and assessment of those alternatives, will reflect their self-interests. The result, as we described earlier in our discussion of strategic choice, is that a decision maker's selection of the best solution is not an optimum choice but one that satisfices. Rather than considering *all* alternatives and listing them, from most preferred to least preferred, the decision maker searches until an alternative emerges that is good enough. Actual decision making, therefore, is not a comprehensive process of searching for an optimum solution. It is an incremental process whereby the decision maker assesses choices until one is found that meets the minimum acceptable level. Once this level is attained, the search stops and the choice is made.

The second argument—that organizations can't be rational—is more complex. To build this argument we need to reflect on Chapter 3 and the competing-values approach to organizational effectiveness.

The competing-values approach proposed that the evaluation of an organization's effectiveness depends on who is doing the evaluating. Different criteria are emphasized by different constituencies. Inherent in this approach is the acknowledgment that organizations have multiple goals. The reality of multiple goals is also an important part of the power-control explanation of how organizations are structured. Basically, the logic is that those who support strategy, size, technology, or environment as structural determinants assume rationality. But rationality is defined as goal-directed behavior. Since organizations have multiple goals that are almost always diverse, rationality does not apply. That is, "since rationality is defined with respect to some preference for outcomes, when there is no consensus on outcome preference it is difficult to speak of rationality."[12] Organizations do not have a singular goal or a hierarchy of multiple goals with which everyone agrees. Thus, even if individual members within an organization could be rational, organizational decision making can't because there is no consistent set of goal preferences.

Divergent Interests

The realities of organizational decision making tell us that the interests of the decision maker and the interests of the organization are rarely one and the same. The traditional decision process, however, assumes them to be. Figure 9–1 depicts reality. Although it would be highly desirable, in terms of organizational effectiveness, for the two circles (representing the individual's interests and the organization's interests) to align perfectly, that is far more likely to be the exception rather than the rule. Given that the two circles do not align, what can we predict and what does it mean to decision making?

Since decision makers act in their self-interests, their choices will reflect only the criteria and preferences compatible with the shaded area. That is, at no time would a decision maker be likely to sublimate his or her own interests to those of the organization. Moreover, if confronted with a set of choices, all of which met the "good enough" criterion, the decision maker would obviously choose the one most beneficial personally. So referring to Figure 9–1, the overlapping area of the circles represents the region in which the decision maker acts consistently with organizational-effectiveness criteria. In this area, for instance, we can expect managers to be

FIGURE 9–1 *Interplay of Decision Maker and the Organization's Interest*

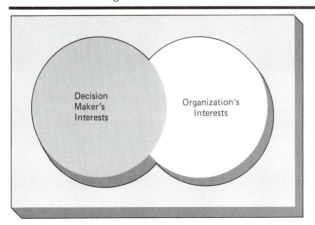

concerned with economic efficiencies and to prefer an organization structure that would facilitate these efficiencies. This area also represents the discretionary range in which, given the constraints of size, technology, and environment, managers still have room for making choices that can be self-serving. The shaded area outside the overlap represents situations in which the decision maker has chosen criteria or preferences that are not compatible with the best interests of the organization but are beneficial to the decision maker.

For instance, phasing out one's department may be in the best interest of the organization, but rarely is it in the best interest of the decision maker. As a result, do not expect managers to make that selection. But *expanding* one's department usually means greater responsibilities, status, and remuneration. Those are rewards that managers value. As a result, we can expect managers to try to increase the size and domain of their units regardless of the effect on the organization. It should be noted that the reward system can be designed to encourage managers to phase out their departments; but it rarely is. It should also be said that the decision to expand the department will be couched in nonpolitical terms. Overt politics is frowned upon in organizations, so self-serving decisions will always be packaged in terms of improving organizational effectiveness.

Dominant Coalitions

While organizations are made up of individuals, they are also made up of coalitions of interests. These coalitions flourish largely because of the ambiguity surrounding goals, organizational effectiveness, and what is thought to be rational.

It is difficult to think of situations in which goals are so congruent, or the facts so clear-cut that judgment and compromise are not involved. What is rational from one point of view is irrational from another. Organizations are political systems, coalitions of interests, and rationality is defined only with respect to unitary and consistent orderings of preferences.[13]

Coalitions form to protect and improve their vested interests. They may have a short-term focus or represent long-term alliances. They can deal with a narrow single issue or a range of broad issues. Probably the most visible coalitions form along departmental lines.

Employees in the marketing department have a common special interest, ensuring that they obtain their share of the organization's resources and rewards. But they are not alone. Accounting, finance, purchasing, and every other department will have their coalitions. Coalitions, of course, are not limited to horizontally differentiated units. Plant managers will have their coalitions, as will different levels of middle managers and even the top management cadre.

The dominant coalition is the one that has the power to affect structure. In a small company, the power coalition and the owners are typically one and the same. In large organizations, top management usually dominates. But not always. Any coalition that can control the resources on which the organization depends can become dominant.[14] A group with critical information, expertise, or any other resource that is essential to the organization's operation can acquire the power to influence the outcome of structural decisions and thus become the dominant coalition. A fuller explanation of the sources of such power appears later in this chapter.

Power

The existence of divergent interests and dominant coalitions leads naturally to the discussion of the role of power in organizations. Simply put, because there is rarely agreement among organizational members on preference outcomes, coalitions wrestle in a power struggle. The power of the various coalitions determines the final outcome of the decision process. Notice that this power struggle comes about because there is dissension concerning preferences or in the definition of the situation.[15] Without this dissension there would be no room for judgment, negotiation, and the eventual politicking that occurs.

Since power and authority are frequently confused by students of management and organization theory, let's clarify the two terms. As you'll see, the differences between them are important because they differentiate the power-control perspective from that of strategic choice.

In Chapter 4, we defined authority as the right to act, or command others to act, toward the attainment of organizational goals. Its unique characteristic, we said, was that this right had legitimacy based on the authority figure's position in the organization. Authority goes with the job. You leave your managerial job and you give up the authority that goes with that position. When we use the term **power** we mean an individual's capacity to influence decisions. As such, authority is actually part of the larger concept of power; that is, the ability to influence based on an individual's legitimate position can affect decisions, but one does not require authority to have such influence.

Figure 9–2 depicts the difference between authority and power.

FIGURE 9–2 *Authority versus Power*

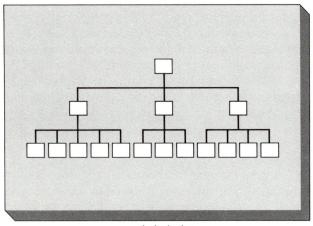

A. Authority

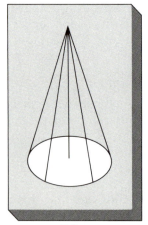

B. Power

The two-dimensional hierarchical arrangement of boxes in Figure 9–2A indicates that there are levels in an organization and that the rights to make decisions increase as one moves up the hierarchy. Power, on the other hand, is conceptualized best as a three-dimensional cone. The power of individuals in an organization depends on their vertical position in the cone and their distance from the center of the cone.

Think of the cone in Figure 9–2B as an organization. The center of the cone will be called the power core. The closer one is to the power core, the more influence one has to affect decisions. The existence of a power core is the only difference between A and B in Figure 9–2. The vertical hierarchy dimension in A is merely one's level on the outer edge of the cone. The top of the cone is equal to the top of the hierarchy; the middle of the cone is equal to the middle of the hierarchy; and so on. Similarly, the functional groupings in A become wedges in the cone. This is seen in Figure 9–3, which depicts the same cone in Figure 9–2B, except that it is now shown from above. Each wedge of the cone represents a functional area. So if the second level of Figure 9–2A contains the marketing, production, and administrative functions of the organ-

FIGURE 9–3 *Bird's-Eye View of the Organization Conceptualized as a Cone*

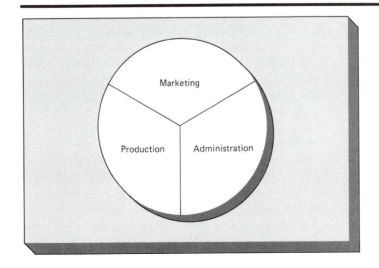

ization, the three wedges of Figure 9–3 are the same functional departments.

The cone analogy allows us to consider these two facts: (1) The higher one moves in an organization (an increase in authority), the closer one automatically moves toward the power core; and (2) it is not necessary to have authority to wield power because one can move horizontally inward toward the power core without moving up.

Ever notice that secretaries of high-ranking executives typically have a great deal of power but very little authority? As gatekeepers for their bosses, they have considerable say as to who can make appointments and who cannot. Additionally, because they are relied upon regularly to pass on information to their bosses, they have some control of what is heard. It's not unusual for $80,000-a-year middle managers to tread very carefully so as not to upset their boss's $25,000-a-year secretary. Why? Because this secretary has power! She is low in the authority hierarchy, but she is close to the power core. Low-ranking employees who have relatives, friends, or associates in high places may be close to the power core. So, too, may the lowly production engineer, with twenty years of experience in the company, who is the only one in the firm who knows the inner workings of all the old production machinery. When pieces of this old equipment break down, no one but this engineer understands how to fix them. Suddenly, this engineer's influence is much greater than would ever be construed from assessing his level in the vertical hierarchy.

The separation of authority and power is obviously very important for understanding the power-control perspective and for differentiating it from strategic choice. It reminds us that those with formal authority may have the clout but, then again, that others in the organization may have created strong power bases that allow them to have even greater influence over decisions. Moreover, because those with the capacity to influence decisions will select criteria and preferences that are consistent with their own self-interests, choices are likely to be highly divergent from those that would occur under strategic-choice conditions. In other words, the power-control position argues that not only will structural decisions be made against different goals, but in contrast to strategic choice, they may be made by a coalition other than those senior executives with the greatest amount of formal authority.

THE ROADS TO POWER

How does an individual or group gain power in an organization? The answer to this question is to keep in mind that power is, first and foremost, a structural phenomenon.[16] It is created by division of labor and departmentation. Horizontal differentiation inevitably creates some tasks that are more important than others. Those individuals or departments performing the more critical tasks, or who are able to *convince* others within the organization that their tasks are more critical, will have a natural advantage in the power-acquisition game. The evidence indicates that there are three roads to the acquisition of power: (1) hierarchical authority, (2) control of resources, and (3) network centrality.[17] Let's take a look at each.

Hierarchical Authority

In spite of our detailed effort earlier in the chapter to differentiate authority and power, we cannot ignore the obvious: formal authority is a source of power. It's not the *only* source of power, but individuals in managerial positions, especially those occupying senior management slots, can influence through formal decree. Subordinates accept this influence as a right inherent in the manager's position.

The manager's job comes with certain rights to reward and punish. Additionally, it comes with prerogatives to make certain decisions. But as we'll see, many managers find their formal influence over people or decisions extremely limited because of their dependence on others within the organization.

Control of Resources

If you have something that others want, you can have power over them. But the mere control of a resource is no guarantee that it will enhance your power. The resource must be both scarce and important.[18]

Unless a resource is scarce within the organization, it is unlikely to be a source of power. With gasoline plentiful, your neighborhood service-station has little ability to influence you. But in the late 1970s, when many people sat in lines for three hours to get five dollars' worth of gas for their cars, station owners had clout. They said, "Jump," and potential customers said, "How high?" The same concept applies in organizations. The mere possession of a resource means nothing if that resource is not scarce.

If resource scarcity increases the power of the resource holder, then the proximity of relevant substitutes for the resource should also be considered. That is, a resource for which there is no close substitute is more scarce than one that has high substitutability. Skills represent an example. Organizations rely on individuals with a wide range of special skills to perform effectively. Those who possess a skill that the organization needs but that no one else in the organization has will obviously be in a more influential position than will one whose skills are duplicated by hundreds of other employees. This describes Johnny Carson's influence at NBC. Probably the most powerful man in American television, Carson is able to negotiate a contract with NBC that pays him in excess of $8 million a year to work only one hour a night, four nights a week, with fifteen weeks of annual vacation! How is Carson able to negotiate such an attractive contract? Because his "Tonight" show draws more than twelve million viewers and is second only to "The Cosby Show" in generating earnings for the network. Most important, the people at NBC believe—rightly or wrongly—that Carson is the scarce and critical resource responsible for generating these high earnings and that there is no close substitute for him.

Similarly, a labor union's power relative to management's is largely a function of its members' ability to restrict management's options. If the organization is highly labor intensive, it will rely heavily on people to get the jobs done. If a company cannot hire someone unless at the time of hiring he or she is already a member of the union, the union could hold the firm captive to its demands. That is why "closed shops" are illegal. Unions obviously would like to hold considerable control over a firm's labor supply. This explains why unions so strongly dislike so-called right-to-work laws that make it illegal for any collective-bargaining agreement to contain clauses calling for compulsory union membership.

These examples indicate another requirement for a resource to give its holder power: The organization must need it! Just being scarce isn't good enough; the resource must also be important. The more a resource approaches criticality for the organization, the more power it gives its holder. To return to a previous example, even when gasoline supplies were limited, if only one station in your town had gas, that station owner would have had power over you only to the degree that you needed gasoline. If you hadn't owned a car, the scarce supply of gasoline would have meant nothing to you. However, if you had been a salesperson who traveled by car, lived in a Sunbelt city where public transportation options were minimal, and depended on having enough gasoline to make your regular calls for your livelihood, that service-station owner would have had a great deal of power. It was just such instances that led to reports of customers in cities such as Los Angeles and Houston paying black market prices of $5 and up per gallon of gas. When you're desperate, you do what you must. Conversely, when others are desperate for what you have, you can use your power to exact a high price for your resource.

In organizations, control and access to information can be a key source of power as long as the information is scarce and important. To illustrate, let's see how control of information can explain why expertise often leads to power and also why many employees go to considerable extremes to cloud what they do in a shroud of secrecy.

Expert knowledge or the possession of special skills is a powerful source of influence, especially in a technologically oriented society. As jobs become more specialized, experts become more indispensable. Therefore, anyone who can develop an expertise that is scarce and important will have power. This increasingly includes, for example, computer specialists, tax accountants, solar engineers, and industrial psychologists. But remember that expertise need not be associated with professionalization. It can be localized knowledge that has little transferability. For instance, suppose that the order clerk in one company (call it XYZ) had developed close ties with a senior purchasing executive at one of the company's major customers (call it ABC). Based on years of telephone contact, the purchasing executive at ABC had instituted the practice of bypassing XYZ's sales personnel, who were responsible for the ABC account. Million-dollar orders were just called in directly to the order clerk at XYZ. This frustrated the sales group at XYZ to no end, but they got credit for the sales and they were not about to upset this prize customer by making him follow XYZ's procedures. The order clerk, meanwhile, capitalized on the situation. He became increasingly knowledgeable of ABC's needs. He even made suggestions to the ABC executive on product modifications that XYZ could make to service ABC better. On the other hand, the salesperson assigned to the ABC account knew nothing of ABC's needs nor had she developed any contacts with key ABC personnel. The result was that this order clerk had become a very powerful figure at XYZ. No one, particularly in the sales department, dared upset him. When he wanted a few extra weeks of vacation, he got them with no questions asked. When he suggested his new son-in-law for a vacancy in the product-design department, the application went through and an offer was made in record time, with noticeable expediting coming from a senior manager in the sales department.

Information, per se, can be a power source. Again, of course, the information must be scarce and important. Secrecy or the lim-

THE RISE OF FINANCIAL PEOPLE TO THE TOP IN LARGE CORPORATIONS

An understanding of power can help to explain the rise of financial personnel in recent years to positions of power in the one hundred largest U.S. corporations.[19]

First, let's look at the facts. Studies that have investigated the background of presidents in large companies have found that manufacturing personnel and enterpreneurs rose to the top in the early part of this century. From the late 1930s to the late 1950s, sales and marketing personnel came to dominate large firms. The period between 1960 and the mid-1980s saw finance personnel increasingly rise to power.

Now let's look at why this occurred. These shifts in the background of corporate presidents essentially reflected changes in the strategy and structure of the organizations, and changes in antitrust laws that promoted an increase in product-related and unrelated mergers after World War II. These changes shifted the power of subunits within corporations, which, in turn, resulted in new leaders coming out of those subunits who could best resolve the problems and uncertainties that the organization faced.

As noted, the early years of this century found corporations run

itation of access to information is used by individuals and groups within the organization to enhance and maintain influence.[20] The information used to make the decision may be kept secret. If others do not know what information went into making a decision, the decision makers can always say that those who did not like the final decision were not privy to all the facts. In effect, as long as information is controlled, it is virtually impossible for anyone to challenge the decision. This describes much of the power attributed to David Stockman, when he was director of the Office of Management and Budget in the Reagan administration. He was the only true expert in the Reagan administration on what was going on within the various federal agencies. In spite of embarrassing the administration with a candid interview, published in the *At-*

by entrepreneurial types and those promoted out of manufacturing. This reflected the production emphasis and single-product strategies of these firms. But after World War II, large corporations began to develop multiproduct strategies and adopt multidivisional structures. This put a premium on sales and marketing expertise and increased promotion opportunities at the top for individuals with these kinds of backgrounds.

A new strategy emerged in the late 1950s that again changed the power position of subunits in large corporations. This was the creation of the conglomerate—a set of many, autonomous companies, operating in unrelated businesses. Conglomerates like Textron, LTV, ITT, and Litton Industries were, in actuality, merely shells that contained dozens of other companies. Of course, in addition to the emergence of conglomerates, the federal government was also becoming more tolerant of large-scale mergers. As a result, corporations changed their strategies from growth through increased market shares to growth through acquisitions of different product lines. These forces—the growth of conglomerates and mergers—put less importance on the type of goods produced and sold. The emphasis had shifted to rapid growth through acquisitions and maximization of short-term profits. When large corporations are seeking rapid growth and investing in dissimilar businesses, the only criterion that could be used to evaluate investment decisions and the performance of business units was financial. So those with a financial background found themselves in the preferred track on the road to the top.

lantic Monthly, in which Stockman openly admitted great personal apprehension with the same economic policies he was openly supporting in public, Reagan chose only to give him a mild reprimand. Because the interview almost completely undermined Stockman's credibility as a spokesperson for the administration, you would have normally expected Stockman to be fired on the spot. But he held his job in the Reagan administration until he resigned nearly four years later. Why? Because Reagan simply could not replace Stockman. He might have become a liability because of his candid remarks, but the reality was that Stockman's control of information made him an irreplaceable resource.

In addition to maintaining secrecy over the information used in the decision, it is also possible to keep the decision-making process itself secret or occasionally even the results of the process secret. The former may involve not divulging the names of the decision makers or the process of deliberation. The latter is exemplified best by the practice, in many organizations, of keeping salaries secret.

This discussion on using expertise and information as power tools provides insights into employee actions that are often seen as irrational. When placed in the context of controlling scarce and important resources, behaviors such as destroying the procedure manuals that describe how your job is done, refusing to train people in your job or even to show others exactly what you do, creating specialized language and terminology that inhibits others from understanding your job, or operating in secrecy so that the tasks you perform will appear more complex and difficult than they really are suddenly appear to be very rational actions.

Network Centrality

Being in the right place in the organization can be a source of power.[21] Those individuals or groups with **network centrality** gain power because their position allows them to integrate other functions or to reduce organization dependencies. Of course, being in "the right place" is not a random phenomenon. Who has centrality depends on the organization's strategy and the problems it faces at any given moment.[22] Functional departments within an organization take on different degrees of importance relative to the strategy the organization is pursuing and the critical problems that arise. This means that an organization's primary strategic orientation is an influence on who has the power. In an organization that is market oriented—like Procter & Gamble—marketing personnel will be more powerful than, say, accountants or research-and-development people. We would also expect accounting to be more powerful in organizations that rely heavily on financial data—such as banks and brokerage firms—or when the organization faces critical financial or control problems.[23] When an organization is financially healthy, the accounting function is generally less critical to the immediate needs of the organization. But when the organization is in a financial crisis, accounting's concerns become the major concern of the entire organization. Not surprisingly, when the financial crisis diminishes, accounting will become less critical and, thus, less powerful. Students of Chrysler Corporation watched between 1979 and 1984 as the power of the company's accounting and financial staff rose and fell inversely with Chrysler's financial performance.

The power of different functions can be seen in a study comparing hospitals with insurance firms.[24] The hospitals' strategies emphasized efficiency and cost control, while the insurance firms sought product and market innovation. Consistent with the role of centrality, the researcher found that the accounting, process-improvement, and operations functions had the most power in the hospitals; and the marketing and product-development functions had the most power in the insurance companies.

A study of a production plant in France gives us additional insights into how being in the right place in an organization can be a source of power.[25] The researcher observed that the maintenance engineers in this plant exerted a great deal of influence even though they were not particularly high in the organizational hierarchy. The researcher concluded that the breakdown of the machinery was the only remaining uncertainty confronting the organization. The maintenance engineers were the only personnel who could cope with machine stoppage, and they had taken the pains to reinforce their power through control of information. They avoided written procedures for dealing with breakdowns; they purposely disregarded all blueprints and maintenance directions; and so on. Not even the supervisors in the plant had adequate knowledge to check on these engineers.

We can even predict, based on the network-centrality theme, that those holding power will occasionally resort to inventing problems that they can handle just to remind others in the organization how critical they are to the organization's success.[26] In the French factory, if the machines never broke down, the maintenance engineers would have no opportunity to demonstrate the organization's dependence on them. This reasoning can explain why industrial relations departments occasionally allow a strike to occur when an impasse could be resolved. What better way is there to remind everyone within a company just how important the industrial relations department is than to have a strike that closes most of the company down and *requires* the skills of the industrial relations' labor negotiators to resolve the conflict?

SYNTHESIZING THE POWER-CONTROL VIEW

The previous discussions on nonrational decision making, dominant coalitions, divergent interests, and power allows us now to synthesize power-control's view of how organization structures are derived.

We can begin our synthesis by restating the power-control thesis: An organization's structure, at any given time, is to a large extent the result of those in power selecting a structure that will, to the maximum degree possible, maintain and enhance their control. As we'll see, the power-control perspective doesn't ignore the impact of size, technology, or other contingency variables. Rather, it treats them as constraints that must be met in what is otherwise a political process.

Structural Decisions as a Political Process

Power-control advocates think of an organization's structure as the result of a power struggle between special-interest coalitions, each arguing for a structural arrangement that best meets its own needs instead of organizationwide interests—all the time, of course, couching its arguments and preferred criteria in terms of organizational effectiveness. In such a setting, politics will determine the criteria and preferences of decision makers.

Politics refers to efforts of organizational members to mobilize support for or against policies, rules, goals, or other decisions in which the outcome will have some effect on them. Politics, there-fore, is essentially the exercise of power. You may appropriately ask, Why is the structural decision a political one? The answer is that the choice of any structure will automatically favor some coalitions and disadvantage others. A coalition's location in a struc-ture will determine such things as its influence in planning, its choice of technology, the criteria by which it will be evaluated, allocation of rewards, control of information, its proximity to sen-ior executives, and its ability to exercise influence on numerous decisions in which it has a stake in the outcome.

So what happens when organization structure is viewed as the outcome of a political process rather than as a result of rational decision making? Those with the power call the shots! This can change the players who make the structural decision as well as the criteria and preferences they use. The dominant coalition, which may or may not include top management, become the key players. "Good enough" replaces maximization as the criterion of effec-tiveness. And the self-interests of the dominant coalition determine the preferred outcome, not the interests of the organization.

Contingency Factors as Constraints

It's important to keep in mind that power-control acknowledges a role for technology, environment, and the other contingency vari-ables. But that role is not as imperatives; that is, they don't *deter-mine* structure. Like strategic choice, the power-control view treats the contingency variables as constraints.

Strategy, size, technology, and environment act as general con-straints on structure to narrow decision-making choices. They set the general parameters for organizational effectiveness. But within the parameters, there is still a lot of room left for maneuvering, especially since organizational effectiveness is a problematic state, and the structural choice only has to satisfice.

The Power-Control Model

Figure 9–4 depicts how power-control advocates perceive the cre-ation of an organization's structure. The choice of a structure is constrained by the organization's strategy, size, technology, en-vironment, and the required minimal level of effectiveness. These

ETHICS AND THE USE OF POWER

Are members of the dominant coalition acting *unethically* when they seek to use their power to enhance their control? In today's business environment—where unethical behavior has become an increasing concern of executives, the media, academics, students of management, and the general public—this question at least needs to be addressed.[27]

Ethics refers to rules or principles that define right and wrong conduct.[28] This, then, begs the question: Is the use of power, per se, wrong? Many contemporary behavioral scientists would argue that it isn't. They note that power is a natural part of human interactions—"we influence, or try to influence, other people every day under all sorts of conditions"—that carries over into organizational life.[29]

Power really has two faces—one negative and the other positive.[30] The negative side is associated with abuse—when, for example, powerholders exploit others or use their power to merely accumulate status symbols. The positive side is characterized by a concern for group goals, helping the group to formulate its goals, and providing group members with the support they need to achieve these goals.

If the dominant coalition chooses a structure that satisfices rather than maximizes goal-attainment, has it acted unethically? Is satisficing an abuse of the system? Does satisficing exploit employees, stockholders, or other relevant constituencies? Is any self-serving action by the dominant coalition that suboptimizes the organization's effectiveness an unethical act or has the dominant coalition acted ethically if the organization's performance merely meets the "good enough" standard? Undoubtedly, people will disagree on answers to these questions. But it is answers to questions such as these that will determine whether the power-control perspective describes unethical practices.

forces combine to establish the set of structural alternatives from which the decision will be made. Who will make the decision? The dominant coalition! How will this dominant coalition make the decision? By imposing its self-interests on the criteria and preferences in the decision. The result is the organization's emergent structure.

FIGURE 9–4 *The Power-Control Model*

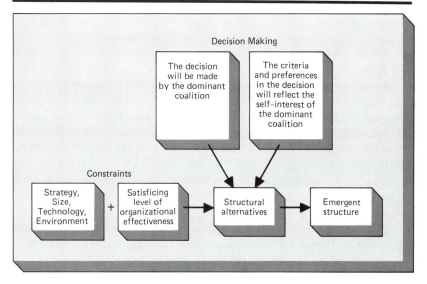

IMPLICATIONS BASED ON THE POWER-CONTROL VIEW

It is now time to translate our insights from the power-control perspective into implications for the structuring of organizations. We begin by considering a power-control interpretation of technology and environment's role on structure.

Technology and Environment

"The picture of the organization as an adaptive, responsive entity, proximately affected by the demands of technology or environment, is probably as misleading as the parallel portrait of the competitive organization in classical economic theory."[31] Power-control advocates argue that an organization's structure, at any given time, will be one that allows those in power to maintain the control they have. In terms of technology and environment, therefore, the dominant coalition can be expected to seek routine technologies and attempt to manage their environment to reduce uncertainty. Let us expand briefly on each of these points.

Technology does not *cause* structure. It is chosen. The choice of a domain tends to constrain the organization's technology, but the domain is also chosen. Within a given domain, a range of technologies almost always exists. Which type of technology will be selected? That which is most routine and relies most heavily on mechanization and automation. Routine technologies make individual workers more substitutable for each other and hence more easily replaceable. Routinization also serves the interest of top management by facilitating centralization of power. Given that technology is chosen, routine technologies will be most prevalent because they enhance control.

The organization will seek to manage its environment to reduce uncertainty. It can, for example, insulate its technologies to reduce the impact of uncertainty; establish more favorable relationships with those elements in the environment that pose potential difficulties; or shift to a more favorable environment by changing domains. The view that structure is a response to the environment implies that changes in structure occur to improve organizational effectiveness. When the organization responds to external demands, it usually does so under extreme duress. "The organization that appears to be innovative or responsive is so, we would argue, because such a course of action enhances the influence and resource position of those in control of the organization's activities."[32]

When is the environment likely to be an overpowering constraint in the structural decision? When opportunities in the organization's environment are scarce or limited[33] and when there is a minimal degree of organizational slack.[34]

Scarcity in the environment would include situations where there was intense competition or limited opportunities for growth. An abundant environment, on the other hand, would describe an industry that could adequately support all current competitors and where there were considerable opportunities for growth. In the scarce environment, the organization's options or strategic choices would be fewer, and less room would be available for the dominant coalition to maneuver.

Organizational slack is that cushion of actual or potential resources that enables an organization to adjust to environmental change.[35] These are the resources in excess of those required for the organization to achieve a minimal level of effectiveness. They include things like extra cash, a large credit line, underutilized plant capacity, untapped management potential, discretionary funds for travel and entertainment, or earnings that far exceed the industry average. The less slack an organization has, the tighter the parameters are within which the structural decision must be made.

Stability and Mechanistic Structures

These comments lead us to additional extensions. Because organizations seek routinization and management of uncertainty, power-control advocates propose that structural change should be minimal. Those in power can be expected to try to maintain their control. If the current structure is effective in maintaining control, why should they want to change? They will not, except when forced. The argument made by power-control advocates is that significant changes represent, in effect, quasi-revolutions.[36] They are likely to occur only as a result of a political struggle in which new power relationships evolve. This kind of political struggle rarely happens. When it does, it usually follows a major shake-up in top management or indicates that the organization is facing obvious and direct threats to its survival. When changes in structure occur, they are more typically incremental.[37] Incrementalism maintains stability by keeping changes small and never deviating much from the previous structural arrangement. A look at the organization structures of Ford Motor Co., the U.S. Air Force, or the *New York Times* in 1959 and 1989 shows each substantially unchanged over the thirty-year period and that change has been evolutionary rather than revolutionary.

The power-control view of structure predicts that not only will structural arrangements be relatively stable over time, but mechanistic structures will dominate. This is consistent with the conclusions drawn in Chapter 8. If stability, routinization, and centralized control are sought, it seems logical that mechanistic structures will rule. And observations of structures, as we noted in Chapter 8, concur with this prediction. Figure 9–5 expands the "Structural Alternatives" box presented in Figure 9–4. Structural

FIGURE 9–5 *Decision Discretion in the Power-Control Model*

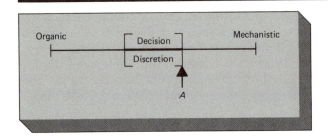

options range along an organic-mechanistic continuum. Those in power will choose structures that maintain their control. So given that organizational effectiveness is a range rather than a point, there will be some decision discretion available to the dominant coalition. Within its discretionary range, it will select the most mechanistic alternative (point *A* in Figure 9–5). This anticontingency position flies in direct opposition to the theme "there is no one best way to organize." The contingency advocates' theme of "no one best way" uses performance as the standard. The mechanistic structure *is* the "one best way" if best refers to maintenance of control rather than performance.

Interestingly, there is even evidence that in dynamic environments, where there is rapid change, mechanistic structures emerge.[38] Contrary to the contingency view that dynamic environments would be matched with organic structures, decision makers appear to prefer control over increased effectiveness. Of course, this should be true only when a certain minimal level of organizational effectiveness has already been achieved.

Complexity

Increased differentiation—horizontally, vertically, or spatially—leads to difficulties in coordination and control. Management would prefer, therefore, all things being equal, to have low complexity. But, of course, all things are not equal. Size, technology, and environmental factors do make high complexity efficient in many cases. So compromise is required. The "imperatives" set the parameters. Management can then be expected to choose the lowest degree of complexity (to maximize control) consistent with the satisficing criterion for organizational effectiveness.

It has been noted that information technology can permit the development of more elaborate and complex structures without necessarily foresaking management's control.[39] Sophisticated information systems utilizing computer technology allow senior executives to receive continual communications. Management can monitor a large range of activities many levels down the hierarchy or thousands of miles away and still maintain close control over those activities. The fact that an executive in Atlanta can punch eight keys on the computer terminal at his desk and get an immediate readout on the current status of an inventory item in a company warehouse in Seattle means that this executive can monitor inventories more closely than managers in Seattle could have twenty years ago.

Formalization

Those in power will influence the degree of rules and regulations under which employees work. Because control is a desired end for those in power, organizations should have a high degree of formalization.

If technology were nonroutine or if environmental uncertainty could not be managed, we would expect that high formalization—while desired by those in control—could not be implemented without disastrous effects on organizational performance. But as we have concluded, management will make extensive efforts to routinize tasks and manage uncertainty. Since technology and environments are chosen by those in power, we can expect them to select ones that are compatible with high levels of formalization and maintenance of control. In those cases where factors require low formalization—because of an extremely turbulent environment that cannot be managed or highly professionalized personnel—those in power can be expected to rely on sophisticated information technology as a control device that can be substituted for rules and regulations.

Centralization

From earlier discussions on centralization, we know that it is preferred when mistakes are very costly, when temporary external threats exist, or when it is important that decisions reflect an understanding of the "big picture." To these we can add: when those in control want to make the decisions. In fact, power-control advocates claim decentralization should occur infrequently. Even when it does, it may be pseudodecentralization. That is, top management will create the appearance of delegating decisions downward but use information technology for feedback. This feedback allows those in control to monitor lower-level decisions closely and to intercede and correct at any time the decisions they do not like.

If persons are allowed discretion, but are permitted the opportunity to make decisions because their performance can be rapidly and accurately assessed, it seems that there has been no real sharing of control, influence, or power in the organization. It is conceivable, then, that the introduction of information technology can make possible the appearance of decentralization while maintaining effective centralized control over organizational operations.[40]

It can also be argued that those in power maintain control in decentralized situations by defining the parameters of decisions. For example, university faculty members perceive themselves as operating in a heavily decentralized environment. Important decisions, such as hiring, are made by faculty members at the department level. But the decision that a vacancy exists typically lies with the college- or university-level administrators. The president decides which departments will be given new positions to staff and also decides the disposition of slots that open up as a result of resignations or retirements. While it's true that department members select their colleagues, top-level university administrators maintain considerable control through their power to allocate positions among campus units and their ultimate right to veto candidates of whom they do not approve.

SUMMARY

No more than 50 to 60 percent of the variability in structure can be explained by strategy, size, technology, and environment. A substantial portion of the residual variance may be explained by the power-control view of structure, which states that an organization's structure, at any given time, is largely the result of those in power selecting a structure that will, to the maximum degree possible, maintain and enhance their control.

The other determinants of structure assume rationality. However, for rationality to prevail an organization must have either a single goal or agreement over the multiple goals. Neither case exists in most organizations. As a result, structural decisions are not rational. The structure decision is a power struggle between special-interest groups or coalitions, each arguing for a structural arrangement that best meets their own needs. Strategy, size, technology, and environment define the minimal level of effectiveness and set the parameters within which self-serving decision choices will be made.

Power is the central theme in the power-control perspective. Structural choices will be made by those who hold power—the group that we have called the dominant coalition. This is usually the senior management, but it need not be. Power can be acquired by holding hierarchical authority, or by controlling resources that are scarce and important in the organization, or by having a central position in the organization.

The argument is made that both technology and environment are chosen. Thus, those in power will select technologies and environments that will facilitate their maintenance of control. Organizations, therefore, should be characterized by routine technologies and environments in which uncertainties are relatively low. To enhance control further, those in power will seek to choose structures that are low in complexity and high in both formalization and centralization.

FOR REVIEW AND DISCUSSION

1. "Strategy, size, technology, and environment are irrelevant in explaining an organization's structure." Do you agree or disagree? Discuss.
2. Contrast strategic choice and power control.
3. What flaws can you identify in the strategic choice argument?
4. Describe the traditional decision-making process. What assumptions does it make?
5. Who makes up an organization's dominant coalition?
6. Contrast power with authority.
7. How is it possible for someone low in the organization to obtain power?
8. How does control over decision premises give power to a person?
9. Some positions in an organization are essentially powerless. Why? Are certain functions in organizations typically more powerful? Less powerful?

10. What type of functional background do you think will be held by individuals who will be running large corporations during the decade of the 1990s? Support your answer.

11. How is the structural decision a political process?

12. Using the power-control perspective, describe how most organizations are structured.

13. "Power is derived from the division of labor that occurs as task specialization is implemented in organizations." Build an argument to support this statement.

14. How would advocates of the power-control view explain the existence of an organic structure?

15. The president of a large corporation hires an impartial consultant to analyze the organization's structure. After a long and careful analysis, the consultant submits a report to the corporation's board of directors that suggests several small changes but leaves the current structure substantially in place. Explain the president's decision to use a consultant and the consultant's conclusions from a power-control perspective.

NOTES

[1] Adapted from Michael Korda, *Power! How to Get It, How to Use It* (New York: Random House, 1975), pp. 75–77.

[2] Jeffrey D. Ford and John W. Slocum, Jr., "Size, Technology, Environment and the Structure of Organizations," *Academy of Management Review*, October 1977, pp. 561–75.

[3] John Child, "Organization Structure, Environment and Performance: The Role of Strategic Choice," *Sociology*, January 1972, pp. 1–22; and Derek S. Pugh, "The Management of Organization Structures: Does Context Determine Form?" *Organizational Dynamics*, Spring 1973, pp. 19–34.

[4] Child, "Organization Structure, Environment and Performance."

[5] Ibid.

[6] Herbert A. Simon, *Administrative Behavior*, 3d ed. (New York: Free Press 1976).

[7] Paul Hirsch, "Organizational Effectiveness and the Institutional Environment," *Administrative Science Quarterly*, September 1975, pp. 327–44.

[8] Howard E. Aldrich, *Organizations and Environments* (Englewood Cliffs, N.J.: Prentice Hall, 1979), pp. 149–59.

[9] Danny Miller and Cornelia Dröge, "Psychological and Traditional Determinants of Structure," *Administrative Science Quarterly*, December 1986, pp. 539–60.

[10] James G. March, "The Technology of Foolishness," in J. G. March and J. P. Olsen, *Ambiguity and Choice in Organizations* (Bergen, Norway: Universitetsforlaget, 1976), p. 71.

[11] James G. March and Herbert A. Simon, *Organizations* (New York: John Wiley, 1958).

[12] Jeffrey Pfeffer, *Organizational Design* (Arlington Heights, Ill.: AHM Publishing, 1978), p. 8.

[13] Ibid., pp. 11–12.

[14] Eva C. Chu, "Dominant Coalition as a Mediating Mechanism Between the Rational Model and the Political Model in Organization Theory." Paper presented at Annual Academy of Management Conference, Anaheim, Calif., August 1988.

[15] Jeffrey Pfeffer, "Power and Resource Allocation in Organizations," in Barry M. Staw and Gerald R. Salancik, eds., *New Directions in Organizational Behavior* (Chicago: St. Clair Press, 1977), p. 240.

[16] Jeffrey Pfeffer, *Power in Organizations* (Marshfield, Mass.: Pitman Publishing, 1981), p. 4.

[17] W. Graham Astley and Paramjit S. Sachdeva, "Structural Sources of Intraorganizational Power: A Theoretical Synthesis," *Academy of Management Review*, January 1984, pp. 104–13.

[18] Pfeffer, "Power and Resource Allocation," pp. 248–49.

[19] Neil Fligstein, "The Intraorganizational Power Struggle: Rise of Finance Personnel to the Top Leadership in Large Corporations, 1919–1979," *American Sociological Review*, February 1987, pp. 44–58.

[20] Pfeffer, "Power and Resource Allocation," p. 246.

[21] Daniel J. Brass, "Being in the Right Place: A Structural Analysis of Individual Influence in an Organization," *Administrative Science Quarterly*, December 1984, pp. 518–39; Judith D. Hackman, "Power and Centrality in the Allocation of Resources in Colleges and Universities," *Administrative Science Quarterly*, March 1985, pp. 61–77; and Hanna Ashar and Jonathan Z. Shapiro, "Measuring Centrality: A Note on Hackman's Resource-Allocation Theory," *Administrative Science Quarterly*, June 1988, pp. 275–83.

[22] Donald C. Hambrick, "Environment, Strategy, and Power within Top Management Teams," *Administrative Science Quarterly*, June 1981, pp. 253–75; and M. A. Hitt, R. D. Ireland, and K. A. Palia, "Industrial Firms' Grand Strategy and Functional Importance: Moderating Effects of Technology and Uncertainty," *Academy of Management Journal*, June 1982, pp. 265–98.

[23] Keith G. Provan and Germain Boer, "Beyond Strategic Contingencies Theory: Understanding Departmental Power in Organizations." Paper presented at the Annual Academy of Management Conference, Boston, Mass., August 1984.

[24] Hambrick, "Environment, Strategy, and Power."

[25] Michael Crozier, *The Bureaucratic Phenomenon* (Chicago: University of Chicago Press, 1964).

[26] Pfeffer, "Power and Resource Allocation," p. 257.

[27] My thanks to Bernie Hinton for suggesting the importance of this question.

[28] Keith Davis and William C. Frederick, *Business and Society: Management, Public Policy, Ethics,* 5th ed. (New York: McGraw-Hill, 1984), p. 76.

[29] Harold J. Leavitt and Homa Bahrami, *Managerial Psychology: Managing Behavior in Organizations,* 5th ed. (Chicago: University of Chicago Press, 1988), p. 121.

[30] David C. McClelland, "The Two Faces of Power," *Journal of International Affairs,* Vol. 24, No. 1, 1970, pp. 29–47.

[31] Pfeffer, *Organizational Design,* p. 225.

[32] Ibid.

[33] Barry M. Staw and E. Szwajkowski, "The Scarcity-Munificence Component of Organizational Environments and the Commission of Illegal Acts," *Administrative Science Quarterly,* September 1975, pp. 345–54.

[34] Richard M. Cyert and James G. March, *A Behavioral Theory of the Firm* (Englewood Cliffs, N.J.: Prentice-Hall, 1963), p. 36.

[35] L. J. Bourgeois III, "On the Measurement of Organizational Slack," *Academy of Management Review,* January 1981, p. 30.

[36] Pfeffer, *Organizational Design,* p. 176.

[37] Ibid., p. 14.

[38] L. J. Bourgeois III, Daniel W. McAllister, and Terence R. Mitchell, "The Effects of Different Organizational Environments upon Decisions about Organizational Structure," *Academy of Management Journal,* September 1978, pp. 508–14.

[39] Pfeffer, *Organizational Design,* pp. 73–75.

[40] Ibid., pp. 72–73.

10

ORGANIZATIONAL DESIGN OPTIONS

AFTER READING THIS CHAPTER, YOU SHOULD BE ABLE TO:

1 Explain why there should be a limited set of structural configurations.
2 Define the five basic parts of any organization.
3 Describe the five basic structural configurations.
4 List the strengths and weaknesses of each of these configurations.
5 Explain when each configuration should be used.
6 Classify each of the configurations in terms of their structural characteristics.

Introduction
IS EVERY ORGANIZATION REALLY UNIQUE?

In one way, organizations are like fingerprints. Each has its own unique structure. Coca-Cola and PepsiCo, for instance, are both large corporations that derive most of their income from soft drinks. But a careful review of their organizations finds that their structures are not identical clones of each other. Yet, again like fingerprints, no structure is *truly* unique. All fingerprints, for instance, have common properties that allow them to be classified around common elements. If we look at the organizations that currently exist, it's quickly obvious that they too have common elements. To make our point, PepsiCo, B.F. Goodrich, Citicorp, and Phelps Dodge are all in very different industries. However, a close look at their structures reveals that they share at least two things in common—each is high in complexity and high in formalization. So while there may be four million or more organizations today in North America, there certainly aren't four million *different* forms or configurations. Like fingerprints, many have common elements that, once identified, allow for the development of a classification framework.

The purpose of this chapter is to build such a classification framework. If we are to be able to recommend preferred structural designs to managers, we need to know our options. By the time you finish reading this chapter, you'll have an understanding of the five basic design options from which decision makers can choose and the conditions under which each is preferred.

THE CASE FOR STANDARD CONFIGURATIONS

Since the late 1970s, there has been a growing search to identify some common organizational types or configurations.[1] Inherent in this search is the belief that, in fact, there does exist some limited set of configurations that are significantly *alike* within their category, yet meaningfully *different* from organizations in other categories. Every **configuration** would contain a complex clustering of elements that are internally cohesive and where the presence of some elements suggest the reliable occurrence of others.[2]

The goals that call for the set of configurations to be limited and for each to be internally cohesive are important. If that set were, for example, made up of five hundred or one thousand configurations, it would be nearly impossible for anyone to fully understand them, never mind use them in any useful way. It would create a classic case of "information overload." While there is no scientifically derived cut-off that would separate a *manageable* set of configurations from an *overwhelming* set, any number beyond a half-dozen or so would undoubtedly detract from the creation of a useful categorization scheme. Similarly, if the elements within each configuration were unrelated, then the likelihood of finding a manageable set is unlikely. So, to illustrate, if there were five key elements on which organizations differed and each one could be rated as either "high," "moderate," or "low," there could potentially be 243 (3^5) different configurations if the elements were unrelated.

Of course, it might be unreasonable to question the basic belief that there actually exists, in the total population of organizations, a limited set of internally cohesive configurations that could be identified. We'll argue that this belief *is* valid based on (1) the natural-selection phenomenon, (2) the search by organizations for internal consistency, and (3) the propensity for organizations to follow what's in fashion.

The natural-selection argument was developed in Chapter 8 in our discussion of population ecology. It resurfaces here for us to point out that the environment may encourage only relatively few organizational forms to survive in the same setting.[3] To be cost efficient and competitive, an organization may need to adopt structural properties similar to those of other organizations in its industry or its market niches or that are following similar strategies. The natural-selection thesis, for example, might predict that successful fast-food franchises or the Big Six public accounting firms would have similar "industry" structures. Those that developed structures different from the industry norm would be less successful and, over the long run, die off.

The second argument is that organizations may be driven toward a given configuration to achieve consistency in their internal characteristics and to fit with their situation.[4] For example, the extensive use of division of labor, standardization, and the employment of unskilled personnel to do repetitive tasks tends to be associated with high formalization. Internal inconsistencies will lead to reductions in performance. So, over time, organizations should develop a set of structural characteristics that fit well together. This should lead to a limited set of configurations in which internal consistencies are achieved.

Finally, the number of viable configurations that are in use will be limited by fashion or what is currently in vogue.[5] Organizational decision makers are not immune from the influence of other organizational decision makers. Just as what we wear, eat, and drive are influenced by peers, the media, and other sources, so is an organization's design. Decision makers like to think they are current and progressive. If the current fashion favors adaptive, decentralized organizations, there will be pressures on organizations to look contemporary. If for no other reason, such imitation conveys to strategic constituencies—like bankers, labor unions, and security analysts—that management is up to date on current management practices. A contemporary organization design symbolically conveys to constituencies that the organization is striving for effectiveness.

COMMON ELEMENTS IN ORGANIZATIONS

While there is no universally agreed-upon framework for classifying organizations, Henry Mintzberg's recent work probably gets closest to it.[6]

Mintzberg argues that there are five basic parts to any organization. They are shown in Figure 10–1 and defined as follows:

1. **The operating core.** Employees who perform the basic work related to the production of products and services.
2. **The strategic apex.** Top-level managers, who are charged with the overall responsibility for the organization.
3. **The middle line.** Managers, who connect the operating core to the strategic apex.
4. **The technostructure.** Analysts, who have the responsibility for effecting certain forms of standardization in the organization.
5. **The support staff.** People who fill the staff units, who provide indirect support services for the organization.

Any one of these five parts can dominate an organization. Moreover, depending on which part is in control, a given structural configuration is likely to be used. So, according to Mintzberg, there are five distinct design configurations, and each one is associated with the domination by one of the five basic parts. If control lies with the operating core, decisions are decentralized. This creates the *professional bureaucracy.* When the strategic apex is dominant, control is centralized and the organization is a *simple structure.* If middle management is in control, you'll find groups of essentially autonomous units operating in a *divisional structure.* Where the analysts in the technostructure are dominant, control will be through standardization, and the resultant structure will be a *machine bureaucracy.* Finally, in those situations where the support staff rules, control will be via mutual adjustment and the *adhocracy* arises.

Each of these design configurations has its own unique set of

FIGURE 10–1 *Five Basic Elements of an Organization*

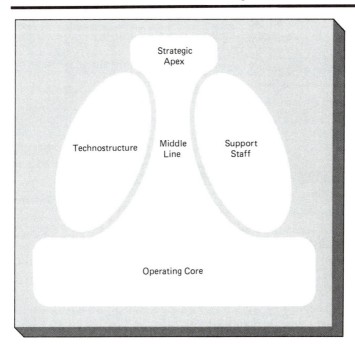

Henry Mintzberg, *Structure in Fives: Designing Effective Organizations,* © 1983, p. 262. Reprinted by permission of Prentice Hall, Englewood Cliffs, NJ.

pluses and minuses. Consistent with the contingency philosophy, each is the preferred configuration under certain conditions. In the remainder of this chapter, we'll describe each configuration, its strengths and weaknesses, and what those conditions are that make it the preferred option.

THE SIMPLE STRUCTURE

What do a small retail store, an electronics firm run by a hard-driving entrepreneur, a new Planned Parenthood office, and an airline in the midst of a companywide pilot's strike have in common? They probably all utilize the simple structure.

The simple structure is said to be characterized most by what

FIGURE 10–2 *The Simple Structure*

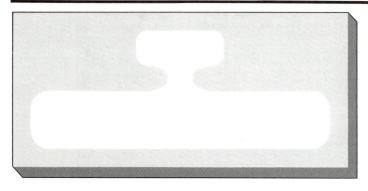

Henry Mintzberg, *Structure in Fives: Designing Effective Organizations,* © 1983, p. 11. Reprinted by permission of Prentice Hall, Englewood Cliffs, NJ.

it is not rather than what it is. The simple structure is not elaborated.[7] It is low in complexity, has little formalization, and has authority centralized in a single person. As shown in Figure 10–2, the **simple structure** is depicted best as a flat organization, with an organic operating core and almost everyone reporting to a one-person strategic apex where the decision-making power is centralized.

Figure 10–3 illustrates an application of the simple structure. Notice that this organization, Fashion Flair retail stores, is flat. Decision making is basically informal—all important decisions are

FIGURE 10–3 *Fashion Flair Stores*

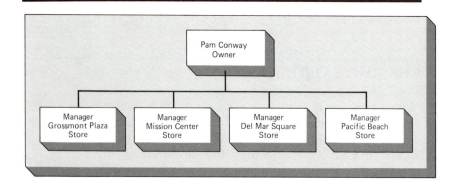

centralized in the hands of the senior executive, who because of the low complexity is able to obtain key information readily and to act rapidly when required. This senior executive is the owner-manager of Fashion Flair. The senior executives in the simple structure typically have a wide span of control.

Strengths and Weaknesses

The strength of the simple structure lies in its simplicity. It's fast and flexible and requires little cost to maintain. There are no layers of cumbersome structure. Accountability is clear. There is a minimum amount of goal ambiguity because members are able to identify readily with the organization's mission, and it is fairly easy to see how one's actions contribute to the organization's goals.

The simple structure's predominant weakness is its limited applicability. When confronted with increased size, this structure generally proves inadequate. Additionally, the simple structure concentrates power in one person. Rarely does the structure provide countervailing forces to balance the chief executive's power. Therefore, the simple structure can easily succumb to the abuse of authority by the person in power. This concentration of power, of course, can work against the organization's effectiveness and survival. The simple structure, in fact, has been described as the "riskiest of structures hinging on the health and whims of one individual."[8] One heart attack can literally destroy the organization's decision-making center.

When Should You Use It?

When are you likely to find a simple structure? If the organization is small or in its formative stage of development, if the environment is simple and dynamic, if the organization faces high hostility or a crisis, if the senior manager is also the owner, or if the senior executive either wants to hoard power or has power thrust upon him by his or her subordinates.

The simple structure is effective when the number of employees is few. Small size usually means less repetitive work in the operating core, so standardization is less attractive. Informal communication is convenient. As long as the structure remains small, the "one-person show" can effectively oversee all activities, be knowledgeable about key problems, and carry out all important decisions.

The simple structure also meets the needs of organizations when they are in their formative years. "The *new organization* tends to adopt the Simple Structure, no matter what its environment or technical system, because it has not had the time to elaborate its administrative structure."[9] Almost all organizations, therefore, pass through the simple-structure stage. For those that remain small in size, the simple structure may be permanent rather than transitory.

Simple and dynamic environments tend to be associated with the simple structure's flat organization with centralized decision making and organic operating core. Why? A simple environment is comprehended easily by a single individual and, therefore, enables the individual to control decision making effectively. A dynamic environment requires an organic structure so that it can react to unpredictable contingencies.

Regardless of size, when an organization suddenly confronts a hostile environment, management is likely to resort to the simple structure. The reason for this is logical. When survival is threatened, top management wants control. Further, since the hostility disrupts the standard operating procedures, the SOPs are likely to be suspended. The result is a temporary flattening out of the organization.

Our discussion of the power-control position in the previous chapter leads us to the prediction that senior decision makers would have a strong preference for the simple structure. Why? Because it is an excellent vehicle for concentrating power in a single place. While large size typically excludes the possibility of a permanent simple structure, this configuration should be used by medium- and small-sized organizations, where power is consolidated. A look at most small- and medium-sized owner-managed organizations confirms this prediction. Owner-managers have considerable power. They assert that power by maintaining a structure that allows them the greatest control. That, of course, is the simple structure.

Similarly, regardless of size, when the top executive hoards power and purposely avoids high formalization so as to maximize the impact of his or her discretion, that executive will, in effect, design a simple structure for the organization. Power and the simple structure are again correlated when organizational members defer power to the chief executive. That is, even if the senior executive does not crave power, if subordinates do not want to be involved with decision making, they force it back to the executive. The result is the same as if the power had been sought by the executive: decision making becomes centralized in one person at the top, and the organization takes on simple-structure characteristics.

It has been proposed that the classic case of the simple structure is the entrepreneurial firm.[10] It continually searches for risky environments where large and established organizations hesitate to operate. These entrepreneurial firms are usually small, so they can remain organic, and their entrepreneurs can maintain tight control. Of course, the high risk translates into a high attrition rate. Thus, the entrepreneurial firm rarely stays that way long. The weak ones die. The successful ones tend to grow and become increasingly risk aversive. When this happens, the simple structure tends to be replaced by either a machine or professional bureaucracy.

THE MACHINE BUREAUCRACY

Standardization! That's the key concept that underlies all machine bureaucracies. Take a look at the bank where you keep your checking account; the department store where you buy your clothes; or the government offices that collect your taxes, enforce health regulations, or provide local fire protection. They all rely on standardized work processes for coordination and control.

The **machine bureaucracy** has highly routine operating tasks, very formalized rules and regulations, tasks that are grouped into functional departments, centralized authority, decision making that follows the chain of command, and an elaborate administrative structure with a sharp distinction between line and staff activities. Figure 10–4 depicts this configuration, using Mintzberg's framework. Rules and regulations permeate the entire structure. While not explicitly evident from Figure 10–4, the key part of this design is the technostructure. That's because this is where the staff analysts who do the standardizing—the time-and-motion engineers,

FIGURE 10–4 *The Machine Bureaucracy*

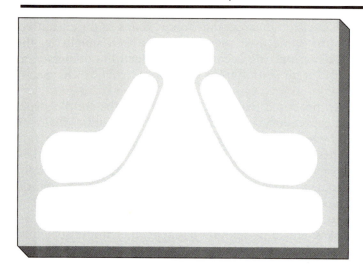

Henry Mintzberg, *Structure in Fives: Designing Effective Organizations*, © 1983, p. 170. Reprinted by permission of Prentice Hall, Englewood Cliffs, NJ.

job-description designers, planners, budgeters, accountants, auditors, systems-and-procedures analysts—are housed.

Figure 10–5 illustrates the machine-bureaucracy form as utilized at the Maytag Company. Notice the reliance on functional departmentation, with similar and related occupational specialties grouped together. In a machine bureaucracy, activities such as marketing, research and development, manufacturing, and personnel are typically grouped under functional executives. These executives oversee their occupational specialties but are, in turn, responsible to a central headquarters that acts as an overall coordinator.

Strengths and Weaknesses

The primary strength of the machine bureaucracy lies in its ability to perform standardized activities in a highly efficient manner. Putting like specialties together results in economies of scale, minimization of duplication of personnel and equipment, and comfortable and satisfied employees who have the opportunity to talk "the same language" among their peers. Further, machine bureau-cracies can get by nicely with less talented—and, hence less costly—middle- and lower-level managers. The pervasiveness of rules and regulations substitute for managerial discretion. Standardized op-erations, coupled with high formalization, allow decision making to be centralized. There is little need, therefore, for innovative and experienced decision makers below the level of senior executives.

One of the major weaknesses of the machine bureaucracy is illustrated in the following dialogue between four executives in one company: "Ya know, nothing happens in this place until we *produce* something," said the production executive. "Wrong," com-mented the research-and-development manager, "nothing happens until we *design* something!" "What are you talking about?" asked the marketing executive. "Nothing happens here until we *sell* some-thing!" Finally, the exasperated accounting manager responded, "It doesn't matter what you produce, design or sell. No one knows what happens until we *tally up the results!*"

This conversation points up the fact that specialization creates subunit conflicts. Functional unit goals can override the overall goals of the organization.

The other major weakness of the machine bureaucracy is some-thing we've all experienced at one time or another when having to deal with people who work in these organizations: obsessive concern with following the rules. When cases arise that don't pre-cisely fit the rules, there is no room for modification. The machine bureaucracy is efficient only as long as employees confront prob-lems that they have previously encountered and for which pro-grammed decision rules have already been established.

When Should You Use It?

The machine bureaucracy is most efficient when matched with large size, a simple and stable environment, and a technology that contains routine work that can be standardized. You see its effec-tiveness when you go into the main post office in any major city. Employees are assigned specific responsibilities—sorting letters and packages, making local deliveries, picking up mail from de-posit boxes, and the like. Procedures govern the way sorting is to be carried out and the path mail deliveries are to follow. If you bring in a package to be mailed, the clerk will follow a preset

FIGURE 10–5 *Maytag Company*

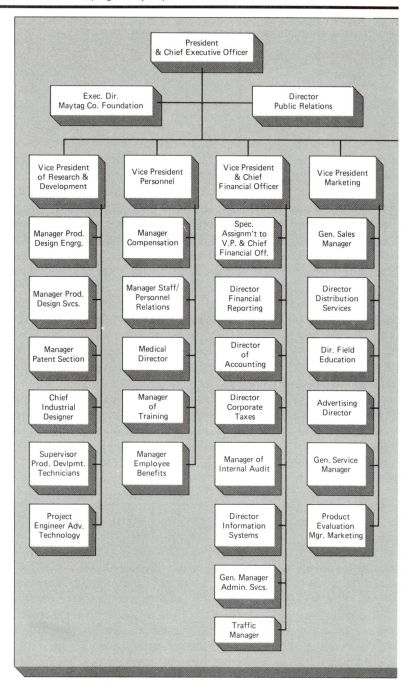

Courtesy of Maytag Company.

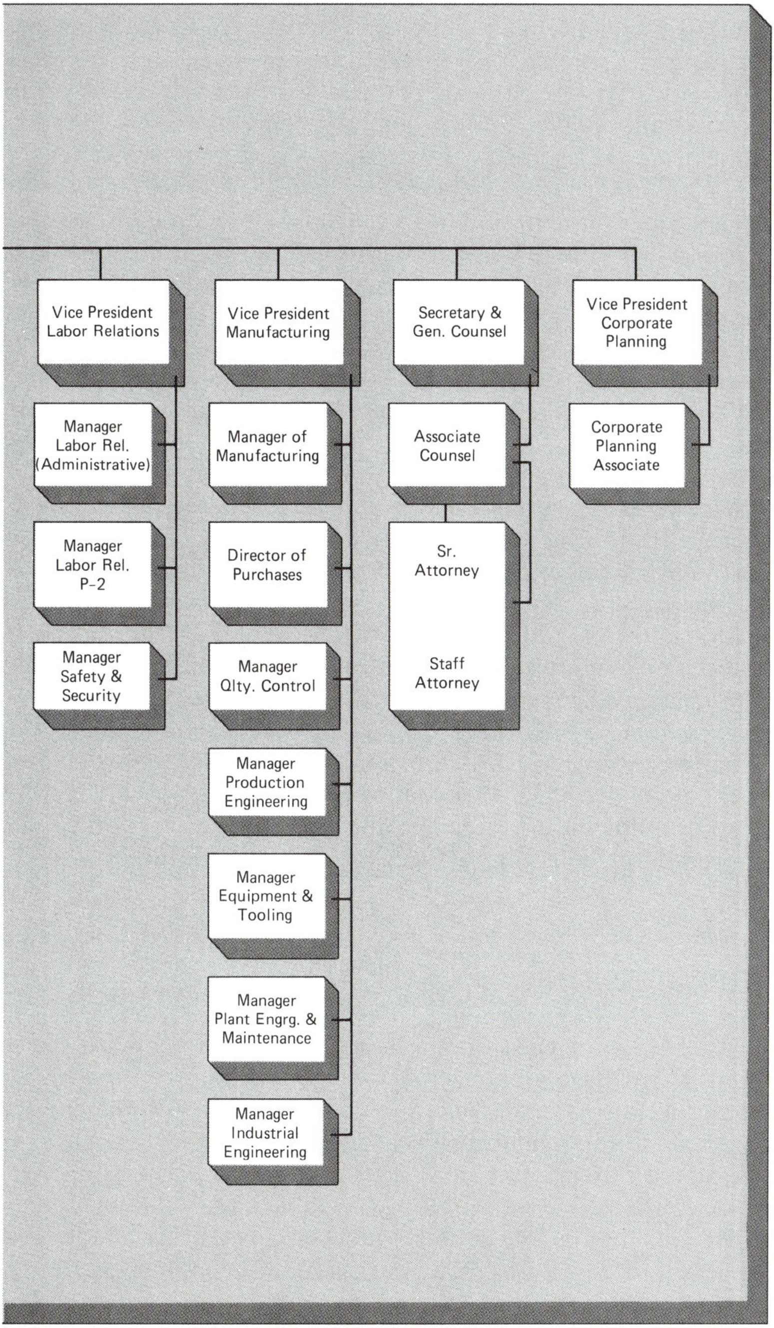

Vice President Labor Relations
Manager Labor Rel. (Administrative)
Manager Labor Rel. P-2
Manager Safety & Security
Vice President Manufacturing
Manager of Manufacturing
Director of Purchases
Manager Qlty. Control
Manager Production Engineering
Manager Equipment & Tooling
Manager Plant Engrg. & Maintenance
Manager Industrial Engineering
Secretary & Gen. Counsel
Associate Counsel
Sr. Attorney
Staff Attorney
Vice President Corporate Planning
Corporate Planning Associate

routine to determine: Did you wrap the package with the proper paper? Did you use the right kind of tape? Is the addressee's identification clearly written? When do you want the package to get to its destination? Do you want a signed receipt of delivery? Do you want insurance? Despite the billions of pieces of mail handled every day, the post office is reasonably efficient. It is, however, only as long as its environment remains stable and its technology routine. The post office, like all machine bureaucracies, is very poor at making changes. This design configuration is just not conducive to making changes either rapidly or efficiently. That can be seen in the efforts to automate the post office's operations. The process took decades rather than months.

Where are you likely to find machine bureaucracies? In mass-production firms, such as those in the automobile and steel industries; service organizations with simple, repetitive activities, such as prisons or insurance and telephone companies; government agencies with routine work, such as post offices and tax collection department; and organizations that have special safety needs, such as airlines and fire departments. All these organizations have routine and highly standardized activities. Most of their contingencies have occurred many times before and are therefore predictable and amenable to formalized procedures. You would not, for instance, want to fly with an airline that was not organized as a machine bureaucracy. How comfortable would you be if you knew the "maintenance men did whatever struck them as interesting instead of following precise checklists, and the pilots worked out their procedures for landing in foggy weather when the need arose?"[11]

THE PROFESSIONAL BUREAUCRACY

The last quarter of a century has seen the birth of a new structural animal. It has been created to allow organizations to hire highly trained specialists for the operating core, while still achieving the efficiencies from standardization. The configuration is called the **professional bureaucracy,** and it combines standardization with *decentralization.*

The jobs that people do today increasingly require a high level of specialized expertise. An undergraduate college degree is required for more and more jobs. So, too, are graduate degrees. The knowledge explosion has created a whole class of organizations that require professionals to produce their goods and services. Obvious examples include hospitals, school districts, universities, museums, libraries, engineering design firms, social service agencies, and public accounting firms. This has created the need for an organizational design that relies on social specialization rather than functional specialization; that is, as you'll remember from Chapter 4, specialization that is based on the possession of individual skills rather than division of labor.

Figure 10–6 illustrates the configuration for professional bureaucracies. The power in this design rests with the operating core because they have the critical skills that the organization needs, and they have the autonomy—provided through decentralization—to apply their expertise. The only other part of the professional bureaucracy that is fully elaborated is the support staff, but their activities are focused on serving the operating core.[12]

You can see what a professional bureaucracy looks like in Figure 10–7. The San Diego State University Library relies on the technical skills of acquisition, cataloging, reference, government documents, and similar specialists. These professionals acquired their skills through years of study leading up to the receipt of their master's in library science degrees. These professionals perform their activities relatively autonomously, but the structure is high in complexity, and there are lots of rules and regulations; however, the formalization is internalized rather than imposed by the or-

FIGURE 10–6 *The Professional Bureaucracy*

Henry Mintzberg, *Structure in Fives: Designing Effective Organizations,* © 1983, p. 159. Reprinted by permission of Prentice Hall, Englewood Cliffs, NJ.

FIGURE 10–7 *San Diego State University Library*

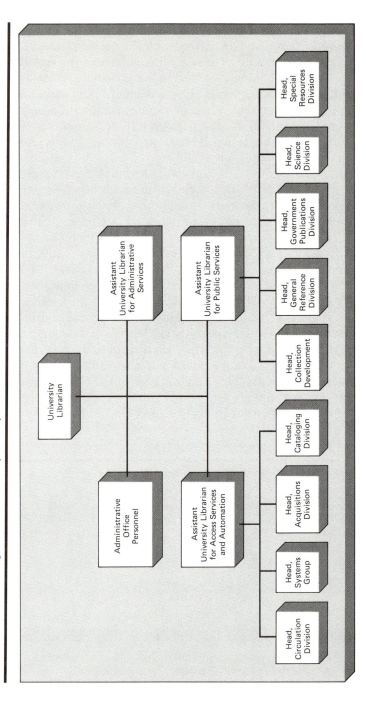

ganization itself. The library example also illustrates a fact about most professional bureaucracies, and that is that they also typically include machine bureaucracies within them. In libraries, for example, the support staff that assists the professionals—secretaries, clerks, people who stack the shelves, and the like—will not have decentralized authority, and their formalization will be externally imposed.

Strengths and Weaknesses

The strength of the professional bureaucracy is that it can perform specialized tasks—ones that require the skills of highly trained professionals—with the same relative efficiency as the machine bureaucracy can. Why then, you may ask, didn't management just choose the latter? It's not because management wouldn't *prefer* the machine form! In power-control terms, the professional bureaucracy requires top management to give up a considerable degree of control. But what's their alternative? The professionals need the autonomy to do their jobs effectively.

The weaknesses of the professional bureaucracy are the same as for the machine form. First, there is the tendency for subunit conflicts to develop. The various professional functions seek to pursue their own narrow objectives, often sublimating the interests of other functions and the organization as a whole. Second, the specialists in the professional bureaucracy, like their counterparts in the machine form, are compulsive in their determination to follow the rules. Only the rules in professional bureaucracies are the making of the professionals themselves. Standards of professional conduct and codes for ethical practices have been socialized into the employees during their training. So, for example, while lawyers or nurses have autonomy on their jobs, their professional standards of how their work is to be done can be a hindrance to an organization's effectiveness when the standards are rigid and unable to adjust to unique or changing conditions.

When Should You Use It?

The professional bureaucracy is at its best when matched with large size, a complex and stable environment, and a routine technology internalized through professionalization. The organization's operating core will be dominated by skilled professionals who have internalized difficult-to-learn but nevertheless well-defined procedures. The complex and stable environment means that the organization requires the use of difficult skills that can be learned only in formal education and training programs, but there is enough stability for these skills to be well defined and standardized.

The knowledge explosion made the professional bureaucracy a fashionable choice in the 1980s. As organizations hired more and more technical specialists, they were forced to come up with an alternative to the machine bureaucracy. The professional bureaucracy provided such an alternative by decentralizing decision making while maintaining the other advantages of the machine form. From the power-control perspective, the professional bureaucracy is obviously inferior to the machine bureaucracy. However, it is clearly preferable to the more free-form adhocracy that we discuss later in the chapter.

THE DIVISIONAL STRUCTURE

General Motors, Hershey Foods, Du Pont, Burlington Industries, and Xerox are examples of organizations that use the divisional structure.

As Figure 10–8 illustrates, the power in the divisional structure lies with middle management. The reason is that the **divisional**

FIGURE 10–8 *The Divisional Structure*

FIGURE 10–9 *General Motors Corporation*

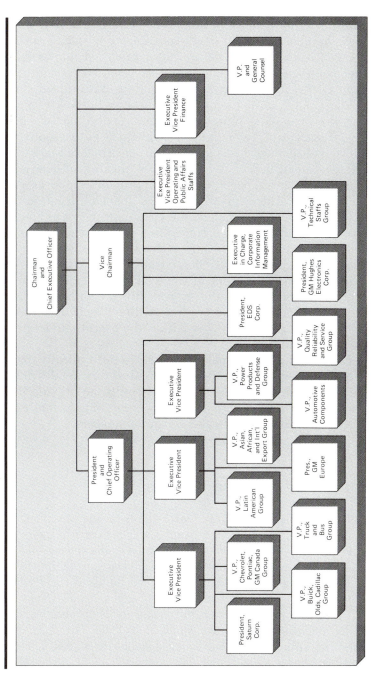

structure is actually a set of autonomous units, each typically a machine bureaucracy unto itself, coordinated by a central headquarters. Since the divisions are autonomous, it allows middle management—the division managers—a great deal of control.[13]

Figure 10–9 shows how the divisional form is utilized at General Motors. Each of its major chains—groups headed by a president or vice president—represents a separate division. As with all divisional structures, each division is generally autonomous, with the divisional managers responsible for performance and holding complete strategic and operating decision-making authority. This form also has a central headquarters that provides support services to the divisions. This typically includes financial, legal, and tax services. Additionally, of course, the headquarters act as an external overseer, evaluating and controlling performance. Divisions, therefore, are autonomous within given parameters. Most continue to follow the dictum of Alfred Sloan, who originated the divisional structure at General Motors in the 1920s, that there should be "decentralized operations and responsibilities with coordinated control." Division managers are free to direct their divisions any way they see fit as long as it is within the overall guidelines set down by headquarters.

A closer look at divisional structures reveals typically that the divisions represent a set of "little companies" that are designed as machine bureaucracies. The divisions tend to be organized into functional groups, with high division of labor, high formalization, and centralized authority in the division managers.

Strengths and Weaknesses

One of the problems associated with the machine bureaucracy is that the goals of the functional unit tend to override the organization's overall goals. One of the strengths of the divisional structure is that it seeks to remedy this problem by placing full responsibility for a product or service in the hands of the divisional manager. So one of the advantages to the divisional structure is that it provides more accountability and focus on outcomes than does the machine bureaucracy alone.

Another strength of the divisional structure is that it frees up the headquarters staff from being concerned with the day-to-day operating details so they can pay attention to the long term. Big-picture, strategic decision making is done at headquarters. At GM, for instance, senior executives in Detroit can wrestle with the world's

PROCTER & GAMBLE'S NEW CATEGORY STRUCTURE

For more than fifty-five years, Procter & Gamble was organized around brands. Each brand—such as Tide, Crisco, Head & Shoulders, and Scope—had its own brand manager, who was singularly accountable for his or her brand's performance. The brand-management structure fostered internal competition and established strong incentives to excel. But having brands compete directly against each other created conflicts and inefficiencies. As competitors expanded (for instance, between 1979 and 1988, the number of detergent brands increased from 27 to 46) and market growth slowed (during that same period, unit sales in the detergent market were up just 17 percent) in the packaged-goods business, P&G decided it needed to reorganize in order to get its brands to work better together. In what has been described as "the biggest management change in more than thirty years," P&G introduced a derivative of the divisional form that it calls the category structure.[14]

The new design leaves the brand managers intact but adds a new layer of management over the brand managers. Products have been segmented into 39 categories—from diapers to cake mixes—each run by a category manager. This manager has direct profit responsibility and oversees all advertising, sales, manufacturing, research, engineering, and other activities related to his or her category. The category manager for laundry detergents, for example, becomes a mini–general manager, accountable for his or her entire product line, with direct responsibility over the half-dozen or so brand managers of laundry detergent products.

The major advantage of this new structural design is it allows P&G to create marketing strategies that encompass entire categories and fit brands together. For instance, now a category manager decides how to position advertising for Tide and Cheer in order to avoid confusion in the minds of consumers.

future transportation needs while the division managers can go about the business of producing Chevrolets and Buicks as efficiently as possible.

It should be obvious that the autonomy and self-containment characteristics of the divisional form make it an excellent vehicle for training and developing general managers. This is a distinct advantage over the machine bureaucracy and its emphasis on specialization. That is, the divisional structure gives managers a broad range of experience with the autonomous units. This individual responsibility and independence gives them an opportunity to run an entire company, with its frustrations and satisfactions. So a large corporation with fifteen divisions has fifteen division managers who are developing the kind of generalist perspective that is needed in the organization's top spot.

Another strength of the divisional form is that its autonomous units can be lopped off with minimal effect on the entire organization. Ineffective performance in one division has little effect on the other divisions. As such, the divisional structure spreads the risk by reducing the chance that a poorly performing part of the organization will take down other parts of the organization with it.

It's evident that the real strengths of the divisional form come from its creation of self-contained businesses "within a business." The divisions have the responsiveness, the accountability, and the benefits of specialization and are able to process information as if they were organizations unto themselves. Yet they also have the benefits of large size that allow economies of scale in planning, acquisition of capital, and spreading of risk. Returning to our example of General Motors, when Saturn Corporation needs $500 million to build a new plant, GM is able to borrow that money at a rate several percentage points below what Saturn could negotiate if it were not part of General Motors. Similarly, that division can be provided with legal expertise that could never be available "in house" if Saturn were a separate corporation independent of GM.

Let us turn now to the weaknesses of the divisional structure, of which there is no shortage. First is the duplication of activities and resources. Each division, for instance, may have a marketing research department. In the absence of autonomous divisions, all the organization's marketing research might be centralized and done for a fraction of the cost that divisionalization requires. So the divisional form's duplication of functions increases the organization's costs and reduces efficiency.

Another disadvantage is the propensity of the divisional form to stimulate conflict. There is little incentive with this structural design to encourage cooperation among divisions. Further conflicts are created as divisions and headquarters argue about where to locate support services. The more the divisions succeed in having these services decentralized to their level, the less dependent they are on headquarters and, hence, the less power headquarter's personnel can wield over them.

The autonomy of the divisions, to the degree that it is more theory than practice, can breed resentment in the division managers. While the structure gives general autonomy to the divisions, the autonomy is exercised within constraints. The division manager is being held fully accountable for results in his or her unit, but because he or she must operate within the uniform policies imposed from headquarters, the manager is likely to be resentful and argue that his or her authority is less than the responsibility.

Finally, the divisional form creates coordination problems. Personnel are frequently unable to transfer between divisions, especially when the divisions operate in highly diverse product or service markets. Du Pont employees in the Remington Arms Division, for instance, have little transferability to the Textile Fibers or Petro-Chemicals divisions. This reduces the flexibility of headquarters' executives to allocate and coordinate personnel. Additionally, the divisional form may make coordination of customer relations and product development a problem. If the divisions are in competing or closely adjoining markets, they may compete with each other for the same sale. To many prospective automobile buyers, Pontiacs and Oldsmobiles are nearly interchangeable products. Yet since the two are produced by separate General Motors divisions and have substantially distinct dealer networks, competition to get the sale is as intense between Pontiac and Oldsmobile as between Chevrolet and Ford. Similarly, the competition between divisions over product development can be dysfunctional. The classic illustration is the NDH—not developed here—syndrome. An innovation developed by one division and then authorized by headquarters to be instituted in all divisions frequently fails because it was NDH. This rivalry and territorial protectionism by the individual divisions can make coordination by headquarters extremely difficult.

When Should You Use It?

The primary criterion determining the use of the divisional structure is product or market diversity. When an organization chooses
a diversification strategy—to become a multiproduct or multi-
market organization—the divisional form becomes preferable to a
machine bureaucracy. When an organization diversifies, conflicts
along the horizontal dimension between functions become too great
and a change in structural design becomes necessary.

Other contingency factors include size, technology, and environment. As size increases, it becomes more difficult to coordinate
functional units and to keep members' attention focused on the
organization's goals. Organizational size and goal displacement
appear to be highly correlated. So increases in size encourage
movement to the divisional structure. All technologies are not compatible with the division form. To be applicable, the organization's
technology must be divisible. "Divisionalization is possible only
when the organization's technical system can be efficiently separated into segments, one for each division."[15] Thus, it is difficult,
for instance, for Bethlehem Steel to divisionalize because economies of scale and the commitment of hundreds of millions of
dollars to very high fixed-cost technical systems basically precludes divisibility. Finally, the environment affects preference for
the divisional form. The divisional structure works best where the
environment is neither very complex nor very dynamic. Why? Highly
complex and dynamic environments are associated with nonstan-
dardized processes and outputs, yet the divisional form is a lot like
the machine bureaucracy in its emphasis on standardization. So
the divisional form tends to have an environment that is more
simple than complex and more stable than dynamic.

THE ADHOCRACY

When Steven Spielberg or George Lucas goes about making a film,
he brings together a diverse group of professionals. This team—
composed of producers, scriptwriters, film editors, set designers,
and hundreds of other specialists—exists for the singular purpose
of making a single movie. They may be called back by Spielberg

or Lucas when they begin another film, but that is irrelevant when the current project begins. These professionals frequently find themselves with overlapping activities because no formal rules or regulations are provided to guide members. While there is a production schedule, it often must be modified to take into consideration unforeseen contingencies. The film's production team may be together for a few months, or in some unusual cases, for several years. But the organization is temporary. In contrast to bureaucracies or divisional structures, the filmmaking organizations have no entrenched hierarchy, no permanent departments, no formalized rules, and no standardized procedures for dealing with routine problems. Welcome to our last design configuration: the **adhocracy.** It's characterized by high horizontal differentiation, low vertical differentiation, low formalization, decentralization, and great flexibility and responsiveness.

Horizontal differentiation is great because adhocracies are staffed predominantly by professionals with a high level of expertise. Vertical differentiation is low because the many levels of administration would restrict the organization's ability to adapt. Also, the need for supervision is minimal because professionals have internalized the behaviors that management wants.

We have already found professionalization and formalization to be inversely related. The adhocracy is no exception. There are few rules and regulations. Those that exist tend to be loose and unwritten. Again, the objective of flexibility demands an absence of formalization. Rules and regulations are effective only where standardization of behavior is sought. In this context, it may be valuable to compare the professional bureaucracy with adhocracy. Both employ professionals. The key difference is that the professional bureaucracy, when faced with a problem, immediately classifies it into some standardized program so that the professionals can treat it in a uniform manner. In an adhocracy, a novel solution is needed so that standardization and formalization are inappropriate.

Decision making in adhocracies is decentralized. This is necessary for speed and flexibility and because senior management cannot be expected to possess the expertise necessary to make all decisions. So the adhocracy depends on decentralized teams of professionals for decision making.

The adhocracy is a very different design from those we've encountered earlier. This can be seen in Figure 10–10. Because the adhocracy has little standardization or formalization, the technostructure is almost nonexistent. Because middle managers, the support staff, and operatives are typically all professionals, the traditional distinctions between supervisor and employee and line and staff become blurred. The result is a central pool of expert talent that can be drawn from to innovate, solve unique problems, and perform flexible activities. Power flows to anyone in the adhocracy with expertise, regardless of his or her position.[16]

Adhocracies are best conceptualized as groups of terms. Specialists are grouped together into flexible teams that have few rules, regulations, or standardized routines. Coordination between team members is through mutual adjustment. As conditions change, so do the activities of the members. But adhocracies don't have to be devoid of horizontally differentiated departments. Frequently, departments are used for clarity, but then department members are deployed into small teams—which cut across functional units—to do their tasks.

Applied Data Research (see Figure 10–11) is a New Jersey firm that designs, develops, and markets computer software packages

FIGURE 10–10 *The Adhocracy*

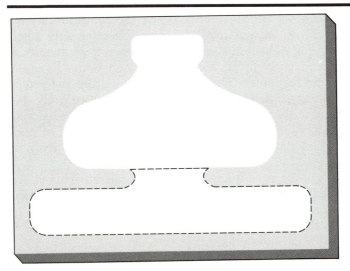

Henry Mintzberg, *Structure in Fives: Designing Effective Organizations,* © 1983, p. 262. Reprinted by permission of Prentice Hall, Englewood Cliffs, NJ.

FIGURE 10–11 *Applied Data Research*

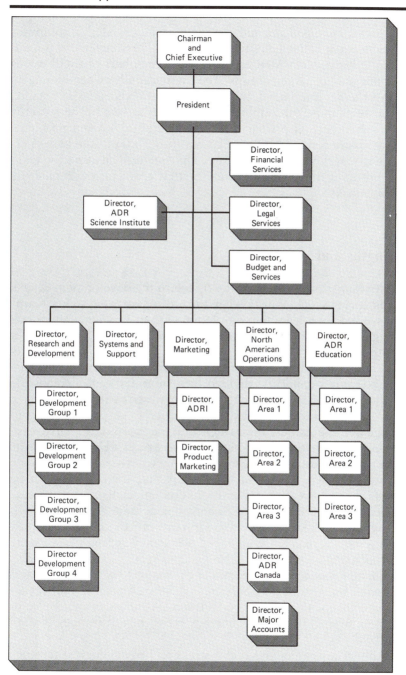

Courtesy of Applied Data Research.

and provides consulting and research services related to computer systems. ADR relies heavily on the flexibility inherent in the adhocratic form. Most ADR employees are members of small teams that are part of larger groups. The distinction between managers and workers is minimized since the organization is essentially staffed by professionals. All employees enjoy a great deal of autonomy. ADR's structure is primarily designed around solving problems rather than narrow functional specialities. Rather than being permanently part of a team, employees have tenure on a specific team depending on how long it takes for that team to accomplish its current tasks.

Strengths and Weaknesses

The history of adhocracy can be traced to the development of task forces during World War II, when the military created ad hoc teams that were disbanded after completion of their missions. There was no rigid time span for their existence: teams could last a day, a month, or a year. Roles performed in the teams were interchangeable, and, depending upon the nature and complexity of the mission, the group could be divided into subunits, each responsible for different facets of the job to be performed. The advantages of these ad hoc teams included their ability to respond rapidly to change and innovation and to facilitate the coordination of diverse specialists. More than forty-five years have passed since World War II, but the advantage of ad hoc teams, or what we call adhocracy, continues today. When it is important that the organization be adaptable and creative, when individual specialists from diverse disciplines are required to collaborate to achieve a common goal, and when tasks are technical, nonprogrammed, and too complex for any one person to handle, the adhocracy represents a viable alternative.

On the negative side, conflict is a natural part of adhocracy. There are no clear boss-subordinate relationships. Ambiguities exist over authority and responsibilities. Activities cannot be compartmentalized. In short, adhocracy lacks the advantages of standardized work.

Adhocracy can create social stress and psychological tensions for its members. It is not easy to set up and quickly dismantle work relationships on a continuing basis. Some employees find it difficult to cope with rapid change, living in temporary work systems, and having to share responsibilities with other team members.

In contrast to bureaucracy, adhocracy is clearly an inefficient configuration. It is also a vulnerable design. As one author noted, "Many of them either die early or else shift to bureaucratic configurations to escape the uncertainty."[17] So why, you might ask, would it ever be used? Because its inefficiencies, in certain circumstances, are more than offset by the need for flexibility and innovation.

When Should You Use It?

The adhocracy is certainly not every organization's "cup of tea." The factors that determine when adhocracy will be effective are the organization's strategy, technology, environment, and life stage.[18]

The adhocracy is associated with strategies of diversity, change, and/or high risk. Such strategies demand the flexibility inherent in adhocracy.

The technology in an adhocracy will be nonroutine. A nonroutine technology must be used to respond to the changing strategies that the organization will be employing. The technology will contain little formalization, relying on the expertise of professionals to provide the "right" response. Additionally, the technology will be complex in that it will draw on the talents of diverse specialties. This, in turn, requires coordination and integration of specialized and heterogeneous skills. The adhocracy is the preferred mechanism for facilitating this integration.

The adhocracy's environment will be dynamic and complex. That is because innovative work, being unpredictable, is associated with a dynamic environment and because innovative work, which is sophisticated, links with a complex environment—one that is difficult to interpret and comprehend.[19]

The adhocracy form is preferred in the early years of an organization's life cycle. Why? This is the time when the organization needs the greatest flexibility as it attempts to identify its market niche and determine precisely how it is going to go about achieving its goals. Innovation is high in an organization's formative years as it struggles to survive. Of course, the lack of prior precedents and entrenched vested interests fosters experimentation with new and different approaches. It has been argued that adhocracy is most evident in those industries that are relatively young—ones that basically developed since World War II.[20] This would include, for example, organizations engaged in aerospace, electronics, consulting, and research.

A final point regarding the adhocracy is its current trendiness. During the 1970s and 1980s, this design has been particularly susceptible to managers' propensity to follow fashion. It fits well with the notion, held by many managers today, that environments are dynamic and complex. Add to this the fact that organizations are increasingly being staffed by technical experts, and it becomes fashionable for management to choose work designs that emphasize decentralized teams and task forces.

SUMMARY

While our society is populated by millions of organizations, they can essentially be reduced into one of five general configurations: the simple structure, the machine bureaucracy, the professional bureaucracy, the divisional structure, and the adhocracy.

As Table 10–1 demonstrates, the simple structure and adhocracy are essentially organic structures, while the other three are more mechanistic in form. Yet each is unique and preferable to the other four under certain conditions.

The simple structure is recommended for small organizations, for those in their formative stage of development, for organizations in environments that are simple and dynamic, as a response to times of crisis, or when those in control desire power to be centralized.

The machine bureaucracy is designed to effectively handle large size, a simple and stable environment, and a technology that is composed of routine and standardized work. Its professional counterpart is also designed for large organizations with a routine technology. However, the professional bureaucracy's members are technical specialists confronting a complex environment. To effectively operate with these professionals and a complex environment, a decentralized bureaucratic design is necessary.

The divisional structure looks a lot like the machine bureaucracy. However, it has been designed to respond to a strategy that emphasizes market or product diversity, where the organization is large, technologies are divisible, and the environment tends to be simple and stable.

The adhocracy requires top management to give up the most control. In power-control terms, therefore, it is the least desirable of the five con-

TABLE 10–1 *Summary of the Five Configurations*

CHARACTERISTIC	SIMPLE STRUCTURE	MACHINE BUREAUCRACY	PROFESSIONAL BUREAUCRACY	DIVISIONAL STRUCTURE	ADHOCRACY
Specialization	Low	High functional	High social	High functional	High social
Formalization	Low	High	Low	High within divisions	Low
Centralization	High	High	Low	Limited decentralization	Low
Environment	Simple and dynamic	Simple and stable	Complex and stable	Simple and stable	Complex and dynamic
General structural classification	Organic	Mechanistic	Mechanistic	Mechanistic	Organic

figurations. When will management select the adhocracy? With diverse, changing, or high-risk strategies or when the technology is nonroutine and the environment is both dynamic and complex. It is also effective in dealing with the problems that are typically encountered when an organization is in the formative years of its life cycle. However, since the simple structure is also well designed to deal with the problems in an organization's formative period—while maintaining centralized control—the simple structure is likely to be more widely adopted in an organization's early years.

FOR REVIEW AND DISCUSSION

1. What is a configuration?
2. Define the five common elements in any organization.
3. How do coordination and control change in each configuration?
4. Describe the simple structure. When would you use it?
5. Describe the machine bureaucracy. When would you use it?
6. Describe the professional bureaucracy. When would you use it?
7. Describe the divisional structure. When would you use it?
8. Describe the adhocracy. When would you use it?
9. Contrast the simple structure and adhocracy.
10. Review the five configurations from the power-control perspective.
11. If management was concerned with developing future top management talent, which organizational design would be preferable? Why?
12. The professional bureaucracy and adhocracy were both described as currently fashionable designs. Why?
13. When might management blend designs; for example, combining the machine bureaucracy with adhocracy?
14. How is a university designed? Explain why it has such a configuration.
15. How is the New Avanti Corp., described in Chapter 7, designed? Explain why it has such a configuration.

NOTES

[1] Henry Mintzberg, *The Structuring of Organizations* (Englewood Cliffs, N.J.: Prentice Hall, 1979); William McKelvey, *Organizational Systematics: Taxonomy, Evolution, Classification* (Berkeley: University of California Press, 1982); John E. Oliver, Jr., "An Instrument for Classifying Organizations," *Academy of Management Journal*, December 1982, pp. 855–66; Danny Miller and Peter H. Friesen, *Organizations: A Quantum View* (Englewood Cliffs, N.J.: Prentice Hall, 1984); and Mariann Jelinek, "Organization Structure: The Basic Conformations," in M. Jelinek, J. A. Litterer, and R. E. Miles

(eds.), *Organizations By Design: Theory and Practice*, 2d ed. (Dallas: Business Publications, 1986), pp. 125–39.

[2] Miller and Friesen, *Organizations: A Quantum View*, p. 12.

[3] Ibid., p. 21.

[4] Ibid.

[5] Henry Mintzberg, "Organization Design: Fashion or Fit?" *Harvard Business Review*, January–February 1981, pp. 103–16.

[6] See, for example, Henry Mintzberg, *Structure in Fives: Designing Effective Organizations* (Englewood Cliffs, N.J.: Prentice Hall, 1983).

[7] Ibid., p. 157.

[8] Mintzberg, *Structuring of Organizations*, p. 312.

[9] Ibid., p. 308.

[10] Mintzberg, *Structure in Fives*, pp. 160–61.

[11] Mintzberg, *Structuring of Organizations*, p. 332.

[12] Mintzberg, *Structure in Fives*, p. 194.

[13] Ibid., p. 217.

[14] "The Marketing Revolution at Procter & Gamble," *Business Week*, July 25, 1988, pp. 72–76.

[15] Mintzberg, *Structuring of Organizations*, pp. 397–98.

[16] Mintzberg, *Structure in Fives*, p. 261.

[17] Miller and Friesen, *Organizations: A Quantum View*, p. 85.

[18] Henry Mintzberg, "Structure in 5's: A Synthesis of the Research on Organization Design," *Management Science*, March 1980, pp. 336–38.

[19] Mintzberg, *Structuring of Organizations*, p. 449.

[20] Mintzberg, "Structure in 5's," p. 338.

11

BUREAUCRACY:
A CLOSER LOOK

AFTER READING THIS CHAPTER, YOU SHOULD BE ABLE TO:

1 Define Weber's bureaucracy.
2 Outline the advantages to Weber's bureaucratic model.
3 Contrast markets and hierarchies.
4 List negative consequences of bureaucracy.
5 Describe Bennis' argument for the demise of bureaucracy.
6 Summarize Miewald's counterargument that bureaucracy is in good health.
7 Explain why bureaucracies are so popular in practice.

Introduction
IS SMALL REALLY BEAUTIFUL?

Small is in! It has become the accepted thesis of contemporary management gurus to recommend that organizations create small, adaptive, and autonomous units. Decentralization has become *de rigueur*. The list of companies that now are organized into smaller, "more manageable" units includes many of the most successful corporations in America—IBM, 3M, Hewlett-Packard, Nucor, Mars, General Foods. Heaven help the current manager who argues for the value of centralizing decision making or, worse yet, acts to make his or her organization *more* bureaucratic! Yet, while it's true that smaller craft are more responsive to shifting currents, better able to navigate in uncertain waters, and less susceptible to catastrophic loss than ocean liners, the way to get one thousand passengers around the world in comfort and safety is not necessarily to put them in one hundred schooners.[1]

Maybe bureaucracy hasn't gotten a fair shake. Few terms in organization theory carry a more negative connotation than *bureaucracy*. However, both the machine and professional forms of bureaucracy are widely evident in practice. This suggests we take a closer look at this structural design.

Let's begin by stating, without qualification, that bureaucracy is *not* synonymous with inefficiency. If I were to say that "the Internal Revenue Service is a bureaucracy," my statement would immediately conjure up for most people a host of attributes that imply inefficiency—rigid application of rules; buck passing; impersonal; paper shuffling; redundancy of effort; a lethargic attitude toward change; empire building; and the like. If this is what you think of when you hear the term bureaucracy, forget these prejudices! Bureaucracy is merely a type of structure. It is not, in and of itself, good or bad. In some situations, it *is* inefficient. In others, as we saw in the previous chapter, it can be highly efficient.

WEBER'S BUREAUCRACY

The classic perspective on bureaucracy was proposed by German sociologist Max Weber (pronounced *vay-ber*) at the beginning of this century.[2] He sought to describe an ideal organization—one that would be perfectly rational and would provide maximum efficiency of operation.[3] As you read through this section on Weber, you will recognize that our description of the machine bureaucracy in the previous chapter is a very close adaptation of what Weber meant when he used the term bureaucracy.

Weber's Original Definition

The following characteristics form the essence of Weber's **bureaucracy** or ideal organization. Keep in mind, however, that Weber's bureaucratic model was a hypothetical rather than a factual description of how most organizations were structured:

☐ *Division of labor.* Each person's job is broken down into simple, routine, and well-defined tasks.

☐ *Well-defined authority hierarchy.* A multilevel formal structure, with a hierarchy of positions or offices, ensures that each lower office is under the supervision and control of a higher one.

☐ *High formalization.* Dependence on formal rules and procedures to ensure uniformity and to regulate the behavior of job holders.

☐ *Impersonal nature.* Sanctions are applied uniformly and impersonally to avoid involvement with individual personalities and personal preferences of members.

☐ *Employment decisions based on merit.* Selection and promotion decisions are based on technical qualifications, competence, and performance of the candidates.

☐ *Career tracks for employees.* Members are expected to pursue a career in the organization. In return for this career commitment, employees have tenure; that is, they will be retained even if they "burn out" or if their skills become obsolete.

☐ *Distinct separation of members' organizational and personal lives.* The demands and interests of personal affairs are kept completely separate to prevent them from interfering with the rational impersonal conduct of the organization's activities.

These characteristics illustrate Weber's "ideal type" of rational and efficient organization. Goals are clear and explicit. Positions are arranged in a pyramidal hierarchy, with authority increasing as one moves up the organization. The authority lies in the positions rather than in the people who occupy them. Selection of members is based on their qualifications rather than on "who they know"; requirements of the position determine who will be employed and in what positions; and performance is the criterion for promotions. Commitment to the organization is maximized and conflicts of interest eliminated by providing lifetime employment and separating members' off-the-job roles from those required in fulfilling organizational responsibilities.

Sounds good, doesn't it? No politicking, no emotional involvement with individual personalities, no conflicts over goals or criteria for defining effectiveness, decisions based solely on objective criteria, and nice clear lines of authority. Does this jibe with the bureaucracies you know? Probably not! But remember: Weber was not describing the average or typical organization. He was defining the characteristics that established the "ideal type," the ultimate efficiency machine. As Weber said:

Experience tends universally to show that *the purely* bureaucratic type of *administrative organization* . . . is, from a *purely technical point of view,* capable of attaining the *highest degree of efficiency* and is in this sense formally the most rational known means of carrying out imperative control over human beings. It is superior to any other form in precision, in stability, in the stringency of its discipline, and in its reliability. It thus makes possible a particularly high *degree of calculability* of results for the heads of the organization and for those acting in relation to it. It is finally superior both in intensive efficiency and in the scope of its operations, and is formally capable of application to all kinds of administrative tasks.[4]

We consider the problems with bureaucracy later in this chapter—and there are certainly plenty of them—but before doing that, it is important to understand fully the implications of Weber's model. Weber's bureaucracy has some strong and positive qualities.

Positive Qualities in Weber's "Ideal Type"

Weber's bureaucracy included a number of characteristics that, it can be argued, are highly desirable. Specifically, we can single out the attempt to eliminate the use of irrelevant criteria for choosing employees; the use of tenure to protect employees against arbitrary authority, changes in skill demands, and declining ability; the establishment of rules and regulations to increase the likelihood that employees will be treated fairly and to create stability over time; and the creation of a vertical hierarchy to ensure that clear lines of authority exist, that decisions are made, and that accountability over decisions is maintained.[5]

Weber's model seeks to purge the organization of favoritism. He fought against prejudice and discrimination more than half a century before civil rights legislation. One major plus of bureaucracy, therefore, is that it sought to bring objectivity to employee selection by reducing nepotism and other forms of favoritism by decision makers and replacing it with job-competence criteria.

The idea of giving employees security through tenure is often attacked on the grounds that it makes employees complacent. Why work hard when your job is literally guaranteed? The potential costs of complacency are real, but they must be compared with the benefits that tenure provides. These benefits include commitment to the organization, protections against arbitrary actions of senior management, and inducement to master skills that may have limited marketability. By offering employees security in employment, they can pursue those activities and learn those skills that may have little value outside the organization but that, nevertheless, are important for the organization's success. You are much more likely to accept spending a year or more learning the idiosyncracies of your firm's accounting system if you recognize that the firm is committed to providing a career for you regardless of whether the accounting system changes or there is a significant decline in the company's business. A glance at the historical management-labor relationship in Japan supports the value of tenure. Japanese employees have traditionally been granted permanent employment, regardless of the business cycle. In response, Japanese firms have some of the most loyal and productive employees in the world.

Rules and regulations may be constraints on what you can and cannot do, but they reduce ambiguity and increase uniformity of actions. Without a policy, for instance, how does a manager know when he or she can make a decision? Absence of policy, therefore, leaves the manager open to reprimand for any decision made, however trivial. Similarly, if I do something wrong, I want to be assured that I am not unduly penalized. Bureaucracy's high formalization provides the mechanism with which to facilitate this standardization of discipline practices.

Finally, while the vertical hierarchy may be seen as a vehicle for "buck passing," its positive qualities are often overlooked. It answers such questions as, To whom do I take my problems? How much authority does that manager have? Whom do I have to see to get this decision made? The importance of these issues is revealed in a survey of managers in industrial firms. They were found to be decidedly "in favor of more, rather than less, clarity in lines of authority, rules, duties, specification of procedures, and so on."[6] These managers recognized that only when the structure and relationships are clear can authority be delegated.

Summarizing Weber's Contribution

The central theme in Weber's bureaucratic model is standardization. The behavior of people in bureaucracies is predetermined by the standardized structure and processes. The model, itself, can be dissected into three groups of characteristics: those that relate to the structure and function of the organization, those that deal with

MARKETS VERSUS HIERARCHIES: AN EXPLANATION FOR THE EXISTENCE OF BUREAUCRACIES

Why do bureaucracies exist? Based on earlier discussions in this book, you might argue that large size, routine technologies, and stable environments make bureaucracies the most efficient means to accomplish goals. Another answer to this question is: Bureaucracies exist because markets fail.

A **transaction-cost model** of organizations, based on microeconomic theory, has been proposed, which views markets and hierarchies as alternative ways to coordinate economic activity.[7] **Markets** are defined as a means for allocating resources based on bargaining over prices. This, for example, would describe the process you would probably use if you needed to hire someone for a couple of days to paint your house. Because there is competition among painters, the transaction is likely to be perceived as efficient, with both you and the painter feeling an equitable bargain has been struck.

But markets become too costly, and hence inefficient, when transactions become overly complex or ill defined. Such might be the case if you owned forty or fifty buildings and needed the on-going services of dozens of painters, electricians, plumbers, and similar tradespeople. What if you happen to be a large chemical manufacturer or own a dozen new car dealerships? To reduce uncertainty, you'd seek the services of accountants, forecasters and planners, and personnel specialists and would want a sophisticated information system to minimize transaction costs. Under high uncertainty, then, **hierarchies** often become more efficient and replace markets by allocating resources through rules and authority relationships. Rules create job classifications, outline compensation schedules, identify people in authority, determine who can interact with whom, and the like.

The transaction-cost model demonstrates that hierarchies arise because they reduce costs by establishing rules and coordinating positions that are not found in markets. The model can help to explain the existence of large bureaucratic organizations, widespread use of multidivisional structures, and management's desire to control uncertainties through vertical integration.

means of rewarding effort, and those that deal with protection for individual members.[8]

Weber's model stipulates a hierarchy of offices, with each office under the direction of a higher one. Each of these offices is differentiated horizontally by division of labor. This division of labor creates units of expertise, defines areas of action consistent with competence of unit members, assigns responsibilities for carrying out these actions, and allocates commensurate authority to fulfill these responsibilities. All the while, written rules govern the performance of members' duties. This imposition of structure and functions provide a high level of specialized expertise, coordination of roles, and control of members through standardization.

The second group of characteristics in Weber's model relates to rewards. Members receive salaries in relation to their rank in the organization. Promotions are based on objective criteria such as seniority or achievement. Since members are not owners, it is important that there be a clear separation of their private affairs and property from the organization's affairs and property. It is further expected that commitment to the organization is paramount, the position in the organization being the employee's sole or primary occupation.

Finally, Weber's model seeks to protect the rights of individuals. In return for a career commitment, members receive protection from arbitrary actions by superiors, clear knowledge of their responsibilities and the amount of authority their superior holds, and the ability to appeal decisions that they see as unfair or outside the parameters of their superior's authority.

DYSFUNCTIONAL CONSEQUENCES OF BUREAUCRACY

Bureaucracies have received more than their share of unfavorable publicity. In this section, we review these criticisms.

Goal Displacement

Bureaucracy is attacked most frequently for encouraging **goal displacement**—the displacement of organizational goals by subunit or personal goals. This general theme has been packaged in a number of forms.

The most general argument has been proposed by Robert Merton.[9] After acknowledging that bureaucratic rules and impersonality produce a high degree of reliability and predictability, he pointed out that conformity can be detrimental because it reduces flexibility. Rules and regulations become so emphasized that they take on a symbolic meaning of their own. The rules become more important than the ends that they were designed to serve, the result being goal displacement and loss of organizational effectiveness. Occasionally you will see this phenomenon in large retail clothing stores. Rules about keeping shelves fully stocked and neat, instituted to increase sales, can be followed so compulsively by the sales personnel that customers are ignored. Similarly, people in the registrar's office in some colleges become so enamored of making students follow the rules for adding and dropping courses that they forget that they are there to help students get the class schedule they want and clear the path to getting their degrees.

Philip Selznick also believed that means could become ends through goal displacement.[10] He emphasized that specialization and differentiation create subunits with different goals. The goals of each separate subunit become primary to the subunit members. What happens as a result of the conflict between these subunits is that achievement of subunit goals becomes more important than accomplishment of the organization's goals. This was illustrated in one manufacturing firm, where marketing secured a very large and profitable order. The sale came with a tight deadline and required production personnel to give the order special handling outside the normal routine. Despite the profits that this sale would bring to the company, the production manager balked because the order would disturb his unit's efficiency ratios. He succeeded in dragging his feet long enough so that the order was lost to a competitor.

A third perspective on goal displacement was offered by Alvin Gouldner.[11] Gouldner proposed that rules and regulations not only define unacceptable behaviors but also define *minimum* levels of acceptable performance. If the organization's goals are not internalized and made a part of the employee's behavior, the rules encourage apathy. That is, people will do just the bare minimum to get by. The rules, therefore, become interpreted as setting the minimum standards for performance rather than identifying unacceptable behaviors. You will see this phenomenon operating when students take a course on a "pass-fail" basis rather than for a letter grade. The instructor's cutoff separating passing from failing becomes the point of attention. Students rarely exert more effort than is necessary to get just into the passing range.

A final goal-displacement argument has been proposed by Victor Thompson.[12] Thompson sees the highly formalized bureaucracy as creating insecurities in those in authority that lead to what he has called **bureaupathic behavior.**[13] Decision makers use adherence to rules to protect themselves from making errors. Instead of high formalization facilitating decision making, the rules and regulations provide protection to hide behind: "Don't blame me. I was just following rules!" Thompson suggested that as persons in hierarchical positions become increasingly dependent upon lower-level specialists for achievement of organizational goals, they tend to introduce more and more rules to protect themselves against this dependency.

Inappropriate Application of Rules and Regulations

Related closely to the problem of goal displacement is the undesirable effect of members' applying formalized rules and procedures in inappropriate situations; that is, responding to a unique situation as if it were routine, resulting in dysfunctional consequences. Merton suggested that over time, bureaucracies breed such devotion to rules that members blindly repeat decisions and actions that they have made a number of times before, unaware that conditions have changed.[14] Of course, actions and decisions based on past training and experience may be very inappropriate under different conditions. This leads to errors, as many of us have observed firsthand in dealing with government agencies. The clerk who processes drivers' license applications in a state motor vehicle office may know how to handle applicants who have never driven before, renewals, and out-of-state applications. When confronted with an applicant who had a valid foreign license (your author), the clerk handled the application as if I had come from out of state. Only six weeks later did I find, upon receipt of a letter from the state capitol, that the clerk had failed to use a special procedure for applicants who were coming from out of the country. We can conclude that bureaucracies' high formalization makes it difficult to respond to changing conditions.

Employee Alienation

A major cost of bureaucracy is employee **alienation.** Members perceive the impersonality of the organization as creating distance between them and their work. As a "cog in the wheel," it is frequently difficult to feel committed to the organization. High specialization further reinforces one's feeling of being irrelevant—routine activities can be easily learned by others, making employees feel interchangeable and powerless. In professional bureaucracies, formalization must be lessened; otherwise the risk of employee alienation is very high.[15]

Concentration of Power

The concentration of power in senior executives of bureaucracies has been targeted by some. Although this criticism is subjective—it depends on whether one considers concentration of power undesirable—undoubtedly it flies in the face of those social scientists who want to equalize power in organizations to make them more humanistic.[16] It is a fact that bureaucracy generates an enormous degree of power in the hands of a very few. If you perceive this as undesirable or counter to the values of a democratic society, as some do, you will find this attribute a negative consequence of the bureaucratic form.

Nonmember Frustration

The last negative consequence that we address relates to those outside the organization who must deal with the bureaucracy. Members are remunerated for their work in bureaucracies. If it takes six weeks to process an internal requisition for a dozen typewriter ribbons, it may be frustrating to the employee who needs those ribbons. But he or she is paid to be in the office forty hours a week—and that pay is received whether the ribbons are there or not. So while bureaucracies may alienate some of their members—in the name of efficiency—the members' compensation is some salve for the wounds. But clients and customers of bureaucracies must meet the impersonal "monster" and its occasional hassles without being paid to do so. If the bureaucracy is a business firm, with viable competitors, you can always take your business some place else if the bureaucracy fails to satisfy your needs. But reality reminds us that, in all probability, the competitors also use the bureaucratic form. Moreover, if the organization is a government agency or a regulated monopoly (such as the electric company), you have little choice. When you move and need to have your gas or electricity turned on, you deal with the bureaucracy on its terms. Often they will not tell you exactly when they will be at your residence other than to say it will be between 8 A.M. and 5 P.M. on a given day. So *you* stay home and wait, although they profess that they exist to serve you. Every college student who has undergone the rigors of registration and has confronted the school's impersonal and rule-dominated "system" can relate to the frustration that nonmembers feel who must deal regularly with bureaucracies.

IS BUREAUCRACY A STRUCTURAL DINOSAUR?

"Bureaucracy had its time, but those days are gone. If bureaucracy is not already dead, it is gasping its last breath." "Bureaucracy is alive and well. It is still the most efficient way to organize activities."

These positions reflect two perspectives on bureaucracy. Which is correct? Let us present the arguments; then, you be the judge.

The Coming Death of Bureaucracy

One of the best-known arguments presented against the machine bureaucracy was made by social psychologist Warren Bennis.[17] While published more than twenty years ago and since modified,[18] it nevertheless represents a succinct analysis of the antibureaucracy attack. The following summarizes Bennis's argument that bureaucracy has become obsolete.

Every age develops an organizational form appropriate to its needs, and the one that dominated in the latter part of the nineteenth century and first half of the twentieth century was known by sociologists as bureaucracy and by most business managers as "damn bureaucracy." That form is now out of step with contemporary realities.

The bureaucratic model was developed as a reaction against the personal subjugation, nepotism and cruelty, and the capricious and subjective judgments that passed for acceptable managerial practices during the early days of the Industrial Revolution. Bureaucracy emerged out of the need by organizations for order and precision and demands by workers for impartial treatment. It was an organization form ideally suited to the values and demands of the Victorian era. Today's conditions are inconsistent with those values and demands. At least four factors are direct threats to bureaucracy:

1. *Rapid and unexpected change.* Bureaucracy's strength is its capacity to manage efficiently routine and predictable activities that take place in a stable and predictable environment. Bureaucracy, with its nicely defined chain of command, its rules and its rigidities, is poorly adapted to the rapid change the environment now demands.

2. *Growth in size.* While in theory there may be no natural limit to the height of a bureaucratic pyramid, in practice the element of complexity is almost invariably introduced when there is a considerable increase in size. Increased administrative overhead, tighter controls, greater impersonality, outmoded rules—all are examples of what happens in bureaucracy as size increases—act to hinder organizational growth.

3. *Increasing diversity.* Today's activities require persons of very diverse, highly specialized competence. Hurried growth, rapid change, and increased specialization are incompatible with bureaucracy's well-defined chain of command, rigid rules and procedures, and impersonality.

4. *Change in managerial behavior.* Managers are undergoing a subtle but perceptible change in philosophy. These changes are undermining the ideology that surrounded and supported bureaucracy. Specifically, managers have (a) a new concept of human beings, based on increased knowledge of their complex and shifting needs, which replaces an oversimplified, innocent, push-button idea of men and women; (b) a new concept of *power*, based on collaboration and reason, which replaces a model of power based on coercion and threat; and (c) a new concept of *organizational values*, based on humanistic-democratic ideals, which replaces the depersonalized mechanistic value system of bureaucracy.

In summary, Bennis saw the bureaucratic structure as too mechanical for the needs of modern organizations. He argued that the structure has become obsolete because it is designed to deal with stable environments, whereas the contemporary need is for a structure that is designed to respond effectively to change.

The Greatly Exaggerated Death of Bureaucracy

Robert Miewald has offered a counterargument to Bennis.[19] His major contention is that bureaucracy can adapt to changing and dynamic environments. The following summarizes Miewald's response.

Warren Bennis has caught the fancy of many by describing conditions that, he argues, are bringing about the death of bureaucracy. Certainly there can be no doubt that the organization is changing, but these changes are not leaving bureaucracy behind. In fact, the forces of bureaucracy have never been stronger.

Our perspective on bureaucracy has been influenced strongly by the characteristics identified by Max Weber. Genius though he was, Weber was not a soothsayer. He could not have foreseen all the many forms that the essence of bureaucracy could take. His formulation of the concept of bureaucracy provided an invaluable tool for the analysis of organizational problems in a society that was making the adjustment to industrialization. However, rather than make the superficial assumption that *postindustrial* means *postbureaucratic,* it might be wiser to inquire whether bureaucracy can adjust to the so-called New Age. Is bureaucracy restricted to the mechanical? In many cases it would appear that external bureaucratic controls have simply been replaced by more subtle influences on the individual. The end result in either case is the same: a high degree of predictability about human behavior in large, complex organizations.

Weber never implied that his ideal type was the universal, eternal form. His intention, rather, was to make the affairs of people more amenable to rational calculation. Given the technology of the nineteenth century and his familiarity with the authoritarian tendencies of the Germans, it is little wonder that Weber described bureaucracy as he did. He would hardly be surprised, however, to learn that more sophisticated means of controlling behavior have been invented. All he wanted was a scientifically derived concept of efficiency and certainly would not be aghast to find that his model had been modified to reflect new ways in which to improve on efficiency. At the peak of its influence, machine bureaucracy was the most efficient means for applying rationality to organizational life. Of all social structures, it promised the maximization of scientifically correct decision making.

Is the so-called postbureaucratic situation of today really different from the conditions implied in Weber's model? No! It does not differ at all in any significant sense, and one might go on to argue that in the most critical areas, the postbureaucratic system is nothing more than the Weberian model with all the most sophisticated modifications. Despite the contortions through which organizational theorists have put themselves in the twentieth century, the remarkable fact remains that there has been no substantial change in their basic premises. The guiding belief still is that regularities exist that, on one level or another, may be learned and acted upon.

Bureaucracy is not dead. If Weber were here today, he would conclude that bureaucracy is still very much alive and well. Specific elements of his model are poorly adjusted to our times and must be modified. But that is a reasonable concession to the fact that conditions do change. It is one thing to say that bureaucracy must be *eliminated* and another to admit that it has *changed with the times*.

How has it changed? Most obviously it had to develop an alternative to deal with organizations where authority is based on knowledge. The professional bureaucracy is a clear example of such a modification. Rational discipline, rather than imposed externally, is internalized through the professionalization of employees. Authority from above is replaced with self-regimentation. This, of course, does not result in the end of bureaucracy. One can argue, in fact, that the professional bureaucracy has merely substituted the arrogance of high training for the arrogance of high office.

In summary, Miewald has argued that Weber never meant bureaucracy's characteristics to endure for eternity. Weber's major objective was to create a rational and efficient form. That *form* is bureaucracy. Whatever form is required to maintain rationality and efficiency results in bureaucracy. The development of the professional bureaucracy is a perfect example of bureaucracy's characteristics being modified to represent the most rational and efficient way in which to structure knowledge-dominated organizations.

OT
CLOSE-UP

SLIMMING DOWN BUREAUCRACIES

The *new* corporate bureaucracy is leaner and more efficient than its equivalent of ten or even five years ago. This is probably most evident in smaller corporate headquarters staffs.[20]

Bureaucracies in multibusiness corporations have a tendency to become bloated with support staff at headquarters. It has not been unusual for some of the *Fortune* 100 firms to employ 10,000 or more people at head office. AT&T, for example, had over 30,000 people in the early 1980s in corporate staff jobs such as planners, economists, marketers, central purchasing agents, real estate managers, futurologists, and human-resources specialists. They have since eliminated 12,000 of these positions.

The current trend is to decentralize activities to operating units, reduce the "big brother" role of headquarters, and buy services outside whenever possible rather than employing full-time staffs to provide them. The result is a corporate headquarters staff that acts like a small merchant bank or holding company, investing capital among various enterprises, monitoring the profitability of each against projections, replacing underachieving top managers, and constantly looking for new investment opportunities.

A number of companies are setting high standards for keeping their headquarters staff lean. For instance, Borg-Warner employs 82,000 people, yet has only 175 employees at its headquarters. Transamerica employs in excess of 15,000 people and has sales of over $7 billion a year, but gets by with a headquarters staff that numbers only 100. Nucor, the mini-steel operator, has 4000 people working in its mills, but it has only 17 people at its North Carolina headquarters.

YOU CANNOT IGNORE THE OBVIOUS: BUREAUCRACIES ARE EVERYWHERE!

Despite the criticism directed at bureaucracy, you cannot ignore the obvious. Bureaucracies are everywhere! The vast majority of large organizations are predominantly bureaucratic in structure, and for all but a few, bureaucracy represents the most efficient way for them to organize.[21]

This conclusion runs counter to what *should* prevail if, as some claim, we now live in times where change is constant and dynamic, standardized technologies have been replaced by customized processes, and humanistic practices and the goal of reducing employee alienation demand the elimination of the rigidities of bureaucracy. Why is it, then, that the bureaucratic form is thriving? There appears to be no simple answer to this question. We can propose a number of possible explanations:

1. *It works.*   Forgetting the contingency factors that would predict nonbureaucratic structures for a moment, it is obvious that bureaucracy works. Regardless of technology, environment, and so on, bureaucracies are effective in a wide range of organized activities: manufacturing, service firms, hospitals, schools and colleges, the military, and voluntary associations. As one proponent remarked, bureaucracy is "a form of organization superior to all others we know or can hope to afford in the near and middle future.[22]

2. *Large size prevails.*   Organizations that succeed and survive tend to grow to large size. And we know that bureaucracy is efficient with large size. Small organizations and their nonbureaucratic structures are more likely to fail, so over time, small organizations may come and go but large bureaucracies stay. It may also be that size is the dominant criterion determining structure and, therefore, that increased size may *cause* bureaucracy.

3. *Natural selection favors bureaucracy.*   The natural-selection thesis, which was the basis of the population ecology model discussed in Chapter 8, can also be used to explain the rise and proliferation of bureaucracies.[23]

There are potentially many types of organizations in our society. But although they differ, they all retain certain design elements because those elements are inherently more efficient and able to compete more effectively. Bureaucracy's structural features are the ones that are selectively retained because they achieve reinforcing consequences, while nonbureaucratic features are selectively eliminated. Once proven to be efficient, bureaucracies then force their form on other organizations in their environment. Those organizations that fail to adopt this design will be less efficient and will eventually be driven out in the competition for resources. So bureaucracies will eventually dominate in our society because this design, in contrast to all others, tends to be the most efficient, and it drives out organizations that use any other form.

4. *Societal values are unchanging.* A counterpoint to Bennis's position that management's philosophy is shifting to greater humanism is that North American values favor order and regimentation. North Americans have traditionally been goal-oriented and comfortable with authoritarian structures. Parents are controlling in the home; the church seeks order and rationality in parishioner behaviors; and schools reinforce order, regularity, and being part of the "system." Employees in organizations look with disfavor on jobs that are ambiguous and where job responsibilities are vague. While North Americans believe strongly in individual freedoms, it is generally acknowledged that freedom requires obedience to a set of rules and regulations. "Your freedom to swing your fists ends where my nose begins." Bureaucracy is consistent with the values of order and regimentation.

5. *Environmental turbulence is exaggerated.* As discussed in Chapter 8, environments may not be as dynamic as assumed. The media project that "the times, they are changin'." A more correct observation might be that (a) changes are no more dynamic now than at any other time in history, and (b) the impact of uncertainties in the environment on the organization are substantially reduced as a result of managerial strategies.

6. *The professional bureaucracy has emerged.* The professional bureaucracy provides the same degree of standardization and control as does Weber's machine bureaucracy. The increased need for technical expertise in organizations and the rapid expansion of knowledge-based industries has been handled neatly by the professional bureaucracy. The bureaucratic form has demonstrated the ability to adjust to its greatest threat—the knowledge revolution— by modifying itself. The goal of standardization has proven to be achievable by more than one path.

7. *Bureaucracy maintains control.* High standardization, preferably with centralized power in the hands of the dominant coalition, is desired by those in control. Bureaucracy obviously meets that end. From the power-control perspective, therefore, we would predict bureaucracy to be the preferred structure because it is the most effective mechanism structurally for maintaining control of large organizations. Consistent with this conclusion is the observation that a moderate degree of routineness pervades all organizations.[24] Since technology is chosen, it is logical to conclude that those in power would select technologies (and a matching structural form) that would maintain and enhance their control.

Those elements, when taken together, lead us to the inevitability of bureaucracy. It is the dominant structural form in North America, and the probability of doing away with it or significantly changing it in our lifetime is very likely close to zero.

EVEN PRISONERS SEEM TO LIKE BUREAUCRACY!

In December of 1987, Cuban detainees at the Atlanta Federal Prison took control of the penitentiary for ten days. When prison officials finally regained control from the prisoners, they were astonished to find that the rebels had set up their own bureaucracy.[25] They printed up stationery, circulated interoffice memos among their command posts, and set up a reward system that allocated chits, good for commissary purchases, only to detainees who were sympathetic to the takeover. Prison officials even found a sword that had been manufactured in the prison workshop. Its function? It was an authority symbol, kept by the rebel commander, to convey clearly to all detainees who was in charge.

SUMMARY

Bureaucracy refers to a type of organizational structure characterized by division of labor, a well-defined authority hierarchy, high formalization, impersonal relations, employment decisions based on merit, career tracks for employees, and distinct separation of members' organizational and personal lives. This definition originated from the work of German sociologist Max Weber.

There are basically two types of bureaucracy. The one identified by Weber is what we would now call machine bureaucracy. It is characterized structurally by high complexity, high formalization, and centralization.

Professional bureaucracy, the other type, is preferred when the organization employs highly skilled professionals. The professional bureaucracy achieves the same end as the Weberian model, but it relies on extensive decentralization and the replacement of external formalization with internalized professional standards.

The strength of the bureaucratic form lies in standardization. The organization is more efficient because employee behavior is controlled and predictable. Organizational members benefit by knowing that they will be treated fairly.

The critics of bureaucracy have argued that it results in goal displacement, inappropriate application of rules and regulations, employee alienation, the concentration of power in the hands of a few, and frustrations for the clients and customers who must deal with the impersonality and rule-bound behavior of bureaucrats.

Our conclusion is that bureaucracy is the dominant organizational form in society and has achieved its distinction because it works best with the type of technologies and environments that most organizations have. Importantly, it is also consistent with maintaining control in the hands of the organization's dominant coalition.

FOR REVIEW AND DISCUSSION

1. Define bureaucracy. How does this compare with the layperson's definition of the term?
2. "Weber's 'ideal type' is a standard. No real organizations are like this model." Do you agree or disagree? Discuss.
3. What role do rewards play in Weber's bureaucracy?
4. What role does power play in Weber's bureaucracy?
5. Can you give an example of an organization with one thousand or more employees that is not a bureaucracy? What kind of structure does this organization have? Why is it designed this way?
6. Contrast Weber's ideal type of organization with a professional bureaucracy.
7. "Providing employees with permanent employment leads to ambivalence and eventually organizational ineffectiveness." Build an argument to support this statement. Then refute your argument.
8. As an employee in a bureaucracy, what benefits does this structural form provide you with?
9. From society's point of view, is the efficiency and productivity of large organizations sufficiently important that we can sacrifice some employee satisfaction?
10. If you had your choice between working in a machine bureaucracy, a professional bureaucracy, or an adhocracy, which would you choose? Why? How do you think your answer compares with most college students? Most North Americans?

11. How do you explain the popularity of the bureaucratic form?
12. What conditions foster the development of (a) a machine bureaucracy? (b) a professional bureaucracy?
13. Give an example of goal displacement in a bureaucracy that you have observed personally.
14. Gouldner said that rules and regulations in a bureaucracy not only define unacceptable behaviors but also "define *minimum* levels of acceptable performance." What does this mean?
15. "There are only two types of organizations: those that are newly formed and bureaucracies." Do you agree or disagree? Discuss.

NOTES

[1] Franck A. De Chambeau, "Keeping the Corporate Tall Ships Afloat," *Across the Board*, March 1987, pp. 54–56.

[2] Max Weber, *The Theory of Social and Economic Organizations*, ed., Talcott Parsons, trans., A. M. Henderson and Talcott Parsons (New York: Free Press, 1947).

[3] Since Weber wrote in German, what he said is subject to bias and errors when translated into English. Interpretations of what Weber actually meant by the term bureaucracy have been the subject of debate. See, for example, J. Cohen, L. Hazelrigg, and W. Pope, "De-Personizing Weber: A Critique of Parsons' Interpretation of Weber's Sociology," *American Sociological Review*, April 1975, pp. 229–41; and R. M. Weiss, "Weber on Bureaucracy: Management Consultant or Political Theorist?" *Academy of Management Review*, April 1983, pp. 242–48. However, our description currently represents the dominant interpretation.

[4] Weber, *The Theory of Social and Economic Organizations*, p. 337. (Author's emphasis)

[5] The following discussion is adapted from Charles Perrow, *Complex Organizations: A Critical Essay* (Glenview, Ill.: Scott, Foresman, 1972), pp. 8–44.

[6] Cited in Perrow, *Complex Organizations*, p. 37.

[7] This box is based on Oliver E. Williamson, *Markets and Hierarchies: Analysis and Antitrust Implications* (New York: Free Press, 1975); Oliver E. Williamson and William G. Ouchi, "The Markets and Hierarchies and Visible Hand Perspectives," in Andrew H. Van de Ven and William F. Joyce, eds., *Perspectives on Organization Design and Behavior* (New York: John Wiley, 1981), pp. 347–70; and James A Robins, "Organizational Economics: Notes on the Use of Transaction-Cost Theory in the Study of Organizations," *Administrative Science Quarterly*, March 1987, pp. 68–86.

[8] Perrow, *Complex Organizations*, p. 59.

[9] Robert K. Merton, "Bureaucratic Structure and Personality," *Social Forces*, May 1940, pp. 560–68.

[10] Philip Selznick, *TVA and the Grass Roots: A Study in the Sociology of Formal Organizations* (Berkeley: University of California Press, 1949).

[11] Alvin W. Gouldner, *Patterns of Industrial Bureaucracy* (New York: Free Press, 1954).

[12] Victor Thompson, *Modern Organizations* (New York: Knopf, 1961).

[13] Ibid., p. 154.

[14] Merton,"Bureaucratic Structure and Personality."

[15] George A. Miller, "Professionals in Bureaucracy, Alienation among Industrial Scientists and Engineers," *American Sociological Review*, October 1967, pp. 755–68.

[16] See, for example, Chris Argyris, *Personality and Organization: The Conflict Between System and the Individual* (New York: Harper & Row, 1957).

[17] Warren G. Bennis, "The Coming Death of Bureaucracy," *Think*, November–December 1966, pp. 30–35.

[18] See Warren G. Bennis, "A Funny Thing Happened on the Way to the Future," *American Psychologist*, July 1970, pp. 595–608; and "Conversation: An Interview with Warren Bennis," *Organizational Dynamics*, Winter 1974, pp. 50–66.

[19] Robert D. Miewald, "The Greatly Exaggerated Death of Bureaucracy," *California Management Review*, Winter 1970, pp. 65–69. With permission.

[20] Thomas Moore, "Goodbye, Corporate Staff," *Fortune*, December 21, 1987, pp. 65–76.

[21] Perrow, *Complex Organizations*, p. 5; and Howard E. Aldrich, *Organizations and Environments* (Englewood Cliffs, N.J.: Prentice Hall, 1979), p. 9.

[22] Perrow, *Complex Organizations*, p. 7.

[23] John Langton, "The Ecological of Bureaucracy: The Case of Josiah Wedgwood and the British Pottery Industry," *Administrative Science Quarterly*, September 1984, pp. 330–54.

[24] Perrow, *Complex Organizations*, p. 175.

[25] Reported in *U.S. News & World Report*, January 4, 1988, p. 19.

12

ADHOCRACY:
A CLOSER LOOK

AFTER READING THIS CHAPTER, YOU SHOULD BE ABLE TO:

1 Describe the strengths and weaknesses of the matrix.
2 Identify the characteristics of Theory Z organizations.
3 Describe how structure can facilitate innovation.
4 Explain how network structures work.
5 Contrast temporary and permanent forms of adhocracy.
6 Assess the role that adhocracies will play in the design of future organizations.

Introduction
TELEVISING THE OLYMPIC GAMES

NBC paid $300 million for the American rights to televise the 1988 Summer Olympic Games from Seoul, South Korea. It's not an assignment that happens regularly at NBC. In fact, the last time the network televised an Olympics was the 1972 Winter Games from Sapporo, Japan.

NBC spent three years planning for the two-week extravaganza. But what made the project uniquely challenging was its complexity.[1] First, all preparations had to be in addition to NBC's normal broadcasting operations. None of the planning effort for the Olympics could interfere with the day-to-day broadcasting of NBC's regular programs. If it was necessary to take people off their normal jobs to work on the Olympics, someone had to be found to fill in for them. Second, the project was immense. The physical distance of Seoul from NBC's New York headquarters plus language and cultural differences made the job particularly challenging. A sixty-thousand-square-foot broadcast center had to be erected in Seoul. Sixty-million dollars in state-of-the-art technical equipment had to be shipped to South Korea and set up. More than eleven hundred NBC employees—five hundred in engineering, three hundred in production, and three hundred in management and clerical positions— were needed to run the 100-monitor control rooms, the 15 edit rooms, the 150 tape machines, the 100 NBC cameras, the 17 mobile units, and coordinate operations. Third, televising the Olympic Games demands high flexibility because unexpected, world-class performances can occur at almost any time. There were 220 events taking place at 23 different locations throughout Seoul. In many cases, a half dozen or more events were going on simultaneously, and NBC had to be able to switch from one site to another instantly if something noteworthy was occurring. Finally, NBC had a lot at stake in the Games. It was competing against ABC's successful record of televising past summer and winter Olympics. Moreover, it had sold some 1750 minutes of advertising time at an average of $660,000 a minute in prime time. Sponsors were expecting high ratings, and, if they didn't materialize, there was the possibility that NBC would have to return part of this money to advertisers. If ratings slacked, the estimated $50 to $75 million in profits that NBC was estimating from the Games could quickly turn to a loss. Of course, a successful performance in the ratings would have a positive effect, giving the network's fall schedule a strong boost.

How did NBC organize the task of broadcasting the Games? They utilized an adhocracy. While NBC is essentially a machine bureaucracy, the structure used to plan and operate the Olympics had few formal rules and regulations. Decision making was decentralized, although carefully coordinated by NBC's executive producer for Olympic operations. The need to bring together more than a thousand technical specialists, who could apply their skills on a temporary project in a dynamic environment requiring the ability to respond rapidly to change, led NBC to use an adhocracy. To have used any other design would have lessened the company's effectiveness in achieving its objectives.

The conditions that demand the flexibility of an adhocracy may not occur every day nor be applicable to most organizations, but that doesn't reduce the adhocracy's importance. As organizations take on increasingly demanding, innovative, and complex activities, they will very likely turn to the adhocracy, or some variant of it, as a necessary means to complete these activities successfully. This chapter looks at a number of designs that are, in varying degrees, forms of adhocracy. However, keep in mind that, like Weber's "ideal" bureaucracy, the pure adhocracy is also an abstraction. That is, there is probably no such thing as a *pure* adhocracy. An organization's design may be *generally* adhocratic or *moving toward* adhocracy, but no organization is likely to have all the characteristics attributed in Chapter 10 to the pure adhocracy model.

THE MATRIX

The **matrix** is a structural design that assigns specialists from specific functional departments to work on one or more interdisciplinary teams, which are led by project leaders. The matrix adds a flexibility dimension to bureaucracy's economies of specialization. And it's the flexibility dimension—created by the use of multidisciplinary teams—that places the matrix into the adhocracy classification.

Figure 12–1 illustrates the matrix form as used by an aerospace firm. Notice that there are traditional functional departments: design engineering, manufacturing, contract administration, purchasing, accounting, and personnel. These are shown across the top of Figure 12–1. Overlapping these functional departments are four projects. Each of these projects is directed by a manager who staffs his or her project with people from the functional departments. Are the horizontal and vertical axes in a matrix always made up of functional units and projects? For the most part, matrix designs evolve around functional units. However, the vertical axis might be products or programs as well as project groups. The box on p. 332 describes how General Mills utilizes the matrix to coordinate its thirty-three consumer products.

The most obvious structural characteristic of the matrix is that it breaks the unity of command concept—a cornerstone of bureaucracy—which requires every employee to have one and only one boss to whom he or she reports. Employees in the matrix have two bosses—their functional department manager and their project manager. The matrix has a dual chain of command. There is the normal vertical hierarchy within functional departments, which is "overlaid" by a form of lateral influence. So the matrix is unique

THE MATRIX AT GENERAL MILLS

There is no shortage of name brands at General Mills: Cheerios, Bisquick, Trix, Betty Crocker cake mixes, Stir 'n Frost, Total, Hamburger Helper, Gold Medal flour. Each of the thirty-three consumer-food brands at General Mills has its own product manager: The product managers act as business managers—they collect all the internal and external information that might affect the brand, set goals for it, and establish strategies and tactics to achieve these goals. They are responsible for identifying key issues, thoroughly reviewing their business and their competitors, and formulating an operating plan that includes a sales forecast; itemization of costs to meet the forecast; and advertising, pricing, and trade tactics. The plan is submitted to, and negotiated with, a marketing director, who is responsible for several product managers.

Once a plan is approved, executing it is the product manager's responsibility. But with that task goes almost no formal authority. He or she has control over the budget, but little else and must therefore be a master of persuasion. If the product manager needs special support from the sales force or increased output from the plant to gear up for a big advertising campaign, he or she has to sell the idea to people who report to functional managers in charge of sales and manufacturing. Similarly, if the manager thinks that the product needs different packaging, a more focused television commercial, or a reformulation of ingredients, he or she must impress the appropriate support groups with the importance of paying particular attention to that brand.

In summary, General Mills uses the matrix structure as a way to give brand managers a feeling of running their own show, in spite of their being part of an established, hierarchical company with sales of over $4 billion a year.[2]

in that it legitimates lateral channels of influence. Project managers have authority over those functional members who are part of that manager's project team. Referring back to Figure 12–1, the purchasing specialists who are responsible for procurement activities on the Gamma project, would be responsible to both the manager of purchasing and the Gamma project manager. Authority is shared between the two managers. Generally, this is done by giving

FIGURE 12–1 *A Matrix Organization in an Aerospace Firm*

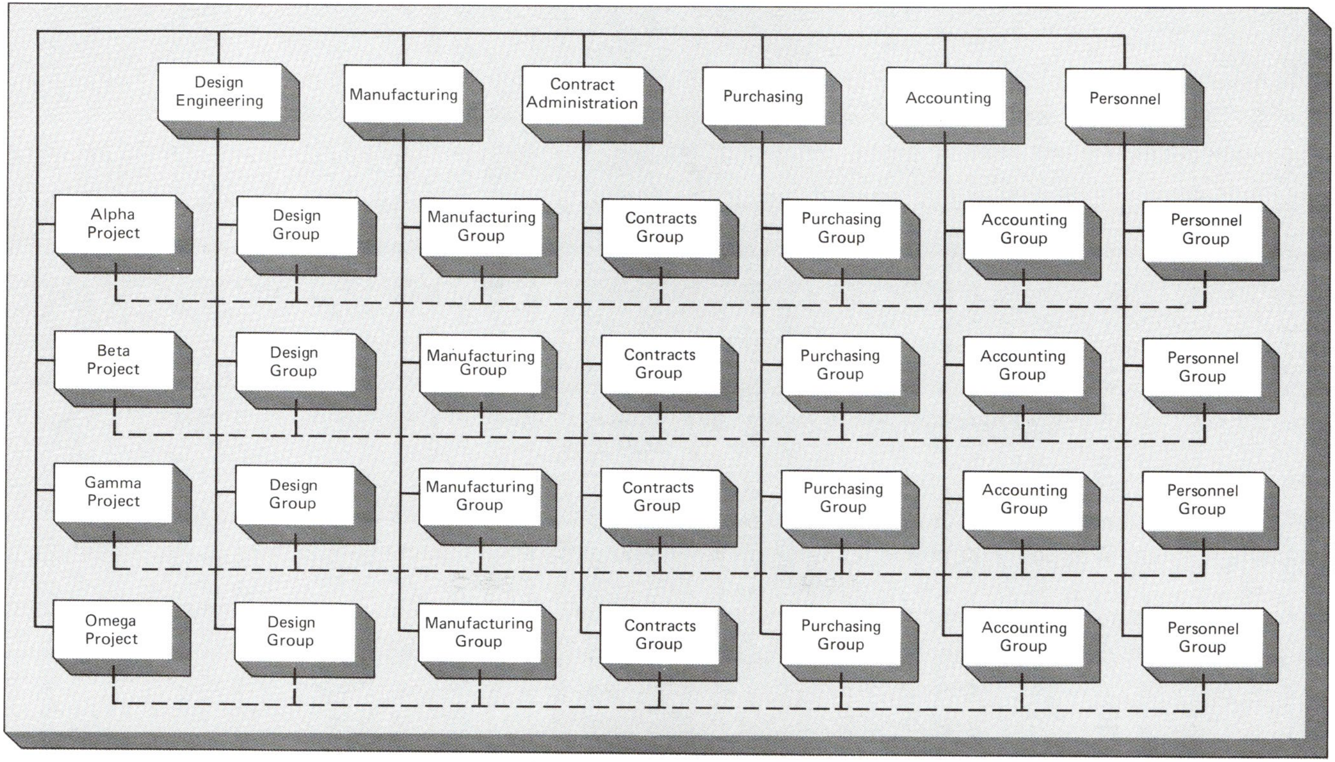

the project managers authority over project employees relative to the project's goals. Decisions such as promotions, salary recommendations, and the annual review of each employee typically remain a part of the functional manager's responsibility.

When Should You Use the Matrix?

The matrix has been popular for more than twenty years. Today you'll find it being used in advertising agencies, aerospace firms, research-and-development laboratories, construction companies, hospitals, government agencies, universities, management consulting firms, and entertainment companies.[3] But what do these organizations have in common that would lead to the use of the matrix design? The evidence indicates three conditions that favor the matrix: (1) environmental pressure from two or more critical sectors; (2) interdependence between departments; and (3) economies of scale in the use of internal resources.[4]

The typical matrix is designed to have a dual focus, such as functions and products. An advertising agency, for example, may have to maintain its technical knowledge (the functional focus) while being responsive to client needs (the product focus). The matrix allows the agency to create a team for a client that would be overseen by an account executive and composed of functional specialists from the firm's copy writing, media development, and marketing research departments. The duality might also be created by the need to respond to geographic differences. So you might find a matrix designed around function and geography or product and geography. Again, to illustrate, an insurance company may meet its competition by offering a variety of products—i.e., life, health, fire, automobile—and respond to area differences by establishing regional offices. The key, however, is that if environmental pressure is coming from only a single sector, there should be no need for a dual hierarchy.

The second requirement is interdependence between departments. In our previous advertising agency example, the services of copy writers, media developers, and marketing researchers were needed to meet the client's needs. The job could not be done by any one of the specialties alone. The degree of interdependence, of course, changes in response to demands from the environment.

The mix of people on any project team will reflect the objectives of the project at that particular time.

The final condition that favors the matrix is internal economies of scale. The organization's activities could be structured solely around its projects. For example, reflecting back on Figure 12–1, each of the aerospace firm's projects could have its own design engineers, contract administrators, and the like. They would be permanently attached to a given project and work solely on that project. But such a design tends to be inefficient where the organization is of moderate size, and personnel are not easily divisible. The matrix would allow our aerospace firm to allocate design engineers temporarily to several projects. The company would be able to take advantage of specialization that accrues to large size— for example, employing a number of design engineers with a wide range of unique skills and experiences—but could never be justified if the specialists worked only on a single project team. In fact, if projects tended to be small and employees were rigidly assigned to a single project, it would be very likely that some projects would not have an adequate talent pool to complete their work successfully.

Two Types of Matrix Structures

The projects or products in a matrix can be undergoing change continuously or they can be relatively enduring. The first typifies the temporary matrix; the second represents the permanent matrix.

The aerospace example depicted in Figure 12–1 illustrates the temporary matrix. When new contracts are secured, project teams are created by drawing members from functional departments. A team exists only for the life of the project on which it is working. While each project might last half a dozen or more years, the fact that such companies as McDonnell-Douglas or General Dynamics may have a large number of projects operating simultaneously means that the makeup of the matrix changes constantly. New contracts demand the formation of new projects so that at any one time you might find several projects winding down while others are in their infancy.

The projects or products in the permanent matrix stay relatively intact over time. Large colleges of business use the permanent matrix when they superimpose project structures—undergraduate programs, graduate programs, research bureaus, and executive development programs—over the functional departments of accounting, finance, management, marketing, and the like. Directors of the product structures utilize faculty from the departments to achieve their goals. The director of the graduate business program staffs his courses with members from the various departments. Notice that the products do not change; thus we say that this is a permanent matrix. Why use this type of structure? It provides clear lines of responsibilities for each product line. The success or failure, for instance, of the executive development program in a college of business lies directly with its director. Without the matrix, it is difficult to find anyone who can coordinate and take responsibility for the effective performance of the development program.

Permanent matrix structures also are evident in some large retail chains such as Sears, Roebuck and J. C. Penney.[5] These chains create dual lines of authority when they establish store managers (equivalent to product managers) and merchandise managers (equivalent to functional managers). The former is responsible for the performance of his or her store. The latter's responsibility relates to the purchasing of appropriate merchandise for these stores. The women's lingerie buyer, for instance, will purchase merchandise for many of the company's stores. These dual lines of authority create two sets of permanent managers who have separate responsibilities and report up separate lines of authority.

Strengths and Weaknesses of the Matrix

The strength of the matrix lies in its ability to facilitate coordination when the organization has a multiplicity of complex and interdependent activities. As an organization gets larger, its information-processing capacity can become overloaded. In a bureaucracy, complexity results in increased formalization. The direct and frequent contact between different specialties in the matrix can make for better communication and more flexibility. Information permeates the organization and more quickly reaches those people who need to take account of it. Further, the matrix reduces bureaupathologies. The dual lines of authority reduce tendencies of departmental members to become so busy protecting their "little worlds" that goals become displaced.

There are other advantages to the matrix. As we noted, it facilitates the efficient allocation of specialists. When individuals with highly specialized skills are lodged in one functional department or project group, their talent is monopolized and underutilized. The matrix achieves the advantages of economies of scale by providing the organization with both the best resources and an effective way of ensuring their efficient deployment. Further advantages of the matrix are that it creates (1) increased ability to respond rapidly to changes in the environment, (2) an effective means for balancing the customer's requirements for project completion and cost control with the organization's need for economic efficiency and development of technical capability for the future, and (3) increased motivation by providing an environment more in line with the democratic norms preferred by scientific and professional employees.[6]

The major disadvantages of the matrix lie in the confusion it creates, its propensity to foster power struggles, and the stress it places on individuals.[7] When you dispense with the unity of command concept, ambiguity is significantly increased and ambiguity often leads to conflict. For example, it's frequently unclear who reports to whom, and it is not unusual for project managers to fight over getting the best specialists assigned to their projects. Confusion and ambiguity also create the seeds for power struggles. Bureaucracy reduces the potential for "power grabs" by defining the rules of the game. When those rules are "up for grabs," power struggles between functional and project managers result. For individuals who desire security and absence from ambiguity, this environment can produce stress. Reporting to more than one boss introduces role conflict, and unclear expectations introduce role ambiguity. The comfort of bureaucracy's predictability is absent, replaced by insecurity and stress.

THEORY Z

It's no secret that the Japanese have been very successful at producing high-quality products at competitive prices. Part of their success is due to the way that large Japanese organizations are designed. Table 12–1 summarizes the characteristics in the typical, large American bureaucracy (the Theory A organization) and the characteristics inherent in the typical large Japanese company (the Theory J organization). William Ouchi of UCLA has found that several American companies, whether knowingly or not, have developed systems that have many of the characteristics evident in Japanese firms. He found, for instance, that IBM, Procter & Gamble, Eastman Kodak, and Hewlett-Packard have a lot in common with the Japanese system. Ouchi has coined the term Theory Z to describe the Americanized version of the Japanese model.[8] Let's briefly overview the characteristics of American bureaucracies in order to have a point of reference for comparing Theory J and Theory Z organizations.

The **Theory A** bureaucracy is designed to control employees through a tightly monitored structural system. It is adapted to handle high rates of employee turnover. Jobs are defined narrowly, and employees are required to specialize. An employee's specialized skills lend themselves to transferability between organizations, thus encouraging mobility. If employees become frustrated, they have ready alternatives in employment opportunities with other organizations. Similarly, organizations can hire employees from other firms and give them considerable responsibility and competitive salaries because these individuals' skills are trans-

TABLE 12–1 *Characteristics of Theory A and Theory J Organizations*

THEORY A	THEORY J
Short-term employment	Life-time employment
Specialized career paths	Nonspecialized career paths
Individual decision making	Consensual decision making
Individual responsibility	Collective responsibility
Frequent appraisal	Infrequent appraisal
Explicit, formalized appraisal	Implicit, informal appraisal
Rapid promotion	Slow promotion
Segmented concern for people	Comprehensive concern for people

Adapted from W. G. Ouchi and A. M. Jaeger, "Type Z Organizations: Stability in the Midst of Mobility," *Academy of Management Review*, April 1978, p. 308. With permission.

ferable, allowing them to become quickly productive for their new employer.

In a system where members are transient, it is important to minimize interdependencies. Therefore, Theory A organizations individualize decision making and responsibility.

High levels of turnover also create regular vacancies. Opportunities for promotion are plentiful. Because supervisors know little about their employees beyond their job-related activities, appraisals tend to be formalized and impersonal and relate only to specific measures of job performance. These appraisals, made on at least an annual basis, then become the input from which promotion decisions are made.

When employees come and go quickly, are required to assume individual responsibilities, pursue specialized career paths, and are appraised on impersonal criteria, they have little motivation to identify with the organization or to exert energy toward forming friendships. The organization responds to this individualistic ethic by treating people as just another input cost. Employees, then, are not significantly different from a drill press or a fork-lift truck. You purchase them to obtain utility of service and can discard them if they break or become obsolete.

The Japanese model (**Theory J**) is a very different structural animal, and that difference is essentially a function of low turnover.[9] When employees are hired with the belief that the marriage is a permanent one, management can justify developing an organization in which control is maintained through a socialization process that indoctrinates the organization's philosophy into every employee. While this is a much slower process, it results in a structure that is much more likely to mirror an adhocracy than the mechanistic bureaucracy that Theory A creates.

Movement in Japanese organizations tends to be far more horizontal than vertical. Instead of emphasizing vertical promotions, Japanese employees are rotated around the organization. This creates employees that are generalists rather than specialists. The creation of generalists encourages teamwork and cooperation, and fosters informal communication networks that help to coordinate work activities across functional areas.

Decision making in Japanese organizations is not "participative" in the American sense of the term. That is, it is not characterized by frequent group meetings and negotiations between manager and subordinates. In the Japanese model, the manager discusses and consults informally with all who may be affected. When all are familiar with the proposal, a formal request for a decision is made, and as a result of the previous informal preparations, it is almost always ratified. The key is not so much agreement with a decision as it is for those concerned to have the opportunity to be advised about it and to have their views heard fairly. The Japanese

OT
CLOSE-UP

BUT THINGS ARE CHANGING IN JAPAN!

The Theory J model is undergoing change in Japan. As recently as the early 1980s, the idea of Japanese employees changing companies in mid-career was almost heresy, but that is no longer true.[10] In 1987, for instance, 2.7 million people, or 4.4 percent of the Japanese workforce, changed jobs. That was up 80 percent from 1982.

Japan's "lifetime employment" system—or at least its spirit—is unlikely to disappear in the near future, but job-hopping by employees is tending to undermine it. And these changes may have longer-term effects on Japan's traditional work culture. Employees may be less patient in waiting for promotions, less willing to sublimate their needs for individual recognition to achieve group harmony, and less willing to place their fates in the hands of their employers.

What has brought about this change in Japan? A number of forces seem to be at work. First, Japan is plagued with labor shortages. So many companies, desperate for trained professionals, are hiring people from the competition. Second, some Japanese firms have sought to shake up their complacent organizational cultures. Hiring outsiders, who bring a fresh perspective, can stimulate new ideas. Third, an increasing number of foreign employers—like Lotus Development, Daimler Benz, and BMW—have set up operations in Japan and have brought a different philosophy toward hiring. Fourth, some large Japanese companies, facing slower growth, have been increasingly encouraging senior employees to take early retirement. The result has been that many workers are sensing that the system of lifetime employment isn't what it used to be. Finally, a number of Japanese workers have grown impatient with the traditional system. They are looking for more money, more challenges, and greater job responsibilities. Changing employers provides a quick means of achieving these goals.

system also emphasizes organizing work tasks around groups rather than individuals. Tasks are assigned to groups, and there is collective responsibility for outcomes.

Japanese employees are appraised against a number of criteria, only one of which is current output or performance. These appraisals are also less frequent and more informal than in American firms. Regular and frequent performance appraisals are necessary in Theory A organizations because of member mobility and the need to have adequate data from which to make promotion decisions. Lifetime employment and slow promotion result in appraisals that emphasize ability to get along with others and being a good team player.

Finally, the Theory J organization has a holistic concern for the well-being of employees. Management considers its human resources, not its financial or physical resources, to be *most* important in the search for long-run success. Managers will be found spending a great deal of their time talking to employees about everyday matters. Even senior managers in Japan regularly spend time with operating personnel to learn their concerns.

The **Theory Z** organization is the Japanese model adapted to fit into American culture. Table 12–2 identifies its attributes. For the most part, as you can see, it very closely parallels the Theory J model. However, it has been modified to reflect American values such as individualism and allocating rewards on the basis of performance.

Firms like IBM and Procter & Gamble don't guarantee their employees lifetime jobs. What they do offer, however, is a long-term commitment to provide stable employment. Layoffs result only from severe economic setbacks. These Theory Z–type companies treat their employees as a valuable and scarce resource, to be nurtured over the long term.

The Japanese system, in attempting to ensure that employees fit in properly, overtly discriminates. Culturally dissimilar types, particularly women and minorities, are selectively excluded from the mainstream. Such actions are unacceptable in the United States. Theory Z organizations, therefore, contain a less homogeneous labor force than Theory J firms. Employees in Theory Z firms are also appraised once or twice a year, and the process emphasizes objective measures of actual job performance rather than informal or subjective assessments.

Just as Theory A organizations are bureaucratic, the Theory Z

HEWLETT-PACKARD IN SAN DIEGO

Hewlett-Packard, an electronics company, was founded in 1939; the firm was committed early on to give meaning to work as well as to making a profit. Part of that commitment was to provide long-term employment and establish a generous profit-sharing plan. The H-P plant in San Diego, which designs and manufactures computer plotters, follows that original H-P commitment.

Plant management is committed to not laying off employees. For instance, in the early 1970s, during a recession, everyone at H-P took a 10 percent pay cut. As a result, no one was laid off. Management also downplays authority and strongly supports group decision making. H-P employees, for example, meet weekly to resolve production problems. But the H-P plant seeks to blend the American concern for individualism with the Japanese collectivism. In contrast to Japan, there are no morning inspirational speeches or calisthenics nor does anyone wear a uniform to identify rank. Pay raises at H-P are based on merit and seniority. Performance appraisals occur four times a year, and evaluations are based on teamwork and ability to meet or exceed individual quotas.

H-P plants are held to under two thousand employees to keep them manageable. The San Diego facility employs fifteen hundred. The internal culture is informal. Everyone, including management, dresses casually. Managers and operatives alike are addressed on a first-name basis. Flexible work hours are used so that employees can adjust their hours individually. Machines are set up to allow individuals to work at their own speeds. The work areas are open, the personnel department being the only office in the plant that has a door. If employees have a problem, they are encouraged to air it openly. Employees can take their grievance to anyone, up to and including the plant's general manager. Stories circulate that some employees have even called H-P's president with a problem.

Based on "Hewlett-Packard's San Diego Division," a research paper prepared by Leslie Beams, Susan Eubanks, and Arthur Turner under the supervision of Professor Stephen P. Robbins. San Diego State University, 1981.

TABLE 12–2   *Characteristics of Theory Z Organizations*

Long-term employment
Moderately specialized career paths
Consensual decision making
Individual responsibility
Infrequent appraisal
Implicit, informal appraisal with explicit, formalized measures
Slow promotion
Comprehensive concern for people

Adapted from W. G. Ouchi and A. M. Jaeger, "Type Z Organizations: Stability in the Midst of Mobility," *Academy of Management Review*, April 1978, p. 311. With permission.

organizations are essentially adhocratic. Complexity is low since excessive layers of management are unnecessary. Formalization is also low. The concern with the long term, organizational loyalty, and teamwork acts to regulate employee behavior. Operating decisions are made by work teams. The result is an organization design that is significantly more like those popular in Japan than the traditional mechanistic structure that has historically dominated the American scene.

THE COLLATERAL FORM

America has rediscovered the value of entrepreneurship. It is now fashionable to want to start up a small company, to take risks, to be innovative. The simple structure is the ideal mechanism within which entrepreneurship can flourish. But the large company needn't be left out in the cold. Companies such as General Electric, Du Pont, Texas Instruments, IBM, and AT&T are experimenting with collateral organization designs that allow **intrapreneuring;** that is, creating the spirit and rewards of entrepreneurship within or alongside a large bureaucracy.[11]

3M INSTITUTIONALIZES INNOVATION

Few companies have succeeded like 3M in creating an organizational structure that stimulates innovation among its scientific and engineering personnel.[12]

3M is a huge company. It employs 82,000 people, more than 6000 of whom are scientists and engineers; it has sales in excess of $10 billion a year; and it has a product line that encompasses some sixty thousand items (most notably, Scotch-brand tapes). New products are generated at the extremely high rate of more than two hundred a year from its research labs. And the company does a pretty good job of achieving its goal of having 25 percent of any year's sales coming from products that didn't exist five years previously. For instance, Post-it Notes—those little sticky pieces of colored paper that don't damage surfaces when they're pulled off—were introduced in 1980 and, within five years, were generating annual sales in excess of $200 million.

If there is a single secret to 3M's success, it's the company's ability to stimulate intrapreneurship among its scientists and engineers. 3M's dozens of divisions are organized into groups, and the groups are divided into four sectors, or categories. Yet the structure is highly decentralized, and researchers are given a great deal of discretionary latitude with their projects. In fact, since the 1920s, 3M has had a policy allowing its researchers to spend up to 15 percent of their time on projects of their own choosing. Moreover, the company encourages its employees to take risks and rewards them well when they succeed. Of course, 3M is well aware that creating an intrapreneurial climate means having a different breed of employee. Because they're interested in change and making things happen, 3M researchers don't readily accept rules and regulations, and they challenge authority, ask embarrassing questions, circumvent the chain of command, and often behave in ways incongruent with bureaucracy. But 3M considers these disruptions a small price to pay to keep innovation alive within its overall mechanistic structure.

The **collateral form** is a loosely structured organic appendage designed to coexist side by side with a bureaucracy on a relatively permanent basis.[13] They are typically small teams or separate business units that are given the independence and resources to experiment. They can pursue their own ideas without the rules, time-consuming analysis, and approvals from multiple levels of management that are required in bureaucracies.[14] In contrast to the bureaucratic mainframe, which is designed to solve the organization's structured problems effectively, the collateral appendage has the flexibility to solve ill-structured problems. Innovative ideas to unique problems can be tried; and if they fail, the costs to the overall organization are usually relatively small.

The strength of the collateral form is the achievement of the advantages from bureaucracy's high efficiency through standardization while, at the same time, obtaining the flexibility from intrapreneurship. By creating adhocracies within bureaucracies, a large corporation can stimulate creativity and innovation, cut product-development time, and hold on to bright and achievement-oriented employees who might otherwise leave to work for another firm or start their own small firm.

Innovation doesn't come without a price. That price, for organizations that adopt the collateral form, is usually disorder. Meshing bureaucratic and organic units creates a clash of cultures—one valuing order and the other flexibility. The primary challenge lies with top management in the bureaucracy. While intrapreneuring is currently fashionable and the potential for the big "breakthrough" is alluring, it is usually difficult for top management to let free spirits go off on their own with little centralized control. It takes a unique type of top management—which itself has been nurtured in bureaucracy's rules, checks and balances, and intolerance for failure—to leave the intrapreneurial units alone and let them take risks and make mistakes.

THE NETWORK STRUCTURE

A new form of organization design is currently gaining popularity. It allows management great flexibility in responding to new technology, fashion, or low-cost foreign competition. It is the **network**

structure—a small central organization that relies on other organizations to perform manufacturing, distribution, marketing, or other crucial business functions on a contract basis.[15]

Some very large companies (such as Nike, Esprit de Corp apparel, Emerson Radio, and Schwinn Bicycle) have found that they can sell hundreds of millions of dollars of products every year and earn a very competitive return with few or no manufacturing facilities of their own and only a few hundred employees. What they have done is to create an organization of relationships. They connect with independent designers, manufacturers, commissioned sales representatives, or the like to perform, on a contract basis, the functions they need.

The network stands in sharp contrast to more traditional structures where there are multiple vertical levels of management and where organizations seek to control their destiny through ownership. In such organizations, research and development is done in-house, production occurs in company-owned manufacturing plants, and sales and marketing are performed by their own employees. To support all this, management has to employ extra personnel such as accountants, human resource specialists, and lawyers. In the network structure, most of these functions are bought outside the organization. This gives management a high degree of flexibility and allows the organization to concentrate on what it does best. For most American firms, that means focusing on design or marketing and buying manufacturing capability outside. Emerson Radio Corporation, for example, designs and engineers its TVs, stereos, and other consumer electronic products, but it contracts out their manufacture to Asian suppliers.

Figure 12–2 shows a network structure in which management contracts out all of the primary functions of the business. The core of the network organization is a small group of executives. Their job is to oversee directly any activities that are done in-house and to coordinate relationships with the other organizations that manufacture, distribute, and perform other crucial functions for the network organization. The dotted lines in Figure 12–2 represent those contractual relationships. So, in essence, managers in network structures spend most of their time coordinating and controlling external relations.

The network organization is not appropriate for all endeavors. It fits industrial companies like toy and apparel firms, which re-

FIGURE 12–2 *A Network Structure*

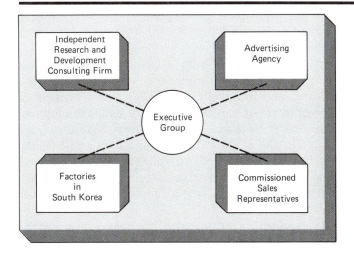

quire very high flexibility in order to respond quickly to fashion changes. It also fits firms whose manufacturing operations require low-cost labor that is available only outside the United States and can best be utilized by contracting with foreign suppliers. On the negative side, management in network structures lacks the close control of manufacturing operations that exists in more traditional organizations. Reliability of supply is also less predictable. Finally, any innovation in design that a network organization acquires is susceptible to being "ripped off." It's very difficult, if not impossible, to closely guard innovations that are under the direction of management in another organization. Yet, with computers in one organization now interfacing and communicating with computers in other organizations, the network structure is becoming an increasingly viable alternative.

OTHER EXAMPLES OF ADHOCRACY

The design of adhocratic structures is limited only by the creativity of the designers. But in addition to those designs we have already discussed, three other examples of adhocracies have gained popularity in the OT literature. These are the task force, the committee structure, and the collegial structure.

The Task Force

The **task force** is a temporary structure formed to accomplish a specific, well-defined and complex task that involves a number of organizational subunits.[16] It can be thought of as a scaled-down version of the temporary matrix or a temporary version of the organic appendage in the collateral form. Members serve on the task force until its goal is achieved, at which time the task force is disbanded. Then the members move on to a new task force, return to their permanent "home" departments in the organization, or leave the organization.

When an organization is confronted with a task whose success is critical to the organization, which has specific time and performance standards, is unique and unfamiliar, and requires functions that are interdependent, a task force can be desirable. These conditions explain why Ford Motor Co. went to the task-force concept in the early 1980s to develop the Taurus.[17]

Dubbed "Team Taurus," this task force took a completely different approach than traditionally followed in the U.S. auto industry. In the past, Ford had developed their cars sequentially: first design drew it, then engineering made it work, then manufacturing figured out how to build it, and finally, service looked for some way to fix it. Every time the job was handed to the next department, the next unit discovered something they didn't like and made changes. This lack of coordination tended to produce defective cars, with each department blaming the others for any problems that surfaced.

Team Taurus included representatives from all the various units—planning, design, engineering, advertising, public relations, manufacturing—and even outside suppliers that made incidental parts. They worked together, from the beginning, to create a car that could compete head-on, in terms of quality and design, with the best from Japan and Europe. When the project was completed in 1985, Team Taurus was disbanded. The Team Taurus task force proved highly effective. The Ford Taurus and its sister, the Mercury Sable, have been products that have sold almost as fast as they could be produced, and *Consumer Reports* rated the Taurus higher than any domestic car it had ever tested.

Note how Ford exploited the major advantage of the task force. It allowed the company to be adaptive, yet, at the same time, maintain its efficient bureaucracy. By attaching task-force structures to the mechanistic mainframe, organizations like Ford can get the best of both worlds: flexibility and efficiency.

The Committee Form

Another example of adhocracy is the **committee form** of organization. When it is desired that a broad range of experience and backgrounds be brought to bear on a decision, when those who will be affected by a decision are allowed to be represented, when it is believed desirable to spread the work load, or during periods of management transition when no single individual is ready to lead the organization, committee structures may be highly effective.

Committees may be temporary or permanent. A temporary committee typically is one and the same with a task force. Permanent committees, however, facilitate the bringing together of diverse inputs like the task force plus the stability and consistency of the matrix. When permanent committees are established at the top level of the organization, we frequently refer to the positions as forming a plural executive. Such a structure brings diverse perspectives into top-level decision making and permits the heterogeneous tasks of the chief executive's job to be divided up and parceled out according to the background and skills of the plural executive group. Du Pont, for example, has utilized the plural-executive concept for a number of decades. Westinghouse and General Electric, similarly, use a three-person management committee at the top. Each person still retains certain lines of authority, but all work as a group on planning and attacking long-range strategic problems of a nonoperating nature. Some universities and state governments have also introduced the plural-executive committee. A number of universities have an "office of the president" rather than the position of president and several states have an "office of the governor" instead of a singular position.

The Collegial Form

A structural form of adhocracy fashionable in universities, research labs, and other highly professional organizations is the **collegial form.** Its unique characteristic is full democracy in the making of all important decisions. This is in contrast to the task force or committee structures that utilize representative decision making.

The best example and most widespread use of the collegial structure is the design of academic departments in major universities. All key decisions are made by the department as a whole. Typically, even the department head carries no more weight than his or her one vote. The selection of new members, contract renewals, allocation of teaching assignments, performance appraisals, granting of tenure, modifications in curriculum, grading policies, and similar decisions are made by the department as a whole.

The collegial structure represents the utmost in decentralization. In universities, faculty members act with only minimal guidelines. These guidelines—university policies and procedures—tend to allow a great deal of leeway for departmental discretion. In the research units at Eastman Kodak or Bell Labs, you similarly find a structure that provides employees with extremely high autonomy, a minimum of formalization, and collegial decision making, which allows highly skilled professionals to adapt rapidly to the changing needs of their work.

TWO CONTEMPORARY VIEWS ON TOMORROW'S ORGANIZATIONS

Management gurus Peter Drucker and Tom Peters both agree that tomorrow's organizations are going to be flatter, less hierarchical, and more decentralized. In a word, they're going to be more *adhocratic.* Whether Drucker and Peters are right is another issue, but it is interesting to consider how they arrive at their conclusions and the specific form they think future organizations will take. As you'll see, Drucker essentially proposes a technology explanation: Future organizations will look more like large *symphony orchestras* than the traditional pyramid-shaped corporate bureaucracies because the typical organization will have become information-based.[18] An information-based technology will require adhocracy. Peters, on the other hand, offers an environmental uncertainty argument. He says that unprecedented change and uncertainty in the environment will require organizations to cherish impermanence. They will thrive on chaos and appear to be something akin to *focused anarchies.*[19]

Drucker sees computer technology changing the composition of tomorrow's organizations. Knowledge-based organizations will be composed largely of specialists who direct and discipline their own performance through organized feedback from colleagues, customers, and headquarters. These organizations will function much like a large symphony orchestra. Instead of doing things sequentially—research, development, manufacturing, and marketing—they'll be done by *synchrony.* Clear, simple, common objectives will allow the chief executive to "conduct" directly hundreds of employees or musicians. The CEO will be able to have a wide span of control because each employee will be a specialist who knows his or her part.

Peters sees the world as being in a state of revolutionary change. Every business has—and continues to confront—new competitors. In many cases, management doesn't even know where tomorrow's competitor will come from. It might come from Southeast Asia or from a couple of young entrepreneurs working in their garage in California. Add the uncertainty created by such things as exchange rates, interest rates, rates of inflation, and prices of energy, and you have a constantly gyrating environment.

Peters' solution is for management to create flexible, porous, team-based adhocracies. They will be low in formalization. Written rules will be replaced by a strong competitive vision and by managers who lead by example. These organizations will be low in complexity. Top managers will set the tone by breaking down both vertical hierarchical barriers and functional walls. Managers will feel comfortable leaping two or three levels in the organization to communicate with other members and crossing traditional functional boundaries to get things done quickly. The organizations will also be decentralized, with employees serving on multiple task force teams that will focus on quality or productivity improvement. Finally, Peters' idea of tomorrow's organizations is one where porous boundaries separate the organization and its members from outsiders. Employees will regularly communicate with people in their organization's specific environment and members of the specific environment will be actively involved in organizational activities. The barriers that separate the organization from its environment will be ripped away, leaving it virtually impossible to identify the outside organizational boundaries. This organization will be fluid, action-oriented, and able to adapt quickly to chaotic changes in the environment. Of course, in so doing, it will itself become a form of purposeful, or focused, anarchy.

"IT'S NICE IN THEORY, BUT . . ."

Do you see a disparity between the conclusions drawn about bureaucracy and the direction of this chapter? Regarding bureaucracy, we said that it was thriving, inevitable, and "the dominant structural form in North America." In this chapter, however, we have described a variety of organizations that use adhocracy and have implied that it is found, in some form, in most dynamic environments where flexibility is necessary for survival. Both these observations are correct. However, they are not contradictions.

Usage in a wide *range* of organizations should not be confused with wide *acceptance*. First, adhocracies are the dominant structure in only a small minority of industries. Second, the form is used most popularly as an adjunct to bureaucracy. Third, adhocracies that require top management to give up control will face strong, constant resistance. Finally, where adhocracy is found it is often more accurate to conceive of it as a "vehicle" propelling the organization toward bureaucracy or failure rather than as an ongoing structure.

One must be careful in generalizing from a few examples. It is true that many small electronic firms, some large aerospace companies, most research laboratories, and almost all "think tank" consulting firms are organized as adhocracies. But these examples also comprise basically the entire set of adhocracies. In terms of impact—whether you use sales, number of personnel employed, or any other standard criterion—these industries are not the mainstay of organized activity in North America.

Adhocracy is most likely to emerge as an addendum to the bureaucratic form. At times survival will demand that the bureaucratic organization respond rapidly to change. Management does this in two ways. First, it makes wide use of the professional-bureaucracy form. Second, it uses organic appendages like task forces to foster innovation and flexibility. Both essentially allow those in power to maintain control.

Some forms of adhocracies appear to require management to give up its control. We would argue that such designs will be strongly resisted by top management. For example, experience with collateral forms finds that the autonomy of intrapreneurial units may not be as extensive as the theory suggests. As one venture capitalist put it, "Even the best of organizations cannot keep its management's finger out of the pie."[20] It has also been noted that Theory Z–type organizations only give the appearance of reducing top management's control.[21] An employee's psychological commitment to the Theory Z organization for his or her work life makes the employee more likely to tolerate conditions about which he or she might otherwise complain; employee power is reduced through job rotation; and management chooses the size of work teams, the members who will be on each team, and the job-rotation patterns between teams, ensuring that no individual or team gains too much influence.

Finally, and perhaps most important, when adhocracy does emerge as the dominant structure in an organization, don't expect it to stay that way long. Success and progression in its life cycle drive the organization toward stability and standardization. As an organization settles in on what it does best, it is encouraged to repeat these activities. Standardization, differentiation, and formalization result. Of course, there is another alternative. The organization may die. Adhocracies will exist in dynamic environments where, unfortunately, the risk of failure is great. Changes in consumer tastes, breakthroughs by competitors, and the like, are threats to survival. Adhocracies, therefore, are more vulnerable than bureaucracies are.

At the societal level, organizations that succeed take on bureaucratic characteristics. Those that fail may be summarized best by this antecdote. Chris Argyris, a consistent proponent of democracy in organizations, studied two hundred American companies. After looking at his results, he was disheartened to find them all authority conscious. Commenting on the findings, one of his colleagues remarked: "Chris, did it ever occur to you that the reason you didn't get a chance to study the organizations which are democratic is because they didn't stay in business long enough?"[22]

Our conclusion from the previous chapter still holds: Bureaucracies are the dominant structural form. Adhocracies are few in number and in spite of those such as Peter Drucker and Tom Peters who believe that adhocracy is the structure best adapted to the technologies and environments of the next decade, there is no reason to believe that the adhocratic form is anything other than a structural design that is right for certain organizations at a certain stage in their life cycles or as an addendum to a bureaucracy. Our analysis suggests that adhocracy should rarely be an organization's dominant structure and that it is unlikely to become tomorrow's primary structural form.

SUMMARY

What bureaucracy was to the mechanistic model, adhocracy is to the organic. An adhocracy is a rapidly changing, adaptive, usually temporary system organized around problems to be solved by groups of relative strangers with diverse professional skills.

Adhocracies are excellent vehicles for responding to change, facilitating innovation, and coordinating diverse specialists. However, they create internal conflicts and tend to be less efficient than bureaucracies.

Examples of adhocracies include the matrix, Theory Z, the collateral form, network, task force, committee design, and collegial form. When should these types of designs be considered? With diverse, changing, or high-risk strategies or where the technology is nonroutine and the environment is both dynamic and complex. It is also the preferred structural design when an organization is in the formative years of its life cycle.

Despite the attention given to adhocracies in recent years, it continues to be an atypical organizational form. Adhocracies are the dominant structure in only a minority of industries. When used, it is usually as an adjunct to bureaucracy. Organizations that are adhocracies in their early years tend to either evolve into bureaucracies or die off.

FOR REVIEW AND DISCUSSION

1. "The adhocracy rates low on all three structural components." Do you agree or disagree? Discuss.
2. Describe the type of organizations that might be organized as adhocracies. Why?
3. Under what conditions would adhocracy be preferable to the professional bureaucracy?
4. Explain the matrix structure. What conditions should exist before it is implemented?
5. Present the advantages and disadvantages of the matrix.
6. What is the role of authority in the matrix?
7. Contrast the matrix with the professional bureaucracy. How are they similar? Different?
8. Contrast the pure Japanese organization system with Theories A and Z.
9. How is permanent employment a cornerstone of the Theory Z organization?
10. Is Theory Z at odds with the power-control position?
11. Is your college organized along bureaucratic or adhocratic lines? How did you draw your conclusion? What are the critical determinants that affect your college's structure?
12. Contrast the collateral form with the task force. How are they similar? Different?
13. Why would an adhocracy be inefficient where the organization utilized a routine technology and faced a stable environment?
14. Is adhocracy compatible with large size? Support your position.
15. "Adhocracy is the organizational structure of the 21st century." Build an argument to support this position. Then build an argument to refute this position.

NOTES

[1] This section is based on Rudy Martzke, "Olympic TV," *USA Today*, September 16, 1988, p. 3E; and Richard Zoglin, "NBC's Bid For TV Glory," *Time*, September 19, 1988, p. 76.

[2] Ann M. Morrison, "The General Mills Brand of Managers," *Fortune*, January 12, 1981, pp. 99–107.

[3] Stanley M. Davis and Paul R. Lawrence, "The Matrix Diamond," *Wharton Magazine*, Winter 1978, pp. 19–27.

[4] Stanley M. Davis and Paul R. Lawrence, *Matrix* (Reading, Mass.: Addison-Wesley, 1977) pp. 11–24.

[5] Leonard R. Sayles, "Matrix Organization: The Structure with a Future," *Organizational Dynamics*, Autumn 1976, pp. 2–17.

[6] Kenneth Knight, "Matrix Organization: A Review," *Journal of Management Studies*, May 1976, pp. 111–30.

[7] Ibid., and Stanley M. Davis and Paul R. Lawrence, "Problems of Matrix Organizations," *Harvard Business Review*, May–June 1978, pp. 131–42.

[8] William G. Ouchi, *Theory Z: How American Business Can Meet the Japanese Challenge* (Boston: Addison-Wesley, 1981).

[9] Nina Hatvany and Vladimir Pucik, "An Integrated Management System: Lessons from the Japanese Experience," *Academy of Management Review*, July 1981, pp. 469–74.

[10] Masayoshi Kanabayashi, "In Japan, Employees Are Switching Firms For Better Work, Pay," *The Wall Street Journal*, October 11, 1988, p. 1.

[11] Gifford Pinchot III, *Intrapreneuring* (New York: Harper & Row, 1985).

[12] See, for example, Art Fry, "The Post-It Note: An Intrapreneurial Success," *SAM Advanced Management Journal*, Summer 1987, pp. 4–9; and "Keeping the Fires Lit Under the Innovators," *Fortune*, March 28, 1988, p. 45.

[13] David Rubinstein and Richard W. Woodman, "Spiderman and the Burma Raiders: Collateral Organization Theory in Action," *Journal of Applied Behavioral Science*, Vol. 20, 1984, pp. 1–21.

[14] "Here Come the Intrapreneurs," *Time*, February 4, 1985, pp. 36–37.

[15] See "And Now, the Post-Industrial Corporation," *Business Week*, March 3, 1986, pp. 64–67; Raymond E. Miles and Charles C. Snow, "Organizations: New Concepts for New Forms," *California Management Review*, Spring 1986, pp. 62–73; and Jeffrey Pfeffer and James N. Baron, "Taking the Workers Back Out: Recent Trends in the Structuring of Employment," in Barry M. Staw and L. L. Cummings, eds., *Research in Organizational Behavior*, Vol. 10 (Greenwich, Conn.: JAI Press, 1988), pp. 257–303.

[16] William J. Altier, "Task Forces—An Effective Management Tool," *Sloan Management Review*, Spring 1986, pp. 69–76.

[17] "How Ford Hit the Bull's-Eye with Taurus," *Business Week*, June 30, 1986, pp. 69–70; and Patrick Bedard, "Recall Roulette," *Car and Driver*, August 1986, p. 128.

[18] See Peter F. Drucker, "The Coming of the New Organization," *Harvard Business Review*, January–February 1988, pp. 45–53.

[19] See Tom Peters, "Restoring American Competitiveness: Looking for New Models of Organizations," *Academy of Management Executive*, May 1988, pp. 103–9.

[20] As quoted in "Here Come the Intrapreneurs," p. 37.

[21] Stephen P. Robbins, "The Theory Z Organization From a Power-Control Perspective," *California Management Review*, January 1983, pp. 67–75.

[22] "McClelland: An Advocate of Power," *International Management*, July 1975, p. 28.

13

MANAGING THE ENVIRONMENT

AFTER READING THIS CHAPTER, YOU SHOULD BE ABLE TO:

1 Explain why management seeks to control its organization's environment.

2 Compare internal and external environmental control strategies.

3 Describe the most comprehensive action management can take when faced with an unfavorable environment.

4 Define environmental scanning.

5 Identify several techniques for buffering the organization from the input side.

6 Explain how organizations smooth out fluctuations in the environment.

7 Describe when an organization would apply rationing.

8 Differentiate between coopting and coalescing.

9 List reasons for the popularity of interlocking directorates.

10 Explain the role of political action committees in helping industries manage their environment.

Introduction
ATTENTION FORD MOTOR CO.: DON'T MESS WITH VIC POTAMKIN!

In the late 1940s, Victor Potamkin opened a single Lincoln-Mercury dealership in Philadelphia. Like other automobile dealers at the time, he was restricted by his supplier—in this case, the Lincoln-Mercury Division of the Ford Motor Company—from selling any competitor's products.

General Motors, Chrysler, and American Motors also had similar policies banning their dealers from selling other domestic car lines. This practice made dealers, like Potamkin, totally dependent on their suppliers. If you were a Chevrolet dealer, for instance, and Chevys were poorly made, too expensive, or had an outdated design in a given year, there was nothing you could do about it. Moreover, the domestic manufacturers made dealers like Potamkin sign long-term contracts that governed the number and type of cars they were allowed to receive (important for hot items), the cars they had to receive (important for disposing of the "dogs"), how much of the cost of failures they had to absorb under the warranty, how much they could charge for repairs, and how much advertising they had to do. The manufacturers set the wholesale and retail prices. When demand was high for Lincolns, for example, Potamkin was told he would get only so many cars. When demand was low, he was told how many cars he was required to take. In this way, companies like Ford and GM forced their dealers to protect the manufacturers from fluctuations in the market for their cars and from the yearly gamble on model changes and new-product entries.[1]

Things started to change in 1979. Auto sales in the United States were plummeting at about the same time consumers were discovering the higher quality in imported cars. To protect their sales volumes, many dealers of domestic brands added import franchises. Potamkin was one of these. Today, he and his sons run a chain of auto dealerships that include all models made by Ford and Chrysler (the U.S. manufacturers were forced in the early 1980s to ease their restrictions on dealers selling domestic competitors), plus Cadillac, Chevrolet, Isuzu, Hyundai, Subaru, Toyota, Mitsubishi, and Volkswagen. Potamkin has become the largest automobile dealer in the United States, selling nearly 40,000 new cars and trucks each year and 26,000 used vehicles. His annual sales exceed three-quarters of a *billion* dollars!

One of the more interesting outcomes of Potamkin's having become a super-dealer is that he is no longer beholden to a single automobile manufacturer. The Lincoln-Mercury Division of Ford no longer has the power to force him to sell any car it wants to make. He can pick and choose his franchises. If the quality or sales level of a particular manufacturer's product declines, he can drop it and not be forced out of business. When you sell fourteen different brands, which Potamkin now does, no one manufacturer controls your destiny. In fact, the dependency relationship between Potamkin and the automobile manufacturers has become completely reversed. They now are dependent on him for sales. Potamkin and the more than 250 super-dealers like him around the country are calling the shots with domestic and foreign auto manufacturers. While there are still thousands of small, single-brand auto dealers in the United States, more and more of them are taking on multiple dealerships to increase their bargaining clout with the car manufacturers.

Every organization—regardless of the industry it's in or whether it's profit seeking or not for profit—faces some degree of environmental uncertainty. Why? Because no organization is completely able to generate internally all the resources it needs to sustain itself.[2] Every organization, for example, requires financial and human resources as inputs and clients or customers to absorb its outputs. But just because an organization confronts environmental uncertainty does not mean that management has to meet this uncertainty empty handed. As the Potamkin case illustrates, there *are* things managers can do to lessen the impact of the environment on the organization's operations. They can attempt to *manage* their environment![3]

MANAGEMENT'S QUEST TO CONTROL ITS ENVIRONMENT

In Chapter 1, we acknowledged that real-life organizations are open systems. Not only do they interact with their environment, but this interaction is necessary for the organization's viability and survival. However, we know managers don't like uncertainty.[4] They don't like being dependent on other organizations. If management had its way, it would prefer to operate in a completely predictable and autonomous environment. In such a perfect world, there would be no need for contingency plans because there would be no surprises; and the organization would be impervious to influences from other organizations. Yet all organizations face some uncertainty, and many environments are quite dynamic. It should not be surprising, therefore, to find that managers want to act so as to reduce this uncertainty. But can the environment be managed?

The population-ecology perspective, presented in Chapter 8, argues that management can't affect its environment. The environment is treated as a given, and management is depicted as helpless in reacting to it. But as we pointed out in our criticism of this theory, management is not always impotent. Managers have discretion over the strategies they choose and the ways in which organizational resources are distributed. Moreover, large and powerful organizations clearly have the means to shape major elements in their environment.

This chapter stands as a counterpoint to the population-ecology view. Large organizations consistently demonstrate by their actions that they are not captives of their environments and that they have the means to lessen their environmental dependence. They reduce labor uncertainty by locating in states where unions exert little power or by building plants in countries where there is an abundant supply of low-cost labor. They engage in joint ventures to lessen competition. They lobby state and federal legislators to support laws that benefit them and to defeat those that are perceived as detrimental. The larger an organization is, the more resources, skills, and influence it will typically have at its disposal. But environmental-management strategies are not only available to large and powerful organizations. Many of the techniques we'll discuss can be and are used by small and uninfluential organizations. But keep in mind that large size is positively associated with increased power to reduce environmental uncertainty.[5]

CLASSIFYING STRATEGIES

In very simplistic terms, managers have two general strategies they can take in their attempt to lessen environmental uncertainty. They can respond by adapting and changing their actions to fit the environment, or they can attempt to alter the environment to fit better with the organization's capabilities. The former approach we call **internal strategies** and the latter **external strategies**.

When management selectively cuts prices or recruits executives from its competitors, management is making internal adjustments to its environment. The environment doesn't change, but the fit between the organization and the environment is improved. The result is that the organization's dependence on the environment is reduced.

External strategies are efforts designed to actually *change* the environment. If competitive pressures are cutting an airline's profitability, it can merge with another airline to gain a more syn-

TABLE 13–1   *Internal and External Strategies*

INTERNAL STRATEGIES	EXTERNAL STRATEGIES
Domain choice	Advertising
Recruitment	Contracting
Environmental scanning	Coopting
Buffering	Coalescing
Smoothing	Lobbying
Rationing	
Geographic dispersion	

ergystic network of routes. If changes suggested in a federal tax reform proposal threaten a small life insurance company, it might use its membership in a trade association to lobby against tax changes that will negatively affect the life insurance industry.

Using the internal-external dichotomy, we can categorize a number of uncertainty reduction techniques. Table 13–1 summarizes the internal and external strategies that we'll now elaborate upon.

INTERNAL STRATEGIES

Management doesn't actually have to change the environment in order to lessen the organization's dependence on it. The following internal strategies demonstrate that there are actions that almost any organization can take—the small as well as the large—to match it better with its environment; and in so doing, lessen the impact of the environment on the organization's operations.

Domain Choice

The most comprehensive action management can take when faced with an unfavorable environment is to change to a domain with less environmental uncertainty.[6] Management could consider, for instance, staking out a niche that has fewer or less powerful competitors; barriers that keep other competitors out as a result of high entry costs, economies of scale, or regulatory approval; little regulation; numerous suppliers; no unions; less powerful public-pressure groups, and the like. Unfortunately, because there are not many opportunities for organizations to become unregulated monopolies, most domain-choice decisions substitute one set of environmental uncertainties for another.

If management can't change to a more favorable domain, it might choose to broaden its strategy to take a generalist format. The logic here is that the more general an organization's objectives, structure, and activities, the more slack resources it will have available and the greater flexibility it will have in responding to environmental change.[7]

Generalists, in contrast to specialists, can exploit a number of segments of the environment. They do a lot of different things and employ individuals with greater versatility. This flexibility, of course, does not come without costs. Generalists tend to be less efficient than specialists because the latter have a minimal amount of slack resources, rely on more standardized technologies, and achieve economies through high formalization. If the environment is stable, the advantage goes to the specialists. But when the environment is dynamic, the generalist's flexibility allows management to internally redirect resources to take advantage of opportunities in the environment. You can see this in the aerospace industry. When defense contracts decline, McDonnell-Douglas can still operate profitably by redirecting resources from its defense projects into its commercial aviation programs. But Northrop—which relies almost exclusively on government defense contracts—finds its profitability is singularly tied to the Pentagon budget.

Recruitment

The recruitment of the right people can lessen the influence of the environment on an organization. In 1984 Boston University's administration lured former Boston mayor, Kevin White, to teach at their university for $100,000 a year. Were there more talented academics available for less money? Probably. But White had contacts and political clout! His visibility could attract donors to build BU's endowment and improve links between the university and the powers at City Hall.

The practice of selective hiring to reduce environmental uncertainty is widespread. Corporations hire executives from competing firms to acquire information about their competitor's future plans. High-tech firms entice scientists from competitive firms with large salary increases and stock options to gain the technical expertise held by their competition. However, the greatest media attention tends to be reserved for private organizations that recruit former government officials. Business and legal firms regularly hire such officials, often at exorbitant salaries, to acquire their favorable ties with influential decision makers and knowledge of government operations. The major New York and Washington law firms, for instance, are full of former influential members of Congress and high-ranking presidential appointees.

Environmental Scanning

Environmental scanning entails scrutinizing the environment to identify actions by competitors, government, unions, and the like, that might impinge on the organization's operations. To the extent that this scanning can lead to accurate forecasts of environmental fluctuations, it can reduce uncertainty. It allows management to anticipate change and make internal adjustments rather than react after the fact. The manufacturing firm that can anticipate changes in demand for its products correctly can plan or schedule operations of its technical core ahead of time and thereby minimize the impact of these changes. Similarly, the consulting firm that can forecast accurately which contracts it will win during the next six months is better prepared in having the right number and mix of consultants available to handle these projects.

Who does environmental scanning? Boundary spanners! **Boundary spanners** are persons who operate at the periphery or boundary of the organization, performing organizational relevant tasks and relating the organization to elements outside it.[8] Boundary spanners function, in effect, as exchange agents between the organization and the environment. Examples of typical boundary-spanning jobs include sales representatives, marketing researchers, purchasing agents, lobbyists, public relations specialists, and personnel recruiters.

What do those who occupy boundary-spanning roles do? Quite a lot! They handle input acquisition and disposal of output transactions, filter inputs and outputs, search and collect information, represent the organization to the environment, and protect and buffer the organization. "It is through the reports of boundary agents that other organization members acquire their knowledge, perceptions, and evaluations of organization environments. It is through the vigilance of boundary agents that the organization is able to monitor and screen important happenings in the environment."[9]

BALLARD'S SALES PEOPLE EFFECTIVELY SCAN THE ENVIRONMENT

Ballard Medical Products is a small firm, with sales of around $10 million a year, that makes products for the hospital-supply industry.[10] Because the company has to compete against giants like American Hospital Supply and Johnson & Johnson, Ballard has developed a strategy to find and dominate small niches in its market. This requires identifying customer needs that others don't see and the ability to quickly turn customer needs into new-product innovations. Ballard has made its strategy work by using its sales representatives as boundary spanners.

Ballard has thirty-five sales reps whose job, in addition to selling the company's current product line, is to listen to customers and watch them at work. What new products do they need? How can existing products be improved? This information isn't gathered by written surveys or asking direct questions. Rather, Ballard's reps actually observe doctors, nurses, and medical personnel using the company's products. They personally get to know their users, build friendships with them, and then look and listen as they put the products to daily use.

Ballard has turned their sales reps into effective boundary spanners and the company's principal intelligence-gathering mechanism. They go beyond merely meeting with hospital purchasing employees and get inside their customers' organizations. Then they pass what they learn back to company headquarters in Utah, where the information can be used to develop and modify Ballard's product line.

Buffering

Buffering reduces the possibility that the organization's operations will be disturbed by insuring supplies and/or absorption of outputs. By buffering its operating core from environmental influences at the input or output side, management allows the organization to operate as if it were a closed system.

On the input side, buffering is evident when organizations stockpile materials and supplies, use multiple suppliers, engage in preventive maintenance, or recruit and train new employees. Each of these activities is designed to protect the operating function of the organization from the unexpected. The appliance manufacturer that stockpiles a ninety-day supply of steel allows itself to continue to operate for several months in event of a strike in the steel industry. The newspaper that purchases newsprint from three or four different paper companies reduces its dependence on any one firm. Preventive maintenance substitutes known costs for the unknown. Just as you may take your car in every few months for a checkup and precautionary service to avoid the surprise and expense of the unexpected breakdown, organizations can do the same. Buffering can also be done with human resources. Since organizations require trained personnel, their unavailability or lack of appropriate skills can mean a loss in productive efficiency. Management can meet this uncertainty through recruitment and training.

Buffering at the output level allows fewer options. The most obvious method is through the use of inventories. If an organization creates products that can be carried in inventory without damage, then maintaining warehouse inventories allows the organization to produce its goods at a constant rate regardless of fluctuations in sales demand. Toy manufacturers, for example, typically ship most of their products to retailers in the early fall for selling during the Christmas season. These manufacturers, of course, produce their toys year-round and merely stockpile them for shipping during the fall.

Buffering provides benefits by reducing environmental uncertainties. We would predict management's propensity to buffer to be related directly to the degree of routinization in the organization's technology. However, the benefits must be appraised against the costs. The more obvious of these costs are the increased carrying expense of buffering activities and the risk of obsolescence inherent in stockpiling.

Smoothing

Smoothing seeks to level out the impact of fluctuations in the environment. Organizations that use this technique include telephone companies, retail stores, car rental agencies, magazines, and sports teams. The heaviest demand on telephone equipment is by business between the weekday hours of 8A.M. and 5P.M. Telephone companies have to have enough equipment to meet peak demand during this period. But the equipment is still there during the rest of the time. So what do they do? They smooth demand by charging the highest prices during their peak period and low rates, to encourage you to call "home," during the evenings and on weekends. Retail clothing stores know that their slowest months are January (following the Christmas "blitz") and August (prior to "back-to-school"). To reduce this "trough" in the revenue curve, retail stores typically run their semiannual sales at these times of the year. Car rental agencies make extensive use of smoothing. The same car that rents for $40 a day during the week is frequently half that price on the weekend. The reason is that business people are heavy users of rental cars and their usage is during the week. Rather than have the cars sit idle on weekends, the rental agencies smooth demand by cutting prices. Magazine publishers frequently give you a substantial discount—sometimes up to 50 percent off newsstand prices—if you become a mail subscriber. Why do they do this? It smooths demand. Finally, we suggest that sports teams usually give fans reduced prices when they buy season tickets covering all the home games. Even if the team has a very poor win-loss record, management has assured itself of a certain amount of income.

Rationing

When uncertainty is created by way of excess demand, management may consider **rationing** products or services; that is, to allocate output according to some priority system. Examples of rationing can be found in hospitals, colleges, post offices, and restaurants. Hospitals often ration beds for nonemergency admissions. And when a disaster strikes—earthquake, fire, flood—beds are made available only to the most serious cases. College administrators frequently use rationing to allocate students to popular programs. Recently, for instance, the demand for business courses has exceeded the supply of seats available at many colleges and universities. In response, entrance requirements have frequently been raised as a way to limit demand. The post office resorts to rationing, particularly during the peak Christmas rush. First-class mail takes priority, and lesser classes are handled on an "as available" basis. It is not unusual for better restaurants to require reservations. The use of reservations acts to both ration and smooth demand for dining tables.

OT
CLOSE-UP

A MEN'S STORE THAT PRACTICES RATIONING

Bijan's of Beverly Hills and New York City is a men's store, but not like any you or I are likely to frequent. The store's founder and owner, Bijan, came to the U.S. from Iran in the mid-1960s. He believed there was a market among the very rich, for expensive, high-quality men's clothing and furnishings. His success has proved him right. His stores now have annual sales of $40 million, and they have made Bijan a multimillionaire.

The term *expensive* doesn't do justice to Bijan's merchandise. Ties start at $120 each. Suits average $3000 apiece. You can buy a nice alpaca sport coat for $10,000. Or how about a six-piece alligator travel set for $75,000? Sales of $40,000 to $100,000 to a single customer are routine.

In addition to being expensive, there is something else unique about Bijan's. You need an appointment to get in! His customers number about fifteen hundred, but they just can't walk in the door. Everyone must call ahead for an appointment. What this does, of course, is allow Bijan to develop highly accurate forecasts of daily demand, eliminate any "peak periods," and permit Bijan to schedule sales and support personnel so as to minimize their nonproductive time.

Geographic Dispersion

Environmental uncertainty sometimes varies with location. There is clearly more political uncertainty for a business firm operating in Beirut, Lebanon, than for one operating in Salinas, Kansas. To lessen location-induced uncertainty, organizations can move to a different community or lessen risk by operating in multiple locations.

Historically, unions have been strongest in the northeastern United States and weakest in the south. Many business firms have responded by moving their operations to the south. In so doing, they have reduced one uncertainty—union-induced strikes or walkouts—from their environment. On the international level, environmental uncertainty created by the U.S. government's changing policies on import restrictions and the fluctuating value of the dollar are undoubtedly the primary reasons why Japanese car manufacturers like Honda, Nissan, and Mazda have built, or are currently building, factories in the United States.

EXTERNAL STRATEGIES

Now we turn to strategies that directly seek to change the environment to make it more favorable for an organization. These include everything from the use of advertising to shape consumer tastes to illegal agreements with a rival to restrict competition.

Advertising

Procter & Gamble spends hundreds of millions of dollars each year to promote Tide, Ivory soap, Folger's coffee, and the dozens of other P&G products. Through extensive advertising, P&G's management seeks to reduce competitive pressures, stabilize demand, and allow it the opportunity to set prices with less concern for the response of its competitors.

The organization that can build brand loyalty has lessened its dependence on consumers. So regardless of the brand-name product or service—whether it's a Sony video recorder, the American

Express card, Diet Coke, Revlon Nailgloss, Bic disposable razors, or Federal Express overnight delivery—when you see it actively promoted through advertising, keep in mind that this advertising is a device that management uses to reduce its dependence on fickle consumers and new alternatives offered by the competition.

Maybe the classic example of advertising's creating a following and sustaining demand for a product over time is Bayer Aspirin. The content of aspirin is the same regardless of brand name. Yet the manufacturer of Bayer has convinced a significant segment of the aspirin-buying public that Bayer's "pure aspirin" is superior to its competitors and justifies a price from two to five times higher than generic brands.

Contracting

Contracting protects the organization from changes in quantity or price on either the input or output side. For instance, management may agree to a long-term fixed contract to purchase materials and supplies or to sell a certain part of the organization's output. Airlines contract with oil companies to buy fuel on a fixed-term contract, thus reducing their susceptibility to fluctuations in availability and price. A major soap manufacturer—whose products are household names—contracts to sell ten thousand cases a month of its standard detergent to a large discount chain that will be marketed under the chain's private label. This assures the soap manufacturer of a certain amount of sales and reduces its dependency on the fluctuating preferences of consumers.

Coopting

Organizations may resort to **coopting** their uncertainties; that is, absorbing those individuals or organizations in the environment that threaten their stability. This is most frequently accomplished in business firms through selective appointments to the organization's board of directors.

Research demonstrates that the composition of a corporation's board can be explained by considering the organization's requirements for various types of environmental support.[11] If an organization's primary need is capital, you can expect to find a greater percentage of directors from banks, insurance companies, and other financial institutions. Regulated industries are overseen by government agencies and these industries respond by disproportionately loading their boards with lawyers. Following this theme, you can expect organizations facing labor uncertainties to appoint union officers to their boards; those whose survival depends on government contracts to seek former government officials for their boards; organizations that are vulnerable to public sentiment to respond by appointing board members who are consumer advocates, prominent women, or minority spokespersons; and the board of organizations whose legitimacy is in question to include winners of the Nobel Prize, prominent military heroes, or similarly accomplished individuals. If you were head of a major securities firm that had just pleaded guilty to several thousand counts of fraud and misrepresentation, you might try to restore some of your lost reputation by trying to entice someone with unquestioned credentials for honesty and integrity—like a Walter Cronkite—to join your board of directors.

The **interlocking directorate,** where two or more organizations share one or more directors in common, has been described as the most widely used environmental management strategy.[12] There is no shortage of studies that seek to explain the prevalence of interlocks and the benefits it can provide to management.[13]

The evidence demonstrates extensive interlocking in the U.S., particularly among the largest corporations with headquarters in New York, Chicago, or Los Angeles.[14] For example, of America's 797 largest firms, only 62 have no interlocks with the remaining 735 firms.[15] That's a scant 8 percent! Among the top 130 U.S. corporations, representatives from 13 firms consistently reappear on boards.[16] Among these 13 were 5 banks (Bank of America, Citibank, Chase Manhattan, Manufacturer's Hanover, and Morgan), 3 oil firms (Exxon, Mobil, and Texaco), 2 insurance companies (Prudential and Metropolitan Life), and 2 auto giants (General Motors and Ford).

Why are interlocking directorates so popular? The general answer is that they coopt market constraints. More specifically, its been argued that they can (1) facilitate horizontal coordination, (2) facilitate vertical coordination, (3) provide expertise, and (4) enhance the organization's reputation.[17] Horizontally interlocked organizations can gain advantages through pricing, advertising, and research and development. They can act as an informal means to coordinate plans between organizations. Such interlocks, however, can violate antitrust laws. Vertical coordination, such as frequently exists between a firm and one of its suppliers, increases the likelihood that needed resources will be available. Expertise is provided when outside directors hold information about other organizations or industry activities. These can help the focal organization formulate its strategies more accurately. Finally, an organization's reputation can be affected by who serves on its board and those board members' organizational connections. Prestigious board members provide a more favorable image for the organization and can attract sought-after customers as well as avoid problems with financial institutions, government regulatory agencies, or the like.

Coalescing

During the 1980s, dozens of *Fortune* 500 corporations were merged into other companies. These mergers often brought about economies of scale by eliminating redundant administrative personnel and by providing opportunities for merging technical and managerial expertise. But it would be naive to ignore the reality that many mergers reduce environmental uncertainty by lessening interorganizational competition and dependency. Chevron's acquisition of Gulf Oil created one less player in the big-oil game. Ford Motor's purchase of First Nationwide Financial expanded Ford's ability to offer credit to its new-car buyers and lessened its dependency on other financial institutions.

When an organization combines with one or more other organizations for the purpose of joint action, it is called **coalescing**. Mergers are an example. So, too, are joint ventures and cooperative (though illegal) agreements to fix prices or split markets.

One of the most publicized joint ventures in the past decade has been the teaming up of General Motors and Toyota to produce the Chevrolet Nova in northern California. The reasoning underlying this alliance is that GM wanted to learn how the Japanese firm produced such high-quality cars so efficiently, while Toyota sought the American company's marketing expertise. Their joint venture allows each to improve its competitive posture (see Table 13–2 for recent examples of joint ventures).

Mergers and joint ventures are legal means for organizations to manage their environment. In contrast, while illegal cooperative activities for managing the environment are certainly not condoned here, we have to acknowledge their existence. In the late 1950s, America was shocked to learn that executives from General Electric, Westinghouse, and several other large electrical-equipment manufacturers secretly met annually and agreed to a price-fixing scheme that divided up that year's major bid contracts among the conspirators and allowed the "winner" of each extremely high profits. When the scheme was uncovered, the companies were fined, and some senior executives in these firms were actually imprisoned. Undoubtedly such illegal tactics continue to go on today, but catching the culprits and proving restraint of trade is difficult. As a case in point, many states make it illegal for real-estate agents to conspire to set a fixed sales-commission rate. Yet within these states, agents' commissions almost never deviate from the 6 or 7 percent "norm." Selling real estate requires cooperation among many agents. Most use multiple-listing services. This creates the

TABLE 13–2   *Examples of Recent Joint Ventures*

General Motors/Suzuki: Manufacturing and distributing of subcompact GEOs.
Ford/Mazda: Building Ford Probes and Mazda MX-6 models jointly in Michigan.
Caterpillar/Mitsubishi: Manufacturing giant earthmovers.
Norton Co./Torrington Co.: Designing, developing, manufacturing, and marketing of hybrid ceramic bearings.
General Electric/Fanuc Ltd.: Producing robotic machine tools.
IBM/Cincinnati Milacron: Developing software programs for factory automation.
Hewlett-Packard/Northern Telecom: Developing and marketing of corporate information systems.
Du Pont/Phillips: Developing, producing, and selling optical-storage discs.
Henley Group/Empresa Nacional del Petroleo: Building the world's second-largest methanol plant in Chile.

opportunity for implicit cooperate agreements to develop. More-over, any agent who undercuts the norm will find other agents uncooperative. The result is that the real-estate-sales industry es-sentially operates with fixed prices.

COMPAQ AND OTHERS JOIN FORCES AGAINST IBM

Compaq Computer Corp. is the leading maker of IBM-compatible personal computers. Like many other clone makers, Compaq had profited on IBM's early decision to make its PC specifications available to the competition at a very low cost. The maximum licensing royalty any clone maker paid to IBM was 1 percent. However, when IBM introduced its Personal Systems 2 computers in 1987, it also introduced a new and innovative "bus"—the device that controls how various parts of the computer communicate with one another—called the Micro Channel. And to lessen competition for the PS/2, IBM set licensing royalties on the Micro Channel as high as 5 percent. IBM's logic, of course, was that since they set the industry standard, competitors had no choice but to negotiate licensing agreements on IBM's terms. But IBM was mistaken. There was another option open to the clone-makers. They could break with IBM and set their own standard. In the fall of 1988, led by Compaq, nine clone-makers did just that. They announced that they had agreed on standards for a bus that would meet or exceed the capabilities of IBM's Micro Channel.[18]

IBM controls 22 percent of the PC market. But the nine clone-makers—Compaq, Tandy, Zenith Data Systems, AST Research, Wyse Technology, Hewlett-Packard, Italy's Ing C. Olivetti, Japan's NEC, and Epson America—have 26.6 percent of the market. Individually they knew they could not challenge IBM, but their combined clout could allow them to reduce their dependence on IBM. Their alternative design standard will mean that there will be three main competitors in this market: the "group of nine's" new standard, IBM's Micro Channel, and NuBus, which is inside Apple Computer's Macintosh. Ironically, if this strategy works, IBM could end up having to clone the cloners.

Lobbying

The U.S. automobile industry wants the federal government to do those things that will increase the sale of American cars. In this quest, the industry can stand passively by and hope legislators will voluntarily take action to protect the interests of U.S. automobile manufacturers. On the other hand, it can actively take its case directly to key Washington decision makers. Not surprisingly, the latter choice is the one that the auto industry has chosen. The major automobile producers individually, and collectively through their trade associations and political action committees (PACs), actively seek to influence legislators to pass laws favorable to the U.S. auto industry's interests. These lobbyists argue, for example, for the imposing of import restrictions, the removal of safety-equipment requirements and overall corporate average-fuel-economy regulations, and favorable tax treatment.

The automobile industry is not alone. **Lobbying**—using influence to achieve favorable outcomes—is a widespread practice used by organizations to manage their environment.

The 1980s saw a marked increase in the use of PACs as lobbying vehicles. PACs, for instance, are now a major source of funds for political candidates. Organizations that seek particular advantages can direct money through PACs to those candidates that will support their interests.

Trade and professional associations actively lobby on behalf of their members. The Tobacco Institute and the National Rifle Association fight hard in Washington to reduce uncertainties that might affect tobacco and gun interests, respectively. For example, the NRA, with just three million members, has been enormously successful in blocking federal and state gun-control legislation. Some organizations even use the power of the government to stablize relationships in an industry. Doctors, chiropractors, and other professionals lobby state licensing boards to restrict entry, regulate competition, and keep their professions more stable. The airlines and trucking industries historically were regulated, and many firms lobbied hard (though usually quietly) to maintain that regulation. In contrast to the notion that regulation exists to protect the interests of the general public, a strong counter-argument can be built that government regulation maintains monopoly power (and thus reduces environmental uncertainty) in the hands of the regulated.

GUIDELINES FOR MANAGING THE ENVIRONMENT

Success in managing the environment requires analyzing the source of uncertainty and then selecting a strategy that the organization can effectively implement. As we noted at the beginning of the chapter, large size facilitates environmental influence. Certainly, a Du Pont or Eastman Kodak is going to have more clout in controlling its relationships with suppliers than is a small chemical firm or a local business offering one-hour film developing. Yet most of the strategies presented in this chapter have wide applicability.

Table 13–3 presents some responses managers can make to reduce environmental uncertainty. The examples of strategic actions are only examples. They don't purport to be *all* or the *only* options available to management.

Let's take a look at an industry we've discussed before—tobacco (in Chapter 5)—to see the actions firms in that industry have pursued to manage their environment. The major area of uncertainty facing this industry has been government regulation. Since the late 1960s, tobacco firms have responded by essentially expanding their domain through horizontal diversification. Most recently, R.J. Reynolds Industries purchased Nabisco Brands, and Philip Morris bought General Foods and Kraft. The merged companies are now more food companies than cigarette manufacturers. Another response of tobacco firms has been to spend heavily on lobbying. They have fought hard to defeat such legislation as that which would limit smoking in public areas and at the work place. Individual tobacco firms and the Tobacco Institute (which is supported by tobacco companies) have also contributed funds for research on the relationship between smoking and cancer. The companies realize that it is statistically unlikely that the research will "prove" that smoking causes cancer, thus giving the tobacco firms more data to cloud the controversy. Moreover, if such research is unfavorable to tobacco interests, the researchers have no strong motivations to publicize their findings widely. Why kill the goose that lays the golden eggs? Finally, it is important to note that tobacco firms are now using advertising in a very selective fashion to counter antismoking forces. They seek to demonstrate that their advertis-

TABLE 13–3 *Matching Sources of Uncertainty with Strategic Actions*

SOURCE	EXAMPLES OF STRATEGIC ACTIONS
Government	Lobby for favorable treatment Recruit former government officials Bribe government officials Relocate to a different governmental jurisdiction
Competition	Advertise to build brand loyalty Select a less competitive domain Merge with competition to gain larger market share Negotiate a cooperative agreement with competition
Unions	Negotiate a long-term collective-bargaining agreement Hire professionals to keep unions out Build facilities in countries with a large, low-cost labor supply Appoint prestigious union official to board of directors
Suppliers	Use multiple suppliers Inventory critical supplies Negotiate long-term contracts Vertically integrate through merger
Financial institutions	Appoint financial executives to board Establish a line of credit to draw upon when needed Diversify by coopting a financial institution Use multiple financial sources
Customers	Advertise Use a differentiated price structure Ration demand Change domain to where there are more customers
Public pressure groups	Appoint critics to board Recruit critics as employees Engage in visible activities that are socially conscious Use trade association to counter criticism

ing does not want to convert nonsmokers. Rather, the intention is to get current smokers to switch to their brand. This is probably best exemplified in the Carlton ad campaign that merely states, in very large letters, "IF YOU SMOKE, please try Carlton."

SUMMARY

Every organization faces some degree of environmental uncertainty. However, in contrast to the population-ecology view that organizations are powerless to affect their environments, this chapter has sought to demonstrate that management can reduce the impact of environmental uncertainty on the organization.

There are essentially two approaches available to management. The first is to adapt and change its actions to fit the environment. These are internal strategies and include changing domain, recruiting executives and technical specialists with links to the environment, scanning the environment to anticipate changes, buffering the operating core, smoothing out fluctuations in demand, rationing products or services, and geographic dispersion. The second approach is to alter the environment to fit better with the organization's capabilities. These are external strategies such as advertising, contracting with suppliers or customers, co-opting individuals or organizations through absorption, coalescing with other organizations, and lobbying to achieve favorable outcomes. While technically only the latter actually changes the environment, both strategies together create the techniques we say are available for *managing the environment.*

FOR REVIEW AND DISCUSSION

1. Contrast the population-ecology view of organizations with this chapter's theme.
2. Why do organizations seek to manage their environment?
3. Which strategies—internal or external—are more likely to involve interorganizational cooperation? Why?
4. Contrast the advantages of both specialist and generalist stratagies.
5. Who are boundary spanners? What role do they play in managing environmental uncertainty?
6. How does smoothing reduce environmental uncertainty?
7. Is managing the environment illegal? Explain.
8. Is product differentiation a strategy for reducing environmental uncertainty? Explain.
9. Contrast coopting and coalescing.
10. What advantages accrue to an organization whose board members are widely interlocked with other organizations?
11. Is it easier for a profit-making business to manage its environment than for a not-for-profit organization?
12. Is it easier for a manufacturing organization to manage its environment than for a service organization?

13. For each of the following organizations, what do you think are their major environmental uncertainties?
   a. a radio station
   b. an automobile dealer
   c. a college bookstore
   d. a law firm
   e. a large home-building firm
14. Explain how the management of each of the previous organizations might attempt to manage its environment.
15. If organizations try to manage their environment, why don't they try to manage their technology?

NOTES

[1] See William J. Hampton, "The New Super-Dealers," *Business Week*, June 2, 1986, pp. 60–66; and Charles Perrow, *Complex Organizations*, 3rd ed. (New York: Random House, 1986), p. 252–53.

[2] Howard E. Aldrich, *Organizations and Environments* (Englewood Cliffs, N.J.: Prentice Hall, 1979), p. 266.

[3] Jeffrey Pfeffer, "Beyond Management and the Worker: The Institutional Function of Management," *Academy of Management Review*, April 1976, pp. 36–46; and Jeffrey Pfeffer and Gerald R. Salancik, *The External Control of Organizations: The Resource Dependence Perspective* (New York: Harper & Row, 1978).

[4] William R. Dill, "Environment as an Influence on Managerial Autonomy," *Administrative Science Quarterly*, March 1958, pp. 409–43.

[5] John Kenneth Galbraith, *The New Industrial State* (Boston: Houghton Mifflin, 1967).

[6] See, for example, James D. Thompson and William J. McEwen, "Organizational Goals and Environment: Goal-Setting as an Interaction Process," *American Sociological Review*, February 1958, pp. 23–31.

[7] John H. Freeman and Michael T. Hannan, "Niche Width and the Dynamics of Organizational Populations," *American Journal of Sociology*, May 1983, pp. 1116–45.

[8] Richard Leifer and André Delbecq, "Organizational/Environmental Interchange: A Model of Boundary Spanning Activity," *Academy of Management Review*, January 1978, pp. 40–41.

[9] Dennis W. Organ, "Linking Pins Between Organizations and Environments," *Business Horizons*, December 1971, p. 74.

[10] Tom Richman, "Seducing the Customer," *INC.*, April 1988, pp. 96–104.

[11] See, for example, Jeffrey Pfeffer, "Size and Composition of Corporate Boards of Directors: The Organization and Its Environment," *Administrative Science Quarterly*, March 1972, pp. 218–28; and Mark S. Mizruchi and Linda Brewster Stearns, "A Longitudinal Study of the Formation of In-

[11] See, for example, Jeffrey Pfeffer, "Size and Composition of Corporate Boards of Directors: The Organization and Its Environment," *Administrative Science Quarterly*, March 1972, pp. 218–28; and Mark S. Mizruchi and Linda Brewster Stearns, "A Longitudinal Study of the Formation of Interlocking Directorates," *Administrative Science Quarterly*, June 1988, pp. 194–210.

[12] Max H. Bazerman and F. David Schoorman, "A Limited Rationality Model of Interlocking Directorates," *Academy of Management Review*, April 1983, p. 206.

[13] See, for example, Johannes M. Pennings, *Interlocking Directorates* (San Francisco: Jossey-Bass, 1980); Beth Mintz and Michael Schwartz, "The Structure of Intercorporate Unity in American Business," *Social Problems*, December 1981, pp. 87–103; Mark Mizruchi, *The Structure of the American Corporate Network* (Beverly Hills, Calif.: Sage, 1981); and Michael Ornstein, "Interlocking Directorates in Canada: Intercorporate or Class Alliance?," *Administrative Science Quarterly*, June 1984, pp. 210–31.

[14] Ronald S. Burt, Kenneth P. Christman, and Harold C. Kilburn, Jr., "Testing a Structural Theory of Corporate Cooptation: Interorganizational Directorate Ties as a Strategy for Avoiding Market Constraints on Profits," *American Sociological Review*, October 1980, p. 821.

[15] Johannes M. Pennings, *Interlocking Directorates*, pp. 188–91.

[16] Senate Committee on Governmental Affairs, *Interlocking Directorates Among the Major U.S. Corporations* (Washington, D.C.: U.S. Government Printing Office, 1978).

[17] F. David Schoorman, Max Bazerman, and R. S. Atkin, "Interlocking Directorates: A Strategy for Reducing Environmental Uncertainty," *Academy of Management Review*, April 1981, pp. 243–51.

[18] Katherine M. Hafner, "Score One For the Clones," *Business Week*, September 19, 1988, p. 33.

14

MANAGING ORGANIZATIONAL CHANGE

AFTER READING THIS CHAPTER, YOU SHOULD BE ABLE TO:

1 Define planned change.
2 List reasons that might precipitate a structural change.
3 Describe the four categories of intervention strategies.
4 Explain the three-step change process.
5 Describe organizational designs that foster innovation.
6 Explain why stability, not change, characterizes most organizations.

Introduction
SYSTEM-WIDE CHANGE AT GENRAD

Founded in 1915 by a group of engineers from MIT, the General Radio Company was established to produced highly innovative and high-quality (but expensive) electronic test equipment.[1] Over the years, General Radio developed a consistent organization to accomplish its mission. It hired only the brightest young engineers, built a loose functional structure dominated by the engineering department, and developed its own unique "General Radio culture." This culture valued management by consensus, an absence of interpersonal and intergroup conflict, and slow growth. General Radio's strategy and associated structure, systems, and people were very successful. By World War II, General Radio was the largest test-equipment firm in the United States.

After World War II, however, increasing technological and cost-based competition began to erode General Radio's market share. Al-

381

though management made numerous incremental changes, General Radio remained fundamentally the same organization. In the late 1960s, when CEO Don Sinclair initiated strategic changes, he left the firm's structure and systems intact. This effort at doing new things with established systems and procedures was less than successful. By 1972, with annual sales at $44 million, the company incurred its first loss.

In the face of this sustained performance decline, Bill Thurston (a long-time General Radio executive) was made president. As president, Thurston began a series of changes that could only be called "comprehensive" or "system-wide." General Radio adopted a more marketing-oriented strategy. Its product line was cut from twenty different lines to three; much more emphasis was given to product-line management, sales, and marketing. Resources were diverted from engineering to revitalize sales, marketing, and production. During 1973, the firm moved to a matrix structure, increased its emphasis on controls and systems, and went outside for a group of executives to help Thurston run this revised General Radio. To perhaps more formally symbolize these changes and the sharp move away from the "old" General Radio, the company changed its name to GenRad. By the mid-1980s, GenRad's sales had exploded to over $200 million.

After nearly sixty years of incremental changes around a constant strategy, Thurston and his executive team had introduced systemwide changes in the company's strategy, structure, people, and processes. While traumatic, these changes were instrumental in leading to a dramatic turnaround in GenRad's performance.

GenRad illustrates that organizational effectiveness often demands implementation of change. Almost all organizations continuously introduce small, adaptive changes. But as shown at GenRad, sometimes management has to initiate broad, painful, and comprehensive systemwide change.

This chapter looks at what managers can do to actively facilitate change. Our basic tenet will be that an effective organization "is not a stable solution to achieve, but a developmental process to keep active."[2] Of course, the importance of change in the structure and design of organizations should come as no surprise to you. Our previous review of the literature on strategy, technology, environment, adhocracy—to take the more obvious cases—made constant reference to change. Strategies that entailed a great deal of change had different implications on structure than did those that were stable. Nonroutine technologies entail more change than do routine ones, and, to ensure effectiveness, the nonroutine type requires a more flexible structure. Similarly, organizations facing rapidly changing environments will look for flexibility in their structures. Adhocracy was introduced as the model most compatible with change. Change demands flexibility, innovation, and rapid responsiveness. Organizations facing a high degree of change, it was argued, will be most effective with an adhocratic structure or at least a structure with a number of adhocracy's primary characteristics.

SOME DEFINITIONS

The title of this chapter, "Managing Organizational Change," has been carefully chosen to limit our discussion. Organization theorists are not interested in *all* changes. Changes can "just happen," or can be "planned." Similarly, change agents can direct their efforts at changing people as well as structures. Our attention will be with change that is managed or *planned* and will be limited to *structural* concerns.

Planned Change

Some organizations treat change as an accidental occurence. However, we'll be addressing change activities that are planned or purposeful.

The objective of planned change is to keep the organization current and viable. As long as organizations confront change—current products and services reach maturity in their life cycles and become obsolete; competitors introduce new products or services; government regulations and tax policies affecting the organization are changed; important sources of supply go out of business; a previously nonunionized labor force votes for union representation—the organization either responds or accepts the inevitable decline in effectiveness. Organizations that persist in "keeping their heads in the sand" eventually find themselves running going-out-of business sales, in bankruptcy court, or just fading from the scene. This is illustrated in Table 14–1. Among U.S. cor-

TABLE 14–1   *Survival Rates for U.S. Corporations*

AGE IN YEARS	PERCENTAGE SURVIVING TO THIS YEAR
5	38
10	21
15	14
20	10
25	7
50	2
75	1
100	0.5

Source: Adapted by permission of publisher, from Paul C. Nystrom and William H. Starbuck, "To Avoid Organizational Crises, Unlearn," *Organizational Dynamics*, Spring 1984, p. 54. American Management Association, New York. All rights reserved.

porations, 62 percent failed within their first five years and 90 percent were gone after twenty years. Although it is undoubtedly true that most of these were small and relatively young firms, large established organizations are not immune to failure. Studebaker, W. T. Grant, and Railway Express were billion-dollar corporations that went under. In recent years, we've seen the fall or near fall of such companies as Laker Airways, Sambo restaurants, Wheeling-Pittsburgh Steel, Pizza Time Theatres, Lionel Corporation, Storage Technology, Wilson Foods, Win Enterprises, and Coleco Industries. To this list can be added hundreds of large, but less visible, organizations whose survival has been threatened because management has failed to successfully respond to a changing environment. Because organizations are open systems—dependent on their environments—and because the environment does not stand still, organizations must develop internal mechanisms to facilitate planned change. Change efforts that are **planned**—proactive and purposeful—are what we mean by *managing* change.

Structural Change

The types of change that management seeks to create are varied. The type of change depends on the target. At the individual level, managers attempt to affect an employee's behavior. Training, socialization, and counseling represent examples of change strategies that organizations use when the target of change is the individual. Similarly, management may use interventions such as sensitivity training, survey feedback, and process consultation when the goal is to change group behavior. Individual and group change, which is typically studied in organizational-behavior courses under the heading of "organizational development," is outside the province of this text.

Our concern is with structural change. We focus on techniques that have an impact on the organization's structural system. This means that we will be looking at changing authority patterns, access to information, allocation of rewards, technology, and the like. Of course, the fact that behavioral-change considerations are avoided should in no way diminish their importance. Managers can and should use behavioral techniques to bring about change along with structural techniques. Together, the two represent a complete "tool kit" for managing change. However, in this text we concern ourselves solely with the structural side.[3]

A MODEL FOR MANAGING ORGANIZATIONAL CHANGE

Figure 14–1 represents a model for organizational change. It can be broken down into a set of steps. Change is initiated by certain forces. These forces are acted upon in the organization by a change agent. This change agent chooses the intervention action; that is, he or she chooses *what* is to be changed. Implementation of the intervention contains two parts: *what* is done and *how* it is done. The *what* requires three phases: unfreezing the status quo, movement to a new state, and refreezing the new state to make it permanent. The *how* refers to the tactics used by the agent to implement the change process. The change itself, if successful, improves organizational effectiveness. Of course, changes don't take place in a vacuum. A change in one area of the organization is likely to initiate new forces for other changes. The feedback loop in Figure 14–1 acknowledges that this model is dynamic. The need for change is presumed to be both inevitable and continual.

FIGURE 14–1 *A Model for Managing Organizational Change*

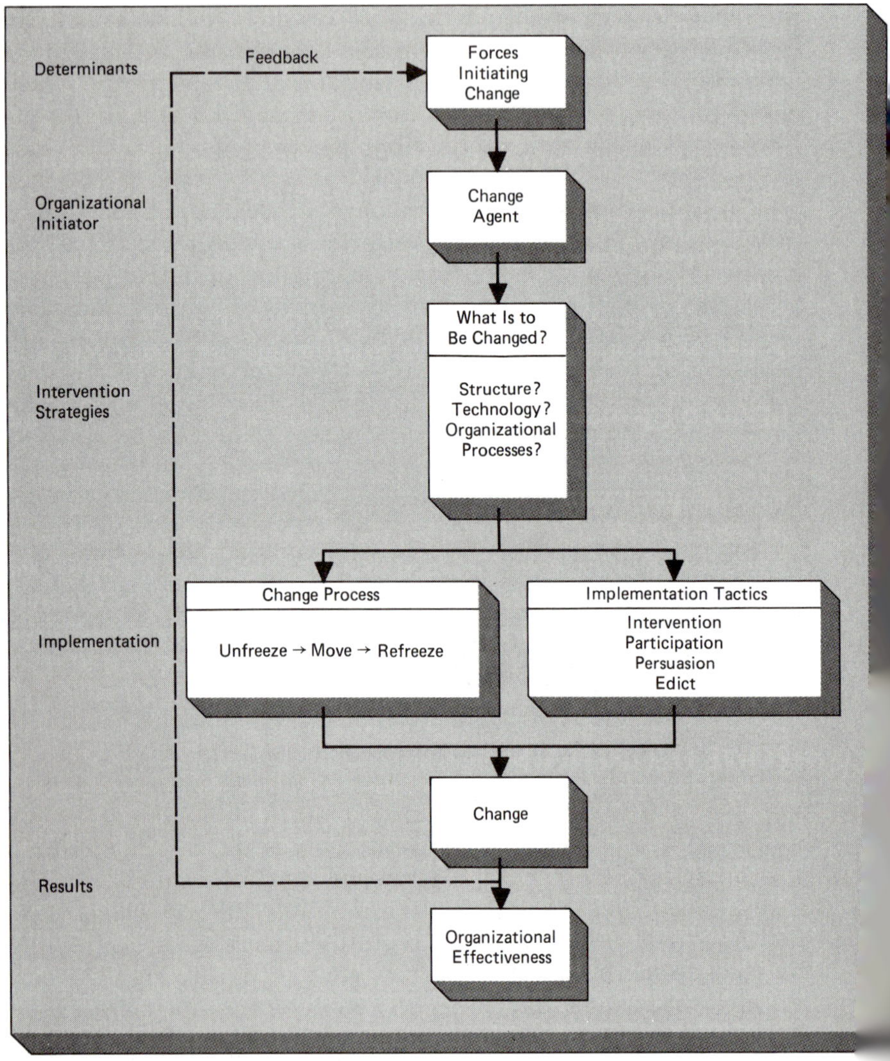

Determinants

How does an organization know that change is necessary? It may be the identification of an opportunity upon which management wants to capitalize. More often, however, it is in anticipation of, or in reaction to, a problem. These opportunities and problems may exist inside the organization, outside the organization, or both.

The factors capable of initiating structural change are countless. While it is tempting to create several categories in which most of the factors can fall neatly, such efforts dramatize quickly that the impetus for change can come from anywhere. Table 14–2 summarizes a number of the more visible reasons for an organization's considering a change in structure. This list, of course, is far from comprehensive. The seeds of structural change can come from an unlimited set of sources. But there should be no doubt in your mind that changes in strategy, size, technology, environment, or power can be the source of structural change.

TABLE 14–2   *Some Determinants of Structural Change with Examples*

- *Change in objectives.* Consistent with the strategy imperative, if an organization chooses to move from being an innovator to being a follower, its structure will likely need to become more mechanistic.
- *Purchase of new equipment.* Consistent with the technology imperative, new equipment that increases capital intensity and standardizes internal processes will tend to require the organization to become more mechanistic.
- *Scarcity of labor.* Labor shortages can result in changes in technology. The shortage of tax lawyers, systems analysts, nurses, and similar professionals has forced managers to make their organization more organic. Because these professionals are in short supply, they have been able to negotiate a greater voice in decision making, less direct supervision, and fewer rules and regulations.
- *Implementation of a sophisticated information-processing system.* When organizations introduce sophisticated information processing, the centralization dimension is typically altered.
- *Government regulations.* The passage of new laws creates the need to establish new departments and changes the power of current departments.
- *The economy.* When interest rates went from around 7 percent into the high teens during the late 1970s, a number of organizations responded by expanding the discretion of purchasing personnel and decentralizing authority to allow them to respond more quickly to changes in inventory needs.
- *Unionization.* Large, geographically dispersed organizations that suddenly become unionized will tend to centralize labor relations activity to faciliate coordinating negotiation of companywide collective bargaining agreements.

(Continued)

TABLE 14–2   *(Continued)*

- *Increased pressures from consumer-advocate groups.* In response to consumer pressure groups, some organizations have created or expanded their public relations department, whereas others have upgraded the authority of personnel in the quality-control function.
- *Mergers or acquisitions.* Duplicate functions will be eliminated, and new coordinating positions are typically created.
- *Actions of competitors.* Aggressive action by competitors can lead to the expansion of boundary-spanning roles and an increase in decentralization.
- *Decline in employee morale.* Overly structured jobs can be a source of low job satisfaction. Redesigning the technology of these jobs by increasing task variety, autonomy, feedback, and the like can improve morale.
- *Increase in turnover.* Organizations that are losing employees that are good performers and who are difficult to replace often modify their reward system and redesign jobs to make them more challenging.
- *Sudden internal or external hostility.* Temporary crises are typically met by management centralizing decision making.
- *Decline in profits.* When a corporation's profits drop off, management frequently resorts to a structural shakeup. Personnel will be shuffled, departments added and/or deleted, new authority relationships defined, and decision-making patterns significantly altered.

The Organizational Initiator

Who initiates structural change? Change agents! But who are they? **Change agents** are those in power and those who wish either to replace or constrain those in power.[4] This typically includes senior executives, managers of major units within the organization, internal staff-development specialists, and powerful lower-level employees. It also includes consultants brought in from the outside.

Figure 14–1 depicts change agents as the intermediaries between the forces initiating change and the choice of an intervention strategy. They are important for who they are and the interest they represent. As our discussions of organizational effectiveness and the power-control perspective demonstrated, decision making in organizations is *not* value free. You should expect, therefore, that every change agent will bring along his or her own self-interests.

OT
CLOSE-UP

WHEN THINGS TURN BAD, DO ORGANIZATIONS GO OUTSIDE FOR A NEW CEO?

One of management's roles in an organization is to provide symbolic meaning.[5] Even though senior management clearly cannot control all the forces that influence an organization's performance, constituents such as stockholders, brokerage firms, bankers, and employees aren't comfortable with management explanations such as "it wasn't our fault" when things go bad. When companies run into hard times and performance significantly drops, the board of directors typically replaces the CEO. Of course, there is a positive side to this scenario, and that's when top management "lucks into" a favorable situation. They are rewarded for the good performance as if they were the major cause of it. This, for instance, describes what happened to U.S. oil company executives in the mid-1970s when the OPEC countries raised the price of oil from $2.25 to $11 a barrel in a matter of days. Profits at companies like Exxon and Chevron skyrocketed, and their CEOs received huge performance bonuses. But let's take a closer look at where the new CEOs come from when organizational performance significantly drops and stock prices tumble.

It has been commonly assumed that when a company performs poorly, the new CEO will come from outside the firm. The logic is that an outsider is essential for a successful turnaround. Insiders, on the other hand, have been thought to be promoted only when performance is satisfactory and a maintenance strategy is sought. Interestingly, the research doesn't fully confirm these predictions.[6]

It's true that when organizational performance has been good to excellent, insiders are chosen. But very poor performance doesn't seem to lead to outsider succession. Why? Any answer can only be speculative, but two have promise. First, it may be difficult to attract viable outside candidates to take the CEO position in a company whose past performance has been extremely poor. Second, given that the board does the selecting and since 40 to 50 percent of the typical board is made up of internal, high-ranking company executives, endorsing outside succession may jeopardize their own jobs. Consistent with the power-control perspective, these officers are reluctant to bring in an outside CEO because, as senior inside managers, they are the most likely to be replaced in a turnaround strategy.

What one manager considers a situation "in need of change" may be fully within the acceptable range for another. It is not unusual for employees in any given function to politick actively for someone from their area to be selected for the organization's top spot. If successful, they can typically expect favored treatment. A CEO who rose through the ranks of the marketing staff can be expected to be more receptive to marketing's problems. He or she is also more likely to recognize marketing's contribution to the organization's effectiveness. As long as effectiveness is appraised in terms of who is doing the evaluating, the background and interests of the change agent are critical to the determination of what is perceived as a condition in need of change.

The outside consultant, who takes on the change agent role, can be looked at from two perspectives. From the rational point of view, the outside consultant brings to the organization objectivity to analyze the organization's problems and the expertise to offer valuable suggestions for change. From the power-control perspective, however, the outside consultant becomes nothing other than the "hired gun" brought in to confirm and legitimate changes that might otherwise be perceived as self-serving.[7]

Management can use outside experts to give the appearance of impartiality. When might outside consultants be used this way? When management is seen as biased toward a specific change action. The outside consultants can be used as a manipulative means to achieve management's preferred solution. This tends to work because consultants are typically perceived as objective and expert. This ensures the legitimacy of their advice. Moreover, because they are not permanently attached to the organization, they are perceived as fostering less visible self-interest in their recommendations.[8] Add to this the fact that smart consultants realize that the best way to ensure that they are asked back for further advice is to provide those who hired them with the conclusions they want to hear, and the outside consultant begins to take on the appearance of a tool with which those in power provide legitimacy to their self-serving decisions.

JAN CARLZON: THE CHANGE AGENT AT SCANDINAVIAN AIRLINES

When Jan Carlzon took over as president of Scandinavian Airlines (SAS), the company was losing $20 million a year. In one year, he turned the company around to where it earned $54 million in profits. He achieved this dramatic reversal by accepting the role of change agent and initiating a complete upending of the organization.[9]

Carlzon calculated that each of the ten million people who fly SAS came in contact with approximately five SAS employees and that each contact lasted only an average of fifteen seconds. In these fifty million "moments of truth" lay the success or failure of SAS, since, to the customers, these short contacts would be the basis upon which they would decide whether or not they would fly SAS again. To Carlzon, this analysis meant that not only the performance of SAS but its future lay in the lands of frontline people like ticket agents, flight attendants, and baggage handlers. So he decided SAS needed to change the way it did business. It had to become customer-driven. And to do this, he had to dramatically change SAS's structure. He took it as his job to communicate his new vision of SAS throughout the company.

What Carlzon did was to turn the organization structure upside down. Operational decisions would no longer be made by management. They would be delegated to the bottom level of the pyramid. Since these frontline people are the ones who most directly influence the customer's impression of the company during those "moments of truth," they must have the authority to solve problems on the spot, as soon as they arise. No front line employee should have to wait for a supervisor's permission to do what is right for the customer. As Carlzon put it, "No passenger boards the plane while still worried or dissatisfied." And what is management's role in the new SAS? Simply to *enable* the front line to serve the customer. Rather than get in the way, management does the planning, coaching, and other support activities to allow the front line to do its job well.

Intervention Strategies

The term **intervention strategies** is used to describe the choice of means by which the change process takes place. Strategies tend to fall into one of four categories: people, structure, technology, and organizational processes. Since we are concerned with structural issues in this volume rather than with behavior, we can omit from our discussion the topic of changing people.

Structure. The structure classification includes changes affecting the distribution of authority; allocation of rewards; alterations in the chain of command; degree of formalization; and addition or deletion of positions, departments, and divisions. Procter & Gamble's category innovation, discussed in Chapter 10, was a reorganization change that added another vertical level and reduced the span of control at the top. This reduced top management's involvement in day-to-day operating activities, created greater flexibility for growth, and provided more opportunities for training those candidates most likely to assume the company's top slot.

Technology. The technology classification encompasses modifications in the equipment that employees use, interdependencies of work activities among employees, and changes that affect the interrelationships between employees and the technical demands of their jobs.

For instance, the business faculty at a junior college in the Midwest decided that all introductory courses—basic management, marketing, finance, accounting—would be converted from the lecture format to self-paced videocassette learning modules. Each course required students to listen to forty one-hour cassette tapes and complete a programmed learning text designed especially for the course and coordinated with the tapes. Faculty members designed the courses, made the tapes, wrote the accompanying texts, provided one-on-one tutorials, and devoted an increased amount of time to preparing for and teaching more advanced courses. This major change in technology dramatically reduced the need for new faculty, altered the characteristics required of new faculty in that new members needed greater specialization to handle the advanced courses, eliminated the variance in the information that students received when they took the same course from different instructors, and allowed department heads to effectively supervise a greater number of faculty.

Organizational Processes. The final strategy considers changing organizational processes such as decision making and communication patterns. If a change agent, for instance, introduces task forces into a machine bureaucracy with the intent of improving the transmission of information between functional units and allowing representatives from each unit to participate in decisions that will affect each of them, the change agent will have altered the organization's decision-making processes.

Implementation

Referring again to Figure 14–1, once forces for initiating change exist, someone has assumed the change-agent role, and it has been determined what it is that is to be changed, we need to consider *how* to implement the change. We begin by looking at the steps in the change process. Then we turn our attention to implementation tactics.

The Change Process. Successful change requires *unfreezing* the status quo, *moving* to a new state, and *refreezing* the change to make it permanent.[10] Implicit in this three-step **change process** is the recognition that the mere introduction of change does not ensure either the elimination of the prechange condition or the fact that the change will prove to be enduring.

The management of a large oil company decided to reorganize its marketing function in the western United States. The firm had three divisional offices in the West, located in Seattle, San Francisco, and Los Angeles. The decision was made to consolidate the divisions into a single regional office to be located in San Francisco. The reorganization meant transferring more than 150 employees, the elimination of some duplicated managerial positions, and the institution of a new hierarchy of command. As you might guess, a move of this magnitude was difficult to keep secret. Rumors about it preceded the announcement by several months. The decision itself was made unilaterally. It came from the executive offices in New York. The people affected had no say whatsover in the choice. For those in Seattle or Los Angeles, who may have disliked the decision and its consequences—the problems inherent in transferring to another city, pulling youngsters out of school, making new friends, having new co-workers, the reassignment of responsibilities—their only recourse was to quit. This actual case history of an organizational change will be used to illustrate the unfreezing-moving-refreezing process.

The status quo can be considered an equilibrium state. To move from this equilibrium—to overcome the pressures of both individual resistance and group conformity—**unfreezing** is necessary. This can be achieved in one of three ways. The *driving forces*, which direct behavior away from the status quo, can be increased. The *restraining forces*, which hinder movement from the existing equilibrium, can be decreased. A third alternative is to *combine the first two approaches*.

Using the reorganization example cited, management can expect employee resistance to the consolidation. To deal with that resistance, management can use positive incentives to encourage employees to accept the change. For instance, increases in pay can be offered to those who accept the transfer. Very liberal moving expenses can be paid by the company. Management might offer low-cost mortgage funds to allow employees to buy new homes in San Francisco. Of course, management might choose to unfreeze acceptance of the status quo by removing restraining forces. Employees could be counseled individually. Each employee's concerns and apprehensions could be heard and clarified specifically. Assuming that most of the fears are unjustified, the counselor could assure the employees that there was nothing to fear and then demonstrate, through tangible evidence, that restraining forces are unwarranted. If resistance is extremely high, management may have to resort to both reducing resistance and increasing the attractiveness of the alternative if the unfreezing is to be successful.

Once unfreezing has been accomplished, the change itself can be implemented. This is where the change agent introduces one or more intervention strategies. In reality, there is no clear line separating unfreezing and moving. Many of the efforts made to unfreeze the status quo may, in and of themselves, introduce change. So the tactics that the change agent uses for dealing with resistance may work on unfreezing and/or moving. Six tactics that managers or change agents can use for dealing with resistance to change are described in Table 14–3.

Assuming that a change has been implemented, if it is to be

TABLE 14–3   *Tactics for Dealing with Resistance to Change*

1. *Education and communication.* Resistance can be reduced by communicating with employees to help them see the logic of a change. This tactic assumes basically that the source of resistance lies in misinformation or poor communication. If employees receive the full facts and clear up any misunderstandings, the resistance will subside. This can be achieved through one-on-one discussions, memos, group presentations, or reports.
2. *Participation.* It's difficult for individuals to resist a change decision in which they have participated. Assuming that the participants have the expertise to make a useful contribution, their involvement can reduce resistance, obtain commitment, and increase the quality of the change decision.
3. *Facilitation and support.* Change agents can offer a range of supportive efforts to reduce resistance. When employee fear and anxiety are high, employee counseling and therapy, new skills training, or short, paid leaves of absence may facilitate adjustment.
4. *Negotiation.* This tactic requires the exchange of something of value for a lessening of the resistance. For instance, if the resistance is centered in a few powerful individuals, a specific reward package can be negotiated that will meet their individual needs.
5. *Manipulation and cooptation.* Manipulation refers to covert influence attempts. Twisting and distorting facts to make them appear more attractive, withholding undesirable information, or creating false rumors to get employees to accept a change are all examples of manipulation. Cooptation is a form of both manipulation and participation. It seeks to "buy off" the leaders of a resistance group by giving them a key role in the change decision. The advice of those who have been coopted is sought not to result in a better decision but only to get their endorsement.
6. *Coercion.* This tactic is the application of direct threats or force upon the resisters. Examples include threats of transfers, loss of promotions, negative performance evaluations, or a poor letter of recommendation.

Source: Adapted from John P. Kotter and Leonard A. Schlesinger, "Choosing Strategies for Change," *Harvard Business Review*, March–April 1979, pp. 106–14.

successful, the new situation needs to be refrozen so that it can be sustained over time. Unless this last step is attended to, there is a very high likelihood that the change will be short-lived and employees will attempt to revert to the prior equilibrium state. The objective of **refreezing,** then, is to stabilize the new situation by balancing the driving and restraining forces.

How is refreezing done? Basically, it requires systematic re-placement of the temporary forces with permanent ones. It may mean formalizing the driving or restraining forces: for instance, a permanent upward adjustment of salaries or the permanent re-moval of time clocks to reinforce a climate of trust and confidence in employees. The formal rules and regulations governing behavior of those affected by the change should be revised to reinforce the new situation. Over time, of course, the group's own norms will evolve to sustain the new equilibrium. But until that point is reached, the change agent will have to rely on more formal mechanisms.

Are there key factors that determine the degree to which a change will become permanent? The answer is "Yes." A review of change studies identified a number of relevant factors.[11] The *reward allocation system* is critical. For instance, if rewards fall short of expectation over time, the change is likely to be short-lived. If a change is to be sustained, it needs the *support of a sponsor*. This individual, typically high in the management hierarchy, provides legitimacy to the change. Evidence indicated that once sponsorship is withdrawn from a change project, there are strong pressures to return to the old equilibrium state. People need to know what is expected of them as a result of the change. Therefore, *failure to transmit information* on expectations should reduce the degree of refreezing. *Group forces* is another important factor. As employees become aware that others in their group accept and sanction the change, they become more comfortable with it. *Commitment* to the change should lead to greater acceptance and permanence. As noted earlier, if employees participate in the change decision, they can be expected to be more committed to seeing that it is successful. Change is less likely to become permanent if it is implemented in a singular unit of the organization. Therefore, the more *diffusion* in the change effort, the more units that will be affected and the greater legitimacy the effort will carry.

These factors remind us that the organization is a system and that planned change will be most successful when all the parts within the system support the change effort. What is more, suc-cessful change requires careful balancing of the system. The con-solidation of three divisional units into a singular regional office obviously carries with it a wide range of reverberating effects. But the impact of even small changes (i.e., when a multibillion-dollar consumer-products firm creates a new department of public affairs staffed with only a handful of personnel) can be expected to be widespread. Other departments and employees will be threatened. Still others will feel that a portion of their responsibilities has been taken from them. All changes, regardless of how small, will have an impact outside the area in which they were implemented. No change can take place in a vacuum. A structural modification in unit A will affect other structural variables within unit A as well as structural variables in units B,C, and so forth. This systems perspective makes it imperative that change agents consider any and all interventions as having a potential impact on a far greater territory than the specific point where the change was initiated.

Implementation Tactics. Paralleling the change process in the implementation stage is the decision of what tactics should be used to install the planned change. Research has identified four tactics that change agents use. One author has called these tactics intervention, participation, persuasion, and edict.[12]

The use of the **intervention** tactic is characterized by change agents *selling* their change rationale to those who will be affected. They argue that current performance is inadequate and establish new standards. The agents cite comparable organizations or units with better performance to justify the need for change and then often explicitly describes how current practices can be improved. To assess more fully inefficient or poorly designed procedures, change agents using the intervention tactic frequently form task forces made up of effected personnel. But change agents retain power to veto any of the task force's recommendations.

In **participation,** change agents *delegate* the implementation decision to those who will be affected. Change agents stipulate the need for change or the opportunities change can provide, create a task force to do the job, assign members to the task force, and then delegate authority for the change process to the task force with a statement of expectations and constraints. Change agents who use this tactic give full responsibility to the task force for implementation and exercise no veto power over its decisions.

Some change agents handle change by essentially *abdicating* the decision to experts. Change agents identify the need or opportunity for change. But because they are disinterested, lack knowledge, or feel others can handle the job better, they take a relatively passive role. What they do is to allow interested internal staff—or qualified outside experts—to present their ideas for bringing about change. The internal or external experts then use **persuasion** to sell their ideas. Change agents become active only after various ideas have been presented. They listen and often ask for supporting documentation. But those who will be affected choose the best ideas for implementing the change.

The final tactic was used in the oil-company reorganization example presented earlier. Top management made their structural change decision unilaterally. They avoided any participation and *told* those effected what the change would be. This is called implementation by **edict**. When this tactic is used, change agents merely announce changes and use memos, formal presentations, or the like to convey their decision.

In practice, how popular is each of these implementation tactics? A study of ninety-one cases found persuasion to be most widely used, occurring in 42 percent of the cases.[13] Edict was the next most popular with 23 percent, followed by intervention and participation with 19 and 17 percent, respectively.

Results

The model in Figure 14–1 culminates with change taking place and a resulting effect on organizational effectiveness. Whether that effect is positive, negative, temporary, or permanent depends on each of the earlier steps.

Research on implementation tactics demonstrates that there are real differences in their success rates.[14] Change directives by managerial fiat are clearly inferior to other options. Edict was successful just 43 percent of the time. Participation and persuasion achieved success rates of 84 and 73 percent, respectively. Intervention, while used in only 19 percent of the cases, attained a perfect 100 percent success rate.

Regardless of the outcome, the model shown in Figure 14–1 is dynamic. The need for change is continuous, hence the need for the feedback loop. Successful change agents have little time to sit back and reflect on their achievements. New forces will already be working to make additional changes necessary. The change model we have proposed, therefore, is never at rest.

THE INNOVATING ORGANIZATION

A recent *Fortune* magazine cover story declared that innovating "has become the most urgent concern of corporations everywhere."[15] "Innovate or die" is the new battle cry in industries as diverse as office equipment, automobiles, home building, publishing, and financial services. In industries such as these, where dynamic environments have become a fact of life, innovation has become closely linked with organizational effectiveness. But is *innovation* the same as *change*? And what type of organization is best designed to stimulate innovation?

Anything different represents a change. **Innovation,** however, is the adoption of ideas that are new to the adopting organization.[16] All innovations, therefore, represent a change, but not all changes are innovative. The innovative change breaks new ground for the organization and hence is more threatening and more likely to be resisted by the organization's members.

Innovation typically takes one of two forms: technological or administrative.[17] **Technological innovation** is what most of us usually think about when we think about innovative change. These innovations encompass the use of new tools, techniques, devices, or systems to produce changes in products or services or in the way those products are produced or services rendered. The introduction of modular workstations at an IBM facility in Austin, Texas, which allows IBM to build computers entirely with robots, is an example of technological innovation. On the other hand, **administrative innovation** is the implementation of changes in an organization's structure or its administrative processes. This would include changes like the introduction of flextime work schedules or a matrix organization design.

The organization's strategy sets the overall framework for the importance of innovation. Prospectors, for example, tend to foster more innovation. Reactors, in contrast, tend to be low innovators. But clearly certain structures are better than others for stimulating innovation.[18]

The machine bureaucracy is least likely to stimulate or be accepting of innovation. Of course, one could argue that, because it tends to be associated with stable environments, bureaucracy is least in need of innovation. Its value lies in efficiency through standardization, not initiating new and novel ideas. Innovation is most likely to flourish in adhocracies and simple structures. Innovation is stimulated in adhocracies by its personnel, who tend to be professionals; the lack of formalization; and the active involvement of lower-level employees in decision making. The key to innovation in the simple structure, however, lies not in the structure but in its chief executive officer. The evidence indicates that the personality, power, and knowledge of the CEO differentiaties those simple structures that innovate from those that don't. Essentially, CEOs in innovative organizations have personality styles that demonstrate confidence in their abilities to control the environment, have centralized power for maximum control, and possess considerable knowledge about changes taking place in their organization's environment.

TAKING CHANCES AT JOHNSON & JOHNSON

Jim Burke retired as CEO at Johnson & Johnson in 1989, but he left a legacy that breeds innovation.[19] To what does Burke attribute J&J's success at innovating? A corporate culture that encourages risk and creative conflict.

Early in Burke's career at J&J, he championed a children's chest rub that failed dismally. When called into his boss's office, he thought he was going to be fired. "Are you the one who just cost us all that money?" his boss asked. After admitting he was the one, his boss replied, "Well, I just want to congratulate you. If you are making mistakes, that means you are making decisions and taking risks. And we won't grow unless you take risks."

Burke fostered that risk-taking, "you have to lose in order to grow," philosophy during his years at J&J's helm. Additionally, he encouraged what he called "creative conflict" to nurture innovation. J&J people are rewarded for challenging the status quo. Burke claims that a culture that fosters creative conflict without fear of retribution will generate a lot of ideas.

A DESCRIPTIVE VIEW OF ORGANIZATIONAL CHANGE

To this point, most of our discussion on organizational change has been inherently optimistic. While we've alluded to the fact that change is often resisted, the change literature we've described can be criticized as being built on rational assumptions that are essentially naive. For instance, we've implied that managers are motivated to initiate change because they are concerned with effectiveness and that change is a dynamic and continuous process driven by the organization's need to adjust and match itself with the constant changes in its environment.

There is a small but growing set of organization theorists who propose that such assumptions don't mesh with reality. Consistent with our attempt throughout this book to make its contents realistic, this section reviews this descriptive view of organizational change. This view proposes that stability, not change, characterizes most organizations. Moreover, organizations don't make continual adjustments in response to changes in their environment. When change comes, the critics argue, it comes fast and dramatically. To summarize, the theme of this section is that organizations are extremely stable over time; and when change is initiated, it's more revolutionary than evolutionary!

Stability Leads to Inertia

Organizations, by their very nature, are conservative.[20] They actively resist change. You don't have to look far to see evidence of this phenomenon. Government agencies want to continue doing what they have been doing for years, whether the need for their service changes or remains the same. Organized religions are deeply entrenched in their history. Attempts to change church doctrine require great persistence and patience. Educational institutions, which exist to open minds and challenge established doctrine, are themselves extremely resistant to change. Most school systems are using the same teaching technology today as they were fifty years ago. The majority of business firms, too, appear highly resistant to change.

Why do organizations resist change? There are at least four

explanations. First, members fear losing what they already have. Those in power, who are in the best position to initiate change, typically have the most to lose. Second, most organizations are bureaucracies. Such structures have built-in mechanisms that work against change. Third, many organizations can manage their environment and, hence, have buffered themselves against needing to change. Finally, organization cultures resist pressures toward change. Let's elaborate on each of these points.

Any change can be an actual threat to employees' economic well-being, security, social affiliations, or status. Change can result in the loss of money, friends, or work group associates. Since employees have a high investment in specific skills, change also threatens employee self-interest. Few people are prepared to throw away years of job preparation and experience. However, probably the greatest fear is loss of position and privilege by those in the managerial ranks. Top management can legitimately claim to have a great deal to lose from change. One author has noted why senior managers are especially prone to both resist change and misperceive signals that change is needed:

> . . . they have strong vested interests; they will be blamed if current practices, strategies, and goals prove to be wrong; reorientations threaten their dominance; their promotions and high statuses have persuaded them that they have more expertise than other people; their expertise tends to be out-of-date because their personal experiences with clients, customers, technologies, and low-level personnel lie in the past; they get much information through channels which conceal events that might displease them; and they associate with other top managers who face similar pressures.[21]

Add to this the fact that major restructuring almost always includes wholesale replacement of the top managers, and it is not surprising to find senior managers as critical impediments to change.

We have previously concluded that (1) bureaucracies are the most popular structural design in our society, and (2) bureaucracies are designed to handle routine activities as efficiently as possible. The new, the novel, and the nonconforming are anathema to the bureaucratic form. These two facts suggest that change is unlikely to have much of a widespread following. Specifically, bureaucracy's standardized technologies, high formalization, and performance-evaluation and reward systems that strongly penalize risk taking and mistakes discourage doing things differently.

The previous chapter detailed how organizations can manage their environment. Clearly, many large and powerful organizations use their strength to reduce their dependency on their environment. Of course, by doing so, they also reduce their need to adapt to changes in that environment.

The final force that we contend acts to impede change is the organization's culture. As we'll discuss in Chapter 16, every organization has a culture that defines for employees what is appropriate and inappropriate behavior. Once employees learn their organization's culture—and this rarely takes more than a few months—they know the way things are supposed to be done. While culture helps employees understand what's important and what's not, it also creates a consistency of behavior that becomes entrenched and highly resistant to change.

In summary, it appears that planned organizational change gets a lot more attention in textbooks than it gets in practice. The forces against change result in organizational inertia and far more stability than the rational-change literature would predict. Of course, inertia isn't all bad. Organizations need some resistance qualities, otherwise they might respond to every perceived change in the environment. Every organization needs stability to function. If an organization reacted to every change stimulus, it would lose the consistent, goal-directed behavior that makes a group of people into an organization.

Internal Compatibility Requires Revolutionary Change

As we noted in Chapter 10, there are essentially a limited number of basic configurations. Additionally, as we also noted, these configurations have a common and consistent set of elements. If you disturb this consistency by changing one of the elements, the organization's design will become out of balance. At the extreme, if these elements were to change regularly in a piecemeal fashion, there would be too much variety among organizations to allow for a limited set of common configurations. But we know all organizations are not unique. They tend to develop internal consistencies between their technology; authority patterns, span of control; degree of specialization, standardization, and formalization; and other key structural elements.[22] This recognition that an organization's

structural elements need to be consistent and internally compatible has important implications for organizational change. It suggests that when organizations do change, the change will be comprehensive.[23] Let's look at what this means when coupled with our
previous discussion about stability.

Management would prefer to avoid change, if it were possible,
because of its cost, disruptive impacts, and threat to management's
control. If the organization faces a dynamic environment, we should
expect that management will first try to reduce its dependence on
that environment. But even the largest and most powerful organizations cannot completely manage their environment. So management's options are essentially two.[24] It can keep up with the
changes in its environment by changing itself incrementally to
match changes in the environment. This will achieve environmental fit but create internal inconsistencies. The other alternative is
to delay change until it is absolutely necessary and then make it
comprehensive. This maintains internal consistency but at the price
of having a poor environment-structure fit for a period.

This choice between these two options might be a dilemma if
it weren't for management's preference for making as few changes
as possible and the reality that management does not seek to maximize organizational effectiveness. If the choice were between
"change" and "no change," management would be expected to prefer the status quo; but that option is not available. Management
is going to have to accept some changes in order to maintain a
satisficing level of organizational effectiveness. But when the choice
is between continual change and the infrequent variety, the decision is easy. They select the latter.

We can now state the descriptive view of organizational change:
Organizations are characterized by long periods of inertia, punc-
tuated by brief periods of dramatic and comprehensive change that
culminates in a very short period of time.

A Power-Control Footnote

How does the descriptive view of organizational change stack up
with the power-control approach to organization design?[25] Power-
control advocates would agree with the notion of organizational
inertia. They recognize that those in power have little reason to
change the current structure. The status quo maintains control
and furthers the interests of the power holders. But power-control

advocates would ignore any concern for maintaining internal consistency among structural elements and, instead, emphasize the lack of planning in "planned" change and argue that change more likely represents a loss of control by the dominant power coalition than a response to the environment.

Since effectiveness is defined in terms of those doing the evaluating, the rational assumption that "changes in structure will be implemented as needed to ensure high performance" is unrealistic. The power-control position would argue that structural changes that do occur are neither planned nor in response to facilitate technical efficiency or demands of the environment. The following briefly summarizes the power-control view.

Change is most likely a response to pressing demands created by internal and external parties interested in the organization. That is, it is reactive rather than anticipatory. In practice, "planned" change is typically a process of (1) change, followed by (2) the planning that legitimates and ratifies this change. As noted about goals in Chapter 9, meaning is attributed to an action but usually *after* it has occurred. So while change is made in response to demands by powerful interest groups, it is packaged and sold in a more legitimate form: it is rationalized as being consistent with the goals of enhanced organizational effectiveness.

Pressures for change come from anywhere outside the dominant coalition. If those in power are not able to keep those pressures in check, changes will be implemented. It may not be what the dominant coalition wants, but at that point they will have lost control. When these changes are implemented, in response to outside pressures, they will tend to be conveyed as planned and consistent with the organization's goals of improved performance.

SUMMARY

Managing change is concerned with planned structural change. Organizations need to change and adapt in order to be effective.

A wide range of forces can initiate change. The change agent is the individual or individuals who make the structural changes. He or she chooses from structural, technological, or organization process-intervention strategies. The implementation of change requires unfreezing the status quo, moving to a new state, and refreezing the change to make it permanent. Implementation also requires a decision as to the specific tactics to be used.

The evidence indicates that innovating organizations are likely to have a prospector strategy and an adhocratic or simple structure.

Despite all the attention that change has received by organization theorists, organizations are more stable than changing. Organizations can be characterized as having long periods of inertia, followed by brief periods of dramatic and comprehensive change that culminates in a very short period of time. In other words, change is infrequent and revolutionary in nature. The power-control position further states that structural changes, when they occur, are neither planned nor in response to needs for technical efficiency or demands of the environment. Change indicates a loss of control by the organization's dominant coalition.

CHANGE IN A BUSINESS SCHOOL: A POWER-CONTROL INTERPRETATION

The business school at a specific university had experienced very rapid growth. In a period of four or five years, the number of faculty members increased from approximately fifteen to thirty-five. Most of these new members were young, having recently finished their own graduate studies.

The dominant power coalition was made up of the dean and his department heads. All the department heads had been at the university for many years and ruled with considerable strength. Although the dean had come from another university and been in his position only a few years, he was in his late fifties and had been hand-picked by the department chairmen because he was seen as someone who would not "shake up the ship." What the dominant coalition had overlooked, however, was that there were now more young faculty than "old-timers" and that the university's top administrators believed that the future of the business school resided with the new young faculty. Conditions were right for a revolt. The young faculty knew that they had the numbers to overthrow the dominant coalition. The top administration's concern with keeping them at the school enhanced their power. Here is what took place.

Several of the young faculty went to the university's vice president and outlined the business school's problems. They also presented

FOR REVIEW AND DISCUSSION

1. What is the traditional view of change in organizations?
2. What does "managed" change mean?
3. Why do organizations resist change?
4. Describe five determinants of change.
5. Describe the three types of intervention strategies.
6. Contrast driving and restraining forces in unfreezing.
7. Why is "refreezing" of change necessary?

evidence on the poor performance of the dean in dealing with these problems. A few visits with the vice president, followed by his own confirming data, resulted in the dean's being asked to tender his resignation. An acting dean was appointed. Interestingly, few of the dominant coalition saw that a revolt was brewing. It appeared that the department chairmen expected the next dean to maintain the status quo. This, of course, was fine for the chairmen. They were the "fat cats" in the system.

At a faculty meeting several months after the dean's resignation, one of the items on the agenda was nominations to the search committee for selecting a new dean. When that item came up, the young faculty members were ready. Within less than a minute, they had succeeded in nominating and seconding five of their own to the five committee positions. The nominations were closed. Suddenly it became obvious to everyone at the meeting that the young faculty had stacked the deck. You can probably guess what happened from that point on.

The young faculty wanted the power coalition changed, and only those candidates that supported such a change became finalists for the deanship. When the new dean was appointed, the young faculty members took control. All the chair positions were changed. The old-timers were replaced by members of the young faculty coalition. The business school was subsequently reorganized, and the interests of the young faculty were paramount in this structural change. These changes, it was argued, were necessary to improve the effectiveness of the business school. Whether they did is problematic. But there is no question that they furthered the interests of the young faculty by legitimating their power. The young faculty totally revamped the goals and structure of that business school in their interests. To this day, the old-timers have never recovered.

8. Review the various tactics for dealing with resistance to change in power-control terms.
9. Explain why organizations have an inherent bias toward stability.
10. "Bureaucracies have survived because they have proven able to respond to change." Do you agree or disagree? Discuss.
11. "Pressure for change originates in the environment; whereas pressure for stability originates within the organization." Do you agree or disagree? Discuss.
12. "Resistance to change is good for an organization." Do you agree or disagree? Discuss.
13. What type of organizations stimulate innovation? Why?
14. What could the management of a large bureaucracy do to stimulate innovation within their organization?
15. How would you modify Figure 14–1 to reflect the descriptive and power-control views of organizational change?

NOTES

[1] This description of change at General Radio is adapted from Michael Tushman, William Newman, and Elaine Romanelli, "Convergence and Upheaval: Managing the Unsteady Pace of Organizational Evolution," *California Management Review*, Fall 1986, p. 30. By permission.

[2] William H. Starbuck and Paul C. Nystrom, "Designing and Understanding Organizations," in P.C. Nystrom and W.H. Starbuck, eds., *Handbook of Organizational Design*, Vol. 1 (New York: Oxford University Press, 1981), p. xx.

[3] For readers interested in behavioral-change techniques, see Stephen P. Robbins, *Organizational Behavior: Concepts, Controversies, and Applications*, 4th ed. (Englewood Cliffs, N.J.: Prentice Hall, 1989), pp. 544–47.

[4] Daniel Katz and Robert L. Kahn, *The Social Psychology of Organizations*, 2nd ed. (New York: John Wiley, 1978), p. 679.

[5] Jeffrey Pfeffer, "Management as Symbolic Action: The Creation and Maintenance of Organizational Paradigms," in Larry L. Cummings and Barry M. Staw, eds., *Research in Organizational Behavior*, Vol. 3 (Greenwich, Conn.: JAI Press, 1981), pp. 1–52.

[6] Dan R. Dalton and Idalene F. Kesner, "Organizational Performance as an Antecedent of Inside/Outside Chief Executive Succession: An Empirical Assessment," *Academy of Management Journal*, December 1985, pp. 749–62.

[7] Jeffrey Pfeffer, *Power in Organizations* (Marshfield, Mass.: Pitman Publishing, 1981), pp. 142–46.

[8] Ibid.

[9] See Jan Carlzon, "Moments of Truth," *Industry Week*, July 27, 1987, pp. 40–44; and Amanda Bennett, "SAS's Nice Guy Is Aiming to Finish First," *Wall Street Journal*, March 2, 1989, p. B8.

[10] Kurt Lewin, *Field Theory in Social Science* (New York: Harper & Row, 1951).

[11] Paul S. Goodman, Max Bazerman, and Edward Conlon, "Institutionalization of Planned Organizational Change," in Barry M. Staw and Larry L. Cummings, eds., *Research in Organizational Behavior*, vol. 2, (Greenwich, Conn.: JAI Press, 1980), pp. 231–42.

[12] Paul C. Nutt, "Tactics of Implementation," *Academy of Management Journal*, June 1986, pp. 230–61.

[13] Ibid.

[14] Ibid.

[15] Kenneth Labich, "The Innovators," *Fortune*, June 6, 1988, p. 50.

[16] Richard L. Daft, "Bureaucratic Versus Nonbureaucratic Structure and the Process of Innovation and Change," in Samuel B. Bacharach, ed., *Research in the Sociology of Organizations*, vol. 1, 1982, p. 132.

[17] Fariborz Damanpour, "The Adoption of Technological, Administrative, and Ancillary Innovations: Impact of Organizational Factors," *Journal of Management*, Winter 1987, p. 677.

[18] This section adapted from Danny Miller and Peter H. Friesen, *Organizations: A Quantum View* (Englewood Cliffs, N.J.: Prentice Hall, 1984), pp. 176–201. See also James Brian Quinn, "Managing Innovation," *Harvard Business Review*, May–June 1985, pp. 73–84; and Rosabeth Moss Kanter, "When a Thousand Flowers Bloom: Structural, Collective, and Social Conditions for Innovation in Organization," in B. M. Staw and L. L. Cummings (eds), *Research in Organizational Behavior*, Vol. 10 (Greenwich, Conn.: JAI Press, 1988), pp. 169–211.

[19] Based on H. John Steinbreder, "Taking Chances at J&J," *Fortune*, June 6, 1988, p. 60; and "At Johnson & Johnson, A Mistake Can Be a Badge of Honor," *Business Week*, September 26, 1988, pp. 126–28.

[20] Richard H. Hall, *Organizations: Structures, Processes, and Outcomes*, 4th ed. (Englewood Cliffs, N.J.: Prentice Hall, 1987), p. 29.

[21] William H. Starbuck, "Organizations as Action Generators," *American Sociological Review*, February 1983, p. 100.

[22] See, for example, Danny Miller, "Toward a New Contingency Approach: The Search for Organizational Gestalts," *Journal of Management Studies*, January 1981, pp. 1–26.

[23] Miller and Friesen, *Organizations*, pp. 207–47.

[24] Ibid., p. 23.

[25] This section is based on Jeffrey Pfeffer, *Organizational Design* (Arlington Heights, Ill.: AHM Publishing, 1978), pp. 190–92.

15

MANAGING ORGANIZATIONAL CONFLICT

AFTER READING THIS CHAPTER, YOU SHOULD BE ABLE TO:

1 Define conflict.
2 Contrast the traditional and interactionist views of conflict.
3 List the major sources of organizational conflict.
4 Outline the primary techniques for resolving structural conflicts.
5 Identify situations when management should stimulate conflict.
6 List several techniques for stimulating conflict.

Introduction
CONFLICT IN THE EXECUTIVE SUITE

Jennifer Maher produces a situation comedy for the Fox Network in Los Angeles. The quiet in her office was broken by the buzz on her intercom. "Ms. Maher," her secretary blurted, "there's a riot out here. There's a bunch of people who want to see you." Within seconds, a half a dozen of Jennifer's scriptwriters burst through the door. "Jenny," began the spokesperson for the group, "we've had it. You promoted Nick Crane to script supervisor three weeks ago after Christine resigned. Well, we can't work with him! With Christine we were a team. We wrote each script together. We shared ideas. Our scripts were good, damn good, because we all participated in making them that way. Well, Nick has changed the whole thing around. He's split us into two groups, each working on a separate episode. After the three of us have roughed out the general format for the episode, he breaks us up and makes each of us work on one of its three acts. He says it make for better accountability. He thinks he can now find out who the best writers are! Have you ever heard of anything so crazy? Jenny, if you don't do something right now, I'm telling you, we're all gonna quit!"

Two thousand miles away, at the head office of a large chemical company in Chicago, the following telephone conversation was taking place between Bill Douglas and Gary Panek. Bill is vice president of sales. Gary is vice president of research and development

"I don't care how much work you've got down there," Bill was saying, "American Steel is one of our best customers. I told them we'd have a solvent that would meet their needs within thirty days." "I appreciate your dilemma, Bill," Gary replied, "but I've got a dozen projects that have high priority. My staff has only so much time. I think I can put someone on developing a solvent for American in six or seven weeks. Tell American we'll have a product for them within ninety days." "No way," snapped Bill, "we'll lose the whole account." "I'm sorry," Gary said. "If this upsets you so much, Bill, call Henry [the company's president] and tell him, like I've been telling him for the last year, how the R&D group needs a larger staff," Gary lobbied in closing.

Both of the previous incidents have a common thread. They represent organizational conflicts. If we can generalize from a study of middle- and top-level executives by the American Management Association, the average manager spends approximately 20 percent of his or her time dealing with conflict.[1] No study of organizations, therefore, would be complete without an analysis of this topic. We propose that conflict is an inevitable part of organizational life, stemming as much from structural characteristics as from incompatible personalities. Organizations have scarce resources, employees with diverse interests and outlooks, and other attributes that make conflict a constant reality.

DEFINING CONFLICT

There is no shortage of definitions for the term *conflict*. A sampling of the literature describes it as "that behavior by organization members which is expended in opposition to other members";[2] "the process which begins when one party perceives that the other has frustrated, or is about to frustrate, some concern of his";[3] or merely, "whenever incompatible activities occur."[4] Several common themes, however, underlie most definitions.

Conflict must be *perceived* by the parties to it. Whether conflict exists is a perception issue. If no one is aware of a conflict, it is generally agreed that no conflict exists. Of course, conflicts perceived may not be real, whereas many situations that otherwise could be described as conflictive are not because the organizational members involved do not perceive the conflict. For a conflict to exist, therefore, it must be perceived. Additional commonalities among most conflict definitions are the concepts of *opposition, scarcity,* and *blockage* and the assumption that there are two or more parties whose interests or *goals appear to be incompatible.* Resources—whether money, promotions, prestige, power, or whatever—are not unlimited, and their scarcity encourages blocking behavior. The parties are therefore in opposition. When one party blocks the goal achievement of another, a conflict state exists.

Differences between definitions tend to center on *intent* and whether conflict is a term limited only to *overt acts.* The intent issue is a debate over whether blockage behavior must be a determined action or whether it could occur as a result of fortuitous circumstances. As to whether conflict can refer only to overt acts, some definitions, for example, require signs of manifest fighting or open struggle as criteria for the existence of conflict.

Our definition of conflict acknowledges awareness (perception), opposition, scarcity, and blockage. Further, we assume it to be determined action, which can exist at either the latent or overt level. We define **conflict** to be *a process in which an effort is purposely made by A to offset the efforts of B by some form of blocking that will result in frustrating B in attaining his or her goals or furthering his or her interests.*

CONFLICT AND ORGANIZATIONAL EFFECTIVENESS

For most people, the term *organizational conflict* carries a negative connotation. An effective organization is typically thought of as a coordinated group of individuals working toward common goals. In this view, conflict would only hinder the coordination and teamwork necessary to achieve the organization's goals.

IS CONFLICT AT THE USOC COSTING THE UNITED STATES GOLD MEDALS?

In 1978, the United States Olympic Committee was appointed as the principal coordinating group for preparing U.S. athletes for Olympic competition. Between 1978 and 1984, its executive director, F. Donald Miller, did a brilliant job of coordinating the thirty-eight athletic federations that represent the various sports—i.e., basketball, boxing, figure skating—taking part in the games. But the USOC's record since 1984 has been awful. The organization has been rife with conflict and turmoil. One sports-marketing consultant has called it a "national embarrassment." Criticism of the USOC became so vocal that, in early 1988, its president had to assemble an outside task force to study the organization's problems. What happened between 1984 and 1988?[5]

Up until 1984, the separate federations had been poor and completely dependent on the USOC for funds. But in 1984, Miller stepped down. In that same year, the summer games in Los Angeles produced $150 million in profit, most of which went to the USOC. Each federation got $1.2 million. In addition, the climate surrounding amateur athletics was changing, and the federations became more entrepreneurial. They began lining up sponsors. The result was that the federations became less reliant on—and subservient to—the USOC. Efforts to organize joint marketing-licensing programs among the federations, for example, failed. Similarly, several of the federations blatantly defied the USOC's wishes concerning participation in Ted Turner's Goodwill Games in Moscow in 1986. The USOC thought participation would damage USOC sponsorship prospects but the federations went ahead anyway.

Between 1984 and 1988, the USOC had three executive directors. One lasted only nineteen days, complaining he had no choice but to quit, since he couldn't manage the internal squabbling within the USOC. Few experts expected the task force to come up with a sure-fire solution to bring order to this diverse, loosely knit organization, dominated by squabbling amateur sports groups.

But there is another view of conflict. This one argues that conflict improves an organization's effectiveness by stimulating change and improving the decision-making process. Let's look at the arguments underlying each position.[6]

The Traditional View

The **traditional view** of conflict assumes all conflicts are bad. Any conflict, therefore, has a negative impact on an organization's effectiveness.

The traditional approach treats conflict synonymously with such terms as *violence, destruction, and irrationality.* Consistent with this perspective, one of management's major responsibilities is to try to ensure that conflicts don't arise and, if they do, to act quickly to resolve them.

The Interactionist View

An organization totally devoid of conflict is probably also static, apathetic, and nonresponsive to the need for change. Conflict is functional when it initiates the search for new and better ways of doing things and undermines complacency within the organization. As Figure 15–1 illustrates, change doesn't just pop out of thin air. It needs a stimulus. That stimulus is conflict. There must be some dissatisfaction with the status quo before conditions are right to initiate change. So an organization that is completely content with itself—that is, one that is conflict free—has no internal forces to initiate change.

Obviously, the interactionist approach doesn't argue that *all* conflicts are functional. Certainly there are conflicts that negatively affect organizational effectiveness. In such cases, as in the traditional view, management should seek to reduce the conflict. The **interactionist view** implies a wider role for managers in dealing with conflict than does the traditional approach. The manager's job is to create an environment in which conflict is healthy but not allowed to run to pathological extremes. This is depicted in Figure 15–2. In the interactionist view, it is undesirable for conflict levels to be too high or too low. Situation B represents the optimal level. The area from A up to but not including B requires the manager to stimulate conflict to achieve full benefits from its functional properties. The area to the right of B demands resolution efforts to reduce the conflict level.

Managers seem to have little problem in identifying situations where conflict levels are too high and resolution efforts are necessary. But knowing when to stimulate conflict seems to be another

FIGURE 15–1 *Conflict-Survival Model*

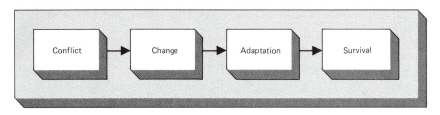

Stephen P. Robbins, *Managing Organizational Conflict: A Nontraditional Approach,* © 1974, p. 20. Reprinted by permission of Prentice Hall, Englewood Cliffs, N.J.

FIGURE 15–2 *Conflict and Organizational Effectiveness*

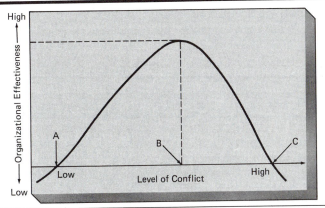

SITUATION	LEVEL OF CONFLICT	TYPE OF CONFLICT	ORGANIZATION'S INTERNAL CHARACTERISTICS	ORGANIZATIONAL EFFECTIVENESS OUTCOME
A	Low or None	Dysfunctional	Apathetic Stagnant Nonresponsive to change Lack of new ideas	Low
B	Optimal	Functional	Viable Self-critical Innovative	High
C	High	Dysfunctional	Disruptive Chaotic Uncooperative	Low

story. For many managers, the whole notion of purposely increasing conflict is difficult to accept. Table 15–1 is offered as a guide to managers in assessing situations where conflict-stimulation efforts may be needed. Affirmative answers to one or more of the questions in Table 15–1 suggest there may be a need for increased levels of conflict.

ANTICONFLICT VALUES PERMEATE OUR SOCIETY

It would be naive to assume that most managers today practice the interactionist approach. Although there is an increasing body of research that attests to the value of conflict, most managers still follow the traditional approach. The interactionist view, therefore, is undoubtedly prescriptive rather than descriptive.

TABLE 15–1   *Is Conflict Stimulation Needed?*

1. Are you surrounded by "yes people"?
2. Are subordinates afraid to admit ignorance and uncertainties to you?
3. Is there so much concentration by decision makers on reaching a compromise that they may lose sight of values, long-term objectives, or the organization's welfare?
4. Do managers believe that it is in their best interest to maintain the impression of peace and cooperation in their unit, regardless of the price?
5. Is there an excessive concern by decision makers for not hurting the feelings of others?
6. Do managers believe that popularity is more important for obtaining rewards than competence and high peformance?
7. Are managers unduly enamored of obtaining consensus in their decisions?
8. Do employees show unusually high resistance to change?
9. Is there a lack of new ideas?
10. Is there an unusually low level of employee turnover?

Stephen P. Robbins, " 'Conflict Management' and 'Conflict Resolution' Are Not Synonymous Terms," © 1978 by the Regents of the University of California. Reprinted from *California Management Review*, Vol. XXI, no. 2, p. 71 by permission of the Regents.

Why is it that managers are uncomfortable with conflict? The answer lies in the fact that tolerance of conflict is counter to most cultures in developed nations. The U.S., Canadian, and advanced European cultures have successfully engendered in their inhabitants a "fear of conflict" and a desire for at least the appearances of agreement and cooperation. Most organizations today reinforce this sentiment.

We are most susceptible to influence in the early years of our development. From the time we reach an age of understanding through the primary school years, we have been inculcated with the value of getting along with others and avoiding conflicts. The home, school, and church are three major institutions that have reinforced anticonflict values during our developing years. In addition, entire countries, such as the United States, have further fostered an anticonflict image by developing a national pride as a peace-loving nation. Multibillion-dollar expenditures are made each year for defense, not offense. Preparation to fight is made only because others may initiate force and therefore protection is justified.

We live in a society that has been built upon anticonflict values. Parents in the home, teachers and administrators in schools, teachings of the church, and authority figures in social groups all traditionally reinforce the belief that disagreement breeds discontent, which acts to dissolve common ties and leads eventually to destruction of the system. Certainly we should not be surprised that children raised to view all conflict as destructive will mature into adult managers who maintain and encourage the same values.

The traditional approach to conflict confuses conflict resolution with conflict management.[7] The "great peacemakers" who take this approach have made a weak basic assumption. They accept the notion that since conflict does exist in organizations, it *must* be in excess of the level that is desired. They assume that it is the manager's role to reduce tensions. Their conclusion then is to initiate actions to reduce conflict. But the goal of management is not harmony and cooperation—it is effective goal attainment! Elimination of conflict is not realistic in complex organizations, nor would such elimination be desirable. As one author has noted, "The individuals or groups who are most vocal in advocating 'harmony and happiness' in an environment devoid of conflict may only be protecting their vested interests in the *status quo*."[8]

SOURCES OF ORGANIZATIONAL CONFLICT

A number of diverse factors can precipitate organizational conflict. Some factors—such as incompatible personalities—are psychological. That is, the conflict is due to the individual characteristics of employees. All that this is really saying is that some people have difficulty getting along with each other and that this difficulty has nothing to do with their job requirements or formal interactions. Our concern, however, is with structurally derived conflicts. The following review reflects the most frequently cited structural sources of conflict.[9]

Mutual Task Dependence

Mutual task dependence refers to the extent to which two units in an organization depend upon each other for assistance, information, compliance, or other coordinative activities to complete their respective tasks effectively. This would describe, for instance, the interactions between the programming and market-analysis groups at a large FM radio station. They depend on each other to determine the right balance in their music format.

The linkage between mutual task dependence and conflict is not direct. What we know is that the former raises the intensity of interunit relations. When forced to interact, there is a definite escalation in the potential for conflict. However, the interaction does not have to lead to conflict. It can also lead to friendly and cooperative relations. If there is a history of antagonism between the units, mutual task dependence will intensify it. Similarly, it will intensify friendly relations as well.

One-Way Task Dependence

The prospects for conflict are much greater when one unit is unilaterally dependent on another. In contrast to mutual dependency, **one-way task dependence** means that the power balance has shifted. The prospects for conflict are decidedly higher because the dominant unit has little incentive to cooperate with the subordinate unit.

The conflict potential in one-way task dependence takes on greater meaning when we recognize that it is far more prevalent in organizations than is mutual dependence. Assembly lines have one-way dependency. This can lead to conflict when "one department's shoddy or incompleted work is left for the next department to complete, with the dependent unit in no position to retaliate."[10] Cooks and waitresses in restaurants are not mutually dependent—the waitress depends more on the cook than vice versa. In business firms, marketing is typically dependent on the credit department for approval of its sales. The medical examiner in a hospital is dependent on the laboratory unit for autopsy results. In fact, almost all line-staff relations are based on one-way task dependence. The staff is required to get along with the line, understand the line's problem, and justify its own existence, whereas none of these requirements is reciprocated by the line groups.

High Horizontal Differentiation

The greater the difference between units, the greater the likelihood of conflict. If units in the organization are highly differentiated, the tasks each does and the subenvironments each deals with will tend to be dissimilar. This, in turn, will lead to significant internal differences between the units. Evidence indicates, for instance, that high horizontal differentiation leads to different goals, time orientations, and management philosophies between units.[11] In a manufacturing firm, the people in production will tend to have a short-term perspective. In contrast, laboratory researchers in the same firm will tend to have a longer-term orientation. Why? Their training has instilled a different time perspective and the demands of their jobs accentuate these orientations. There is truth to the belief that marketing people and accounting people see the organization's "world" through different eyes. It is a natural by-product of specialization. Of course, high differentiation does not automatically lead to conflict. Other factors such as interdependence of tasks and rewards can act to retard or stimulate the latent potential for conflict.

LABOR-MANAGEMENT CONFLICTS

As soon as organizations begin to divide up work, hire specialists, and develop a hierarchical structure, the seeds of conflict are sown. Differentiation, by its very nature, creates a "them" versus "us" mentality. The historical conflict between labor and management, for instance, is embedded in differentiation. Labor-management conflicts have little to do with the inherent personality of union members or managers. The conflict resides in the role perception each holds of the other. An experiment conducted with representatives from both management and labor illustrates this point.[12]

Both the labor and management groups were given a photograph of an ordinary-looking man and asked to describe the individual in the photograph using a long list of personality characteristics. The only difference was that in half the cases the man pictured in the photograph was labeled as a plant manager and in the other half this same person was described as a union official. The descriptions were found to be radically different, depending on whether the man in the photograph was seen as "union" or "management" and, of course, whether the evaluator represented the "union" or "management." Management and labor representatives formed significantly different impressions, each viewing the other as less dependable and more intolerant of diverse points of view than members of their own group.

Low Formalization

Rules and regulations reduce conflict by minimizing ambiguity. High formalization establishes standardized ways for units to interact with each other. Role definitions are clear so that members of units know what to expect from the other. Conversely, where formalization is low, the potential for jurisdictional disputes increases. Departments, for example, jockey for resources and other power bases. Interactions between units, because they are not regulated formally, are characterized by negotiation. In this type of climate, conflicts between units are likely to flourish. Conflicts can still breed in highly formalized structures; however, they are likely to be more regulated and less subversive. As in a hockey game, the rules do not eliminate conflicts. Rather, they allow spectators to better anticipate when conflicts are likely to break out.

Dependence on Common Scarce Resources

Conflict potential is enhanced when two or more units depend on a common pool of scarce resources such as physical space, equipment, operating funds, capital budget allocations, or centralized staff services such as the typing pool. The potential is increased further if unit members perceive that their individual needs cannot be met from the available resource pool when other units' needs are satisfied. When units perceive the situation as "zero-sum"—anything you get comes out of my hide—you can expect interunit conflicts, empire building, monopolizing of resources, and other behaviors that are likely to decrease organizational effectiveness.

Differences in Evaluation Criteria and Reward Systems

The more the evaluations and rewards of management emphasize the separate performance of each department rather than their combined performance, the greater the conflict. We see evidence of this in organizations all the time.

The preference of production units for long, economical runs with its accompanying rewards are in opposition to the rewards provided to sales units for quick delivery to good customers. Production is rewarded for fewer runs that minimize costs, whereas sales is rewarded for speed, which frequently entails the need for a greater number of runs. Similarly, sales is rewarded for selling as much as possible. The credit unit, however, is typically rewarded for minimizing losses. This objective is achieved by curtailing sales to marginal accounts. Many a sales manager spends hours each week trying to convince the credit executive in his or her firm that what the credit department considers a financially unworthy customer is actually "marginally acceptable."

Line-staff conflicts can also stem from differing evaluation criteria and reward systems. Staff units value change, for this is the major way in which they justify their existence. The systems department that suggests no changes is a likely target for elimination. But line units value stability. To line units, change has undesirable repercussions for their operations. Not only is change inconvenient, but it also degrades current methods. Any change suggested by a staff unit implies that the current methods are inadequate, an obviously degrading implication. For further evidence of the conflict that staff units can create, spend a few weeks as an auditor or a quality-control inspector in a manufacturing firm. You don't develop a lot of cooperative relations with personnel in units when you are evaluated and rewarded for finding errors in their work!

Participative Decision Making

The evidence finds that joint decision making, where those who will be affected by a decision are made part of the decision-making body, promotes conflict.[13] The participative process permits a greater opportunity for the expression of existing disputes and allows more occasions for disagreements to arise. This is especially likely to occur when true value differences exist among the participants. The research suggests that the high interaction incurred in participation acts to solidify differences more than facilitate coordination and cooperation. The result is greater differences of opinion and greater awareness of conflict. In many cases, the conflict intensity may be no greater after participation than before, but it tends to move the conflict from latent to overt.

Heterogeneity of Members

The more heterogeneous members are, the less likely they are to work smoothly and cooperatively together. It's been found that personal dissimilarities, such as background, values, education, age, and social patterns lower the probability of interpersonal rapport between unit representatives and in turn decreases the amount of collaboration between their respective units.

Consistent with this notion, we would expect the average tenure of a group to be inversely related to conflict. That is, the longer the group members have worked with each other, the more likely they are to get along well together. Research confirms this hypothesis. For instance, in a school setting, it was found that conflict was highest among the younger and shortest-tenure faculty members and lowest among the older members.[14] We could expect, therefore, that recently established units with all new personnel or those units that have experienced high turnover among members should be more conflict prone.

Status Incongruence

Conflict is stimulated where incongruencies occur in status gradings or from alterations in the status hierarchy. For instance, an increase in conflict was found when the degree to which personal status, or how one perceives oneself, and the level of departmental representation differed in rank ordering of status dimensions.[15] These dimensions include length of service, age, education, and pay. Similarly, in an organization where it was generally acknowledged that research had more prestige than engineering, patterns of initiation and influence were accepted as long as they followed this status ordering. But when this order was abandoned, as for example when low-status industrial engineers needed to direct the higher-status researchers in the implementation of tests, conflict resulted.[16] Further evidence that status inconsistencies lead to conflict is found in William Whyte's classic study of the restaurant industry.[17] Conflict was found to result when low-status waitresses gave "orders" to high-status cooks. Owing to the incongruity between initiation and status, cooks were being perceived in a lower-prestige grade.

Role Dissatisfaction

Closely akin to status incongruence is role dissatisfaction. Role dissatisfaction can come from a number of sources, one of which is status incongruence. When someone feels that she deserves a promotion to reflect her record of accomplishments, she suffers from both role dissatisfaction and perceived status incongruence. In this section, however, we want to emphasize that the ways in which people perceive themselves in their positions can significantly affect their performance and thus the potential for conflict between them and their peers in their own and adjoining units.

When people accept a role, they bring to it a set of hopes and aspirations. When these expectations are not met—for instance, when their work does not prove challenging or the rewards they receive are seen as inadequate—these individuals may display their frustrations in a number of directions. Some resign. Some reduce the effort they exert on the job. Still others choose to fight. This last group can become continuous conflict stimulators—looking for problems, spreading rumors, twisting and distorting facts to instigate disturbances, and similar actions. Such people, and all large organizations have at least one, seem to enjoy upsetting the system. To the degree that they establish allies in their cause, they can become a major source of conflict.

Communication Distortions

One frequently cited source of conflict is communication difficulties. An obvious case is vertical communications. As information is passed up and down the hierarchy, it is susceptible to ambiguity and distortion. But distortions also occur at the horizontal level. For instance, one researcher argued that the less the differing units know about each other's jobs, the less the collaboration that will take place. And this lack of knowledge can lead to unreasonable interunit demands.[18] Animosities observed by your author between a county welfare department and other county agencies in a southern California community appeared to be attributable directly to ignorance on the part of each agency as to the nature of duties of other agencies. In contrast, smooth coordination and relations existed where county employees who did not work for the welfare agency were familiar with the welfare department's responsibilities and contributions.

Semantic difficulties are a frequent problem in organizations. They impede communication essential for cooperative efforts between units. Semantic difficulties can be attributed to the different training, background, and socialization processes that members of units have undergone. It has been reported that the difference in training of purchasing agents and engineers contributes to their conflict.[19] As with physicians and professional hospital administrators, their academic training and orientations differ significantly. Differences in training develop disparate vocabularies and jargon, which impede the effective movement of ideas.

Pragmatism suggests that we also mention that a source of communicative conflicts is the willful withholding of information by one unit from another. As we have noted in previous chapters, information can facilitate the attainment of power. It is only realistic, therefore, to acknowledge that when important information is deliberately kept secret, conflicts can ensue.

If inadequate, distorted, or ambiguous information is a source of conflict, the existence of complete or perfect knowledge might be expected to result in little or no conflict. Interestingly, it does not seem to work that way. Studies demonstrate that interdepartmental conflict increases when departments possess a great deal of knowledge of each other's activities.[20] Why is that so? Complete knowledge makes each party's self-interest fully visible and reveals any and all inequities. Imperfect knowledge, on the other hand, clouds self-interest, diminishes disparities, and makes coordination easier. We can conclude that communication extremes can be sources of conflict. Inadequate or unclear communications stimulate conflict. So, too, does perfect or complete information.

RESOLUTION TECHNIQUES

When the forces of conflict are too great, we say that it is dysfunctional. It has a negative impact on organizational effectiveness. Something needs to be done, therefore, to bring the conflict down to an acceptable level. The following represent structural techniques for reducing conflict intensity.

Superordinate Goals

A **superordinate goal** is a common goal, held by two or more units that is compelling and highly appealing and cannot be attained by the resources of any single unit separately.[21]

A superordinate goal initiates with a definition of a shared goal and the recognition that without the help of the contending parties it cannot be attained. Superordinate goals are highly valued, unattainable by any one group alone, and commonly sought. They must, to be effective, supersede other goals that the units may have individually. They act to reduce conflict by requiring the disagreeing parties to work together in achieving those goals they mutually seek.

After extensive research on resolution techniques, one researcher has concluded that in those instances where conflict has developed from mutually incompatible goals, the use of superordinate goals should increase cooperation.[22] The cooperative environment grows as effort is directed away from concern with separate and independent units to recognition that the conflicting units are part of a larger group, a synergy developing from the collaboration of forces.

A union-management dispute illustrates the functioning of the superordinate goal. In times of economic plenty, unions are frequently adamant in their demands. But in cases where an organization's survival has been seriously threatened by economic pressures, some unions have accepted pay reductions to keep the organization in business. Once the crisis is overcome, demand for higher wages returns. A compelling and highly valued goal—survival—has preceded other individual goals and has temporarily resolved the labor conflict. Evidence supports that superordinate goals, when used cumulatively, develop long-term "peacemaking" potential, thereby reinforcing dependency and developing collaboration.

Reduce Interdependence Between Units

When mutual and one-way interdependence creates conflicts, reduction of this interdependence should be considered as a possible solution. Buffers, for example, can be introduced to reduce interdependence. If the output of department X is department Y's input, then Y is dependent on X. When X is behind schedule, Y will also look bad. One solution involves creating an inventory of X's output as a buffer. The interdependency of X and Y is thus reduced.

Coordination positions can also be effective in reducing inter-dependence between units. On occasions, when industrial firms have interunit conflicts, such as between accounting and engineering departments, they will seek an individual with both an accounting and an engineering background and then create the position of coordinator for him. Because he speaks the language of both, he functions as an integrator between the separate units.

Expanding Resources

When conflict is predicated upon the scarcity of a resource, the easiest manner in which to resolve the confrontation, and the one most satisfying to the conflicting parties, is through expansion of the available resources. Although it may be most undesirable to other parties outside the conflict, its greatest strength as a resolution tool is in its ability to allow each conflicting party a victory.

If the purchasing department in a moderately sized school district is allocated only $800 for monthly salary increases, to be distributed among the department's four members, any individual's gain above $200 is at the expense of others in the unit. If each of the four departmental members expects a $300-a-month raise, then there is a conflict: demand for the fixed resources exceeds its supply. One solution is to allocate more money for salary adjustments. An increase of $400 in the allocation would resolve the conflict.

Expanding resources as a resolution method is extremely successful because it leaves the conflicting parties satisfied. But its use is restricted by the nature of its inherent limitations: organizational resources rarely exist in such quantity as to be easily expanded.

Mutual Problem Solving

Mutual problem solving has been described as the soundest method for resolving intergroup conflicts.[23] This technique requires the conflicting parties to come face to face with the underlying causes for their conflict and share responsibility for seeing that the solution works. The purpose is to solve *the* problem rather than merely to accommodate different points of view.

Mutual problem solving requires that the conflicting units have "the potential to achieve a better solution through collaboration."[24] Although this may be a difficult requirement to meet, where it exists, it relies on seeking fundamental points of difference rather than on determining who is right, who is wrong, who wins, or who loses. Further, through sharing and communicating, the problem is mutually defined. The participants, or at least their representatives, consider the full range of alternatives, and similarities in views become emphasized. Through this process, the causes of doubt and misunderstanding that underlie the conflict become outwardly evident.

Problem solving additionally attempts to "accentuate the positive" by highlighting the commonly held views of the parties. This recognizes an often overlooked side of any conflict—that there exists in almost every instance some issues on which the dissenting parties are in agreement. These similarities are too frequently bypassed and result in what has been referred to as Gresham's law of conflict,[25] which states that similar views and those that work to increase cooperation are pushed out by those views that accentuate differences. Bad forces push out the good. Problem solving seeks to emphasize the similar views and avoid those that breed a hostile climate.

The attempt to resolve differences through the mutual problem-solving approach as described is frequently used and, unfortunately, evidence indicates that it frequently fails. How often we hear someone who is aware of the existence of a conflict say, "What they need to do is sit down and discuss the situation." But problem solving is limited in the types of conflict with which it can deal effectively. Its failures are closely related to its misapplication. Clearly, it is most successful in semantic conflicts. Oppositions that develop from misunderstandings lend themselves to the in-depth analysis of problem solving, definition of terms, and thorough understanding of the opposing parties' ideas.

Appeals Systems

The resolving of conflicts can be handled by creating formal channels for grievances to be heard and acted upon. If an employee or group of employees believe that their rights have been jeopardized by the actions of a superior or a peer, an **appeals system** provides the right of formal redress. The appeal may be made to one's boss's boss, an executive several levels higher in the organization, or a third-party arbitrator.

Unionized organizations present an excellent illustration of the appeals technique. In their grievance procedure, unions have established an elaborate appeals system to resolve conflicts with management. If an aggrieved union member cannot find satisfaction through discussion with a superior, he or she may proceed to appeal the grievance upward through the employing organization; a frequent route in an industrial firm may include presenting the case to the area supervisor, shift supervisor, plant superintendent, industrial relations manager, plant manager, and eventually a neutral, third-party arbitrator, if necessary.

A few organizations, however, have created the position of ombudsman to arbitrate differences. For example, colleges and universities have used the ombudsman to hear and resolve problems among and between faculty, students, and staff. The ombudsman typically begins by using the mutual-problem-solving technique. If this fails, the ombudsman may attempt negotiation or suggest that a senior administrator in the organization—one with authority over both of the conflicting parties—resolve the differences by enforcing a solution.

Formal Authority

The authority that superiors have over the conflicting parties is important enough and its usage spread so widely that it can be singled out as a separate resolution technique.

A disagreement between two nurses that cannot be resolved between them is taken to their supervisor or head nurse for a decision. Similarly, when a conflict develops between sales and production units within a manufacturing firm, it is referred to the two immediate executives responsible for each function and who possess the authority to resolve the differences. If an agreement cannot be reached at this level, their mutual superior will act as the ultimate judge, and in the majority of cases, the authority of the superior will be accepted by both parties.

Individuals in organizations, with rare exception, recognize and accept the authority of their superiors as an acceptable way of resolving conflicts. Although they may not be in agreement with these decisions, they abide by them. Thus, formal authority is highly successful in achieving reductions in conflict.

Increasing Interaction

All other things held equal, the more people interact with each other, the more likely they are to find common interests and bonds that can facilitate cooperation.[26] Certainly, if parties with distinctly opposing values are forced to interact regularly, there is a high probability of conflict. But our point is that continued interaction should reduce the conflict. It may never be as low as management might desire, but the direction should be downward. This can be achieved through transference or exchange of unit members.

By transferring people into or out of a unit, we change its internal structure. The forces that caused conflict in that unit or between that unit and other units may be dissipated by "shaking up" the internal common bonds. Transferring someone out of his or her unit and into an adversary unit can cross-fertilize those areas in conflict and force contact between members.

Cross-fertilization may be achieved more effectively by requiring some personnel in the conflicting units to exchange jobs. Previous organizational barriers are often reduced. A manager at a production plant for a major U.S. aluminum company used employee exchange to reduce conflict in this accounting department. The plant controller attributed the dysfunctional behavior between the general accounting and cost accounting sections to the lack of an information flow between each group. The two units were frequently at odds with each other. To reduce misunderstandings, he had the supervisors of both sections switch jobs for a six-month period. The move expanded the perspective of each supervisor and promoted greater understanding and reduced interunit conflict as the modified views filtered down through the two sections.

Organizationwide Evaluation Criteria and Reward Systems

If separatism in evaluations and rewards creates conflicts, management should consider performance measures that evaluate and reward units for cooperation. Elimination of zero-sum situations should be beneficial. Ensuring, for instance, that quality-control, auditing, and other policing functions are evaluated for their preventive contributions rather than for their success in finding errors will reduce conflicts. Additionally, instituting an organizationwide profit-sharing or bonus plan should assist in reminding people that the organization's primary concern is with the effectiveness of the entire system, not with any singular unit.

Merging Conflicting Units

A final suggestion for resolving conflict is for one of the conflicting units to expand its boundaries and absorb the source of its irritation. This merger technique is exemplified by the solution applied to the conflicts generated when a college of business must rely heavily for its curriculum upon the economics courses offered in the economics department. Historically, economics was located in the college of arts and sciences or liberal arts. The philosophical conflicts that often develop between business and economics can be reconciled through expansion of the business program to include the economics department. The result is the frequently encountered "College of Business and Economics." Elementary and secondary school systems utilize this same technique when they allow persons critical of the curriculum to participate in the review and evaluation of the system's programs and policies. They coopt their critics by merging them into the system.

STIMULATION TECHNIQUES

The interactionist view recognizes that conflict may, at times, be too low as well as too high. When it's too low, managers need to stimulate opposition—to create functional conflict.

Unfortunately, from a theoretical standpoint, we know a great deal more about how to resolve conflicts effectively than we know about stimulating them. This is simply a result of the fact that the notion of stimulating conflict is a relatively recent idea and is just beginning to receive attention from organizational researchers. The following discussion contain some potential stimulation techniques. They have been derived from reviewing the sources of conflict presented earlier in this chapter. They are far more sketchy than our previous discussion of resolution methods; however, do not confuse brevity with unimportance. Stimulation techniques are not more or less important than their resolution counterparts—we just know less about them.

Communications

Managers can manipulate communication messages and channels in such ways as to stimulate conflict. Ambiguous or threatening messages encourage conflict. Information that a plant will close, that a department is to be eliminated, or that a layoff is to be incurred will accelerate conflict intensity. These kinds of messages can be transmitted through the formal authority hierarchy or informal channels. The latter includes all loosely knit and ill-structured networks. "Rumors on the grapevine" refer to unsubstantiated communications following the informal channels. By careful selection of the messages to be distributed through the grapevine and the individuals to carry them, the manager can increase conflict. He can purposely manipulate receivers and message content to add, negate, or make ambiguous the communications that are carried by formal means. How, you may ask, would this produce beneficial results for the organization? It might, for example, reduce apathy, force members to confront their differences, or encourage the reevaluation of current procedures and stimulate new ideas.

Heterogeneity

One way in which to "shake up" a stagnant unit is to add one or more individuals whose background, experience, and values vary significantly from those currently held by members in a unit. Heterogeneity can be synthetic as well as real. The infiltrator may play the role of the proverbial "devil's advocate," who though sharing similar views with other unit members, is assigned the task of questioning, attacking, inquiring and otherwise resisting any homogeneity of views. Either way, the status quo has been disturbed by introducing heterogeneous people.

Competition

Management can stimulate conflict by creating competitive situations between units. Of course, where the stakes in the competition are zero sum, you can expect the conflict to be that much more intense. For instance, when city fire units compete against each other to win the "best firehouse" award, the result is generally a more effective firefighting organization. Equipment is kept in top condition, units respond rapidly to alarms, and teamwork is high. Many companies that continually promote sales contests within their sales staffs believe that this competition leads to a more effective sales force.

Changing the structure by increasing horizontal differentiation has been suggested as an excellent way to create conflict.[27] The example is offered of a school of business made up of just a few departments—accounting, economics, and business administration. The last department included all the faculty who taught management, marketing, and finance courses. This department of business administration was large, having thirty-two members, with a single chairperson, who reported to the dean. When a new dean was hired, he perceived apathy. Faculty members were comfortable with their structural arrangement, sufficiently so that many had become stagnant. As a result, the dean began entertaining the idea of splitting up the business administration department into separate departments of management, marketing, and finance, each with eight to twelve members and a chairperson. The dean's logic is fully consistent with the interactionist view and the value of stimulating conflict. By increasing horizontal differentiation, each area of specialization will be more homogeneous. But there will be differences between units. They will be forced to compete with each other for resources, students, faculty and the like. If you believe in Darwin's survival-of-the-fittest doctrine, then you should find structural decisions like this to be an attractive conflict-stimulation device.

SUMMARY

Conflict is a process in which an effort is purposely made by one person or unit to block another that results in frustrating the attainment of the other's goals or the furthering of his or her interests. Views toward conflict can be labeled as traditional and interactionist. The traditional views all conflict as bad. The interactionist encourages conflict. The interactionist perspective is currently in vogue among theorists, but the traditional perspective dominates in practice.

The most frequently cited structural sources of conflict are mutual task dependence, one-way task dependence, high horizontal differentiation, low formalization, dependence on common scarce resources, differences in evaluation criteria and reward systems, participative decision making, heterogeneity of members, status incongruence, role dissatisfaction, and communication distortions.

Resolution techniques include superordinate goals, reducing interdependence between units, expansion of resources, mutual problem solving, appeals systems, formal authority, increased interaction, organizationwide evaluation criteria and reward systems, and merging of conflicting units. Stimulation of conflict can be achieved by manipulating communication messages and channels, creating heterogeneous units, or creating competition between units.

FOR REVIEW AND DISCUSSION

1. Contrast the traditional and interactionist views of conflict.
2. What forces make the traditional perspective dominant in practice?
3. In what ways can conflict be functional?
4. How does *conflict management* differ from *conflict resolution?*
5. "Units within an organization will always have divergent goals; therefore, all organizations will be characterized by the presence of conflict." Do you agree or disagree? Discuss.
6. Explain the wide prevalence of line-staff conflicts.
7. How does formalization affect conflict?
8. What is the relationship between participative decision making and conflict?
9. What are superordinate goals? Give examples of such goals in three different organizations.
10. "An organization's strategy, if it is clear and widely dispersed, acts as a superordinate goal and retards dysfunctional conflicts." Do you agree or disagree? Discuss.
11. Compare appeals systems and formal authority as conflict-resolution techniques.
12. Give some examples of ways in which to stimulate conflict.

13. What is the relationship between clarity of communication and conflict?
14. What relationships do you see between an organization's structure, change, creativity, and conflict?
15. "Bureaucracies are mechanisms that simultaneously resolve and stimulate structural conflicts." Do you agree or disagree? Discuss.

NOTES

[1] Kenneth W. Thomas and Warren H. Schmidt, "A Survey of Managerial Interests with Respect to Conflict," *Academy of Management Journal*, June 1976, pp. 315–18.

[2] James D. Thompson, "Organizational Management of Conflict," *Administrative Science Quarterly*, March 1960, p. 389.

[3] Kenneth W. Thomas, "Conflict and Conflict Management," in M. D. Dunnette, ed., *Handbook of Industrial and Organizational Psychology* (Chicago: Rand McNally, 1976), p. 889.

[4] Morton Deutsch, *The Resolution of Conflict: Constructive and Destructive Processes* (New Haven, Conn.: Yale University Press, 1973), p. 10.

[5] This is based on Mark Ivey, "If There Were a Gold Medal for Bickering, the U.S. Would Win," *Business Week*, March 21, 1988, pp. 106–8.

[6] This section, and significant parts of this chapter, are based on Stephen P. Robbins, *Managing Organizational Conflict: A Nontraditional Approach* (Englewood Cliffs, N.J.: Prentice Hall, 1974).

[7] Stephen P. Robbins, "'Conflict Management' and 'Conflict Resolution' Are Not Synonymous Terms," *California Management Review*, Winter 1978, pp. 67–75.

[8] Leonard Rico, "Organizational Conflict: A Framework for Reappraisal," *Industrial Management Review*, Fall 1964, p. 67.

[9] A number of these sources were categorized originally in Richard E. Walton and John M. Dutton, "The Management of Interdepartmental Conflict: A Model and Review," *Administrative Science Quarterly*, March 1969, pp. 73–84.

[10] Howard E. Aldrich, *Organizations and Environments* (Englewood Cliffs, N.J.: Prentice Hall, 1979), p. 94.

[11] Paul R. Lawrence and Jay W. Lorsch, *Organization and Environment* (Homewood, Ill.: Irwin, 1969).

[12] Mason Haire, "Role Perceptions in Labor-Management Relations: An Experimental Approach," *Industrial and Labor Relations Review*, January 1955, pp. 204–16.

[13] See Meyer Zald, "Power Balance and Staff Conflict in Correctional Institutions," *Administrative Science Quarterly*, June 1962, p. 22–49; and George Strauss and Eliezer Rosenstein, "Workers Participation: A Critical View," *Industrial Relations*, February 1970, pp. 197–214.

[14] Ronald G. Corwin, "Patterns of Organizational Conflict," *Administrative Science Quarterly*, December 1969, pp. 507–20.

[15] John A. Seiler, "Diagnosing Interdepartmental Conflict," *Harvard Business Review*, September–October 1963, pp. 121–32.

[16] Ibid.

[17] William F. Whyte, *Human Relations in the Restaurant Industry* (New York: McGraw-Hill, 1948).

[18] E. J. Miller, "Technology, Territory, and Time," *Human Relations*, August 1959, pp. 243–72.

[19] George Strauss, "Work-Flow Frictions, Interfunctional Rivalry, and Professionalism: A Case Study of Purchasing Agents," *Human Organization*, Summer 1964, pp. 137–49.

[20] See, for example, Richard E. Walton, John M. Dutton, and Thomas P. Cafferty, "Organizational Context and Interdepartmental Conflict," *Administrative Science Quarterly*, December 1969, pp. 522–42.

[21] Muzafer Sherif, "Experiments on Group Conflict and Cooperation," in Harold J. Leavitt and Louis R. Pondy, eds., *Readings in Managerial Psychology* (Chicago: University of Chicago Press, 1964), p. 410.

[22] Muzafer Sherif, *In Common Predicament: Social Psychology of Intergroup Conflict and Cooperation* (Boston: Houghton Mifflin, 1966), p. 93.

[23] Robert R. Blake, Herbert A. Shepard, and Jane S. Mouton, *Managing Intergroup Conflict in Industry* (Houston: Gulf Publishing, 1964), pp. 99–100.

[24] Ibid., p. 86.

[25] James S. Coleman, *Community Conflict* (New York: Free Press, 1957), p. 14.

[26] Sherif, "Experiments on Group Conflict and Cooperation," pp. 408–21.

[27] James L. Gibson, John M. Ivancevich, and James H. Donnelley, Jr., *Organizations: Behavior, Structure, Processes*, 5th ed. (Dallas: Business Publications, 1985), pp. 311–12.

16

MANAGING

ORGANIZATIONAL

CULTURE

AFTER READING THIS CHAPTER, YOU SHOULD BE ABLE TO:

1 Define organizational culture.
2 List organizational culture's key characteristics.
3 Differentiate the dominant culture from subcultures.
4 Identify characteristics of a strong culture.
5 Explain how a culture is sustained over time.
6 Describe how employees learn an organization's culture.
7 Explain how culture affects the success of mergers and acquisitions.
8 List conditions that favor the successful changing of a culture.

Introduction

THE TEXAS INSTRUMENT CULTURE

Texas Instruments has developed its reputation around state-of-the-art technology.[1] This is the company that invented the integrated circuit, the building block of today's advanced electronics. TI's current product line includes semiconductors, defense electronics, computers, and industrial automation systems. To further attest to its technology focus, ten of TI's top eleven executives, including its CEO, Jerry Junkins, have engineering backgrounds.

Since taking over as CEO in 1985, Junkins has sought to redirect TI's organizational culture from its long-centered, singular focus on technology to one with a stronger marketing orientation. The reason? Junkins recognized that, as a product-driven company, TI's business units were tending to optimize their internal organization, forcing customers to adapt to TI. While this approach might lead to short-term efficiencies in operations, it risks losing touch with the customer and eventually losing sales. Junkins wants TI to adapt to the needs of its customers.

TI is a company with 77,000 employees and sales of $5.6 billion a year. Many of these employees have been with TI for twenty years or more. The TI they know and love is a product-driven company. It emphasizes and rewards technical competence and new product generation. Can Junkins change TI's culture to make it more market-oriented? If it can be changed, how should Junkins go about it?

This chapter introduces the idea that organizations have personalities. We call them organizational cultures. We show how cultures are created and sustained and consider their impact on an organization's effectiveness. However, our main objective in this chapter is to address whether managers like Jerry Junkins can actually change their organization's culture and, if so, how.

WHAT IS ORGANIZATIONAL CULTURE?

There is no shortage of definitions for organizational culture. It's been described, for example, as "the dominant values espoused by an organization,"[2] "the philosophy that guides an organization's policy toward employees and customers,"[3] "the way things are done around here,"[4] and "the basic assumptions and beliefs that are shared by members of an organization."[5] A closer look at the wide array of definitions does uncover a central theme—**organizational culture** refers to a system of *shared meaning*. In every organization there are patterns of beliefs, symbols, rituals, myths, and practices that have evolved over time.[6] These, in turn, create common understandings among members as to what the organization is and how its members should behave.

Culture implies the existence of certain dimensions or characteristics that are closely associated and interdependent. But most researchers make no effort to specify these characteristics. Rather, they talk of culture as some abstract "milieu." If culture exists, and we argue that it does, it should have distinct dimensions that can be defined and measured. Toward that end, we propose that there are ten characteristics that when mixed and matched tap the essence of an organization's culture. While the whole of organizational culture maybe somewhat different from the summation of its parts, the following represent the key characteristics along which cultures differ.[7]

1. *Individual initiative.* The degree of responsibility, freedom, and independence that individuals have.

2. *Risk tolerance.* The degree to which employees are encouraged to be aggressive, innovative, and risk-seeking.

3. *Direction.* The degree to which the organization creates clear objectives and performance expectations.

4. *Integration.* The degree to which units within the organization are encouraged to operate in a coordinated manner.

5. *Management support.* The degree to which managers provide clear communication, assistance, and support to their subordinates.

6. *Control.* The number of rules and regulations, and the amount of direct supervision that are used to oversee and control employee behavior.

7. *Identity.* The degree to which members identify with the organization as a whole rather than with their particular work group or field of professional expertise.

8. *Reward system.* The degree to which reward allocations (i.e., salary increases, promotions) are based on employee performance criteria in contrast to seniority, favoritism, and so on.

9. *Conflict tolerance.* The degree to which employees are encouraged to air conflicts and criticisms openly.

10. *Communication patterns.* The degree to which organizational communications are restricted to the formal hierarchy of authority.

These ten characteristics include both structural and behavioral dimensions. For example, management support is a measure of leadership behavior. Most of these dimensions, however, are closely intertwined with an organization's design. To illustrate, the more routine an organization's technology and the more centralized its decision-making process, the less individual initiative employees in that organization will have. Similarly, functional structures create cultures with more formal communication patterns than do simple or matrix structures. Close analysis would also reveal that integration is essentially an indicator of horizontal interdependence. What this means is that organizational cultures are not just reflections of their members' attitudes and personalities. A large part of an organization's culture can be directly traced to structurally related variables.

PEPSICO VERSUS J. C. PENNEY

PepsiCo and J. C. Penney are both large and successful organizations, but their cultures are clearly different. This can be seen in the diverse way in which they handle poor performance by their employees.[8]

"Everyone knows that if the results aren't there, you had better have your résumé up to date," commented a former PepsiCo manager. Compare that with this statement by a J. C. Penney manager: "Some workers expect us to be a papa and mama and aren't motivated enough to help themselves."

At PepsiCo, rewards are highly contingent on performance. Failure results in punishment. In contrast, at J. C. Penney, poor performers are likely to be treated with consideration and given easier jobs.

DO ORGANIZATIONS HAVE UNIFORM CULTURES?

Organizational culture represents a common perception held by the organization's members. This was made explicit when we defined culture as a system of *shared* meaning. We should expect, therefore, that individuals with different backgrounds or at different levels in the organization will tend to describe the organization's culture in similar terms.

Acknowledgment that organizational culture has common properties does not mean, however, that there cannot be subcultures within any given culture. Most large organizations have a dominant culture and numerous sets of subcultures.[9]

A **dominant culture** expresses the **core values** that are shared by a majority of the organization's members. When we talk about an *organization's* culture, we are referring to its dominant culture. It is this macroview of culture that gives an organization its distinct personality.

Subcultures tend to develop in large organizations to reflect common problems, situations, or experiences that members face. These subcultures can form vertically or horizontally.[10] When one product division of a conglomerate has a culture unique from that of other divisions of the organization, a vertical subculture exists. When a specific set of functional specialists—such as accountants or purchasing personnel—have a set of common shared understandings, a horizontal subculture is formed. Of course, any group in an organization can develop a subculture. For the most part, however, subcultures tend to be defined by departmental designations or geographical separation. The purchasing department, for example, can have a subculture that is uniquely shared by members of that department. It will include the core values of the dominant culture plus additional values unique to members of the purchasing department. Similarly, an office or unit of the organization that is physically separated from the organization's main operations may take on a different personality. Again, the core values are essentially retained but modified to reflect the separated unit's distinct situation.

If organizations had no dominant culture and were comprised only of numerous subcultures, the influence of culture on organizational effectiveness would be far more ambiguous. Why? Because there would be no consistency of perceptions or behavior. It is the "shared meaning" aspect of organizational culture that makes it such a potent concept. But we cannot ignore the reality that many organizations also have distinct subcultures.

CULTURE AND ORGANIZATIONAL EFFECTIVENESS

How does culture affect organizational effectiveness? To answer this question, we need to first differentiate strong cultures from weak ones.

A **strong culture** is characterized by the organization's core values being intensely held, clearly ordered, and widely shared. The more members that accept the core values, agree on their order of importance, and are highly committed to them, the stronger the culture is. Organizations that are young or have constant turnover among their members, almost by definition, will have a weak culture because members will not have shared enough experiences to create common meanings.[11] This shouldn't be interpreted to imply that all mature organizations with a stable membership will have strong cultures. The core values must also be intensely held.

Religious organizations, cults, and Japanese companies are examples of organizations that have very strong cultures.[12] When a James Jones can entice nine hundred members of his Guyana cult to commit mass suicide at Jonestown, we see a degree of sharedness and an intensity of values that allow for extremely high behavioral control. Of course, the same strong cultural influences that can lead to the tragedy of a Jonestown can be directed positively to create immensely successful organizations like IBM, Mary Kay Cosmetics, and Sony.

Maybe the ultimate illustration of a strong culture was that belonging to the old AT&T. Prior to its breakup in 1984, AT&T had a culture uncommon not only in its singleness of purpose and its creation of sense of family but also in its demonstrable contribution to the corporation's success.[13]

AT&T's regulated monopoly of the U.S. telephone market allowed it to focus singularly on the goal of providing the best service possible regardless of cost. Its culture reflected this goal. It emphasized lifelong employment, consensus decision making, communication through hierarchical levels, and avoidance of risk. These cultural values were intensely held, clearly ordered, and widely shared. They clearly met our definition of a strong culture. This strength facilitated AT&T's effectiveness as long as it remained a regulated monopoly. But after the courts broke up AT&T, the company entered the telecommunications industry where it had to compete against the likes of IBM, Xerox, and the Japanese. In this new competitive environment, AT&T's strong culture became a liability. Why? Because the company needed a different, more innovative and risk-taking culture; but strong cultures, like AT&T's, are harder to change than weak ones.

If the culture is strong, how will it influence the organization's effectiveness? The answer is: Effectiveness requires that an organization's culture, strategy, environment, and technology be aligned.[14] The stronger an organization's culture, the more important it is that the culture fit properly with these variables.

The successful organization will achieve a good *external fit*—its culture will be shaped to its strategy and environment. Market-driven strategies, for instance, are more appropriate in dynamic environments and will require a culture that emphasizes individual initiative, risk taking, high integration, tolerance of conflict, and high horizontal communication. In contrast, product-driven strategies focus on efficiency, work best in stable environments, and are more likely to be successful when the organization's culture is high in control and minimizes risk and conflict. Successful organizations will also seek a good *internal fit*, with their culture properly matched to their technology. As noted earlier in the chapter, routine technologies provide stability and work well when linked with a culture that emphasizes centralized decision making and limited individual initiative. Nonroutine technologies, on the other hand, require adaptability and are best when matched with cultures that encourage individual initiative and downplay control.

CULTURE: A SUBSTITUTE FOR FORMALIZATION?

Another result of a strong culture is that it increases behavioral consistency.[15] It conveys to employees what behaviors they should engage in. It tells employees things like the acceptability of absenteeism.[16] Some cultures encourage employees to use their sick days and do little to discourage absenteeism. Not surprisingly, such organizations have much higher absenteeism rates than those organizations where not showing up for work—regardless of reason—is seen as letting your co-workers down.

Given that strong cultures increase behavioral consistency, it's only logical to conclude that they can be a powerful means of implicit control and can act as a substitute for formalization.

We know how formalization's rules and regulations act to regulate employee behavior. High formalization in an organization creates predictability, orderliness, and consistency. A strong culture achieves the same end without any need for written documentation. Moreover, a strong culture may be more potent than any formal structural controls because culture controls the mind and soul as well as the body.

It seems entirely appropriate to view formalization and culture as two different roads to a common destination. The stronger an organization's culture, the less management need be concerned with developing formal rules and regulations to guide employee behavior. Those guides will have been internalized in employees when they accept the organization's culture.

CREATING, SUSTAINING, AND TRANSMITTING CULTURE

An organization's culture doesn't pop out of thin air. Once established, it rarely fades away. What forces influence the creation of a culture? What reinforces and sustains them once they are in place? How do new employees learn their organization's culture? The following summarizes what we've learned about how cultures are created, sustained, and transmitted.

How a Culture Begins

An organization's current customs, traditions, and general way of doing things are largely due to what it has done before and the degree of success it had with those endeavors. This leads us to the ultimate source of an organization's culture: its founders!

The founding fathers or mothers of an organization traditionally have a major impact in establishing the early culture. They have a vision or mission of what the organization should be. They are unconstrained by previous customs of doing things or by ideologies. The small size that typically characterizes any new organization further facilitates the founders' imposing their vision on all organizational members. Because the founders have the original idea, they also typically have biases on how to get the idea fulfilled. The organization's culture results from the interaction between (1) the founders' biases and assumptions and (2) what the original members whom the founder initially employ learn subsequently from their own experiences.[17]

Thomas Watson at IBM, J. Edgar Hoover at the FBI, and Frederick Smith at Federal Express are just a few obvious examples of individuals who have had immeasurable impact in shaping their

RAY KROC'S GHOST STILL OVERSEES McDONALD'S

Ray Kroc began what became the ten-thousand-plus McDonald's restaurant chain in Des Plaines, Illinois, in 1955. Kroc died in 1984, but his ideals can still literally be heard every day in McDonald's Oak Brook, Illinois, headquarters.[18]

Several years before his death, he recorded his ideas on what McDonald's stood for. These, plus tapes of his talk-show appearances, have been put together into a "Talk to Ray" exhibit. McDonald's employees can hear Kroc describe the company's basic principles as he defined them: A commitment to quality, service, cleanliness, and value. Use the best ingredients and the best equipment. Keep bathrooms spotless. Don't compromise.

If you visit McDonald's headquarters, you'll find Ray Kroc being quoted incessantly. Of course, that's what you'd expect in such a strong culture. Kroc's ideals continue to direct management's decisions. He was against diversification and so is current management. He advocated strong support for franchisees, and current management continues this emphasis. Given present management's determination to carry on Ray Kroc's principles—after all, they built an incredibly successful organization that sells more than $14 billion a year of hamburgers, fries, and shakes—you can expect Kroc's influence still to be directing McDonald's well into the 21st century.

organization's culture. For instance, Watson's views on research and development, product innovation, employee dress, and compensation policies are still evident at IBM, even though he died in 1956. Hoover, the original director of the FBI, has been dead for many years, too, but the FBI continues to show remnants of his prejudices and ends-can-justify-the-means philosophy. Federal Express' aggressiveness, willingness to take risks, focus on innovation, and emphasis on service are central themes that founder Smith has articulated from the company's birth.

Keeping a Culture Alive

Once a culture is in place, there are forces within the organization that act to maintain it by giving employees a set of similar experiences. The three forces that play the most important part in sustaining a culture are the organization's selection practices, the actions of top management, and the organization's socialization methods.[19]

Selection. The explicit goal of the selection process is to identify and hire individuals who have the knowledge, skills, and abilities to perform the jobs within the organization successfully. But typically, more than one candidate will be identified who meets any given job's requirements. When that point is reached, it would be naive to ignore the fact that the final decision as to who is hired will be significantly influenced by the decision maker's judgment of how well the candidates will fit into the organization. This attempt to ensure a proper match, whether purposely or inadvertently, results in the hiring of people who have common values (ones essentially consistent with those of the organization) or at least a good portion of those values.[20] Additionally, the selection process provides information to applicants about the organization. Candidates learn about the organization, and if they perceive a conflict between their values and those of the organization, they can self-select themselves out of the applicant pool. Selection, therefore, becomes a two-way street, allowing either employer or applicant to abrogate a marriage if there appears to be a mismatch. In this way, the selection process sustains an organization's culture by selecting out those individuals who might attack or undermine its core values.

Bain & Co., a large Boston management consulting firm, originally hired only new graduates from the Harvard Business School. This practice not only provided bright and talented people; it also reinforced Bain's culture. Many of the values instilled at Harvard—competition, verbal dexterity, hard work, ambition—were also core values at Bain. The selection of recent Harvard graduates increased the likelihood of Bain's having people who would fit in with Bain's culture and contribute to maintaining it.

In contrast, Sony Corporation's Rancho Bernardo facility in California seeks to encourage a family atmosphere.[21] Toward this end, the company selects applicants who lack experience in manufacturing settings. Preference is given to hiring recent high school graduates and housewives who arrive with a "blank slate" regarding how a factory system works. This allows Sony to indoctrinate their employees into the "Sony family" without having to unfreeze their prior experiences.

Top Management. The actions of top management also have a major impact on the organization's culture.[22] Employees observe management's behavior, "such as the time so-and-so was reprimanded for doing a good job just because he was not asked to do it beforehand or the time that so-and-so was fired because she publicly disagreed with the company's position."[23] These incidents then, over time, establish norms that filter down through the organization and convey whether risk taking is desirable; how much freedom managers should give their subordinates; what is appropriate dress; what actions will pay off in terms of pay raises, promotions, and other rewards; and the like.

Socialization. No matter how good a job the organization does in recruiting and selection, new employees are not fully indoctrinated in the organization's culture. Maybe most important, because they are least familiar with the organization's culture, new employees are potentially most likely to disturb the beliefs and customs that are in place. The organization will, therefore, want to help new employees adapt to its culture. As noted in Chapter 4, this adaptation process is called socialization.

All marines must go through boot camp, where they "prove" their commitment. Of course, at the same time, the marine trainers are indoctrinating new recruits in the "marine way." The success of any cult depends on effective socialization. New Moonies undergo a "brain-washing" ritual that substitutes group loyalty and commitment in place of family. New Disneyland employees spend their first two full days of work watching films and listening to lectures on how Disney employees are expected to look and act.

An organization will be socializing every employee throughout his or her career in the organization. However, socialization is most explicit when a new employee enters an organization. This is when the organization seeks to mold the outsider into an employee "in good standing." New employees typically undergo some form of

**OT
CLOSE-UP**

SETTING THE TONE AT ITT

Rand V. Araskog is the president and CEO at ITT—a $20-billion-a-year worldwide conglomerate that is in hundreds of diverse businesses. Araskog has been ITT's chairman since 1979. Since taking the top spot, he has sought to create the company in his image.[24]

Araskog is a "no-nonsense" leader. He frowns on behaviors that he views as unbusinesslike—from drinking and joking to executives who dress inappropriately. He plays by the rules and expects his management team to do likewise. Rising ITT executives are conspicuously upright, proficient at report writing, diligent about meeting projections, and highly suspicious of negativism inside or outside the ranks. Those that successfully emulate their leader find their careers at ITT flourishing.

Araskog's management style has filtered down through the organization's 120,000 employees. There is a high sensitivity to ITT's image. Araskog, for example, makes it clear that there is no room at ITT for compromising on ethical issues. Managers who don't see it the chairman's way find their road up the organization has come to a halt. Similarly, Araskog believes that putting thoughts into writing helps to clarify them. Most of his subordinates are required to submit regular and numerous reports to him. If managers are to do well at ITT, they must demonstrate the ability to make their reports clear and concise.

Mr. Araskog's straight-laced views have strongly influenced ITT's culture. As an illustration, one former vice president related the story of Araskog's visit to his division. Araskog spotted a *Playboy* magazine on a manager's desk and hit the ceiling. Araskog made it clear that he didn't think *Playboy* was appropriate at the office. The lesson, incidentally, was not lost on the former v.p.: "I started making sure that my managers didn't present an image that Mr. Araskog didn't like."

orientation where they are informed on "how things are done around here." Once on the job, a manager or senior colleague often becomes a coach, to further guide and mold the new member. In some cases, a formal training program will even be offered to ensure that the employee learns the organization's culture.

How Employees Learn Culture

In addition to explicit orientation and training programs, culture is transmitted to employees in a number of other forms—the most potent being through stories, rituals, material symbols, and language.

Stories. If you worked at the Ford Motor Co. during the 1970s, you would have undoubtedly heard the story about Henry Ford II reminding his executives, when they got too argumentative, that "it's *my* name that's on the building." The message was clear. Henry Ford II ran the company!

Stories such as this circulate through many organizations. They contain a narrative of events about the organization's founders, key decisions that affect the organization's future course, and the present top management. They anchor the present in the past and provide explanations and legitimacy for current practices.[25]

Rituals. We reviewed rituals previously in Chapter 4 in our discussion of formalization. Just as rituals are used as a formalization technique, they also are a means for transmitting culture. Activities such as recognition and award ceremonies, weekly Friday afternoon beer bashes, and annual company picnics are rituals that express and reinforce the key values of the organization, what goals are important, which people are important and which are expendable.[26]

Material Symbols. Bank of America is a conservative firm. Aggressive risk taking is not central to its culture. Its executives drive four-door, American-made sedans, provided by the bank. Between 1983 and 1987, Bank of America owned the discount brokerage firm of Charles Schwab & Co. In contrast to B of A, Schwab built its reputation on aggressiveness. It sought out and hired only outgoing and what some have called "flashy" brokers. Top executives at Schwab also drove company cars. Only theirs were Ferraris, Porsches, and BMWs. The cars' images fit both the people who drove them and the cultural values Schwab sought to maintain.[27]

Four-dour sedans and Ferraris are material symbols that help to reinforce their organization's culture. The design and physical layout of spaces and buildings, furniture, executive perks, and dress attire are material symbols that convey to employees who is important, the degree of egalitarianism desired by top management, and the kinds of behaviors (i.e., risk taking, conservative, authoritarian, participative, individualistic, social) that are appropriate.

Language. Many organizations and units within organizations use language as a way to identify members of a culture or subculture. By learning this language, members attest to their acceptance of the culture and, in so doing, help to preserve it.

The kitchen personnel in large hotels use terminology foreign to people who work in other areas of a hotel. Members of the U.S. Army sprinkle their language liberally with jargon that readily identifies its members. Many organizations, over time, develop unique terms to describe equipment, offices, key personnel, suppliers, customers, or products that relate to its business. New employees are frequently overwhelmed with acronyms and jargon that after six months on the job become a natural part of their language. But once assimilated, this terminology acts as a common denominator that unites members of a given culture or subculture.

WHEN CULTURES COLLIDE: MERGERS AND ACQUISITIONS

We mentioned previously that Bank of America owned Charles Schwab from 1983 to 1987. What wasn't mentioned was that the acquisition was a failure. The aggressive style of Schwab's personnel did not fit into the conservative and rigid bureaucracy of Bank of America. While B of A's initial strategy seemed sound— Schwab would expand B of A's reach in the financial services business—it failed because the two organization's cultures were too different.

The acquisition of Electronic Data Systems for $2.5 billion in 1984 by General Motors has been a mixed blessing for GM. On the positive side, it has helped to diversify the large automaker and given it a strong source of automation expertise that GM felt it needs to modernize its production plants. However, GM has had problems integrating EDS into its operations.[28] One observer even likened the merger to a Green Beret outfit joining up with the Social Security administration. The basic problem seemed to be that while GM's culture sought to minimize conflict, risk, and personal independence, the EDS culture thrived on competitiveness and aggressiveness. The first two years of this merger were so troublesome that GM even held serious talks with AT&T regarding selling EDS. But that fell through, and GM has made the best to try to make EDS fit into GM's culture.

The preceding examples illustrate that there is more to a successful merger or acquisition than a favorable financial statement or product synergy. If the parties to a marriage both have strong cultures, the potential for "culture clash" becomes very real. In fact, many senior executives are learning the hard way that a cultural mismatch is more likely to result in a disaster than a financial, technical, geographic, product, or market mismatch.[29]

Every year, hundreds of organizations merge with or acquire other organizations. Recent research finds that 90 percent of these mergers fail to live up to the projections originally set by management.[30] Cultural clash is a major cause of this disappointment. The message this carries to management is to spend the time evaluating the culture of any organization that is being considered as a merger or acquisition candidate.

Probably the two most critical factors determining whether a merger or acquisition is successful is the strength of each organization's culture and the degree of differences that exist between the organizations' key cultural characteristics. Let's take a closer look at each of these factors.

In a merger or acquisition, if one or both of the organizations have weak cultures, the marriage is more likely to work. Why? Because weak cultures are more malleable. They can adapt better to new situations. Two strong cultures, on the other hand, can create real problems. This impact of cultural strength on merger success is illustrated by Mellon Corporation's acquisition of Central Counties Bank (CCB) and Girard Bank of Philadelphia.[31] The Mellon-CCB merger met its premerger financial expectations without significant difficulties in personnel or productivity. But CCB had a relatively young, weak, and flexible culture. The Mellon-Girard merger was fraught with communication and hostility problems and characterized by loss of clientele, morale, and productivity. The Girard Bank's culture was much more established, rigid, and older than CCB's. It was more difficult for Girard to blend with Mellon than it was for CCB, not so much because Girard was incompatible with Mellon but because its culture was so well defined.

The merging of two strong cultures needn't present problems if the cultures are highly similar. R.J. Reynolds, for instance, merged with Nabisco with a minimal amount of trauma. Both firms had strong cultures, but their compatibility was high. So strong cultures are likely to hinder effectiveness in the newly merged organization only when the cultures are at odds.

It has been suggested that cultural fit can best be assessed by comparing the two merger candidates on their key cultural characteristics.[32] For example, the ten cultural characteristics presented earlier in this chapter could provide the foundation. Other cultural concerns—such as average age of the board of directors, percentage of promotions from within, number of management levels, or degree of direct customer contact by senior management—could be added to tap additional elements that might aid or hinder integration. If this evaluation indicates a poor fit and if both cultures are relatively strong, management might be well advised to look elsewhere for a merger candidate.

THE KEY DEBATE:
ARE CULTURES MANAGEABLE?

We now turn to the essential issue in this chapter: Are cultures manageable? Clearly, an organization's culture has a marked influence on its employees. But should culture be treated as a given, in which case managers would be advised to understand their organization's culture but reminded that there is nothing they can do to change it? As one author put it, "If we take the concept of culture seriously, we may have to face the possibility that cultural

NKK CORP. TRIES TO CHANGE NATIONAL STEEL

When Tokyo's NKK Corp. spent $292 million in 1984 for a half-stake in American's number-six steelmaker, Pittsburgh based National Steel, some competitors feared a combine so mighty that it could threaten steel giants such as Bethlehem and Inland.[33] NKK planned to spend $1 billion to modernize National's plants, improve quality, and halve the labor required to produce a ton of its steel. After four years, it's clear the competition has nothing to fear in the near term. Despite running at 100 percent of capacity in the best steel market in a decade, the company ranks dead last among major steelmakers in profitability per ton shipped. NKK has been successful in eliminating fewer than 250 jobs, although their original target was 3500. Further, the cooperative partnership that the new management envisioned between the company and union employees hasn't materialized.

While NKK officials still hold expectations that National will someday be America's premier steelmaker, they have found the road to success much harder to travel than expected. What these officials failed to address fully was the difficulty of converting National's culture to fit NKK's way of doing business.

Some of the more difficult problems related to management decision-making practices and involvement of workers in quality circles. NKK set up a nine-member management committee to oversee operations. National's president, frustrated by having to share his authority and by delays in the decision process, took early retirement. NKK also set up monthly quality-circle meetings to work out jobs and develop cheaper ways to do things. But the team culture didn't fit well with National's unionized climate. The quality circles often weren't held or even scheduled. When they were, they tended to be sparsely attended, and participants did little more than just get up and go through the motions.

NKK has learned a tough lesson, but they are not alone. A number of Japanese firms have encountered difficulties in bringing their style of doing business to the United States, especially when Japanese companies buy existing U.S. operations. Unlike start-up facilities, existing plants come with an intact organizational culture. And that culture frequently fits poorly with those typically found in Japanese organizations.

assumptions are virtually impossible to change."[34] Or should culture be taken as a controllable variable that can be adjusted by management, as needed, to align it better with the organization's strategy and environment? As we'll demonstrate, this is *the* critical issue today underlying organizational culture, and there is a great deal riding on the outcome of the debate.[35]

Before we look at this debate in detail, a point of clarification seems appropriate. When we discuss **managing culture,** we mean *changing* the culture. This has grown to become the prevailing definition. Yet as one writer has noted, managing culture need not be the same as changing culture.[36] In a time of transition, for instance, managing an organization's culture may entail sustaining the present culture rather than inducing any change. So, in a very strict sense, managing a culture could entail stabilizing the status quo as well as inducing a shift to another state. For our purposes, however, we'll treat *managing* culture and *changing* culture as synonymous.

The Case For

Management theorists and consultants have a vested interest in demonstrating that they can change undesirable situations. We have, for instance, a large body of literature to improve a manager's leadership style, help managers deal with employees who lack motivation, or guide managers in redesigning inadequate control systems. This same optimism can be applied to organizational culture. As one author put it, "If managers cannot guide their organizations through planned cultural change, the subject has limited practical utility and may be of only academic interest."[37]

An organization's culture may have been appropriate for a certain time and set of conditions. But times and conditions change. Foreign competition, changes in government regulations, rapid economic shifts, and new technologies are examples of forces that may well leave an organization with a culture that hinders its effectiveness. In such cases, management can alter those factors that created and sustain the current culture. That is, just as cultures are learned, they can be unlearned.[38]

We know that the selection process, top management's actions, and the methods chosen for socializing employees sustain a culture.

Similarly, stories, rituals, material symbols, and language are means by which employees learn who and what is important. By changing these factors, we should be able to change the culture. Top management might, for example, fire or demote employees who are

SCOTT PAPER'S CULTURAL TURNAROUND

When Philip Lippincott took over as chief executive at Scott Paper Company in 1981, he immediately set about changing the firm's culture.[39] He inherited a company whose earnings per share had, after adjusting for inflation, declined 8.6 percent since 1974. Scott had become an aging, centralized bureaucracy, with a hold-the-fort mentality. No matter how bad things were, Scott people seemed to be able to rationalize their results by pointing to some company in the industry that was even worse off.

Lippincott believes strongly in the capability of his people. So the first thing he did was decentralize strategy setting. Staffers were shepherded by the hundreds to retreats where they were taught to think strategically. Now, instead of being devised at the head office in Philadelphia, strategy development has been pushed down to the divisions.

Scott has also altered its incentive system. People used to be rewarded based on the size of their unit, their budget, or the assets under their control. In the new system, pay for the company's top six hundred people is substantially based on their contribution to profit. Those who don't produce either shape up or get shown the door, the latter being something that never happened before at Scott.

Lippincott has pared eleven layers of management down to seven. The result has been a 20 percent cut in Scott's administrative component.

It took four years, but by 1985 the company had succeeded in sharply reducing its costs and in transforming its culture. Between 1981 and 1985 profits improved 88 percent, and operating income as a percent of sales went from 11.1 percent to 15.7 percent. By 1987, profits had climbed another 35 percent and the income-to-sales ratio had increased to 17.0 percent. But changing culture is a demanding and long-term effort. As one executive put it, "Every day we run into our old culture; it hits you in the face."

rigidly locked into the current culture and replace them with individuals who accept and promote the values that are sought; or they might institute a new set of rituals that will reinforce a different cultural milieu.

The Case Against

The fact that organization cultures are made up of relatively stable characteristics would imply that they are very difficult for management to change. Cultures take a long time to form. Once established, they tend to become entrenched and resistant to change efforts. Strong cultures are particularly resistant to change because employees become so committed to them.

For employees to *unlearn* years of experiences and memories is a difficult task. That too takes a very long time. So while culture may be theoretically amenable to change, the time frame necessary to unlearn a given set of values and replace them with a new set may be so long as to make the effort realistically impractical. Remember, too, there are a number of forces in an organization that work to maintain its present culture. These would include written statements about the organization's mission and philosophy, the design of physical spaces and buildings, the dominant leadership pattern, past selection practices, entrenched rituals, popular stories about key people and events, the organization's historic performance-evaluation and reward criteria, and the organization's formal structure. To illustrate, past selection practices tend to work against cultural change. Employees chose the organization because they perceived their values to be a "good fit" with the organization.[40] They are comfortable with that fit and will strongly resist efforts that might undermine the predictability and security of the status quo.

A final point in the argument against management's ability to change culture is the reality that if culture could be changed, surely management would do so.[41] If an organization could "install" a culture such as exists at IBM, McDonald's, or other highly successful organizations, wouldn't they do it? Obviously they would! But just because you can describe the type of culture you'd like to have in no way implies that you can implement such a culture.

General Motors has been trying, since the mid-1970s, to create a market-oriented, action-focused culture. So far, they have been relatively unsuccessful, as evidenced by a drop in U.S. market share of 25 percent over the past dozen years.

Understanding the Situational Factors

The foregoing discussion suggests that the real question we should be seeking an answer to is not, Can culture be managed? but rather, Are there *conditions* under which culture can be managed?[42] This leads us to a situational analysis of conditions that are necessary for, or will facilitate, cultural change. The ideas we offer are based on observation as well as substantive research. However, there seems to be increasing agreement among theorists as to the importance of the following situational factors.

A Dramatic Crisis. The condition that is most universally acknowledged as having to exist before culture can be changed is a dramatic crisis that is widely perceived by the organization's members.[43] This is the shock that undermines the status quo. It calls into question current practices and opens the door toward accepting a different set of values that can respond better to the crisis. Examples of such a crisis would include a surprising financial setback, the hostile takeover of the focal organization by another organization, the loss of a major customer (though such a customer would have to represent a significant proportion of the organization's revenues—typically 25 percent or more), or a dramatic technological breakthrough by a competitor. The crisis, of course, need not be real to be effective. The key is that it is *perceived* as real by the organization's members.

Leadership Turnover. Since top management is a major factor in transmitting culture, a change in the organization's key leadership positions facilitates the imposition of new values.[44] But new leadership, per se, is no assurance that employees will accept new values. The new leaders must have a clear alternative vision of what the organization can be; there must be respect for this leadership's ability; and the new leaders must have the power to enact their alternative vision. The result of new leadership without an alternative set of values is likely to be a response that differs in no way from what had proved successful in the past.[45]

Leadership turnover must encompass the organization's chief executive. But it is not limited to this position. The likelihood of successful cultural change typically increases with a purge of all major management positions. Rather than having previous executives accept the new leader's values, it usually is more effective to replace people with individuals who have no vested interest in the old culture.

Life-Cycle Stage. Cultural change is easier when the organization is in transition from the formation stage to the growth stage, and from maturity into decline.

As the organization moves into growth, major changes will be necessary. These changes are more likely to be accepted because the culture is less entrenched. However, other factors will facilitate acceptance of the change. One writer, for instance, has proposed that employees will be more receptive to cultural change if (1) the organization's previous success record is modest, (2) employees are generally dissatisfied, and (3) the founder's image and reputation are in question.[46]

The other opportunity for cultural change occurs when the organization enters the decline stage. Decline typically requires cutbacks and other retrenchment strategies. Such actions are likely to dramatize to employees that the organization is experiencing a true crisis.

Age of the Organization. Regardless of its life-cycle stage, the younger an organization is, the less entrenched its values will be. We should expect, therefore, that cultural change is more likely to be accepted in an organization that is only five years old than in one that is fifty years old.

Size of the Organization. We propose that cultural change is easier to implement in a small organization. Why? In such organizations, it's easier for management to reach employees. Communication is clearer, and role models are more visible in a small organization, thus enhancing the opportunity to disseminate new values.

Strength of the Current Culture. The more widely held a culture is and the higher the agreement among members on its values, the more difficult it will be to change. Conversely, weak cultures should be more amenable to change than strong ones.

Absence of Subcultures. Heterogeneity increases members' concern with protecting their self-interest and resisting change. Therefore, we would expect that the more subcultures there are, the more resistance there will be to changes in the dominant culture. This thesis can also be related to size. Larger organizations will be more resistant to cultural change because they typically tend to have more subcultures.

If So, How?

The previous section reviewed conditions *under which* cultural change is likely to be implemented and accepted. Now we ask the question, If conditions are right, how does management go about enacting the cultural change?

The challenge is to unfreeze the current culture. No single action, alone, is likely to have the impact necessary to unfreeze something that is so entrenched and highly valued. Therefore, there needs to be a comprehensive and coordinated strategy for managing culture.

Cultural Analysis. We suggest that the best place to begin is with a cultural analysis.[47] This would include a cultural audit to assess the current culture, a comparison of the present culture against that which is desired, and a gap evaluation to identify what cultural elements need changing.

The cultural audit should look at the current culture in terms of the ten dimensions identified on page 439. How much individual initiative is there? Is innovation encouraged? To what degree are rewards contingent on performance rather than seniority or politics? Additionally, three basic questions should be answered in order to tap the content of the culture.[48] First, what is the background of the founders and others who followed them? Second, how did the organization respond to past crises or other critical events, and what was learned from these experiences? Third, who are considered deviants in the culture and how does the organization respond to them? Answers to these questions will reveal how particular values came to be formed, the ordering of these values, and where the culture's boundaries are.

The next step in cultural analysis requires that the values sought in the new culture be articulated. What is the preferred culture that is being sought? This desired culture can then be compared against the organization's current values.

The final step in cultural analysis is to identify what cultural dimensions and values are out of alignment and need changing. It's unlikely that all the core values will be found unacceptable. So this step will focus attention only on those specific current values that need modifying. Once the gaps have been identified, consideration can be given to the specific actions that will directly correct the discrepancies.

Specific Suggestions. We have discussed the importance of a dramatic crisis as a means to unfreeze an entrenched culture. Unfortunately, crises are not always evident to all members of the organization. It may be necessary, therefore, to make a crisis more visible. It is important that it be clear to everyone that the organization's survival is legitimately threatened. If employees don't see the urgency for change, it's unlikely that strong cultures will respond much to change efforts.

The appointment of a new top executive is likely to dramatize that "major changes are going to take place." He or she can offer a new role model and new standards of behavior. This executive, however, needs to introduce quickly his or her new vision of the organization and to staff key management positions with individuals loyal to this vision. A large part of Lee Iacocca's success in changing Chrysler's culture is undoubtedly due to his rapid and wholesale shakeup of Chrysler's senior management, bringing in loyal associates with whom he had worked before at Ford. Chrysler's top five executives currently are all former Ford employees.

The responsibility for communicating the new values lies with top management. It has been suggested that this communication must include three basic elements.[49]

1. The state of the business and its competitors, the outlook for the future, and other information that someone with a keen interest in the fortunes of the organization would want to have.

2. The vision of *what* the organization is to become and *how* it will achieve this.
3. The progress of the organization in the areas that are identified as keys to the realization of the vision.

Along with a shake-up among key management personnel, it also makes sense to initiate a reorganization. The creation of new units, the combining of some, and the elimination of others conveys, in very visible terms, that management is determined to move the organization in new directions. Where there are strong subcultures, the extensive use of job rotation will contribute toward breaking them up. Reorganization, when combined with replacing or reassigning people in key positions, can also be used to increase the power of those who accept and espouse the new values.

The new leadership will want to move quickly to create new stories, symbols, and rituals to replace those currently in place. This needs to be done quickly. Delays will allow the current culture to become associated with the new leadership, thus closing the window of opportunity for change.

Finally, management will want to change the selection and socialization processes and the evaluation and reward systems to support employees who espouse the new values that are sought.

Will the implementation of most or all of these suggestions result in an immediate or dramatic shift in the organization's culture? Not very likely! If there is anything that we've learned in recent years about managing culture, it is that it is a lengthy process—measured in years rather than months. Studies suggest that two years would represent a very rapid turnaround in a culture, with four or five years being more the rule.

SUMMARY

Organizations have personalities, just like individuals. We call these personalities organizational cultures. An organizational culture is a system of shared meaning. Its key characteristics are individual initiative, risk tolerance, direction, integration, management support, control, identity, rewards, conflict tolerance, and communication patterns.

Organizations have dominant cultures and subcultures. The former expresses the core values shared by a majority of the organization's members, though most large organizations also have additional values expressed in subcultures. Strong cultures are those where values are intensely held, clearly ordered, and widely shared. Strong cultures increase behavioral consistency. As such, they can act as substitutes for formalization.

The ultimate source of an organization's culture is its founders. It is sustained by the organization's selection and socialization processes and the actions of top management. It is transmitted through stories, rituals, material symbols, and language.

The key debate surrounding organizational culture concerns whether or not it can be managed. Cultures can be changed, but there appear to be a number of conditions necessary to bring about such change. Even where change conditions are favorable, managers should not expect any rapid acceptance of new cultural values. Cultural change should be measured in years rather than months.

FOR REVIEW AND DISCUSSION

1. Define *organizational culture*. Which of its key characteristics are structurally based? Which are behaviorally based?
2. Can an employee survive in an organization if he or she rejects its core values? Explain.
3. What forces might contribute toward making a culture strong or weak?
4. "A strong culture reduces intraorganizational conflict." Do you agree or disagree? Discuss.
5. How is an organization's culture maintained?
6. What benefits can socialization provide for the organization? For the new employee?
7. Can you identify a set of characteristics that describe your college's culture? Compare them with several of your peers. How closely do they agree?
8. What is the relationship between culture and formalization?
9. Why do management theorists and consultants have a vested interest in demonstrating that organizational cultures can be managed?
10. "Culture may change, but the change may not be planned or precipitated by management." Discuss.
11. What factors work against changing an organization's culture?
12. In what stage in an organization's life cycle is cultural change most likely to be accepted? Why?
13. What condition is *most* necessary for cultural change to be accepted?
14. Describe the conditions that would be most conducive to initiating cultural change.
15. A senior executive from a major corporation has hired you to advise her on how she could change her organization's culture. How would you approach this assignment?

NOTES

[1] John H. Sheridan, "Texas Instruments: Looking for 'Easy' Answers," *Industry Week*, May 16, 1988, pp. 66–68.

[2] Terrence E. Deal and Allan A. Kennedy, *Corporate Cultures: The Rites and Rituals of Corporate Life* (Reading, Mass.: Addison-Wesley, 1982).

[3] R. T. Pascale and A. G. Athos, *The Art of Japanese Management* (New York: Simon & Schuster, 1981).

[4] Marvin Bower, *The Will to Manage* (New York: McGraw-Hill, 1966).

[6] Edgar H. Schein, *Organizational Culture and Leadership* (San Francisco: Jossey-Bass, 1985).

[7] Linda Smircich, "Concepts of Culture and Organizational Analysis," *Administrative Science Quarterly*, September 1983, p. 339.

[7] Based on George G. Gordon and W. M. Cummins, *Managing Management Climate* (Lexington, Mass.: Lexington Books, 1979); and Chris A. Betts and Susan M. Halfhill, "Organization Culture: Theory, Definitions, and Dimensions," paper presented at the National American Institute of Decision Sciences' Conference, Las Vegas, Nev., November 1985.

[8] Based on Nirmal K. Sethia and Mary Ann Von Glinow, "Arriving at Four Cultures by Managing the Reward System," in Ralph H. Kilmann et al., eds., *Gaining Control of the Corporate Culture* (San Francisco: Jossey-Bass, 1985), pp. 400–401.

[9] See, for example, K. L. Gregory, "Native-View Paradigms: Multiple Cultures and Culture Conflicts in Organizations," *Administrative Science Quarterly*, September 1983, pp. 359–76.

[10] Meryl Reis Louis, "Sourcing Workplace Culture: Why, When, and How," in Kilmann et al., *Gaining Control*, p. 129.

[11] Edgar H. Schein, "Coming to a New Awareness of Organizational Culture," *Sloan Management Review*, Winter 1984, p. 7.

[12] Charles A. O'Reilly III, "Corporations, Cults and Organizational Culture: Lessons from Silicon Valley Firms," paper presented at the 42nd Annual Meeting of the Academy of Management, Dallas, 1983.

[13] See W. Brooke Tunstall, *Disconnecting Parties: Managing the Bell System Break-Up—An Inside View* (New York: McGraw-Hill, 1985); and Zane E. Barnes, "Change in the Bell System," *Academy of Management Executive*, February 1987, pp. 43–46.

[14] Bernard Arogyaswamy and Charles M. Byles, "Organizational Culture: Internal and External Fits," *Journal of Management*, Winter 1987, pp. 647–59.

[15] Karl E. Weick, "Organizational Culture as a Source of High Reliability," *California Management Review*, Winter 1987, pp. 112–27.

[16] Nigel Nicholson and Gary Johns, "The Absence Culture and the Psychological Contract—Who's in Control of Absence?" *Academy of Management Review*, July 1985, pp. 397–407.

[17] Edgar H. Schein, "The Role of the Founder in Creating Organizational Culture," *Organizational Dynamics*, Summer 1983, pp. 13–28.

[18] Based on Penny Moser, "The McDonald's Mystique," *Fortune*, July 4, 1988, pp. 112–16.

[19] See, for example, Yoash Wiener, "Forms of Value Systems: A Focus on Organizational Effectiveness and Cultural Change and Maintenance," *Academy of Management Review*, October 1988, pp. 541–43.

[20] Benjamin Schneider, "The People Make the Place," *Personnel Psychology*, Autumn 1987, pp. 437–52.

[21] C. Jensen, " 'Family' Keeps Sony in Tune with California," *Cleveland Plain Dealer*, April 15, 1984, p. 1-D.

[22] Renato Tagiuri and G. H. Litwin, *Organizational Climate* (Boston: Harvard University Graduate School of Business Administration, 1968); Jerome L. Franklin, "Down the Organization: Influence Processes across Levels of Hierarchy," *Administrative Science Quarterly*, June 1975, pp. 153–64; and "Handing Down the Old Hands' Wisdom," *Fortune*, June 13, 1983, pp. 97–104.

[23] Ralph H. Kilmann, "Five Steps for Closing Culture Gaps," in Kilmann et al., *Gaining Control*, p. 357.

[24] Based on Monica Langley, "ITT Chief Emphasizes Harmony, Confidence and Playing By Rules," *Wall Street Journal*, September 13, 1984, p. 1.

[25] Andrew M. Pettigrew, "On Studying Organizational Culture," *Administrative Science Quarterly*, December 1979, p. 576.

[26] Ibid.

[27] V. F. Zonana, "The Porsches and Saabs at Schwab Aggravate Some at BankAmerica," *Wall Street Journal*, January 20, 1983, p. 27.

[28] "General Motors' Move to Sell EDS Fails, Highlights Problems of Integrating Unit," *Wall Street Journal*, November 24, 1986, p. 3.

[29] Anthony F. Buono and James L. Bowditch, *The Human Side of Mergers and Acquisitions: Managing Collisions Between People, Cultures, and Organizations* (San Francisco: Jossey-Bass, 1989).

[30] Price Pritchett, *After the Merger: Managing the Shockwaves* (Dallas: Dow Jones-Irwin, 1985), p. 8.

[31] Lee Tom Perry, "Merging Successfully: Sending the 'Right' Signals," *Sloan Management Review*, Spring 1986, pp. 47–57.

[32] Christopher J. Clarke, "Acquisitions—Techniques for Measuring Strategic Fit," *Long Range Planning*, June 1987, pp. 12–18.

[33] Based on J. Ernest Beazley, "In Spite of Mystique, Japanese Plants in U.S. Find Problems Abound," *Wall Street Journal*, June 22, 1988, pp. 1 and 14.

[34] Schein, *Organizational Culture and Leadership*, p. 45.

[35] For three different views on cultural change, see Debra Meyerson and Joanne Martin, "Cultural Change: An Integration of Three Different Views," *Journal of Management Studies*, November 1987, pp. 623–45.

[36] Caren Siehl, "After the Founder: An Opportunity to Manage Culture," in Peter Frost et al., eds., *Organizational Culture* (Beverly Hills, Calif.: Sage Publications, 1985), p. 139.

[37] George G. Gordon, "The Relationship of Corporate Culture to Industry Sector and Corporate Performance," in Kilmann et al., *Gaining Control*, pp. 120–21.

[38] Edgar H. Schein, "Suppose We Took Culture Seriously," *O.D. Newsletter*, 1984, pp. 2–7.

[39] Based on Bill Saporito, "Scott Isn't Lumbering Anymore," *Fortune*, September 30, 1985, pp. 48–49.

[40] Schneider, "The People Make the Place."

[41] Alan L. Wilkins and Kerry J. Patterson, "You Can't Get There from Here: What Will Make Culture-Change Projects Fail?" in Kilmann et al., *Gaining Control*, p. 277.

[42] Joanne Martin, "Can Organizational Culture Be Managed?" In Frost et al., *Organizational Culture*, pp. 95–96.

[43] See, for example, W. Gibb Dyer, Jr., "Organizational Culture: Analysis and Change," in W. G. Dyer, ed., *Strategies for Managing Change* (Reading, Mass.: Addison-Wesley, 1984).

[44] Pettigrew, "On Studying Organizational Culture," pp. 570–81.

[45] W. Gibb Dyer, Jr., "The Cycle of Cultural Evolution in Organizations," in Kilmann et al., *Gaining Control*, p. 216.

[46] Siehl, "After the Founder," pp. 128–29.

[47] Stan Silverzweig and Robert F. Allen, "Changing the Corporate Culture," *Sloan Management Review*, Spring 1976, pp. 33–49; and Michael Albert, "Assessing Cultural Change Needs," *Training and Development Journal*, May 1985, pp. 94–98.

[48] Vijay Sathe, "How to Decipher and Change Corporate Culture," in Kilmann et al., *Gaining Control*, pp. 237–39.

[49] Gordon, "Industry Sector and Corporate Performance," p. 123.

17

MANAGING ORGANIZATIONAL EVOLUTION

AFTER READING THIS CHAPTER, YOU SHOULD BE ABLE TO:

1 Identify four reasons why organizations seek growth.
2 Describe the five-phase model of organizational growth.
3 Define organizational decline.
4 Describe environmental forces that might precipitate organizational decline.
5 Explain how decline affects the administrative component.
6 Outline the steps management is likely to follow in response to decline.
7 Identify potential problems managers face when organizations decline.
8 List specific techniques management can use to reduce personnel.

Introduction
THE DECLINE OF WESTERN UNION

For many generations of Americans, word of momentous personal events—like marriages, births, and deaths—arrived first by Western Union telegram.[1] Founded in 1856, Western Union's management made its first, and maybe most catastrophic, strategic error in the late nineteenth century by refusing to buy Alexander Graham Bell's telephone patents and letting a shaky start-up firm, which was to become the American Telephone & Telegraph Co., get monopoly control of the fledgling telephone business. So, in an odd sort of way, Western Union has been a company in decline for more than a century.

By the early 1970s, AT&T and Western Union owned the only nationwide telecommunication networks and were regulated monopolies.
In addition to the telegram business, Western Union also controlled the
profitable telex business in the U.S. But the environment was dramatically
changing. The telecommunications industry was being deregulated, and
there became a proliferation of competition offering new communications
technologies. In response, Western Union spent hundreds of millions of
dollars to expand its network and diversify into cellular telephony, electronic mail, and even long-distance phone service. Unfortunately, the
company had to borrow nearly a billion dollars to follow this strategy.
The new ventures failed to generate the instant profits needed to support
this huge debt. Yet it was the breakup of AT&T in 1984 that may have
delivered the knockout blow. While the company used its own system
to relay long-distance messages, AT&T owned the local telephone lines
that formed the final link to the customer. The deregulated "Baby Bells"
dramatically increased access charges to their local lines. The result was
that Western Union had to increase its telex and long-distance phone
rates just as AT&T and other competitors were cutting theirs. Not surprisingly, Western Union's business plummeted. To cut costs, sixteen
hundred jobs were eliminated and the remaining eleven thousand employees took a pay cut. The company's best managers began bailing out
en masse. By the late 1980s, whether Western Union had a future was
very much in doubt.

While managers deify growth and often use it as a criterion to
assess organizational effectiveness, the Western Union case illustrates the often overlooked side of the growth-decline cycle. This
other side—specifically, the managing of decline—is becoming an
increasing reality today. Terms like *retrenchment* and *downsizing*
have become staples in many managers' vocabularies. The reality
is that while growth may be widely sought, the contemporary manager is more likely than ever to be managing a shrinking organization.
    This chapter expands on the life-cycle concept introduced in
Chapter 1 to consider the impact of the life-cycle stage on an organization. We demonstrate that the two most significant stages—
growth and decline—create distinctly different organizational
problems and opportunities for managers. We'll begin by taking a
closer look at society's growth bias and presenting a model of
organizational growth.

MANAGING GROWTH

American Values Favor Growth

Traditional American values include optimism about the future. In America, any young person can grow up to be president. You can become rich and successful regardless of the economic status of your family. Parents expect that their children will have more of "the good life" than they had. These notions, while under some attack in the last decade, are relatively accurate descriptions of Americans' fundamental confidence that the future will be better than the present. These optimistic values have permeated our ideas on organizations.[2] Managers and researchers alike have allowed the goal of growth to become a means to express this confidence in an organizational context. Growth came to represent a way to make tomorrow's organizations better than today's.

Bigger Is Better. One of the strong forces for growth has been the "bigger is better" notion in America. Large organizations were desirable, as were large cars and large homes. But large size, when applied to organizations, could also be justified in economic terms. Growth was desirable because with increases in size came economies of scale. Bigger, in fact, was frequently more efficient.

The bigger is better notion, it should be pointed out, still dominates the securities markets. Growth rates continue to be a primary determinant of a stock's value. Stocks that show compounded sales growth rates of 20 percent and higher year after year become the darlings of Wall Street. They frequently carry price-earnings ratios of thirty, forty, or higher. However, let that growth curve flatten, and the stock's price can be expected to dive. Why does this happen? Growth serves as an indicator of an organization's fitness for the future.[3] Since an optimistic future influences the extent to which the organization can obtain continued or increased support from its specific environment, managers are motivated to seek growth.

Growth Increases the Likelihood of Survival. In our discussion of organizational effectiveness, we acknowledged the paramount status accorded to survival. If the organization does not survive, other issues become purely academic. Growth becomes desirable, then, because it increases the likelihood of survival.

Large organizations are not permitted to go out of existence the way small organizations are.[4] In 1980 the U.S. government came to the rescue of Chrysler Corporation by guaranteeing $1.5 billion in loans. Chrysler's large size alone assured it of strong constituencies to fight for its survival. Wherever Chrysler had assembly plants, suppliers, bankers it owed money to, and dealers— which included just about every state in the Union—the company had supporters fighting for government assistance. Your community drugstore or laundromat, should it face financial difficulties, certainly does not attract that kind of support. This same logic, of course, holds for hospitals, colleges, and government agencies. In times of economic crisis, the state of Massachusetts is far more likely to close down Framingham State College, with its 2500 students and 120 faculty members, than it is the University of Massachusetts at Amherst, with its 18,000 students and more than a thousand faculty!

In addition to providing a large constituency, growth facilitates survival by providing more resources with which the organization can buffer itself against uncertainty. Larger organizations can make errors and live to talk about them. General Motors, for instance, has a greater margin for error than does New Avanti Corp. A $100 million mistake at General Motors is an annoyance. The same mistake at Avanti would be a catastrophe. Similarly, more resources provide a buffer in times of setbacks. Growing organizations have slack resources that can be cut more easily than do small or stable organizations. The growing organization that has to reduce its budget by 10 percent can often cut fat without threatening its survival. The stagnant organization is often forced to cut bone. Cosmetic surgery in the first case becomes life-threatening major surgery in the second.

Growth Becomes Synonymous with Effectiveness. What is success? As we noted at the opening of this section, if an organization is getting bigger, it is common to assume that it is being managed effectively.[5]

Business executives flaunt the fact that "sales are up significantly." Hospital administrators produce charts showing that they are handling more patients than ever. College deans brag about having record enrollments. As one business dean remarked, "We must be doing something right. Our enrollments are up more than 15 percent for the fourth year in a row." These examples all illustrate how organizations, rightly or wrongly, use growth as a synonym for effectiveness. If those in the specific environment on whom the organization depends for continued support also equate growth with effectiveness, managers will obviously be predisposed to the values of growth.

The interlacing of growth and effectiveness is seen explicitly in the systems concept, which we discussed in Chapter 1. If you remember, organizations were described as open systems. In this context, organizations are analogous to living organisms, maintaining themselves by acquiring inputs from, and disposing of their output to, the environment. The systems approach favors growth. Growth is sought because it connotes youth and vitality.[6] Growth is evidence that the organization is in good health. And expansion, again consistent with the systems perspective, increases the likelihood that the organization will survive.

Growth Is Power. The arguments that growth can be consistent with economies of scale, can be used by the specific environment to assess the organization's effectiveness, and can increase the likelihood of survival are all economically rational explanations for the pro-growth bias. Now we want to present a political argument in favor of growth.

Growth is almost always consistent with the self-interest of the top management in the organization. It increases prestige, power, and job security for this group. It should certainly be of more than passing interest to know that growth is undoubtedly linked to executive compensation. The evidence indicates that profit rates generally increase in business firms until the organization achieves a reasonably moderate size. Then the profit rate remains stable or declines. As we learned in Chapter 5, size—especially large size—does not necessarily generate economies. The costs of coordination can exceed the benefits from economies of scale. But, and this is what is relevant from a power-control perspective, executive salaries are related to size. Size, in fact, is a better predictor of executive salaries than is profit margin.[7] As a case in point, a recent survey found that the heads of *Fortune* 100 companies made more than twice that of their counterparts at companies ranked in *For-*

tune's 401–500 category.[8] Should we not expect, therefore, top business executives to be motivated toward expanding their firms?

Growth also provides an organization more power relative to other organizations and groups in its environment.[9] Larger organizations have more influence with suppliers, unions, large customers, government, and the like.

This leads us to the obvious conclusion that growth is not a chance occurrence. It is the result of conscious managerial decisions. Growth typically provides both economic benefits to the

OT
CLOSE-UP

HOW DO ORGANIZATIONS GROW?

There are at least four distinct means by which organizations commonly grow.[10]

The first is expansion in the organization's existing domain. Philip Morris followed this strategy in purchasing Kraft. The addition of Kraft food products to Philip Morris' food brands such as Oscar Meyer and Maxwell House coffee gave Philip Morris greater concentration in the foods industry.

Second is growth through diversification into new domains. This appears in a variety of forms, including development of new products and services, vertical integration, and conglomerate diversification. Paramount Communications, which owns such operations as Paramount Pictures, the New York Knicks basketball team, and Simon & Schuster publishers, uses this strategy. So did General Motors a few years back, when it acquired Hughes Aircraft.

Third is growth through technological development. Most large universities, for example, use increased class size as a means to expand. Federal Express has been able to expand rapidly by using computer technology to precisely track packages from receipt to delivery.

Fourth is growth through improved managerial techniques. This strategy seeks to increase the efficiency of the management process. IBM is a good illustration of a firm that has developed a large cadre of outstanding managers, which, in turn, has provided the impetus for growth of the firm.

organization and political benefits to the organization's executive decision makers. As such, strong forces are continually encouraging organizations to grow and expand.

A Model of Organizational Growth

The best-known model of organizational growth was developed in the early 1970s by Larry Greiner.[11] Greiner studied a number of organizations and from his observations proposed that an organization's evolution is characterized by phases of prolonged and calm growth, followed by periods of internal turmoil. The former he called **evolution,** the later **revolution.** Each stage of evolution or growth creates its own crisis. The resolution of the crisis, however, initiates a new evolutionary phase.

This evolution-crisis-evolution process creates the five-phase model shown in Figure 17–1.

Phase 1: Creativity. The first stage of an organization's evolution is characterized by the creativity of its founders. These founders typically devote their energies toward the development of products and markets. Their organization's design tends to look like the simple structure. Decision making is controlled by the owner-manager or top management. Communication between levels in the organization is frequent and informal.

As the organization grows, it becomes difficult to manage by relying only on informal communication. The senior managers become overextended. There comes a *crisis of leadership* as those who run the organization no longer have the skills or interests to direct the organization successfully. Strong professional management is needed that can introduce more sophisticated management and organization techniques.

Phase 2: Direction. If the leadership crisis is resolved, strong leadership will have been acquired. This new leadership will formalize communication and put accounting, budget, inventory, and other systems into place. The organization's design will become increasingly bureaucratic. Specialization will be introduced, as will a functional structure, so as to separate production and marketing activities.

This new direction, however, will create a crisis of its own

FIGURE 17–1 *Five Phases of Growth*

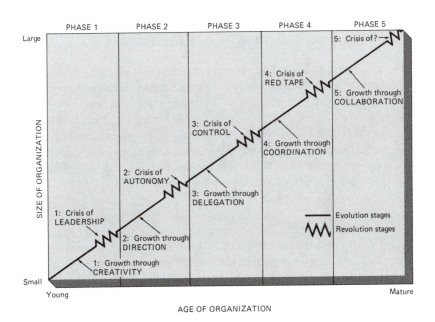

making. Lower-level managers will become frustrated and seek greater influence in decisions that affect them. The new management, though, is reluctant to give up authority. The result is a *crisis of autonomy.* The solution tends to lie in decentralizing decision making.

Phase 3: Delegation. If decisions are decentralized, the crisis of phase two will have been resolved. Lower-level managers will now have relative autonomy to run their units. Top management will devote its energy to long-run strategic planning. Internal control systems will be developed to monitor the decisions of lower-level managers.

Delegation, however, eventually creates a *crisis of control.* Lower-level managers enjoy their autonomy, but top-level managers fear that the organization is going in many directions at the same time. Top management's response is to attempt to return to centralized decision making. Centralization is viewed as the means to provide unity of direction. But this is rarely realistic. Some other means of coordination needs to be found and implemented.

Phase 4: Coordination. The control crisis is solved by implementing staff units to review, evaluate, and control line-management activities and product groups to facilitate coordination.

These coordination devices create their own problems. Line-staff conflicts, for example, begin to consume a great deal of time and effort. Lower-level employees increasingly begin to complain that they are being overwhelmed by too many rules, regulations, and controls. A *crisis of red tape* occurs, and unless it is resolved it can lead to goal displacement.

Phase 5: Collaboration. The solution to the red-tape crisis is strong interpersonal collaboration among the organization's members. A strong culture acts as a substitute for formal controls. Task forces and other group devices are created to perform tasks and solve problems. The organization's structure moves toward the organic form.

Greiner is unclear as to what crisis will evolve out of the collaborative and organic structure. It might well be a return to one of the earlier crises in the model.

The Greiner model demonstrates the paradox that success creates its own problems. As an organization grows, it faces new crises. Each crisis, in turn, requires management to make adjustments in coordination devices, control systems, and organization design. But do organizations grow in standardized time spaces as depicted in Figure 17–1? Moreover, do all organizations grow in the discrete stages that Greiner identifies? The answer to both questions is "No!" Greiner acknowledges that movement between the phases will vary both within and between organizations, but his diagram fails to reflect this. Also, some organizations undoubtedly revert to earlier stages. An increasing number of organizations, as we'll see in a moment, are unsuccessful in responding to a crisis. The result is often the beginning of organizational decline.

ORGANIZATIONAL DECLINE: ACCEPTING THE NEW REALITY

In spite of all the reasons managers have for favoring growth conditions, organizational decline is becoming a fact of life for an increasing number of managers, especially those in large organizations in established industries.[12] In recent years, for instance, Ford cut its work force by more than ten thousand, AT&T Information Systems eliminated twenty-four thousand jobs, CBS cut more than two thousand people, Motorola reduced its semiconductor group by nearly nine thousand employees, and Du Pont sweetened its retirement program to "encourage" thirteen thousand employees to make an early exit. Since the mid-1980s, few of the *Fortune* 500 have escaped this need to reduce the size of their work force. In some U.S. industries—such as steel and textiles—almost every firm has recently closed manufacturing plants and laid off large numbers of employees.

Twenty years ago, few managers or organizational theorists were concerned about decline. Growth was the *natural* state of things, and decline, when it occurred, was viewed as an aberration, a mistake created by poor management, or merely a brief setback in a long-term growth trend. What, then, has changed? Have we merely ignored reality, or have more organizations actually entered the decline stage of their life cycle?

Clarifying Semantics

Before we look at the causes underlying the increase in declining organizations, let's clarify our terminology. When we refer to **organizational decline,** we mean a prolonged decrease in the number of personnel in an organization. It is synonymous with any form of permanent retrenchment. It is *not* meant to describe temporary aberrations in an organization's growth curve.

Another term closely aligned with organizational decline, and sometimes used interchangeably with it, is *downsizing.* But we'll give this term a more specific meaning. By **downsizing,** we mean a slimming down of the organization by reducing the number of vertical levels. Downsizing reduces the number of middle managers, widens the organization's average span of control, and pushes authority downward. When you hear about management reorganizing to become "lean and mean," the organization is typically engaged in downsizing.

The Changing Environment

The preponderance of research and publications on the subject of organization theory took place between the mid-1940s and the mid-1970s. Coincidentally, this same three-decade period was one of relatively uninterrupted growth. It should not be surprising, therefore, to find that the OT literature is heavily growth-oriented, focusing almost exclusively on problems or benefits associated with expansion.

However, beginning around the mid-1970s, we have seen a distinct increase in the number of organizations that have been shrinking their operations. The obvious question is, Why?

One answer is *falling markets.* Bethlehem Steel and the textile maker Celanese Corporation, for example, have found a declining U.S. market for their products. Significantly lower labor costs overseas have been an obvious factor precipitating this market decline. Since 1980, more than two million manufacturing jobs have been lost in the United States to offshore competition. In some cases, foreign governments have interceded, creating falling markets for producers outside their country. Japan, for example, has targeted electronics as an industry in which it wants world influence. To support this commitment, the Japanese government subsidizes many of its electronic firms. This makes it nearly impossible for manufacturers in countries that do not subsidize to compete effectively.

Some organizations, especially those with a single product or those where a single product dominates their sales, have been hit by *the end of the product's life cycle.* Atari, as a case in point, rose and fell with the video-game market. Western Union, as noted at the beginning of this chapter, is another example of an organization that has had to reduce its operations radically as a result of its primary business—telegraph communications—being on the downside of its product cycle.

Some organizations are forced to cut back as a result of *loss of market share.* The total market for their product or services may not be shrinking, but their failure to sustain their share of that market creates the need to retrench. General Motors' loss of market share in the U.S. automobile market is such a case. Deregulation has produced a loss in market share for many firms in the trucking and airline industries. Not surprisingly, most of these large firms have also been undergoing some shrinking of their operations.

The recent rash of *mergers and acquisitions* has created redundancy in many companies. When banks merge or a Chevron acquires a Gulf Oil, efficiencies often dictate consolidating operations and staff personnel in functions such as legal, accounting, purchasing, and human resources.

Local, state, and federal government agencies have additional concerns to worry about. *Reduction of part of their program* can require cutbacks, as occurred at NASA in the 1970s. A *loss in taxpayer support* can require cutbacks, a situation that many school districts have encountered. *A change in government priorities* can require retrenchment. Federal affirmative-action agencies during the Reagan administration were such a case. Finally, geographical areas can be hit by an *erosion in their economic and tax bases*, which requires significant cutbacks. Many of the midwestern farm states have had to reduce their budgets and the services they provide citizens because of a decline in revenue sources.

Is Managing Decline the Reverse of Managing Growth?

Until very recently, there was little research on the decline process. This was undoubtedly due to the growth bias and the reality that organizations undergoing contraction rarely can afford the luxury of sponsoring reflective research, nor does management see much to gain by permitting outsiders to chronicle their organization's decline.[13] Our knowledge today about managing decline is essentially based on some preliminary research evidence and a good deal of insightful speculation.

We begin with the proposition that the management of decline is not merely a matter of reversing the process of managing growth. An organization cannot be reduced piece by piece simply by reversing the sequence of activity and resource building by which it grew.[14] While the research is scant, there does appear to be enough evidence to conclude that activities within same-sized organizations during periods of growth and decline will not correspond

FIGURE 17–2 *The Organization's Life Cycle*

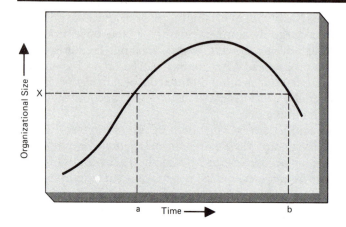

directly. As a generalization, there is a lag that typifies the rate of change in structure during prolonged decline that is not evident in growth.[15] As discussed in Chapter 6, changes in size have a significant impact on structure. But those conclusions were drawn from organizations that were all changing in the growth direction. During decline, size has an impact on structure, but it is not a reverse parallel of the growth pattern. This lag results in the level of structure being greater in the same organization for a given level of size during decline than for the same level of size during growth.[16] Referring to Figure 17–2, the lag thesis would state that at a given size, X, points a and b are not equal. More specifically, at point b in time, the organization should have a greater degree of structure. For instance, we could expect a lag in the degree of formalization. Typically, when an organization goes from one hundred employees to one thousand, there is an increase in formal rules and regulations. But this is not easily reversible. We predict, therefore, that when an organization is contracting, it will tend to have a higher degree of formalization at each size level than it had at the same level in its growth stage. This lag factor is most evident, however, in recent studies of the administrative component in declining organizations.

The Administrative Component Revisited. As described in Chapter 6, the administrative component refers to the number of people in an organization who engage in supportive activities. If there is a lag in decline, one would expect the administrative component to shrink at a slower rate than the whole organization. A number of studies confirm this expectation.[17] In some cases, evidence has been found that the administrative component actually increased while organizations declined.[18] Although the exact nature of the relationship is not well established, it is clear that the relationship between size and the administrative component is different during decline than during growth. Interestingly, either a lag or an increase would be consistent with the conclusion that organizational politics distorts the effect of the decline process on the administrative component.[19] The administrative support group, because of its power, is more effective in resisting cutback pressures. As a result, the ratio of supportive staff to operatives will be higher at the same level of total organizational size in the decline stage.

An Enhanced Case for Power-Control. Organizational size is a major factor in determining an organization's structure during growth but not during decline. So our conclusions in Chapter 6 on the size-structure relationship appear to be relevant only on the upside of an organization's life cycle.

While the evidence is sketchy, we offer the following hypothesis: Size is a key determinant of structure during growth, but it is replaced by power-control in decline. During growth, the actions of vested-interest groups to maintain or enhance their power is not nearly as visible as it is in decline. Slack resources minimize conflicts. Confrontations can be resolved by all parties' winning. However, when the organization is contracting, scarce resources are most dear. Administrative rationality, which can explain the size-structure relationship in growth, is replaced by a power struggle. In decline, therefore, structure is more likely to reflect the interests of those in power, for they are best able to weather a political struggle.

Decline Follows Stages. A final speculation on the decline-structure relationship is based on the assumption that organizations are most likely, initially, to confront what will become a prolonged decline as if it is merely an aberration. If true, prolonged declines should find management treating it in stages.[20] The initial reaction is shock. This first stage, then, is best described as numbed inaction. In the second stage, management will posture itself in defensive

EXPLAINING CUTBACKS IN MIDDLE MANAGEMENT

The research on the administrative component during decline has generated relatively consistent findings: it shrinks at a slower rate than the whole organization. But that conclusion may be dated. A new trend seems to have appeared in the 1980s: cutting back middle-management and white-collar jobs in bad times and good.[21]

Eugene E. Jennings, a Michigan State University professor who has been studying corporate staffing, found that since 1980, eighty-nine of the one hundred largest U.S. companies have reorganized to reduce the number of management levels. This appears to be a new and permanent trend. As W. James Fish, Ford Motor Company's personnel-planning manager put it, "We're looking at a total restructuring of American business."

Of the 24,000 jobs being eliminated at AT&T, 30 percent are in management. Similarly, Texas-based semiconductor manufacturer, Mostek Corporation, has laid off 2600 of its 9800 employees recently, more than 20 percent of them managers.

Why has the administrative component, especially middle management, become the new target for cutbacks? For organizations with financial problems, it's an obvious way to save money. But that motivation has been available for decades. Undoubtedly, increased low-cost competition from overseas has scared many companies into thinning their ranks. A more plausible explanation, however, may be the recent aggressive tactics of corporate raiders bent on taking over companies that appear to be underperforming. These corporate raiders have struck fear into the hearts of the top management in most large corporations. Companies that appear undervalued become prime targets for a takeover raid. Corporate executives have sought to discourage takeovers by keeping their profits up. Reducing management levels to a bare minimum is consistent with this end.

retreat. The decline is ignored or denied. Third, when the facts of decline are evident, it will be reacted to as if it is a temporary crisis. Then, over time, management will begin realistically to make decisions as if it is confronting a prolonged contraction. So only in the fourth stage does management accept the new situation and make the necessary adjustments. From an OT perspective, we would predict that management will make different structural decisions in the third stage than in the fourth.

In the temporary crisis stage, we would predict that management will centralize decision making and resort to a simple structure. This is consistent with the findings presented in Chapter 10. When under attack, management wants control. But this approach cannot result in effective organizational performance when the decline is of a long-term nature. As we learn later in this chapter, one of the major problems that management must face during organizational decline is the propensity for the best employees to leave the organization. To reduce turnover and maintain high levels of employee morale and commitment, management must decentralize and give up autocratic control. When the decline has been diagnosed properly as the long-term variety, management will have to resort to giving employees an increased role in decision making. Increased participation should improve the organization's ability to hold employees and to get necessary input for changes that will almost certainly be necessary. We propose, then, that structure will change during decline. Once decline is recognized, structure will become centralized and take on simple characteristics. However, as it becomes clear that the decline is not temporary, the structure will move toward decentralization.

Potential Managerial Problems When Organizations Decline

Some like the challenge of managing in adversity. Others merely find themselves in a leadership position when facts dictate that the organization has entered its declining phase. While it is undoubtedly easier to manage an organization during growth than during decline, the fact remains that decline is a reality, and when it occurs, managers must be prepared to cope with its consequences. Table 17–1 lists some of these consequences. The remainder of this chapter looks in greater detail at some of these problems and considers what managers can do about them.

Increased Conflict. A manager has the opportunity to really test his or her conflict-management skills during organizational decline. As we have noted before, growth creates slack that acts as a

TABLE 17–1   *Dysfunctional Consequences of Organizational Decline*

Centralization. Decision making is passed upward, participation decreases, and control is emphasized.

No long-term planning. Crises and short-term needs drive out strategic planning.

Innovation curtailed. No experimentation, risk-aversion, and skepticism about noncore activities.

Scapegoating. Leaders are blamed for the pain and uncertainty.

Resistance to change. Conservatism and turf protection lead to rejection of new alternatives.

Turnover. The most competent leaders tend to leave first, causing leadership anemia.

Low morale. Few needs are met, and infighting is predominant.

Loss of slack. Uncommitted resources are used to cover operating expenses.

Fragmented pluralism. Special interest groups organize and become more vocal.

Loss of credibility. Leaders lose the confidence of their subordinates.

Nonprioritized cuts. Attempts to ameliorate conflict lead to attempts to equalize cutbacks.

Conflict. Competition and infighting for control predominate when resources are scarce.

Adapted from Kim Cameron, David A. Whetten, and Myung U. Kim, "Organizational Dysfunctions of Decline," *Academy of Management Journal,* March 1987, p. 128, with permission.

grease to smooth over conflict-creating forces. Management uses this slack as a currency for buying off potentially conflicting interest groups within the organization. Conflicts can be resolved readily by expanding everyone's resources. However, in the decline phase, conflict over resources increases because there is less slack to divvy up. For instance, conflict has been found to be higher in declining school districts than in growing districts.[22]

Consistent with our approach to conflict in Chapter 15, we are not suggesting that the increased conflict evident in decline is necessarily dysfunctional. If managed properly, it can be directed toward slowing the decline. Out of the conflict can come changes that may revitalize the organization: selection of a new domain, the creation of new products or services, and cost-cutting measures that can make the shrunken organization more efficient and viable.

Increased Politicking. Less slack also translates into more politicking. There will emerge many organized and vocal groups actively pursuing their self-interest. As we noted earlier in this chapter, structural changes during decline are more likely to be determined by which coalitions win the power struggle for organizational control than by rational determinants such as size, technology, or environment. Politically naive managers will find their jobs difficult, if not impossible, as they are unable to adjust to the changing decision-making criterion. Remember, under declining conditions, the pie of resources is shrinking. If one department can successfully resist a cut, typically the result will be that other departments have to cut deeper. Weak units not only will take a disproportional part of the cut but may be most vulnerable to elimination. In a "fight-for-life" situation, the standard rules are disregarded. Critical data for decisions are twisted and interpreted by various coalitions so as to further their groups' interests. Such an environment encourages "no holds barred" politicking.

Increased Resistance to Change. The organization responds more slowly to environmental change in decline than in growth.[23] In its effort to protect itself, the dominant coalition fights hard to maintain the status quo and its control. Vested interests thwart change efforts.[24] The unfreezing stage in the change process becomes extremely difficult. Resistance to change seems to be related to the previously discussed "stages of decline."[25] Early in the decline, individuals follow a pattern of "weathering the storm." This is characterized by intensified efforts to follow the old, established procedures and may result in slowing the decline. But if it is truly of the prolonged variety, at best it can only delay the inevitable. So the early part of decline is a period of high resistance to change. Resistance should be reduced as it becomes clear that the decline is not temporary.

One writer has noted that a major force for resisting change during the initial phase of decline will be those vested interests who have benefited most from growth.[26] Since their power base is challenged, they are motivated to continue to push for growth-related policies, even though it no longer makes sense. The writer described research demonstrating this effect in cities that have actively pursued growth—as might have characterized Phoenix, Raleigh, Orlando, and San Diego during the 1980s. Such cities competed with one another for new industry and other preconditions of growth by advertising their low crime rates, low taxes, large labor forces, abundant natural resources, and other favorable features. This growth orientation tended to attract to politics people who had a vested interest in growth—real-estate developers, local business people, educational leaders. These people, in turn, reinforced the drive to increase city size so as to enlarge their share of the local resource pool. They argued, for instance, that growth would increase employment, despite evidence to the contrary; namely, that fast-growing metropolitan areas tend to have higher unemployment rates than do slow-growing ones. Progrowth advocates attempt to push for growth because it supports their interest well beyond the point where the diseconomies of growth overshadow its benefits. If these cities are to change their policies, say, toward stabilizing the population, it will be necessary to dislodge the growth advocates from their power positions and replace them with a new cadre of leaders with a different set of vested interests.[27]

Loss of Top-Management Credibility. In decline, members of the organization will look to some individual or group on which to place the blame for the retrenchment. Whether or not top management is directly responsible for the decline, they tend to become the scapegoat. This, in turn, leads to a loss of top-management credibility. Members compare their organizations with others that are growing or compare their plight with the situation of friends and relatives employed by healthy organizations, and then they look for some place to vent their frustrations. If their organization's senior management were competent, they seem to assume, retrenchment would not be necessary or at least it would be of short duration.

The most overt signs of this loss of credibility is a reduction in employee morale and organizational commitment. During retrenchment, job satisfaction tends to drop significantly as does member loyalty to the organization.

Change in Work-Force Composition. Retrenchment requires personnel cuts. The most popular criterion for determining who gets laid off is seniority; that is, the most recent hirees are first to go. Laying off personnel on the basis of seniority, however, tends to reshape the composition of the work force.

Since newer employees tend to be younger, seniority-based

layoffs typically create an older work force. When organizations operating in mature industries are required to make substantial cuts, the average age of employees may increase ten years or more.

One of the more disheartening results of seniority-based layoffs is that it undermines much of the progress made in the past twenty-five years toward opening up job opportunities for females and minorities. Members of these groups tend to be among the most recently hired and therefore are the first to be let go. The organization's labor force will become more homogeneous, made up again predominantly of white males.

Increased Voluntary Turnover. The other side of employee departures are voluntary quits. This becomes a major potential problem in organizational decline because the organization will want to retain its most valuable employees. Yet some of the first people to voluntarily leave an organization when it enters the stage of decline are the most mobile individuals, such as skilled technicians, professionals, and talented managerial personnel. These, of course, are typically the individuals that the organization can least afford to lose.

Managers are particularly prone to "jump ship" when it is clear that the growth days are over. The opportunities for advancement and increased responsibilities are obviously reduced greatly during decline. The upwardly mobile executive will look for an organization where his or her talents are more likely to be utilized. This suggests that senior management will be challenged to provide incentives to ambitious junior managers if they are to prevent a long, slow decline from snowballing into a rapid descent.

Decaying Employee Motivation. Employee motivation is different when an organization is contracting than when it is enjoying growth. On the growth side, motivation can be provided by promotional opportunities and the excitement of being associated with a dynamic organization. During decline, there are layoffs, reassignments of duties that frequently require absorbing the tasks that were previously done by others, and similar stress-inducing changes. It's usually hard for employees to stay motivated when there is high uncertainty as to whether they will still have a job next month or next year. When their organization is experiencing prolonged decline, managers are challenged to function effectively in an organizational climate typified by stagnation, fear, and stress.

CAUGHT IN THE MIDDLE

How do those middle managers feel who find themselves among the survivors after a major corporate downsizing? Interviews offer some interesting insights.[28]

On the positive side, those who are left find that many of their lower-priority duties have been dropped. They're ending up with more interesting and demanding jobs. Wider spans of control also mean middle managers are operating with more delegated authority and less upper-management control.

But there is a clear and real negative side for these survivors. Many feel overburdened and underappreciated. Even though they escaped the cutting ax, they have difficulty forgetting how their companies treated their peers. They are restless and dissatisfied. One survey of 1200 middle managers found that more than a third believed they would be happier elsewhere. And these managers can't help but wonder if the same fate that befell their colleagues might also strike them sometime down the road.

Regardless of top-management's words or actions, surviving middle managers tend to bemoan the loss of the job security they once had. They have come to recognize the painful truth—middle management's golden age is over. During the 1980s, more than a million U.S. managers and staff professionals lost their jobs as organizations trimmed their management ranks. One expert estimates that more than a third of U.S. middle-management jobs were eliminated. And the stark reality is that these jobs are not coming back. Organizations in the 1990s are going to have significantly fewer middle managers.

What's the Solution?

There are no magic techniques available to management that can overcome the many negative outcomes associated with organizational decline. But some things seem to work better than others.[29] These include clarifying the organization's strategy, increasing communication, centralizing decision making, redesigning jobs, and developing innovative approaches to cutbacks.

Management needs to attack directly the ambiguity that organizational decline creates among employees. This is best done by clarifying the organization's strategy and goals. Where is the organization going? What is the organization's future and potential? By addressing these questions, management demonstrates that it understands the problem and has a vision for what the new, smaller organization will look like. Employees want to believe that management is not content to sit back and run a "going-out-of-business" sale.

Organizational decline demands that management do a lot of communicating with employees. The primary focus of this communication should be downward; specifically, explaining the rationale for changes that will have to be made. But there should also be upward communication to give employees an opportunity to vent their fears and frustrations, and have important questions answered. Remember, management's credibility is not likely to be high. Additionally, rumors will be rampant. This puts a premium on management's making every effort to explain clearly the reasons for, and implications of, all significant changes. That is not going to eliminate employee fears, but it will increase the likelihood that management will be perceived as honest and trustworthy. Under the conditions, that may be about the best one can hope for.

We noted earlier in the chapter that a common action taken by management when decline first begins is to centralize decisions. Such action makes a great deal of sense, and we offer it as a prescription to managers. This suggestion, incidentally, does not contradict our previous recommendation regarding increased communication. The objective is to get people more aware of what is going on, but that doesn't imply a greater role in decision making.

You may also be thinking, Wouldn't decentralization and an increase in participation be a better solution? After all, participation is often proposed as a potent vehicle for facilitating change. We argue against participation during decline, especially on tough resource allocation and cutback decisions, because of the evidence that people can't be rational contributors to their own demise.[30] The self-interest of participants is just too great to provide benefits that exceed the costs. Participation and decentralization should be reintroduced only when it is clear to everyone that the decline has stabilized.

When cuts are made in personnel, it creates the opportunity for management to consolidate and redesign jobs. If the decline appears to be arrested and fears of further layoffs subside, the redesign of jobs to make them more challenging and motivating can turn a problem—eliminating functions and reassigning workloads—into an opportunity. For example, by increasing the variety of work activities and allowing people to do complete jobs, employees can find their new assignments offering a greater diversity of activities and with more whole and identifiable work.

Our final suggestion for managing organizational decline is for management to look for innovative ways to deal with the problems inherent in cutbacks. Some organizations, for example, have offered attractive incentives to encourage employees to take early retirement; have provided outplacement services to laid-off employees; and have imposed work-hour reduction programs to replace layoffs, whereby all employees shared in the cutback by working only twenty-five or thirty hours a week.

SUMMARY

Growth and decline—the two most significant stages in the organization's life cycle—create distinctly different problems and opportunities for managers.

The OT literature has had a growth bias. "Bigger is better" is consistent with the growth bias. So too are the beliefs that growth increases the likelihood of survival, is synonymous with effectiveness, and represents power. This bias can be seen in Greiner's model of organizational growth. In this model, an organization's evolution is characterized by phases of prolonged and calm growth, followed by periods of internal turmoil.

Managing organizational decline is not merely reversing what was done during growth. There is a lag that typifies the rate of change in structure during prolonged decline that is not evident in growth. This lag causes the level of structure to be greater in the same organization for a given size during decline than during growth. In turn, this projects into a larger administrative component during decline; the increased importance of the power-control perspective in explaining structure; and the tendency for management to, first, ignore decline, then to treat it as an aberration and to respond appropriately only after some delay.

In decline, managers are likely to confront higher levels of conflict, increased politicking, increased resistance to change, loss of credibility, changes in work-force composition, higher levels of voluntary turnover, and decaying employee motivation. Suggestions for managing decline include clarifying the organization's strategy, increasing communication, centralizing decision making, redesigning jobs, and developing innovative approaches to cutbacks.

FOR REVIEW AND DISCUSSION

1. Why do American values favor growth?
2. How does growth increase survival?
3. How can growth be conceived as power?
4. What crisis does creativity create? Delegation? Coordination?
5. What criticisms do you have with the organizational growth model?
6. Contrast *organizational decline* and *downsizing.*
7. Describe how organizational decline can be interpreted as a reduction in organizational effectiveness.
8. Is decline more likely to occur in public-sector organizations than in business firms? Explain.
9. "Decline doesn't reduce slack; it increases it! In decline, organizations have *more* personnel and physical resources than they need." Do you agree or disagree? Discuss.
10. How does the administrative component in decline differ from that in growth?
11. Describe how management typically responds to decline.
12. Why might a manager prefer to work in a growing organization than in one that is in decline?
13. What positive outcomes, if any, can you see that retrenchment can provide for an organization?
14. What solutions, other than those mentioned in this chapter, might management implement to manage decline better?
15. Contrast the role of the imperatives in determining an organization's structure (discussed in Part II) during growth and during decline.

NOTES

[1] Based on "The Sad Saga of Western Union's Decline," *Business Week*, December 14, 1987, pp. 108–14.

[2] See, for example, G. Ray Funkhouser and Robert R. Rothberg, "The Dogma of Growth: A Re-Examination," *Business Horizons*, March–April 1985, pp. 9–16; and Dan R. Dalton and Idalene F. Kesner, "Organizational Growth: Big Is Beautiful," *Journal of Business Strategy*, Summer 1985, pp. 38–48.

[3] James D. Thompson, *Organizations in Action* (New York: McGraw-Hill, 1967), p. 89.

[4] Jeffrey Pfeffer, *Organizational Design* (Arlington Heights, Ill.: AHM Publishing, 1978), p. 114.

[5] David A. Whetten, "Organizational Decline: A Neglected Topic in Organizational Science, *Academy of Management Review*, October 1980, p. 578.

[6] William G. Scott, "The Management of Decline," *Conference Board Record*, June 1976, p. 57.

[7] Jeffrey Pfeffer and Gerald R. Salancik, *The External Control of Organizations* (New York: Harper & Row, 1978).

[8] *Fortune*, April 28, 1986, p. 27.

[9] Pfeffer, *Organizational Design*, p. 115.

[10] David A. Whetten, "Organizational Growth and Decline Processes," in Kim S. Cameron, Robert I. Sutton, and David A. Whetten, *Readings in Organizational Decline* (Cambridge, Mass.: Ballinger Publishing, 1988), p. 36.

[11] Larry E. Greiner, "Evolution and Revolution as Organizations Grow." *Harvard Business Review*, July–August 1972, pp. 37–46.

[12] See, for instance, William Weitzel and Ellen Jonsson, "Decline in Organizations: A Literature Integration and Extension," *Administrative Science Quarterly*, March 1989, pp. 91–109.

[13] Whetten, "Organizational Decline," p. 579.

[14] Charles H. Levine, "More on Cutback Management: Hard Questions for Hard Times," *Public Administration Review*, March–April 1979, pp. 179–83.

[15] Jeffrey D. Ford, "The Occurrence of Structural Hysteresis in Declining Organizations," *Academy of Management Review*, October 1980, pp. 589–98.

[16] Ibid., p. 592.

[17] John H. Freeman and Michael T. Hannan, "Growth and Decline Processes in Organizations," *American Sociological Review*, April 1975, p. 215–83; William McKinley, "Complexity and Administrative Intensity: The Case of Declining Organizations," *Administrative Science Quarterly*, March 1987, pp. 87–105; and John R. Montanari and Philip J. Adelman, "The Administrative Component of Organizations and the Ratchet Effect: A Critique of Cross-Sectional Studies," *Journal of Management Studies*, March 1987, pp. 113–23.

[18] Jeffrey D. Ford, "The Administrative Component in Growing and Declining Organizations: A Longitudinal Analysis," *Academy of Management Journal*, December 1980, pp. 615–30.

[19] Michael T. Hannan and John H. Freeman, "Internal Politics of Growth and Decline," in Marshall W. Meyer and Associates, eds., *Environments and Organizations* (San Francisco: Jossey-Bass, 1978), pp. 177–99.

[20] Todd D. Jick, "Process and Impacts of a Merger: Individual and Organizational Perspectives." Doctoral dissertation, Cornell University, 1979.

[21] Based on "Middle Managers Are Still Sitting Ducks," *Business Week*, September 16, 1985, p. 34.

[22] Hannan and Freeman, "Internal Politics of Growth and Decline."

[23] Ibid.

[24] John Gardner, "Organizational Survival: Overcoming Mind-Forged Manacles," in John F. Veiga and John N. Yanouzas, eds., *The Dynamics of*

Organization Theory: Gaining a Macro Perspective, (St. Paul, Minn.: West Publishing, 1979), pp. 28–31.

[25] B. L. T. Hedberg, Paul C. Nystrom, and William H. Starbuck, "Camping on Seesaws: Prescriptions for a Self-designing Organization," *Administrative Science Quarterly,* March 1976, pp. 41–65.

[26] Whetten, "Organizational Decline," p. 582.

[27] H. Molotch, "The City as a Growth Machine: Toward a Political Economy of Place," *American Journal of Sociology,* September 1976, pp. 309–32.

[28] Based on "Caught in the Middle," *Business Week,* September 12, 1988, pp. 80–84.

[29] These suggestions are derived from Ronald Lippitt and Gordon Lippitt, "Humane Downsizing: Organizational Renewal versus Organizational Depression," *S.A.M. Advanced Management Journal,* Summer 1984, pp. 15–21; Lee Tom Perry, "Least-Cost Alternatives to Layoffs in Declining Industries," *Organizational Dynamics,* Spring 1986, pp. 48–61; Cynthia Hardy, "Strategies for Retrenchment: Reconciling Individual and Organizational Needs," *Canadian Journal of Administrative Sciences,* December 1986, pp. 275–89; and George E. L. Barbee, "Downsizing With Dignity: Easing the Pain of Employee Layoffs," *Business and Society Review,* Spring 1987, pp. 31–34.

[30] Charles H. Levine, "More on Cutback Management."

CASE STUDIES

INFORMATION SYSTEMS AT MRS. FIELDS' COOKIES

Based on Tom Richman, "Mrs. Fields' Secret Ingredient," *Inc.*, October 1987, pp. 65–72.

Mrs. Fields' Cookies has nearly five hundred stores in thirty-seven states. In contrast to many food retailers, Mrs. Fields' stores are not franchised operations. Rather, all the stores are owned by Debbi and Randy Fields, and run out of their headquarters in Park City, Utah. The secret to managing this widely dispersed operation is a computer system that is "state of the art."

Mrs. Fields' specialty is fresh and warm chocolate chip cookies. But most of the company's nearly 4500 store employees are young and inexperienced, and know little about the cookie business. Without a knowledgeable owner-manager to guide them, few are skilled enough to know, for example, how many batches of cookie dough to mix each day or when to mix them in order to meet demand and minimize leftovers, how to calculate crew schedules, or how to differentiate applicants who will succeed from those who will fail. So Randy Fields has installed a computer-based information system to do all these things for the store employees.

Each store manager begins his or her day by calling up the Day Planner program on the store computer. The computer will ask the manager a set of questions such as, What day of the week is it? Is it a normal day, school day, holiday, or other? Once these data are entered, the program reviews the store's performance on the last three previous comparable days. It then sets out the day's sales goals, hour by hour and for each product. It states how many customers will be needed each hour and how much each customer will need to purchase. Further, it tells the manager how many batches of cookie dough to make and when to make them. As the day progresses, sales data are entered in the computer hourly. The program can then revise the hourly projections and offer suggestions on how to improve sales. For example, if the average sale is too low, it will provide tips on suggestive selling. If the customer count is down, it might recommend having an employee offer samples to passersby outside. Of course, the individual store computers are linked to Park City, so Randy has almost instant access to how things are going at every store.

This information system also does a number of other functions for store managers. Based on sales projections, it schedules hourly crew needs for two weeks in advance. It has a program that job candidates complete, which, based on answers given by past hirees, provides a valuable profile to the store manager on any applicant's potential to succeed as a Mrs. Fields' employee. The system even has a repair program that helps managers to pinpoint equipment problems. If the problem requires outside repair work, the computer sends a repair request to Park City telling the staff there which machine is broken, its maintenance history, and which vendor to call.

Randy Fields believes this system will allow him, his wife, and their small corporate staff to oversee one thousand stores the same way that they did when they had thirty. He argues that he has created *the* shape of future business organizations that are spatially dispersed—the management hierarchy of the company feels almost flat to store managers, while tight management controls are maintained.

QUESTIONS

1. Describe Mrs. Fields' Cookies in terms of its complexity, formalization, and centralization.
2. Do management information systems, such as the one at Mrs. Fields, alter the conclusion that large size leads to increased vertical differentiation, formalization, and decentralization? Discuss.
3. Are computerized information systems part of an organization's technology? Explain.

4. "This system leads to better store-level decisions." Do you agree or disagree? Support your position.
5. What negative store-level repercussions might result from this system?
6. Explain the potential impact of computerized information systems from the power-control perspective.

_____ CASE 2

SEARS TRIES TO STOP ITS MARKET-SHARE SLIDE

Based on Francine Schwadel, "Its Expansion Lagging, Sears Now Struggles to Stay Independent," *Wall Street Journal,* November 2, 1988, p. 1; Patricia Sellers, "Why Bigger Is Badder at Sears," *Fortune,* December 5, 1988, pp. 79–84; and "Will the Big Markdown Get the Big Store Moving Again?" *Business Week,* March 13, 1989, pp. 110–14.

Sears, Roebuck & Co. once ranked as the premier retailer in the United States. In the 1940s, while competitors played it conservative, Sears management foresaw the growth of suburbia and aggressively located new stores in large suburban shopping centers that offered plenty of parking for the growing number of automobiles consumers were buying. Sears' sales and profits grew impressively. But the company ran into problems in the 1980s. For instance, in 1987, Sears sales grew only 4.3 percent, whereas Wal-Mart's exploded by 34 percent. By the late 1980s, Sears had lost its number-one position in retailing to Kmart, with Wal-Mart closing fast in the third slot. Sears' problems included a bloated structure that created incredibly high operating expenses, an unwieldly system that did a poor job of coordinating and controlling operations, a recent history of inconsistent merchandising and pricing strategies, and an organizational culture that adamantly resisted change.

Sears' selling and administrative expenses represented 30 percent of its sales versus 24 percent at J. C. Penney and Kmart and 17 percent at Wal-Mart. Sears' distribution costs—around 8 percent of sales versus about 2 percent at Wal-Mart and Kmart—were the highest in retailing. These high costs made it hard for Sears to offer competitive prices. General merchandisers like Kmart, single-category discounters such as Toys "R" Us and Circuit City Stores, and hundreds of specialty catalog mail-order firms had attacked Sears from multiple directions by offering a comparable or superior selection of goods at lower prices. Between 1978 and 1988, Sears' share of general merchandise sales in the U.S. fell from 18 to 13 percent. That represented $8.4 billion lost to competitors.

The coordination and control problems of overseeing 825 outlets and 526,000 people seem to have overwhelmed Sears' management. Decision-making had become too centralized. The company's corporate staff occupied 60 percent of the 110-story Sears Tower in Chicago. What once was viewed as "the nice store down the street" had become a remote, powerful corporation. As an example of the coordination and control problems, a visit to a Sears store in New Jersey found that every female mannequin in view— at least ten—had torn stockings. The jewelry department had empty cosmetic racks in it and huge photos of heavily made-up models on the walls even though the conversion of the section from cosmetics to jewelry had taken place six months before. In response, Sears announced in late 1988 that it intended to sell the Sears Tower and move 90 percent of the 8000 corporate staff personnel to cheaper quarters.

One of the more perplexing dilemmas for loyal Sears' customers has been to try to decipher just where Sears stood in the retail hierarchy. Originally, Sears built its reputation on a strategy of offering high-quality, moderate-priced merchandise sold under its own private-label brands. Names like Craftsman, Diehard, and Kenmore had become synonymous with dependability. Its pricing policy was not to be a discount store, but rather to offer hundreds of different items each week on sale. The public learned to watch for these sale items, as attested by the fact that 55 percent of Sears' goods were sold at reduced prices. This image got clouded in the early 1980s when Sears tried to reposition itself as a fashion store. Toward that end, for example, it developed a line of Cheryl Tiegs designer-label clothing. However, its most significant strategic shift was initiated in the spring of 1989. Sears proposed to pursue a strategy of "everyday low pricing." Prices of almost all goods were sharply and permanently cut, and deep-discount promotions were largely eliminated. Sears believed this strategy would cut its administrative overhead and allow it to compete more directly with discounters. Company management believed it would be able to become a low-cost operator by dropping hundreds of styles and models (and thus significantly cutting inventories) and by ending the huge promotional expenses associated with planning, buying, storing, distributing, and advertising the on-going sale goods. Moreover, the new strategy has Sears selling name brands like RCA, Sony, and Maytag alongside its own private-label brands.

Finally, Sears has a long-established culture that has bred arrogance among its employees and management. After dominating the retailing industry for as many years as Sears did, its people saw themselves as working for an American institution. Anything new or different was seen as threatening and, therefore, needed to be resisted. Sears' conservative inbred managers were very slow to respond to any change in the company's environment. Executives, sequestered in the upper floors of the Sears Tower, seemed to be a million miles removed from the needs and concerns of their customers. In response to this static and conservative culture, Sears senior executive have been trying to change their attitudes. For instance, in 1987, 135 of them went to a New Mexico retreat to experience taking risks together with the support of their peers. But the inbreeding and cockiness may be too deep to change easily. In spite of all of Sears' problems, when its CEO was asked in late 1988 what he thought the biggest problem he faced in 1989 was, he replied, "I don't see any huge problems. I feel very good about how we're positioned strategically."

QUESTIONS

1. Describe how Sears' original strategy influenced its structure.
2. Do you think its change in strategy in 1989 should have led to changes in structure? Explain.
3. How has size influenced Sears' structure?
4. Kmart is almost the same size as Sears but is more effective. What structural factors do you think might contribute to Kmart being more effective than Sears?
5. Is Sears a mature or a declining firm? Support your position.
6. What problems does Sears face that Wal-Mart and Kmart don't?

_____ **CASE 3**

MERGING AMC INTO CHRYSLER

Based on "Digesting AMC: So Far, So Good," *Business Week, February 22, 1988, pp. 130–32.*

American Motors Corporation might have been a "little guy" by auto industry standards, but with sales of $3.5 billion, it certainly qualifies as a large organization. When it was bought in August of 1987 by Chrysler Corp., Chrysler chairman Lee Iacocca described the task of merging AMC into Chrysler's operation akin to "swallowing a whale."

Before Japanese firms like Honda and Nissan began producing cars in the United States, AMC regularly held fourth place among the so-called Big Four U.S. automobile manufacturers—behind General Motors, Ford, and Chrysler. AMC had given America cars like the "little Nash Rambler," the Pacer, and the Hornet. But Chrysler wanted AMC predominantly for its highly popular and profitable line of Jeeps and for its new Canadian manufacturing plant. Never a major money-maker, Chrysler was also intent on making AMC more efficient. Iacocca needed not only to merge AMC into Chrysler, but he wanted to cut its operating costs as he had done at Chrysler when he took over in 1980.

The difficulty of merging AMC into Chrysler would not be easy under the best of circumstances, but it was especially challenging in the summer of 1987. Specifically, automobile and truck sales in the United States fell 7 percent that year and U.S. unit sales of Chrysler's line of cars slid 16 percent. Chrysler's pretax profit margin was down to 8.3 percent from 10.2 percent in 1986. Moreover, Japanese carmakers were boosting output at their newly built U.S. factories and Korean automakers, particularly Hyundai, were rapidly expanding their market share. Meanwhile, AMC was preparing to launch the Premier, the first of its new Eagle line of cars, in the fall of 1987.

During the six months following the August 1987 purchase of AMC, Iacocca made every minute count. For example, to boost Jeep production fast at AMC's well-worn Toledo plant, he got workers to work overtime on Saturdays in return for a promise to keep the factory running through 1992; he shut down AMC's 86-year-old Kenosha, Wisconsin, plant, eliminating 5500 jobs and cutting total capacity by 230,000 vehicles; and he began cloning other practices he had used at Chrysler to cut costs, such as reducing steel inventories at stamping plants by 80 percent and eliminating duplications in the production of parts.

QUESTIONS

1. How does the purchase of AMC help Chrysler to manage its environment?
2. If you had been Iacocca in August 1987, what actions would you have taken to reduce resistance among AMC personnel to changes caused by Chrysler's acquisition?
3. At the time of Chrysler's purchase of AMC, was Chrysler a growing, stagnant, or declining organization? How about AMC?
4. Are management efforts to increase efficiency through reductions in staff indicative of an organization in decline? Discuss.
5. How is the acquisition of AMC likely to change Chrysler's organization structure?

_____ CASE 4

HANDS-OFF MANAGEMENT
AT DOVER CORPORATION

Based on Robert McGough, "Hands-Off Managers," _Forbes,_ December 1, 1986, pp. 81–84.

Even though Dover Corp. has annual sales of $1.4 billion, most people have never heard of it. That's because Dover is really a group of 41 different businesses that make such items as bearings, lifts, nozzles, and sucker rods that go into oil pumps, factory controls, and other similar industrial products.

While Dover may not make products with household names, its management knows how to make money. Profits continue to climb each year, and its five-year average return on equity of 21.7 percent is significantly better than well-known conglomerates like ITT. The secret of Dover's success is its unusual organization design. For a company of its size, it has an amazingly small corporate headquarters staff and gives its operating managers an unusual amount of autonomy.

Dover's headquarters office in New York City has only twenty people. The company has no corporate director of sales, personnel, compensation, or corporate planning, and no internal audit staff. The forty-one subsidiaries are divided into five groups, each with its own president and board of directors. These group offices are also small—with only three to five people in each. The head of the subsidiaries rarely have contact with Dover's CEO, unless they initiate the interaction. But when they have a problem or need something from Dover, such as funds to build a new plant, they don't have to communicate through a multilevel bureaucracy. They merely take their concern to their group president. The idea is to let the operating heads of each subsidiary run his or her business independent of external interference. The chief task of Dover headquarters is to take the cash produced by these businesses and buy more like them.

QUESTIONS

1. Most billion-dollar conglomerates have a staff of at least several hundred employees at headquarters. Why?
2. Is Dover's operation undermanaged? Explain.
3. Describe Dover's organization structure. What types of design is management using?
4. How has Dover's strategy influenced its structure?
5. In a conglomerate, what functions, if any, are better performed at corporate headquarters rather than at the unit level? Explain your answer.

_____ **CASE 5**

FORD VERSUS THE GENERAL

Based on Anne B. Fisher, "GM is Tougher Than You Think," _Fortune_, November 10, 1986, pp. 56–64; William J. Hampton and James R. Norman, "General Motors: What Went Wrong," _Business Week_, March 16, 1987, pp. 102–10; Brian S. Moskal, "Glasnost in Dearborn," _Industry Week_, September 21, 1987, pp. 53–55; Alex Taylor III, "Why Fords Sell Like Big Macs," _Fortune_, November 21, 1988, pp. 122–25; and James B.

Treece "GM's Bumpy Ride on the Long Road Back," *Business Week,* February 13, 1989, pp. 74–78.

In the U.S. automobile industry, Ford Motor Co. and General Motors have been giants for more than sixty years. By the late 1920s, they had each become large and inflexible bureaucracies, and they stayed that way until quite recently.

To understand the Ford structure, you have to go back to its founder, Henry Ford. Henry became famous for introducing mass production techniques to the auto industry. But he was a man who feared change and loved control. He stubbornly refused to alter the Model T, even when it was a decade old, and proudly claimed that customers could have "any color car they want, as long as it was black." By the late 1940s, even though Ford Motor Co. had become a massive manufacturing organization, old Henry refused to delegate authority and still tried to make every decision in the company, just as he had done back in its infancy. This historical precedent carried on with later generations of managers. Ford Motor Co. came into the 1980s with a culture built on top-down directives and suppression of any ideas that hadn't originated at the top.

When Alfred Sloan put GM together in the 1920s, he believed in decentralized authority with centralized control. He created separate divisions for Chevrolet, Pontiac, Oldsmobile, Buick, and Cadillac—and each was given a specific market segment within which to compete. Division managers were relatively autonomous but headquarters controlled operations through an extensive reporting system and through its power to allocate financial resources. No one person ran GM. Important decisions required approval by half-a-dozen or more committees and another half-dozen executives. The system worked at culling out poorly reasoned or risky decision options.

By the early 1980s, GM and Ford held very different positions in the automobile industry. GM was on a roll. It controlled 48 percent of the U.S. market and was generating record-breaking profits. Ford, on the other hand, had less than a 16 percent market share. Ford was also losing money—a whopping $3.26 billion between 1980 and 1982 alone. But the companies embarked on different roads during the 1980s and, by the end of the decade, had arrived at very different destinations. GM's market share had fallen to 35 percent, whereas Ford saw its share increase to 22 percent.

More startling was the fact that Ford's earnings had now surpassed GM's, even though its sales were only about two-thirds of the General's. To better understand how this came about, we need to look at the problems each faced entering the 1980s, the strategy they decided to pursue, and the specific actions they took.

Ford's problems in 1980 were many. Its cars were nondescript. A number of its products had reputations for shoddiness. The Japanese were rapidly expanding sales in the United States. And, very importantly, Ford's volume was significantly below GMs. This meant each Ford car had to shoulder a larger percentage of fixed costs than did GM products and resulted in significantly greater per-car profits for GM. Ford executives realized they had to take some drastic actions if the company was to survive. What they did was introduce a broad-based cost-cutting effort, initiate a massive program to change Ford's culture, put renewed emphasis on listening to and working with the people who made Ford products, and change the corporate strategy to become the styling leader among the U.S. "Big Three."

Ford became more efficient by cutting layers of management, getting employees more involved in the production process, and cutting defects by focusing people's attention on improving product quality. Managers and nonmanagers alike took part in a major program to increase their level of participation, commitment, and creativity. Management training particularly emphasized the need to replace the company's autocratic management style with one of participation. Encouraging its design staff to emulate the successes of European stylists, impressively restyled cars began coming off the assembly line in late 1985. The Taurus and Sable, the sporty Probe, and the new models of the Lincoln Continental and Ford Thunderbird became immediate hits with consumers. Meanwhile, by 1987 the company had succeeded in reducing its breakeven point by 40 percent and cutting labor-hours per car down to where the same number of cars could be produced as in 1979 but with 120,000 fewer employees.

General Motors entered the 1980s in a much stronger position than Ford. But GM pursued another strategy—which proved, over time, to be flawed.

Like Ford, GM had high costs and a bloated organization. It, too, had a tradition-bound culture and an internal system that stifled innovation and was slow in reacting to a changing environment. Yet GM had high profits, huge cash reserves, and a pervasive belief that it could do no wrong. So, ironically, GM was a prisoner of its past successes. Its management was cocky and unable to be self-critical.

GM's management assumed that gas prices would rise and fuel shortages would prevail throughout the 1980s, so smaller cars would be highly sought. Aware of the increased competition from Japanese and European manufacturers, GM decided to use its vast financial resources to spend its U.S. and foreign competitors into the ground. For example, it would spend $50 billion between 1980 and 1987 on capital investment—enough to have bought Toyota and Nissan and have a few spare billions left over. GM bought and installed robots, lasers, and computers designed to step up efficiency, boost quality, and make product and engineering changes faster than the old system could. Rather than focus on product styling, it would generate huge economies of scale by building its cars out of common parts. High technology and high volume would enable GM to make cars more cheaply than anyone.

Unfortunately for GM, things didn't work out the way management planned. Fuel prices dropped and, with it, the demand for small cars. Consumers sought large cars, which were being produced in large quantities by Ford and Chrysler. GM spent enough money on capital investment to buy several of its major Japanese competitors, yet the company *lost* market share. The new high-tech factories were hardly more efficient than the old ones. GM found out the hard way that new technology pays off only when combined with changes in the way work is organized on the factory floor. Moreover, the heavy vertical integration at GM—whereby company subsidiaries produced two-thirds of the parts that went into its cars—meant that GM couldn't take advantage of competition among outside suppliers. Ford and Chrysler, using competitive bidding, could buy parts at a significantly cheaper price than GM. The net result was that between 1981 and 1987, GM's break-even point *rose* 30 percent.

GM executives, particularly in the middle-management ranks, resisted any changes. People tended to say, "Hey, we came through this recession and that recession, we survived the oil shocks, we turned a $760-million loss a few years ago into a $4-billion profit. Why would anybody want to come in here and tell us to do anything differently *now*?" Complacency ruled. Attempts to reorganize the car divisions only led to look-alike products—for example, in 1987, it was almost impossible to tell the difference between a $10,000

Oldsmobile Calais and a $26,000 Cadillac Seville—and consumers responded by snubbing GM products. In spite of all of GM's efforts between 1980 and 1988 to expand market share and become more competitive, the company *lost* a significant percent of its market share and took forty-one labor-hours to assemble a midsize car while Ford did it in only twenty-five hours.

By late 1987, GM's executives seemed to have gotten the message. No longer were they pursuing the strategy of expanding market share. Rather, like Ford, they were concentrating on producing more stylish and differentiated cars, and beginning to restructure the company so as to be able to produce fewer cars more efficiently. Plans were being made to close at least four of its twenty-six North American auto assembly plants and slash at least 100,000 jobs from its 600,000-person work force. And this approach seemed to be paying off. In the last half of 1988, GM's profits increased smartly.

QUESTIONS

1. Using competing values, assess why Ford is widely considered more effective than GM. How could GM have used the competing-values approach in the early 1980s to recognize that it had problems?
2. Contrast Ford and GM's strategies. How has each affected their organization's structure?
3. How did GM's technology affect its structure?
4. Assess both company's effectiveness in terms of their "environment-structure" fit.
5. Are there any structural factors that can help to explain why Ford made more money than GM in the late 1980s?
6. Contrast these two organizations' approaches to managing change.
7. Contrast GM and Ford's cultures in 1978 and 1988. What might GM have done in 1980 to reshape its culture and make it better fit its environment?

_____ CASE 6

JOHN PAUL II: CEO OF THE WORLD'S LARGEST ORGANIZATION?

Based on Don A. Schanche, "John Paul II, CEO," *Los Angeles Times Magazine*, September 13, 1987, pp. 9–13.

Pope John Paul II is not a businessperson. He doesn't have to worry about stock performance and production schedules. Yet he is the leader of 840 million Catholics and guardian of one of the world's largest and least understood organizations. Let's look at the Pope's organization and his management strategy.

The basic structure of the Catholic church is deceptively simple. It is composed of a five-step hierarchy: from Pope, to cardinal, to archbishop, to bishop, to parish priest. Worldwide, John Paul commands 405,000 priests, who in turn oversee 30,000 secondary schools, 6000 hospitals and almost 7000 orphanages. Were it not for a decentralized system of management, this huge organization long ago would have sunk into an administrative nightmare. As it is, the Vatican gives only broad direction to the church's 3100 bishops, who have wide authority over all the operations of their dioceses.

Since Pope John Paul II has decided to spend much of his energy taking high-visibility tours of the world, most of the day-to-day administration of the Vatican has been left to ten or so of his chief cardinals. Each has been given charge of a major church office, which are called congregations and resemble a corporate division. There are, for example, the Congregation for Catholic Education and the Congregation for Religious and Secular Institutes. A recent proposal to combine some congregations for economic reasons has produced ferocious infighting among the cardinals.

John Paul, himself, has a clear perception of his organization's goals and has devoted a great deal of time to communicating that perception to others. He has surrounded himself with energetic subordinates who share their leader's vision and he has inspired them to action. He makes it clear to subordinates that he expects nothing less than their very best efforts in everything they do.

The Pope's job has been made more difficult because of the growing numbers of Catholic activists, particularly in the United States, who have challenged the Pope's conservative positions on such emotional issues as divorce, birth control, premarital sex, homosexuality, and the ban on women priests. In contrast to the Catholic church of a hundred years ago, there is considerably less acceptance of a single vision for the church and its goals.

One of the most challenging managerial tasks that have faced John Paul has been managing the church's bureaucracy, known as the Curia. This autonomous, self-protecting apparatus, staffed mostly by Italian clergy, has long resisted papal control. But in the view of most of the members of today's Curia, John Paul has succeeded in banishing that administrative inertia and instead bringing a heightened sense of purpose.

The Pope's "executive desk" is his dining table. He invites subordinates and experts in many fields to join him at virtually every meal. Joaquin Navarro Valls, the Pope's press secretary, has been a frequent guest at the papal table because he plays a key part in getting the Pope's message across to the public. Valls comments that he usually leaves the pontiff's dining room table with a long list of things that he wants done.

Many also say the efficiency and zeal of those who run the Vatican have improved substantially since John Paul took over in 1978, at least in part because the Pope's interest in their work carries an unspoken message of its importance. As Valls noted, "If the Curia was running at 50 rpm in 1978, now it is running at 150 rpm."

Other Popes have thrown up their hands in frustration after attempting—often unsuccessfully—to reshape the bureaucracy to their spiritual goals. John Paul has been a great deal more successful than others, but that is largely due to the groundwork laid by his predecessor, Pope Paul VI. Paul had quietly internationalized the College of Cardinals to create, for the first time, a majority of non-Italians. He had also begun replacing lower-ranking Italians in the Curia, bringing an infusion of new ideas and energies to an administration that had been stuck in place for centuries.

In taking over the church, John Paul has systematically appointed strong men of his own mind to the Curia, told them what he wanted, and let them do their jobs. Similar to a U.S. president's cabinet, the Curia is a collection of organizations that direct the spiritual and temporal affairs of the church. Thus, whoever controls the Curia controls the church.

QUESTIONS

1. How do the following evaluate the Catholic church's effectiveness: (a) the Pope; (b) the Curia; (c) the parish priest; (d) the typical Catholic layperson?

2. Describe the Catholic church's organization today. Has this structure changed under John Paul's leadership?

3. Are there other ways to structure an organization the size of the Catholic church?
4. What has John Paul done to improve the church's effectiveness?
5. Compare and contrast the Pope's role in the Catholic church with the job of corporate CEO, such as Lee Iacocca at Chrysler Corporation.

_____ CASE 7

THE MERCK MAGIC

Based on John A. Byrne, "The Miracle Company," *Business Week*, October 19, 1987, pp. 84–90.

Compared to a company like General Motors, which has sales of $100 billion a year, Merck & Co.'s annual revenues of $5.9 billion seem like small potatoes. But Wall Street places Merck's market value at about $28 billion—which is *more* than the market value of General Motors or other corporate giants like Coca-Cola or Mobil Oil. The major reasons that Merck is valued so highly is that it's in the highly profitable pharmaceutical industry, it generates a considerably higher return on equity than its industry rivals, and its incredible growth potential made possible by a number of new products. Merck is the king of the pharmaceutical industry and is widely acclaimed as one of the best-managed companies anywhere. It owes its success largely to Merck management's long-term focus, strong commitment to research and development, and creation of a highly flexible organization structure that allows its researchers an incredible amount of freedom.

In an era when many corporate leaders are obsessed with immediate results, Merck's management takes a long-term perspective. They don't seek growth by buying up other firms nor do they look for quick profits from their research expenditures. Merck's management spends its money the old-fashioned way, developing new products that may take a decade or longer to bring to market but which, when they arrive, are significantly better than the competition. For example, it spent more than $125 million and three decades of painstaking work to develop and gain FDA approval for its two anticholesterol drugs. The result? Its been estimated that these two drugs could add $1 billion to the company's annual sales only five years after their introduction. This long-term focus has also benefited Merck by providing a large number of successful products. While many of its competitors rely on one or two products for their growth, Merck has 13 major drugs with sales of more than $100 million each.

Merck plows more money into research and development than any of its competitors. In 1988, for instance, the company spent more than $530 million—about one out of every ten dollars spent on pharmaceutical research in the United States. Its R&D division employs 3300 people, more than 10 percent of the company's work force, scattered in eighteen labs in six different countries.

Merck prides itself in the extraordinary freedom it provides its scientists and the informal, project-based structure it uses to develop new products. Its research labs in Rahway, New Jersey, for instance, have the look and feel of a college campus rather than a large corporate research center. The company begins by seeking the best talent available. Then it gives these bright and highly motivated people the freedom to control their own destiny. They are free to decide on an approach and carry it through. And underground projects—those not officially sanctioned—are tolerated and often encouraged. A dual career track is also provided for scientists so that they can pass up promotional opportunities in management without financial penalty. A good researcher can earn $100,000 a year or more working in a lab and without any management responsibilities. Scientists are particularly attracted to Merck not only because of the freedom and rewards that they're offered, but because of the type of work they get to do. Although it is not uncommon for some drug companies to spend up to 80 percent of their R&D budgets to defend existing products through related extensions, Merck devotes the lion's share of its funds to offense—creating future products. This may help to explain the low turnover among Merck's scientists—a mere 5 percent a year.

Merck's structure is informal. Research is divided into 12 therapeutic classes, from antibiotics to cardiovascular drugs. There are also projects that are organized around product candidates. Each potential drug area has a leader—or "champion"—whose job is to keep the laboratories fueled with ideas and excited about the possibilities for drug discovery. Additionally, this leader is charged with selling the program to fellow scientists in various disciplines.

There are scores of microbiologists, biochemists, toxicologists, and others who cluster around a project, but no project team has a budget or a grant of authority. All team members from each discipline must commit their own resources to a project. This requires leaders to persuade specialists such as chemists, pharmacologists, and safety assessors to pledge their own budgets to work on his or her project. The idea is to gain greater collegiality and unity of purpose. As a consensus develops around a project, it gains support—intellectually and financially—from the team's members. One of the hardest tasks for a project leader is to convince others to get involved in his or her project long before the talents of those others are actually needed. Effective leaders learn how to win others over by selling their project's future potential. For example, the leader of the anticholesterol project brought his work to the attention of marketing personnel nearly eight years before the product hit the market. Moreover, because there wasn't much of a market for anticholesterol drugs at that time, the project leader had to sell the "enormous potential" of his product.

QUESTIONS

1. Do Wall Street analysts and Merck's management evaluate Merck's effectiveness similarly? Discuss.
2. Describe Merck's organization structure.
3. What key factors do you think have acted to create this structure?
4. Describe Merck's culture. What does Merck's management do to sustain this culture?

_____ CASE 8

KEEPING THINGS ORGANIC
AT BEN & JERRY'S

Based on Erik Larson, "Forever Young," *INC.*, July 1988, pp. 50–62.

In the summer of 1978, Ben Cohen and Jerry Greenfield opened an ice cream parlor in a renovated Burlington, Vermont, gas station. Their goal was to make and sell super-premium ice cream and have fun doing it. During the next ten years, Ben & Jerry's Homemade Inc. grew into a $45-million-a-year company with 150 employees. Along the way, however, Ben Cohen has become afraid that the company has lost, or at least is losing, its unique culture—

with its emphasis on fun, charity, and goodwill toward fellow workers up and down the line. Ben has begun to wonder whether his firm can be true to its founders' vision of a company that is genuinely sensitive to the needs of its employees and the community while, at the same time, pursuing rapid internal growth.

Ben & Jerry's began as more than just a "profit-making venture." It authentically wanted to act as a force for social change. Ben and Jerry were going to show other people that you could run a business differently from the way most businesses were run. For example, managers would wear jeans and T-shirts, and no executive would be allowed to earn more than five times what the lowest paid employee made. They would hire the handicapped. They would provide free therapy sessions to any employee. They'd stop production so every employee could participate in monthly staff meetings, and they would rely on all employees to participate in company decision making. They'd also donate 7.5 percent of the company's pretax income to socially responsible community causes. And, they would create a work environment that was joyful—where people who liked each other could work hard and have fun at the same time.

Between 1978 and 1986, the company doubled its size each year. In 1987 and 1988, growth "slowed" to a still-healthy 40 percent a year. The company recognized that growth was necessary if the firm was to survive. The market for super-premium ice cream was maturing in the mid-1980s and there was a host of new competitors. The company had to grow to retain its position on supermarket shelves. Another significant factor contributing to Ben & Jerry's growth strategy was the decision, in 1985, to take the company public and sell stock in order to build a new factory with greater capacity. Consistent with the company's community focus, they offered the first shares only to Vermonters, therefore making the community the real owners of the company. Not only did Ben & Jerry's now have stockholders to worry about, but their stockholders were their friends and neighbors. To be socially responsible, they concluded, now meant that the company *had* to grow.

By 1988, Ben Cohen wasn't sure whether growth was compatible with his company's original mission. All he had to do was look around his new plant and offices in his headquarters in Waterbury, Vermont, and see the changes that had taken place. They had a chief operating officer with an M.B.A.! There were cost controls, departments, and memos. Product introductions now took much more effort than they used to and required numerous approvals. Some company managers were wearing ties. While production still stopped for the monthly staff meetings, they were no longer vehicles for two-way communication but, rather, one-way affairs with management telling employees what was happening. Employees also talked about the stress of meeting production goals. On one occasion, work-load pressure got so great that Jerry actually hired a masseuse to come in and give workers massages during their breaks.

Ben was also lamenting the fact that growth had brought malaise. What was once a small group of employees who were like family was becoming an impersonal, and maybe even an inefficient, organization. Employees were no longer privy to every decision management made. Departments were duplicating work. Communications broke down. Employees, for example, found out about the company's new Springfield, Vermont, plant from newspaper accounts. Even the company's most visible egalitarian symbol—the five-to-one salary ratio—was under attack. The highest possible salary in 1988 was $84,240. Consistent with Ben & Jerry's original philosophy, if managers wanted more money, they would first have to raise the lowest salaries. But the director of sales is now complaining that he's making only 60 to 70 percent of what he'd make elsewhere and the chief operating officer says that this policy is making recruiting difficult.

QUESTIONS

1. Has Ben & Jerry's been *forced* to grow? Explain.
2. "This case demonstrates that organizations control people as much or more than people control organizations." Do you agree or disagree with this statement? Discuss.
3. Is Ben & Jerry's original culture now hindering the organization's effectiveness?
4. Can Ben & Jerry's maintain their original culture and, at the same time, continue to grow?
5. What type of structure did Ben & Jerry's have in its early years? Today? What factors brought about this change?
6. If you were a management consultant, what advice would you give Ben Cohen?

SHAKING UP EXXON

Based on John A. Byrne, "Shaking up Exxon," *Business Week,* July 18, 1988, pp. 104–11.

Can you teach an elephant to dance? Lawrence G. Rawl, CEO of Exxon, is out to prove that you can. Since taking charge in January 1987, he has made some bold moves to make Exxon, with 140,000 employees and sales in excess of $83 billion a year, a more efficient company.

Rawl joined Exxon in 1952 and moved up through the ranks. But he was not a typical Exxon executive. Whereas Exxon was a conservative company that was obsessed with conciliation and consensus, Rawl built his reputation on thumbing his nose at Exxon's formality and tradition. For example, as a junior member of Exxon's all-powerful Management Committee in the early 1980s, he'd do things like drape his feet over one of the black leather swivel chairs, swear, and make "smart" remarks. It is ironic that his style may have been an important reason why he was selected as Exxon's CEO. His fellow executives and Exxon's board saw him as a man who got things done. Exxon was lagging behind competitors that had successfully cut costs, and Exxon's stock was languishing. Rawl was seen as one of the few candidates with both the experience and willingness to shake up the company.

For years, Exxon had been one of the largest and most prosperous corporations in the world. It hired quality people and gave them comfortable, high-paying jobs in a protected cocoon that oozed arrogance. Consensus was the dominant decision style. Proposals would make their way through a maze of committees and task forces, plus layers of staff. The consensus style, of course, was safe. If a project didn't work out, no single individual or group could be blamed.

Exxon's corporate headquarter's staff had developed into a complex check-and-balance system for the company's far-flung operations. In New York, highly paid executives examined proposals and decisions from the field, helping to refine them before they came before key corporate committees. But the system only complicated decision making. What resulted was a committee decision process where reams of information would be gathered—far more than anyone could absorb—and where people would come to a meeting of the minds before they ever exposed their positions. No one ever openly questioned proposals; they merely supported them.

In the first 18 months of Rawl's tenure as CEO, Exxon has undergone some major changes. For the most part, they have emphasized disengaging from non–energy and chemical businesses and making Exxon smaller. By the summer of 1988, Exxon was less formal, less certain, and less secure. There were also fewer people and a lot fewer committee meetings.

Between January 1987 and July 1988, employment fell by 30 percent to 100,000. Some 8000 employees left the company. An additional 36,000 were eliminated as businesses were sold off. Nearly 3000 employees were reassigned to other jobs, while some 17,000 saw their jobs redefined. Rawl cleared out several vertical levels in the organization, folded together numerous regional subsidiaries, consolidated worldwide operations, and closed up the company's disastrous attempt at office automation.

Rawl is putting all the company's chips on energy and chemicals. He's betting that oil prices will rise enough in the 1990s to make Exxon's extensive oil and gas reserves more economical to produce. While Exxon has abandoned its investment in nuclear and solar energy, Rawl is relying on Exxon's size to allow it to move into those areas should the need arise. Meanwhile, he's still spending up to $25 million a year in lab work on synthetic fuels. In five years, Exxon has succeeded in cutting the cost of producing synthetic fuels from $60 to $30 a barrel. Still, Rawl is the first to acknowledge that Exxon is held hostage to the volatility in oil markets. As one executive put it, "There's not a helluva lot we can do about oil prices. If the price of oil drops $1 a barrel, our earnings go down $250 million."

So far, Rawl's efforts seem to be paying dividends. His cost-cutting alone added $375 million to Exxon's net in 1987. His trimmed-down work force earns $48,400 per employee in annual profits, more than any other major U.S. corporation. Managers now spend more time running their businesses and less time in meetings. And decisions are now made faster and with less concern about possibly hurting somebody's feelings. The "new" Exxon is tougher and better able to respond to a more competitive world where there's little room for Exxon's former gentlemen managers. Exxon's current executive group realizes that their careers are increasingly on the on the line. If they don't produce, Rawl will have no qualms about replacing them with others who will.

Rawl concedes that there's one major negative to downsizing. The "bench-strength" in management talent that Exxon previously had is no longer there. Senior management jobs have been cut in half—to 250. With fewer high-level slots and regions to send executives to, Exxon's grooming of future leaders will be more difficult. Some of Rawl's critics, however, think there are other negatives. They argue that he's cut too deep and imposed his changes too autocratically. They point out that morale is now extremely low, with many employees concerned about their future with the company. The restructuring not only broke the social contract that implied that Exxon employees had job security but it has also altered expectations about compensation and promotions. Pay raises now rely substantially on performance rather than merely title and, to stay with the company, some managers accepted jobs that were two or even three levels below their previous positions. Some executives complain that they've had to assume the responsibilities previously held by as many as three or four people.

QUESTIONS

1. Contrast Exxon's environment in 1968 and 1988.
2. What, if anything, can Exxon do to manage its environment?
3. How did Rawl carry out his change program? Do you think his approach could have been improved upon?
4. In downsizing Exxon, what problems did Rawl face that could have been predicted based on research on declining organizations?

_____ CASE 10

THE UPHILL BATTLE AT EASTMAN KODAK

> Based on Clare Ansberry, "Eastman Kodak Co. Has Arduous Struggle to Regain Lost Edge," _Wall Street Journal,_ April 2, 1987, p. 1.

Eastman Kodak Co. has some serious problems. Although it once totally dominated the world's film, photo-processing, and camera business, it has recently fallen on hard times. Once the industry innovator, it now seems to let others dictate what it will do. Significant problems have developed with the quality of its products. Competitors have successfully penetrated many of its markets. And, to add insult to injury, over the last four years, top U.S. executives have dropped Kodak from 4th to 70th on *Fortune's* list of the most admired major U.S. corporations.

Twenty years ago, Kodak led the industry in technology. Today, it increasingly chases Japan's Fuji Photo Film Co. For example, Kodak's virtual monopoly of the domestic market for color-negative film has been cut to 82 percent; and Fuji, not Kodak, now produces the the world's fastest color-print still film.

A great deal of Fuji's success has been due to the perception by consumers that Kodak quality isn't what is used to be. Between 1982 and 1987, Kodak's annual photo-finishing sales plunged from $200 million to $60 million, which can largely be attributed to complaints by customers about blurry and grainy quality of prints.

Kodak efforts to expand sales in the camera market have also suffered some serious setbacks. Its introduction of an instant camera in 1976 led to a decade-long patent-infringement suit by Polaroid. Kodak lost the suit and, in addition to paying a huge settlement, had to agree to withdraw from this market. In 1982, in an effort to expand its share of the amateur photography market, Kodak introduced its disk camera. It was easy-to-use and inexpensive, but produced poor-quality pictures. It failed largely because Japanese competitors concentrated on simplifying their high-quality thirty-five-millimeter cameras.

How did Kodak lose touch with its markets? The answer to this question seems to lie in the organization's traditions. The company cultivated fierce loyalty from employees through such practices as rigidly following its "promote-from-within" policy, providing large annual bonuses, and offering free noontime movies. Since Kodak perceived itself as a technology-driven company, promotion criteria favored engineers. As engineers, Kodak executives believed in perfection, no matter how long it took. One classic illustration of this love of tradition was the case of a supervisor who had recently retired. He had kept employment records from the 1930s in his office drawer "because they had always been there."

Management style at Kodak could best be described as centralized, patient, and paternalistic. Decisions percolated to the top for even minor issues. The head of photographic and information products, for instance, could be called upon to make a decision on any one of 50,000 products. This style was effective as long as competitors were impotent, and Kodak's technology and quality standards led the industry. In times of change, however, it made Kodak slow to respond. Even through Kodak was the first choice of the organizers to be the film sponsors for the 1984 Olympic Games, it fussed so long over the contract that the organizers turned to a more amenable and eager Fuji. Kodak executives then were furious when they learned that Fuji had gotten the sponsorship.

The man who has to deal with these problems, Colby Chandler, Kodak's chairman, in many respects mirrors the company for which he works. An engineer by training, he is conservative, down-to-earth, and a genuine "nice guy."

QUESTIONS

1. How has the environment affected Kodak?
2. Describe Kodak's culture in detail.
3. If you were hired as a consultant by Kodak's board, what recommendations would you make to improve the company's effectiveness?

_____ **CASE 11**

THE NEW AT&T

Especially prepared for this volume by Stephen P. Robbins.

In January 1982 the U.S. government announced that it was breaking up the Bell System. Bell's general structure, at that time, is shown in Table 1.

On January 1, 1984, the final step in the breakup became a reality. The "new" AT&T is shown in Table 2. This reorganized company would no longer monopolize the U.S. telephone system. Its operating telephone companies would become independent firms. In return, AT&T would be allowed to compete in the telecommunications and computer markets against the likes of IBM, Xerox, and the Japanese. To understand the impact of this change, you need to know about AT&T's past and its organization culture.

TABLE 1 *The "Old" AT&T (January 1982)*

AT&T corporate headquarters	13,302 employees
Long Lines (interstate long distance)	42,834
AT&T International	530
Bell Labs	24,000
Western Electric	159,862
22 operating companies	798,000
Total	1,038,528

A symbol of AT&T's historic culture is the print of Angus McDonald, a nineteenth-century Bell System lineman, fighting to keep the telephone lines open during a blizzard. A longtime feature of AT&T office decor, the print symbolizes the company's commitment to service. AT&T's culture developed around an incredibly strong service ethic. Employees did what they felt was best for its customers, regardless of what the customers actually wanted. Western Electric, its manufacturing subsidiary, could make phones that would survive falls from twenty-story buildings, and it passed the costs of such phones on to its customers because it had no competition.

Managers, too, were molded to excel in a regulated, monopolistic environment. The road to the top was through operational

TABLE 2 *The "New" AT&T (January 1984)*

AT&T corporate headquarters	2,000 employees
AT&T Communications (interstate and some intrastate long distance)	120,000
AT&T International	900
Bell Labs	19,000
Western Electric	135,000
7 independent regional companies	580,000
Central Services Organization (research and systems engineering group owned by the 7 regionals)	8,800
AT&T Information Systems	110,000
Total	975,700

and technical departments rather than through marketing. The organization was mechanistic, organized around functions, and dominated by engineers. It attracted to its management ranks many who had a high sense of mission and who needed a structural environment and security. Ma Bell took care of its people.

The new AT&T must be a very different company from its predecessor. Its biggest challenge will be to alter its culture to be more competitive and aggressive. Its manufacturing-oriented culture encouraged taking too much time and too much money to make a product. A marketing culture will be geared to supply customers with what they need quickly, and if that includes lower-quality phones and dozens of options, so be it!

AT&T is trying to liberate middle managers by delegating more authority downward, emphasizing teamwork, and encouraging risk taking. But the change does not come easy. AT&T's management seems to be divided into one of two camps: those caught in the past and those living for the future.

QUESTIONS

1. Describe how AT&T's environment, organizational design, culture, and effectiveness are interrelated.
2. What advice would you give AT&T's management for changing its culture?

_____ CASE 12

THE UNITED STATES EMPLOYMENT SERVICE

> From John Rohrbaugh, "The Competing Values Approach: Innovation and Effectiveness in the Job Service," in R. H. Hall and R. E. Quinn, eds., _Organizational Theory and Public Policy_ (Beverly Hills, Calif.: Sage Publications, 1983), pp. 265–80. Copyright © 1983. Reprinted by permission of Sage Publications, Inc.

The U.S. Employment Service (USES) was established in 1933 to facilitate the matching of job-ready workers with available employer openings. The service is jointly administered by the federal government and the states. Each state is responsible for the actual operation of the local Job Service offices within its jurisdiction. To get an idea of its impact, during fiscal 1980, approximately 2600 local Job Service offices filled six million job openings.

The USES would like to match workers and jobs by computer. But this is a major undertaking; something that requires considerable planning and evaluation. In the mid-1970s, the USES developed what it called the Job Service Matching System. It was a nationwide system that included locating computer-based batch processing of matches between applicants and jobs in all large

FIGURE 1 *Performance Profiles of High- and Low-Automation Offices*

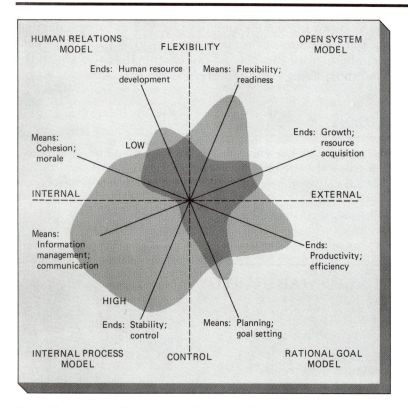

Source: John Rohrbaugh, "The Competing Values Approach: Innovation and Effectiveness in the Job Service," in R. H. Hall and R. E. Quinn, eds., *Organizational Theory and Public Policy* (Beverly Hills, Calif.: Sage Publications, 1983), p. 277. Copyright © 1983. Reprinted by permission of Sage Publications, Inc.

metropolitan areas and real-time processing in selected large metropolitan areas. The system would cost in excess of $250 million.

The USES was concerned with the effectiveness of the matching system in those locations where it had been introduced. A group of consultants were brought in to evaluate the system. The consultants identified 28 USES offices in which to conduct their evaluation. Eleven of these offices reported high levels of use of the information technology and 17 reported low levels of use.

Using the eight factors from the competing values approach to organizational effectiveness, the consultants measured participants' perceptions of their offices' performance. Each of the 28 local Job Service offices was assigned composite performance scale scores on the eight effectiveness criteria. These were obtained from questionnaires administered to the entire staff of each local office investigated. These indices were then plotted on a graph. Figure 1 depicts a composite performance profile of the two sets of Job Service offices—those with high use and those with low use.

QUESTIONS

1. How are the high-use offices performing? What are their problems?
2. How are the low-use offices performing? What are their problems?
3. What can you say in terms of comparing the effectiveness of these two sets of offices?

_____ **CASE 13**

FINDING A PLACE FOR PRODUCT PLANNING

Especially prepared for this volume by Stephen P. Robbins.

This Monday morning's executive committee meeting at Ontario Electronics was certain to be lively. A major decision would be made today.

In addition to being one of the largest electronic component manufacturers in Canada, Ontario Electronics was also one of the fastest growing. Between 1983 and 1988, it had achieved a 55 percent per year compounded growth rate. At its current pace, Ontario Electronics would have sales in excess of $300 million (Canadian) by 1990. Its growth, according to a recent article in a trade journal, was due primarily to heavy outlays for research that had resulted in an ever-expanding product line.

The reason that today's meeting would be interesting was easy enough to predict. At last Wednesday's board of directors meeting, the board gave unanimous approval to the president's suggestion that the company establish a product-planning group. No decision was made as to where this new group would be located. This decision would be made at today's executive committee meeting. The vice presidents of marketing, production, and corporate planning each have come to the meeting prepared to argue that product planning should be placed under their jurisdiction.

"We have a major decision to make today," began the company president, Douglas Harrison. "As you know, the board has approved the creation of a product-planning group. It will be the general mission of this group to identify customer needs and develop product prototypes. Exactly how far they go in terms of market research or design has not been established by the board. They told us to work that out. My preliminary budget for the next year includes $650,000 for this new group. I expect when they are fully operable there will be more than a dozen people in the group."

"I think it's obvious to each of you that product planning belongs in the marketing function," said Veronica Duval, vice president of marketing. "The major thrust of product planning is environment scanning. It must work closely with current and potential customers to identify their product requirements. This is a marketing activity. Since we work with our customers on a daily basis, we know them and are in the best position to interpret and understand their needs."

"I agree with you, Veronica, when you say that the major thrust of product planning is environment scanning," replied Claude Fortier, head of corporate planning. "And environment scanning is precisely what we in corporate planning do on a full-time basis. It's our job to assess where the company is going. Clearly, product planning should be part of our area. Planning is planning, regardless of whether it's at the organization or product level. Our expertise, and I think the company's solid growth is a tribute to our efforts, is in scanning the environment—reading trends, assessing economic changes, evaluating the actions of competitors, and the like. The identification of customer needs is a natural extension of our current activities."

"I can't agree with either of you," was the opening comment of Mitch Jenkins, vice president of production. "The primary emphasis of this company is in production and research. Both these activities are closely related as demonstrated by the fact that production, engineering, and product-research activities are all currently under my direction. This company's success is not due to marketing or corporate planning! Our success has come about because we have shown the ability to develop innovative products that meet high-quality standards. I'm not going to get into a fight over whose function is more important here. The bottom line is that this is a manufacturing firm in a high-technology industry. Its success depends predominantly on generating new quality products and that's precisely what my people do. Doug, I think the decision of where we locate product planning is self-evident. It belongs under production."

Douglas Harrison looked around the table. He reaffirmed to the eight-member committee that he fully expected to resolve the issue of product planning's location at this meeting.

QUESTIONS

1. Where do you think product planning belongs? Why?
2. What insights does this case provide about effectiveness?
3. Why do you think the three vice presidents are so determined to obtain this new group?
4. Describe how the activities of product planning might differ based on which vice president gains jurisdiction.

_____ CASE 14

TRYING TO GET AN AMBULANCE

> From a tape recording made by the Dallas Fire Department under the Texas Open Records Act.

The following conversation took place between Larry Boff and nurse/dispatcher, Billie Myrick, when Boff called the Dallas Fire

Department's emergency number to seek help for his stepmother, Lillian Boff:

NURSE: "And what is the problem here?"

BOFF: "I don't know, if I knew I wouldn't be . . ."

NURSE: "Sir, would you answer my question, please? What is the problem?"

BOFF: "She's having difficulty in breathing."

NURSE: "How old is this person?"

BOFF: "She's 60 years old."

NURSE: "Where is she now?"

BOFF: "She is in the bedroom right now."

NURSE: "Can I speak with her please?"

BOFF: "No, you can't. She seems like she's incoherent."

NURSE: "Why is she incoherent?"

BOFF: "How the hell do I know!"

NURSE: "Sir, don't curse me."

BOFF: "Well, I don't care. Your stupid . . . questions you're asking. Give me someone who knows what they're doing. Why don't you send an ambulance out here?"

NURSE: "Sir, we only come out on life-threatening emergencies."

BOFF: "Well, this is a life-threatening emergency."

NURSE: "Hold on, sir. I'll let you speak with my super . . . uh, officer."

SUPERVISOR: "Hello?"

BOFF: "What do I have to do to get an ambulance out to this house?"

SUPERVISOR: "You have to answer the nurse's questions."

BOFF: "All right! What are they, before she dies will you please tell me what the hell you want?"

SUPERVISOR: "Well, I tell you what, if you curse one more time I'm gonna hang up the phone."

BOFF: "Well, I'll tell you what, what if this were your mother in there and can't breathe, what would you do?"

SUPERVISOR: "You answer that nurse's questions and we'll get you some help."

BOFF: "She's having difficulty in breathing, she cannot talk."

SUPERVISOR: "OK, she's back on the air. Don't you cuss her again."

NURSE: "OK, sir, I need to talk to her still."

BOFF: "You can't. She is incoherent."

NURSE: "Let me talk to her, sir."

BOFF (to his roommate): "Please tell her she's incoherent and cannot talk. (to the nurse) She cannot talk at all."

NURSE: "Why?"

BOFF: "Well, how am I supposed to know?"

NURSE: "Well, give her the phone."

BOFF (to his roommate): "Give her the phone in there. Give her the phone. I know she can't talk. (to the nurse) Forget it. I'll call the main hospital around here, all right?

NURSE: "OK, Bye-bye."

Boff called the nearby Mesquite Hospital but was told it could not send an ambulance to his house in Dallas. With Mrs. Boff's condition worsening, Boff's roommate, Dennis Fleming, placed a second call to the emergency number.

NURSE: "Are you the same man I was talking to earlier?"

FLEMING: "No, that was my roommate."

NURSE: "Uh huh. Why can't I talk to the lady?"

FLEMING: "She cannot talk."

NURSE: "Why?"

FLEMING: "She's in . . . she's just out of it. In fact, he's going in there now. He thinks she's dead."

NURSE: "What do you mean by 'out of it?'"

FLEMING: "She is incoherent."

BOFF (back on the line): "She's dead now. Thank you, ma'am! Would you please send an ambulance? Would you please send an ambulance here?"

QUESTIONS

1. Is the nurse at fault here?
2. Is the supervisor at fault here?
3. Is Mr. Boff at fault?
4. Relate this incident to dysfunctional aspects of bureaucracy.
5. If you were hired as a consultant to review this incident, where would you place the fault?
6. How could the fire department determine if this was a life-threatening emergency in a more effective manner?

_____ **CASE 15**

IMPLEMENTING AN APPOINTMENT SYSTEM

From Peter H. King, "DMV Caught in a Monster Traffic Jam," _Los Angeles Times,_ March 24, 1985, pp. 1, 31–33. Copyright 1985, Los Angeles Times. Reprinted by permission.

In most field offices of the California Department of Motor Vehicles, workers toil within an enclosure formed by three counters and a back wall. The public is kept outside of the perimeter, massing in sloppy ranks to wait a turn at the counter. In both form and function, the design is suggestive of a fort.

Branch managers are under orders to stay out among the troops, so they usually sit against the wall at a desk distinguished by an eight-by-eleven-inch photograph hung overhead. It is a portrait of Gov. George Deukmejian, grinning. Often, and particularly in these days of hectic change at the DMV, his is the only smile in the house.

"Fun?" asked Herman Gupton, 52, who manages the San Francisco DMV branch. "It's not so much fun right now, because of all the pressure in trying to make a program work that had bugs in it from the inception . . . pressure from within and without. I hope it gets to be fun. I hope I don't have to spend the rest of my career fighting alligators, so to speak."

The primary alligator confronting Gupton and his counterparts at the DMV's 154 field offices surfaced last summer in Sacramento with the announcement that the department would no longer deal with its clientele on a first-come, first-served basis. Instead, the public would be required to schedule appointments in advance by telephone.

The new policy, which applies to virtually all DMV transactions, took effect August 6. What has transpired since can be described as a rough transition at best, a bureaucratic fiasco at worst.

"The appointment system quite frankly has put us in a crisis situation," said Thomas R. Weibel, an official in the DMV's Sacramento headquarters. "We are getting some heat."

The system's major flaw became apparent early, and it was so simple that it seemed stunning: Most major field offices did not have enough telephones to make a telephone appointment system work.

People who called for an appointment often discovered that they couldn't get through, so they went to the DMV in person. Because clerks had been instructed to serve only those with appointments, many walk-ins were turned away or given appointments for another day.

Complaints Came Quickly. It did not take long for complaints to pour in, more than a few reaching the man whose smile decorates DMV walls.

"Dear Governor Deukmejian," wrote Elaine L. Boyd, a legal secretary who lives in Lake San Marcos in north San Diego County. "This new 'brillant' system of making appointments for renewal simply DOES NOT WORK! . . . This is the most inexcusable, inefficient and frustrating system that could possibly have been implemented! This is what happens in the Real World when one tries to call DMV for an appointment (as I have for the past three days): A BUSY SIGNAL."

While DMV officials insist that they have made great strides with the system, it was possible two Mondays ago to observe people waiting for an hour in the Santa Monica branch to make an appointment to return in two weeks—and all so they could pay what essentially are taxes.

"Of course it makes me mad," said Caroline Aezrapour, a 24-year-old computer programmer who was on her second trip to the branch to register her car. She had arrived for her appointment, an hour earlier. "It's very slow," she said. "Coming to the DMV is always a headache. The old system was just the same."

Arrived Early. Andrew Varni, 24, showed up for his appointment 10 minutes early. He was rewarded with a $1^1/_4$-hour wait and the grim news that he would need to return with additional registration paper work. "I was here a few years ago," Varni said, "before they had the appointment system. And I got through faster."

Dorothy Caruso was at the end of a line of fifteen people waiting in front of the "Start Here" window. Under the new system, this is where people without appointments are funneled. In some cases they move next to benches where they wait to be squeezed in between appointments, a process that can consume an entire day. Most, however, are given appointments, for another date. Nearly all of the business at the Start Here window would have been accomplished over the telephone—if it were possible to get through.

"I tried calling for six weeks," said Caruso, 42, a schoolteacher. "I sat on the phone. One day I called for five hours straight. I kept track."

Because her newly purchased used car did not have license plates, she began to get tickets. She went in person to the DMV. This was her third trip.

"It stinks," Caruso said of the new system. "This is the most inefficient, slow, snail-like, incompetent, anything-you-want-to-call-it situation. It's maddening. It's like you get caught in a snare they create, and there is nothing you can do about it."

In the beginning, there was the noble goal. And it was a dilly.

After long enduring criticism as what is arguably California's least-loved bureaucracy, the DMV decided to do something about its service. Lines at major branches were spilling out of lobbies and into the streets. Customers were known to wait as long as four hours. It was a mess.

This, of course, comes as no surprise to most Californians. There are nearly seventeen million licensed drivers in the state and twenty million registered vehicles, and the issuance of every license involves some contact with the DMV.

The DMV also had a pragmatic motivation to find a better system. It had begun a $42-million conversion to computers. Terminals were being installed in field offices to process work formerly completed in Sacramento. Entry into the electronic age, ironically enough, was expected to lengthen the time needed to take care of clients at the field office.

"The scope of the project," DMV Director George E. Meese wrote in a report to Deukmejian, "would literally affect every facet of daily operation. And, without some well-defined method of controlling the work flow, the already-diminished service levels would deteriorate even further."

So why not forget the computers and telephone systems and simply add more clerks?

"That," Meese said in an interview, "would just be a never-ending battle of having more and more employees, more and more offices, larger offices, larger parking lots. If you could tell me tomorrow that no one else was going to come into California, then we might be able to do something like that."

After the goal came the innovation. The Santa Barbara DMV branch had solved a temporary parking shortage by requiring appointments. Why, the bureaucrats in Sacramento asked themselves, couldn't this concept be applied statewide? Their response apparently was unanimous: Why not, indeed!

The system requires a customer to first contact an office by telephone. A DMV operator determines which forms the customer needs, and these are sent by mail. If a visit to the office is still needed, an appointment is scheduled. But the emphasis is on keeping office visits to a minimum.

A six-month pilot project was conducted in twenty-four Southern California offices early last year. It demonstrated to the bureaucrats' satisfaction that the new policy would be nothing short of splendid. "The appointment system," an evaluation concluded, "has reduced both customer wait time and the number of customer visits to the field offices."

In retrospect, DMV officials now concede that the pilot study was not a solid test. Some offices had a central telephone system to divert pressure, and it was possible for customers to go to neighboring offices not involved in the trial system.

Nonetheless, out of the project a formula was developed to determine how many telephones were needed to accommodate the new system. The recommended lines were added. And on August 6 a new day dawned for the DMV. And it was not good.

"Grossly Underestimated." "We found out very quickly—very quickly—that the project telephone formulas were grossly underestimated," said Bill Cather, a DMV official in Sacramento.

Telephones were inundated, not only with legitimate calls but also, Meese said, with "those who were merely interested in discussing the pros and cons of the new system."

In some cities, the problem was not placing a call but finding the right number. Telephone information operators did not have the numbers, and they were not printed in phone books.

In other branches, efforts to quickly install new lines were hampered by confusion stemming from the break-up of AT&T and because some DMV switchboards were outdated.

Working on the telephone was something new to most DMV employees. In the past, there had been a strict policy banning any business over the telephone. Workers were known to let phones ring or—in hectic times—take them off the hook. So there was initially some employee resistance as well, officials said.

When frustrated callers began to arrive at the field offices in droves, some managers reacted by taking operators and throwing them into the front lines at the counters. But this created only more difficulty for callers.

In the meantime, the conversion to computers was having its anticipated effect on the speed of individual transactions. And thousands of hours of worker time was being spent in training on the computers, taxing the increasingly burdened staffs.

"I don't know, in retrospect, whether we should have done both changes at the same time," DMV official Weibel said.

Computers Slowed Process. Because the computers were slowing things down, fewer appointments could be scheduled each day, and some customers waited a month for an appointment. Taking care of DMV business is not something many citizens do a month in advance, and so the branches began to fill with the ranks of the unscheduled, all pleading emergency.

A decision had been made that the only way to make the appointment system work would be to apply it statewide, without exceptions. Some clerks enforced this with a vengeance.

Laurel Britton, an aide to Assemblyman Phillip D. Wyman (R-Tehachapi) heard from constituents who drive 40 miles from the foothills or farming communities in the San Joaquin valley to conduct DMV business in Bakersfield. "They would drive their trucks down canyons on wiggly roads and then literally be told that they had to have an appointment," Britton said.

Turned away empty-handed, they would spend the drive home planning angry letters to send to the usual recipients.

Public resistance to the system has been high. Even in offices in which the system is said to be working the best, managers estimate that between 30 percent to 50 percent of customers do not have appointments. Some of this, no doubt, stems from ignorance about the change. But DMV officials also have discovered that some people don't want to make appointments to visit a government office.

"While most Californians appreciate the convenience of appointments," Meese said, "they quite often perceive the appointment programs to be an infringement upon their right to prompt service."

The public reaction to appointments surprised department officials, who tend to compare the system to that found at almost any doctor's office.

"We are not in the business of trying to ram things down people's throats, although we have been accused of that," Weibel said. "We anticipated most people would appreciate the opportunity to avoid coming into a DMV office.

"We had heard the complaints about long lines and the bureaucracy for so many years. We thought, 'Well, this is wonderful.'"

Tough Times. The transition has created tough times for DMV field office workers and managers. Under the old system, clients would get mad waiting in line. Now, they often have their anger up even before they hit the door.

"We have been dealing with the situation at DMV since last fall," said Keïth Hearn, communications director of the California State Employees Assn., which represents most of the department's 7,000 employees. "The main problem is that there is considerable stress on the employees. A lot of them are demoralized due to trying to get the public through the system as fast as possible. . . .

"Another major problem is forced overtime. A lot of these offices have been on mandatory overtime for the past year. This really gets to a lot of people. Last Christmas holiday, a lot of people had scheduled vacations to be with their families, and they had them canceled due to the workload."

Some managers interviewed recalled with irritation their difficulties convincing Sacramento that the new system was in trouble. They believed that their superiors suspected them of loafing, causing problems for what appeared to be an ideal system.

Last year, managers received memos instructing them to place their "most knowledgeable and proficient people" on the new computers.

Then, as the appointment system began, they received memos telling them to put their "most knowledgeable and proficient people" on the telephone banks.

As it became clear that the "Start Here" windows were needed to sort out the large number of clients arriving without appointments, instructions came down for the managers to put their "most knowledgeable and proficient people" at the start window.

"A Standing Joke"

"That became a standing joke among managers," recalled one Sacramento DMV official. "They were saying, 'I ran out of knowledgeable and proficient people back in the automation phase.'"

DMV official Cather said that while most managers defend the system publicly, "a lot . . . would like to see us go back to the old ways and say, 'We gave it a good shot but this just isn't going to work out.' They are not happy. They are tired of fielding complaints."

While nobody is suggesting as yet that the system—now in its eight month—has begun to operate as smoothly as first hoped, the latest word at the DMV is that the toughest period has passed.

"The light at the end of the tunnel is that it is getting better every day," said Toni Gilbert, a DMV regional manager in Long Beach.

Meese said that he expects the system to be working as planned in 30 to 90 days. The goal is to make it reasonably easy to place a call to a field office, schedule appointments within five days and provide service within 15 minutes.

Branches where the system is now said to be working best include the ones hardest hit at first—the downtown Los Angeles branch on Hope Street and Gupton's office on Fell Street in San Francisco.

Hundreds of additional telephone lines have been installed since August. Some troubled offices have been given devices to stack up calls on hold, the same as those employed by airline reservations systems. Another $500,000 worth of these call sequencers are on order.

The appointment system originally was supposed to cost $860,000 to implement. That amount has been exceeded, but officials said they cannot estimate by how much.

While they refuse to entertain any discussion that the system be abandoned, Meese and his top officials have lowered their expectations about overnight efficiency and prompt public acceptance. Instead, they appear resigned to a long haul.

"It has become quite clear," Meese stated in a report presented earlier this year to Deukmejian, "that if we are to reach our ultimate goal of complete public acceptance of the appointment system, we cannot demand immediate compliance."

Adjustments have been made.

Signs on doors of DMV field offices still declare that appointments are mandatory, but some managers have made exceptions since the first day. For instance, Gupton allows people who have lost their license to receive service even without an appointment.

Rural offices have been told to consider the appointment system voluntary.

In late February, Meese distributed a flyer to all branches that set down this order: "Everyone entering a DMV field office is to be served. Appointments are tools for better service. WE DO NOT EXIST to make appointments. The DMV exists to SERVE THE PUBLIC."

At the height of the crisis, which probably peaked in late January, DMV officials heard regularly from state lawmakers who wanted to relay complaints from constituents and ask, as one department official recalled: "What are you turkeys trying to do?"

Legislative interest has dwindled, however. One lawmaker scoffed at recent inquiries, saying "It's just not the major issue of the day."

Perhaps one reason for the Legislature's short interest span rests in the basement of the Capitol Building, Room B-101—a tiny DMV office. That is where many lawmakers and their aides take care of personal DMV transactions.

A reporter dropped in one March morning and found no lines whatsoever.

He asked to renew his license, but was told he must be employed by the Legislature. When he admitted he was not, the would-be renewal applicant was dispatched with a slip of paper. It contained a typed list of telephone numbers. The numbers, it was indicated, should be called in order to schedule appointments at regular DMV field offices in Sacramento.

QUESTIONS

1. Describe the old and new technologies at the DMV.
2. Why is the new technology at the DMV not comparable to that used in a doctor's office?
3. What was wrong with the twenty-four-office pilot study?
4. What problems does this case illustrate about bureaucracies?
5. How has employee resistance to change surfaced in this case?
6. How might this change have been implemented more effectively?

_____ **CASE 16**

WINTHROP HOSPITAL

Adapted from Stephen J. Carroll, Jr., *Cases in Management,* Copyright © 1989 by Kendall/Hunt Publishing Company. Reprinted with permission.

Winthrop Hospital is located in a medium-sized suburban community. A general hospital, it serves a large portion of the surrounding area and is usually operating at, near, or sometimes beyond its capacity. Each floor of the hospital has its own particular structure with regard to the nurses who staff it. This formalized hierarchy runs from the supervisor (who must be a registered nurse) to registered nurses (RNs) to licensed practical nurses (LPNs) to students and nurses' aides. Professionally, there are some duties that are supposed to be performed only by the RNs; these are spelled out in the hospital manual. In practice, however, the LPNs do much of the work that is supposed to be done by the RNs. The RNs are glad for the help because they are very busy with other duties. Through time the work done by the RNs and the LPNs has meshed so thoroughly that one just does the work without thinking of whose job it is supposed to be. The hospital is normally so crowded that, even with everyone performing all types of work, there never seems to be enough time or enough help.

The procedural manual used at Winthrop Hospital was first used in 1971 and has not been revised. Everyone connected with the hospital realizes that it is extremely outdated, and actual practice varies so greatly as to have no similarity to what is prescribed in the manual. Even the courses that the student nurses take teach things entirely differently from what is prescribed in Winthrop's manual.

The vacation privileges of nurses at the hospital show extreme differences for the different types of nurses. RNs receive two weeks' vacation after nine months on the job, whereas LPNs must be on the staff for ten years before receiving their second week of vacation. The LPNs believe this to be extremely unfair and have been trying to have the privileges somewhat more equalized. Their efforts have met with little cooperation and no success. The hospital superiors have simply told them that the terms for vacation are those stated in the hospital manual and that they saw no need to change them.

Some of the individual nurses at Winthrop then began to take matters into their own hands. The LPNs on the fourth floor of the hospital decided that if they couldn't have the extra vacation because of what was written in the manual then they would follow the manual in all phases and go strictly according to the book. Difficulties surfaced as soon as the LPNs began to behave in this manner. The RNs now seemed to have more work than they could handle adequately and the LPNs were just as busy doing solely their "prescribed" duties. The same amount of effort put forth previously was being exerted, but less was being accomplished because of the need to jump around from place to place and job to job in order to work strictly according to the book. An example of this wasted effort occurred in the taking of doctors' orders. Doctors phone in the type of treatment that a patient is to receive—medicines, times for dispensing such, diet, and so forth. These doctors' orders are supposed to be taken by an RN, but in practice whoever was nearest the phone had taken the order. If an LPN took the order she had it signed by the supervisor (stationed at the desk) as a safeguard. This procedure saved the time and effort involved in getting an RN to the phone for every order. Now, however, the LPNs refused to take the doctors' orders and called for an RN. The RN had to leave the work she was doing, go to the phone, take the order, then go back to her unfinished work. This procedure wasted the time of the doctor, the RN, and the LPN who had to locate the RN. The LPNs' practice of going by the book brought about hostile feelings among both groups of nurses and among the doctors who had to work on the floor. The conflicts led to a lessening in the high degree of care that the patients had been receiving.

The conflict initiated by the difference in vacation privileges brought about more complaints from both parties. In the manual the categories for vacation privileges listed "supervisors," "RNs," "lab technicians," and "others." The LPNs resented being placed in the "others" category. They felt that they deserved a separate listing, especially because they had the same amount of training as other groups, such as the lab technicians. Adding further fuel to the fire was the fact that the lab technicians got a second week of vacation after only one year on the job. Another item of controversy was the fact that RNs were allowed to sign themselves in on the job when they reported, whereas the LPNs were required to punch in. The LPNs felt that the RNs thus could hide any incidents of lateness, whereas the LPNs had strict account kept of their time and were docked in salary for any time missed.

The RNs now complained to the hospital superiors more vehemently than ever about being understaffed. They felt that they simply needed more RNs on every floor on every shift to meet what was required of them; this was a demand they had been voicing even before the conflict began. The shortage was especially acute at nights, when unfamiliarity with individual patients often led to mix-ups in the treatments.

The ill feelings led to arguments among the nurses. The LPNs felt that they were always doing more work than the RNs, that they spent more time with the patients because the RNs had more to do at the desk, and that they knew more about treatments because they more often accompanied doctors on their rounds. They now voiced these opinions. The RNs argued superiority on the basis of a longer period of formal training.

All these factors combined to bring about a tremendous drop in morale and a marked decrease in efficiency, and the conflict was in danger of spreading to the other floors in the hospital.

QUESTIONS

1. What is the source of the conflict?
2. If employees work "strictly according to the book" and productivity suffers, what does this tell us about formal organization?
3. "The RNs might be encouraging the conflict to further their self-interests." Explain.
4. What might be done to alleviate the problem?

NAME INDEX

XYZ

ORGANIZATION INDEX

SUBJECT INDEX